SECOND EDITION

Optimizing Cloud Native Java

Practical Techniques for Improving JVM Application Performance

Benjamin J. Evans and
James Gough
Foreword by Holly Cummins

O'REILLY®

Optimizing Cloud Native Java

by Benjamin J. Evans and James Gough

Published by O'Reilly Media, Inc., 1005 Gravenstein Highway North, Sebastopol, CA 95472.

O'Reilly books may be purchased for educational, business, or sales promotional use. Online editions are also available for most titles (*http://oreilly.com*). For more information, contact our corporate/institutional sales department: 800-998-9938 or *corporate@oreilly.com*.

Acquisitions Editor: Brian Guerin	**Indexer:** Potomac Indexing, LLC
Development Editor: Rita Fernando	**Interior Designer:** David Futato
Production Editor: Christopher Faucher	**Cover Designer:** Karen Montgomery
Copyeditor: Emily Wydeven	**Illustrator:** Anna Evans
Proofreader: Piper Editorial Consulting, LLC	

May 2018:	First Edition
October 2024:	Second Edition

Revision History for the Second Edition

2024-10-10:   First Release

See *http://oreilly.com/catalog/errata.csp?isbn=9781098149345* for release details.

978-1-098-14934-5

[LSI]

This book is dedicated to my wife, Anna, who not only illustrated it beautifully but also helped edit portions and, crucially, was often the first person I bounced ideas off.

—Ben Evans

This book is dedicated to my incredible family Megan, Emily, and Anna. Writing would not have been possible without their help and support. I'd also like to thank my parents, Heather and Paul, for encouraging me to learn and their constant support.

I'd also like to thank Ben Evans for his guidance and friendship—it's been a pleasure working together again.

—James Gough

Table of Contents

Foreword

Optimization is a game of "what," and "why," and "where," but mostly "why." Why is my application slow? Where is the time being spent? Why are so many resources being consumed? What metrics matter? What problem am I actually trying to solve? Why is this innocent-looking microbenchmark misleading? Why do my users need this?

Many of us are taught how to program Java, but very few of us are taught how to optimize Java. We may not even know that we need to be able to optimize—until we hit a problem. But optimization is important. There's a saying that "slow is the new down"; outages are terrible, but sluggish performance is expensive, and annoying, and wasteful, and also pretty terrible. There's also sustainability to think about; in general, optimized software consumes less energy and requires less hardware to run. The digital world has a substantial carbon footprint, but we can reduce that by optimizing.

But people are perhaps the most important reason to optimize. Slow applications frustrate users, and in the worst case, may even drive them—and their business—elsewhere. Studies have found even small deterioration in response times can reduce user satisfaction and retention rates.

So how do we make applications go faster? As Ben and James point out in this book, there are no magic fixes or one-click answers. Ben and James do not give a set of recipes for performance tweaks, for the very good reason that this kind of advice goes very stale, very quickly.

Instead, Ben and James focus on principles and methodologies. They begin by introducing the basic observables of performance: throughput, latency, capacity, utilization, efficiency, scalability, and degradation. It is important to know which of these matter to you, because you cannot optimize them all—or at least, not all at the same time. It's exceedingly silly to spend time optimizing throughput if your users actually care about latency, or if the main challenge for your business is hardware costs. Performance is about compromise, and about chasing the right rabbit.

Ben and James give an overview of how to measure performance and how to use statistical analysis to interpret the results. They then dive into a comprehensive overview of how the Java virtual machine works. They cover memory layouts, garbage collection, code execution, and the just-in-time compiler. This is important because performance tuning is a process of discovery and problem-solving, which has to be rooted in an understanding of the whole system. "The whole system" means software, but also hardware, so Ben and James give an excellent primer on modern hardware. In a realistic software deployment, the edge of "the whole" system is not the plastic case of a single computer. Performance analysis must consider the distinctive characteristics of cloud environments and the risks and rewards of distributed computing. It's a lot, but Ben and James cover it. This is a broad book because what a modern software engineer needs to know is equally broad.

When trying to solve a performance problem, it's easy to be distracted by shiny things or influenced by our own pre-judgments. Especially in a complex system, one can easily end up chasing the wrong rabbit. To identify the right rabbit, it's necessary to go wide, across a diffuse and distributed application, and deep, into the internals of Java garbage collection and threading. One must be systematic and rigorous but also, as Ben and James point out, empathetic and business-aware. Performance is not an absolute quantity; slow only matters if it has consequences.

In *Spice World*, Roger Moore's character advised that "when the rabbit of chaos is pursued by the ferret of disorder through the fields of anarchy, it is time to hang your pants on the hook of darkness." With the help of this book, I believe you will be able to chase the right rabbit and hang your pants on the hooks of reason and understanding.

— Holly Cummins
Senior Principal Software Engineer,
Red Hat Middleware

Preface

Why Did We Write This Book?

This book is an updated edition of our *Optimizing Java* title, which was released in 2018. The world has changed markedly since then—in many ways. For Java programmers, the cloud has become ever-more important, and it is now probably more likely than not that Java applications are deployed in the cloud.

Cloud native deployment fundamentally changes a number of aspects of *performance engineering* (or whatever we want to call this specialism), so it seemed appropriate to produce a new edition of the book that reorients the material toward this new reality.

Why Should You Read This Book?

Java developers have, in many cases, not necessarily had a lot to do with the deployment and management of their applications in production. That is, they have tended not to be trailblazers in the adoption of trends like DevOps. With the increasing tide of cloud adoption, this has led to a possible knowledge gap, which this book aims to fix.

Alternatively, DevOps professionals may not have had much exposure to Java/JVM technologies but are now finding themselves needing to manage Java applications, or pieces of infrastructure that are implemented in it (e.g., Cassandra, Infinispan, Kafka, etc.). Java processes are fundamentally different from those implemented in Go, Python, Node.js, etc. To get the best out of them, you need some level of understanding of those differences and how to work with them.

Whichever tradition you have come from, the end goal is the same—to enable you to have confidence in managing your cloud-based production applications and be able to diagnose issues with them as they arise.

Who This Book Is For

Java performance optimization is of interest to several different groups of professionals, not just developers. As such, it is important that we provide on-ramps for people who may be coming from different backgrounds and approaching the subject with a different grounding.

The sorts of jobs that our readers might do include:

- Developers
- Application support and operations staff
- DevOps engineers
- Architects

Each of these groups is likely to have a different focus and take on the material, but they all share a common interest in looking after production business applications in the cloud. They will need to understand the performance behavior of both a single-JVM application and a cloud-deployed, distributed system. In this book we will consider cloud deployments to be public cloud, private cloud, and also a mixture of the two.

An awareness of performance methodology and the relevant aspects of statistics is also important, so that observability and other performance data can be accurately analyzed once it has been collected.

It is also to be expected that the majority of people who read this book will have a need for, or at least an interest in, some of the internals of the systems they support. This understanding is often very important when diagnosing certain types of performance problems, as well as being attractive to the intellectually curious engineer.

What You Will Learn

The material in this book covers a wide variety of topics. This is because this field extends beyond the boundaries of software development and overlaps into a variety of other fields.

What This Book Is Not

You will find almost no discussion of the vendor-specific technologies present on the cloud hyperscalers (AWS, Azure, GCP, OpenShift, and so on) in this book.

This is for two main reasons:

- It would expand the scope of the book and make it unmanageably long.
- It is impossible to stay current with such a large topic area.

The progress made by teams working on those products would make any detailed information about them out of date by the time the book is published. So, instead, in the cloud chapters, we focus on fundamentals and patterns, which remain effective regardless of which cloud your applications are deployed upon.

Conventions Used in This Book

The following typographical conventions are used in this book:

Italic
:   Indicates new terms, URLs, email addresses, filenames, and file extensions.

`Constant width`
:   Used for program listings, as well as within paragraphs to refer to program elements such as variable or function names, databases, data types, environment variables, statements, and keywords.

`<constant width>` *in angle brackets*
:   Shows text that should be replaced with user-supplied values or by values determined by context.

This element signifies a tip or suggestion.

This element signifies a general note.

This element indicates a warning or caution.

O'Reilly Online Learning

O'REILLY® For more than 40 years, *O'Reilly Media* has provided technology and business training, knowledge, and insight to help companies succeed.

Our unique network of experts and innovators share their knowledge and expertise through books, articles, and our online learning platform. O'Reilly's online learning platform gives you on-demand access to live training courses, in-depth learning paths, interactive coding environments, and a vast collection of text and video from O'Reilly and 200+ other publishers. For more information, visit *https://oreilly.com*.

How to Contact Us

Please address comments and questions concerning this book to the publisher:

O'Reilly Media, Inc.
1005 Gravenstein Highway North
Sebastopol, CA 95472
800-889-8969 (in the United States or Canada)
707-827-7019 (international or local)
707-829-0104 (fax)
support@oreilly.com
https://oreilly.com/about/contact.html

We have a web page for this book, where we list errata, examples, and any additional information. You can access this page at *https://oreil.ly/optimizing-java-2e*.

For news and information about our books and courses, visit *https://oreilly.com*.

Find us on LinkedIn: *https://linkedin.com/company/oreilly-media*.

Watch us on YouTube: *https://youtube.com/oreillymedia*.

Acknowledgments

The authors would like to thank a large number of people for their invaluable assistance.

For writing the foreword and technical review:

- Holly Cummins

For providing highly specialized technical help, including information and knowledge not available anywhere else:

- Christine Flood
- Kirk Pepperdine
- Roman Kennke
- Stefan Karlsson
- Jonathan Halliday

- Bela Ban
- Bruno Baptista
- Guus Bosman
- Fabio Massimo Ercoli
- Katia Aresti Gonzalez

For general encouragement, advice, and introductions:

- Stuart Douglas
- José Bolina

Our technical reviewers:

- Tony Mancill
- Dov Katz

- Elspeth Minty

For providing the technical illustrations:

- Anna Evans

The O'Reilly team:

- Rita Fernando
- Brian Guerin
- Zan McQuade

- Jeff Bleiel
- Christopher Faucher
- Emily Wydeven

## CHAPTER 1

Optimization and Performance Defined

Optimizing the performance of Java (or any other sort of code) is often seen as a dark art. There's a mystique about performance analysis—it's commonly viewed as a craft practiced by the "lone hacker, who is tortured and deep-thinking" (one of Hollywood's favorite tropes about computers and the people who operate them). The image is one of a single individual who can see deeply into a system and come up with a magic solution that makes the system work faster.

This image is often coupled with the unfortunate (but all-too-common) situation where performance is a second-class concern of the software teams. This sets up a scenario where analysis is only done once the system is already in trouble and needs a performance "hero" to save it. The reality, however, is a little different.

The truth is that performance analysis is a weird blend of hard empiricism and squishy human psychology. What matters is, at one and the same time, the absolute numbers of observable metrics and how the end users and stakeholders *feel* about them. The resolution of this apparent paradox is the subject of the rest of this book.

Since the publication of the first edition, this situation has only sharpened. As more and more workloads move into the cloud, and as systems become ever-more complicated, the strange brew that combines very different factors has become even more important and prevalent. The "domain of concern" that an engineer who cares about performance needs to operate in has continued to broaden.

This is because production systems have become even more complicated. More of them now have aspects of distributed systems to consider in addition to the performance of individual application processes. As system architectures become larger and more complex, the number of engineers who must concern themselves with performance has also increased.

The new edition of this book responds to these changes in our industry by providing four things:

- A necessary deep-dive on the performance of application code running within a single Java Virtual Machine (JVM)
- A discussion of JVM internals
- Details of how the modern cloud stack interacts with Java/JVM applications
- A first look at the behavior of Java applications running on a cluster in a cloud environment

In this chapter, we will get going by setting the stage with some definitions and establishing a framework for *how* we talk about performance—starting with some problems and pitfalls that plague many discussions of Java performance.

Java Performance the Wrong Way

For many years, one of the top three hits on Google for "Java performance tuning" was an article from 1997–8, which had been ingested into the index very early in Google's history. The page had presumably stayed close to the top because its initial ranking served to actively drive traffic to it, creating a feedback loop.

The page housed advice that was completely out of date, no longer true, and in many cases, detrimental to applications. However, its favored position in the search engine results caused many, many developers to be exposed to terrible advice.

For example, very early versions of Java had terrible method dispatch performance. As a workaround, some Java developers advocated avoiding small methods and instead writing monolithic methods. Of course, over time, the performance of virtual dispatch greatly improved.

Not only that, but with modern JVM technologies (especially automatic managed inlining), virtual dispatch has now been eliminated at a large number—perhaps even the majority—of call sites. Code that followed the "lump everything into one method" advice is now at a substantial disadvantage, as it is very unfriendly to modern just-in-time (JIT) compilers.

There's no way of knowing how much damage was done to the performance of applications that were subjected to the bad advice, but this case neatly demonstrates the dangers of not using a quantitative and verifiable approach to performance. It also provides yet another excellent example of why you shouldn't believe everything you read on the internet.

The execution speed of Java code is highly dynamic and fundamentally depends on the underlying Java virtual machine. An old piece of Java code may well execute faster on a more recent JVM, even without recompiling the Java source code.

As you might imagine, for this reason (and others we will discuss later) this book is not a cookbook of performance tips to apply to your code. Instead, we focus on a range of aspects that come together to produce good performance engineering:

- Performance methodology within the overall software lifecycle
- Theory of testing as applied to performance
- Measurement, statistics, and tooling
- Analysis skills (both systems and data)
- Underlying technology and mechanisms

By bringing these aspects together, the intention is to help you build an understanding that can be broadly applied to whatever performance circumstances you may face.

Later in the book, we will introduce some heuristics and code-level techniques for optimization, but these all come with caveats and tradeoffs that the developer should be aware of before using them.

Please do not skip ahead to those sections and start applying the techniques detailed without properly understanding the context in which the advice is given. All of these techniques are capable of doing more harm than good if you lack a proper understanding of how—and *why*—they should be applied.

In general, there are:

- No magic "go faster" switches for the JVM
- No "tips and tricks" to make Java run faster
- No secret algorithms that have been hidden from you

As we explore our subject, we will discuss these misconceptions in more detail, along with some other common mistakes that developers often make when approaching Java performance analysis and related issues.

Still here? Good. Then let's talk about performance.

Java Performance Overview

To understand why Java performance is the way that it is, let's start by considering a classic quote from James Gosling, the creator of Java:

> Java is a blue collar language. It's not PhD thesis material but a language for a job.[1]
> —James Gosling

That is, Java has always been an extremely practical language. Its attitude to performance was initially that, as long as the environment was *fast enough*, then raw performance could be sacrificed if developer productivity benefited. It was, therefore, not until 2005 or so, with the increasing maturity and sophistication of JVMs such as HotSpot, that the Java environment became suitable for high-performance computing applications.

This practicality manifests itself in many ways in the Java platform, but one of the most obvious is the use of *managed subsystems*. The idea is that the developer gives up some aspects of low-level control in exchange for not having to worry about some of the details of the capability under management.

The most obvious example of this is, of course, memory management. The JVM provides automatic memory management in the form of a pluggable *garbage collection* subsystem (usually referred to as GC), so that memory does not have to be manually tracked by the programmer.

> Managed subsystems occur throughout the JVM, and their existence introduces extra complexity into the runtime behavior of JVM applications.

As we will discuss in the next section, the complex runtime behavior of JVM applications requires us to treat our applications as experiments under test. This leads us to think about the statistics of observed measurements, and here we make an unfortunate discovery.

The observed performance measurements of JVM applications are very often not normally distributed. This means that elementary statistical techniques (especially *standard deviation* and *variance*, for example) are ill-suited for handling results from JVM applications. This is because many basic statistics methods contain an implicit assumption about the normality of results distributions.

---

1 J. Gosling, "The Feel of Java," *Computer*, vol. 30, no. 6 (June 1997): 53–57.

One way to understand this is that for JVM applications, outliers can be very significant—for a low-latency trading application or a ticket-booking system, for example. This means that sampling of measurements is also problematic, as it can easily miss the exact events that have the most importance.

Finally, a word of caution. It is very easy to be misled by Java performance measurements. The complexity of the environment means that it is very hard to isolate individual aspects of the system.

Measurement also has an overhead, and frequent sampling (or recording every result) can have an observable impact on the performance numbers being recorded. The nature of Java performance numbers requires a certain amount of statistical sophistication, and naive techniques frequently produce incorrect results when applied to Java/JVM applications.

These concerns also resonate into the domain of cloud native applications. Automatic management of applications has very much become part of the cloud native experience—especially with the rise of *orchestration technologies* such as Kubernetes. The need to balance the cost of collecting data with the need to collect enough to make conclusions is also an important architectural concern for cloud native apps—we will have more to say about that in Chapter 10.

Performance as an Experimental Science

The initial high-level picture you should have is that the JVM is a fast platform (and generally gets faster with each release), but despite that, Java applications can still be slow. This is because Java/JVM software stacks are, like most modern software systems, very complex.

In fact, due to the highly optimizing and adaptive nature of the JVM, production systems built on top of the JVM can have some subtle and intricate performance behavior. This complexity has been made possible by Moore's law and the unprecedented growth in hardware capability that it represents.

> The most amazing achievement of the computer software industry is its continuing cancellation of the steady and staggering gains made by the computer hardware industry.
>
> —Henry Petroski (attr)

While some software systems have squandered the historical gains of the industry, the JVM represents something of an engineering triumph. Since its inception in the late 1990s, the JVM has developed into a very high-performance, general-purpose execution environment that puts those gains to very good use.

The tradeoff, however, is that like any complex, high-performance system, the JVM requires a measure of skill and experience to get the absolute best out of it.

> A measurement not clearly defined is worse than useless.[2]
>
> —Eli Goldratt

JVM performance tuning is, therefore, a synthesis among technology, methodology, measurable quantities, and tools. Its aim is to effect measurable outputs in a manner desired by the owners or users of a system. In other words, performance is an experimental science—it achieves a desired result by:

1. Defining the desired outcome
2. Measuring the existing system
3. Determining what is to be done to achieve the requirement
4. Undertaking an improvement exercise
5. Retesting
6. Determining whether the goal has been achieved

The process of defining and determining desired performance outcomes builds a set of quantitative objectives. It is important to establish what should be measured and record the objectives, which then form part of the project's artifacts and deliverables. From this, we can see that performance analysis is based upon defining, and then achieving, nonfunctional requirements.

This process is, as has been previewed, not one of interpreting mysterious portents. Instead, we rely upon statistics and an appropriate handling (and interpretation) of results.

In this chapter, we discuss these techniques as they apply to a single JVM. In Chapter 2, we will introduce a primer on the basic statistical techniques required for accurate handling of data generated from a JVM performance analysis project. Later on, primarily in Chapter 10, we will discuss how these techniques generalize to a clustered application and give rise to the notion of observability.

It is important to recognize that, for many real-world projects, a more sophisticated understanding of data and statistics will undoubtedly be required. You are, therefore, encouraged to view the statistical techniques found in this book as a starting point, rather than a definitive statement.

---

2 Eliyahu Goldratt and Jeff Cox, *The Goal* (Gower Publishing, 1984).

A Taxonomy for Performance

In this section, we introduce some basic observable quantities for performance analysis. These provide a vocabulary for performance analysis and will allow you to frame the objectives of a tuning project in quantitative terms. These objectives are the nonfunctional requirements that define performance goals. Note that these quantities are not necessarily directly available in all cases, and some may require some work to obtain from the raw numbers obtained from our system.

One common basic set of performance observables is:

- Throughput
- Latency
- Capacity
- Utilization
- Efficiency
- Scalability
- Degradation

We will briefly discuss each in turn. Note that for most performance projects, not every metric will be optimized simultaneously. The case of only a few metrics being improved in a single performance iteration is far more common, and this may be as many as can be tuned at once. In real-world projects, it may well be the case that optimizing one metric comes at the detriment of another metric or group of metrics.

Throughput

Throughput is a metric that represents the rate of work a system or subsystem can perform. This is usually expressed as number of units of work in some time period. For example, we might be interested in how many transactions per second a system can execute.

For the throughput number to be meaningful in a real performance exercise, it should include a description of the reference platform it was obtained on. For example, the hardware spec, OS, and software stack are all relevant to throughput, as is whether the system under test is a single server or a cluster. In addition, transactions (or units of work) should be the same between tests. Essentially, we should seek to ensure that the workload for throughput tests is kept consistent between runs.

Performance metrics are sometimes explained via metaphors that evoke plumbing. If we adopt this viewpoint, then, if a water pipe can produce one hundred liters per second, then the volume produced in one second (one hundred liters) is the throughput. Note that this value is a function of the speed of the water and the cross-sectional area of the pipe.

Latency

To continue the metaphor of the previous section—latency is how long it takes a given liter to traverse the pipe. This is a function of both the length of the pipe and how quickly the water is moving through it. It is not, however, a function of the diameter of the pipe.

In software, latency is normally quoted as an end-to-end time—the time taken to process a single transaction and see a result. It is dependent on workload, so a common approach is to produce a graph showing latency as a function of increasing workload. We will see an example of this type of graph in "Reading Performance Graphs" on page 11.

Capacity

The capacity is the amount of work parallelism a system possesses—that is, the number of units of work (e.g., transactions) that can be simultaneously ongoing in the system.

Capacity is obviously related to throughput, and we should expect that as the concurrent load on a system increases, throughput (and latency) will be affected. For this reason, capacity is usually quoted as the processing available at a given value of latency or throughput.

For example, if we had a large reservoir at the beginning of our pipe, that would increase our capacity but not our overall throughput. Alternatively, if we had a very narrow ingress into our pipe, and the pipe then opened out, the capacity would be small, because the ingress acts as a choke point.

Utilization

One of the most common performance analysis tasks is to achieve efficient use of a system's resources. Ideally, CPUs should be used for handling units of work rather than being idle (or spending time handling OS or other housekeeping tasks).

Depending on the workload, there can be a huge difference between the utilization levels of different resources. For example, a computation-intensive workload (such as graphics processing or encryption) may be running at close to 100% CPU but be using only a small percentage of available memory.

As well as CPU, other resource types—such as network, memory, and (sometimes) the storage I/O subsystem—are becoming important resources to manage in cloud native applications. For many applications, more memory than CPU is "wasted," and for many microservices, network traffic has become the real bottleneck.

In the scenario where the water pipe has a narrow ingress, although most of the pipe has a large throughput, the overall utilization is low (so water levels in the pipe would be low) because of the capacity restriction represented by the restricted ingress.

Efficiency

Dividing the throughput of a system by the utilized resources gives a measure of the overall efficiency of the system. Intuitively, this makes sense, as requiring more resources to produce the same throughput is one useful definition of being less efficient.

It is also possible, when one is dealing with larger systems, to use a form of cost accounting to measure efficiency. If solution A has a total cost of ownership (TCO) twice that of solution B for the same throughput, then it is, clearly, half as efficient.

Scalability

The throughput or capacity of a system, of course, depends upon the resources available for processing. The scalability of a system or application can be defined in several ways—but a useful definition is the change in throughput as resources are added. The holy grail of system scalability is to have throughput change exactly in step with resources.

Consider a system based on a cluster of servers. If the cluster is expanded, for example, by doubling in size, then what throughput can be achieved? If the new cluster can handle twice the volume of transactions, then the system is exhibiting "perfect linear scaling." This is very difficult to achieve in practice, especially over a wide range of possible loads.

System scalability depends upon a number of factors and is not normally a simple linear relationship. It is very common for a system to scale close to linearly for some range of resources, but then at higher loads to encounter some limitation that prevents perfect scaling.

Degradation

If we increase the load on a system, either by increasing the rate at which requests arrive or the size of the individual requests, then we may see a change in the observed latency and/or throughput.

Note that this change depends on utilization. If the system is underutilized, then there should be some slack before observables change, but if resources are fully utilized, then we would expect to see throughput stop increasing or latency increase. These changes are usually called the degradation of the system under additional load.

Degradation also depends on a system's architecture robustness. For example, if the pipe was made out of the same material as children's balloons, the degradation under load would be pretty catastrophic. Once the load increased past a certain level, throughput would go to zero.

On the other hand, a more robust system would show a more realistic degradation scenario. For example, leaks that spring and get worse as pressure increases, or requests that are rejected before going into the system, are similar to having the tap on too hard and water splashing out and not getting into the pipe.

Correlations Between the Observables

The behavior of the various performance observables is usually connected in some manner. The details of this connection will depend upon whether the system is running at peak.

For example, in general, the utilization will change as the load on a system increases. However, if the system is underutilized, then increasing load may not appreciably increase utilization. Conversely, if the system is already stressed, then the effect of increasing load may be felt in another observable.

As another example, scalability and degradation both represent the change in behavior of a system as more load is added. For scalability, as the load is increased, so are available resources, and the central question is whether the system can use them. On the other hand, if load is added but additional resources are not provided, degradation of some performance observable (e.g., latency) is the expected outcome.

> In rare cases, additional load can cause counterintuitive results. For example, if the change in load causes some part of the system to switch to a more resource-intensive but higher-performance mode, then the overall effect can be to reduce latency, even though more requests are being received.

To take one example, in Chapter 6 we will discuss HotSpot's JIT compiler in detail. To be considered eligible for JIT compilation, a method has to be executed in interpreted mode "sufficiently frequently." So it is possible at low load to have key methods stuck in interpreted mode, but for those to become eligible for compilation at higher loads due to increased calling frequency on the methods. This causes later calls to the same method to run much, much faster than earlier executions.

Different workloads can have very different characteristics. For example, a trade on the financial markets, viewed end to end, may have an execution time (i.e., latency) of hours or even days. However, millions of them may be in progress at a major bank at any given time. Thus, the capacity of the system is very large, but the latency is also large.

However, let's consider only a single subsystem within the bank. The matching of a buyer and a seller (which is essentially the parties agreeing on a price) is known as *order matching*. This individual subsystem may have only hundreds of pending orders at any given time, but the latency from order acceptance to completed match may be as little as one millisecond (or even less in the case of "low-latency" trading).

In this section, we have met the most frequently encountered performance observables. Occasionally slightly different definitions, or even different metrics, are used, but in most cases these will be the basic system numbers that will normally be used to guide performance tuning and act as a taxonomy for discussing the performance of systems of interest.

Reading Performance Graphs

To conclude this chapter, let's look at some common patterns of behavior that occur in performance tests. We will explore these by looking at graphs of real observables, and we will encounter many other examples of graphs of our data as we proceed.

The graph in Figure 1-1 shows sudden, unexpected degradation of performance (in this case, latency) under increasing load—commonly called a *performance elbow*.

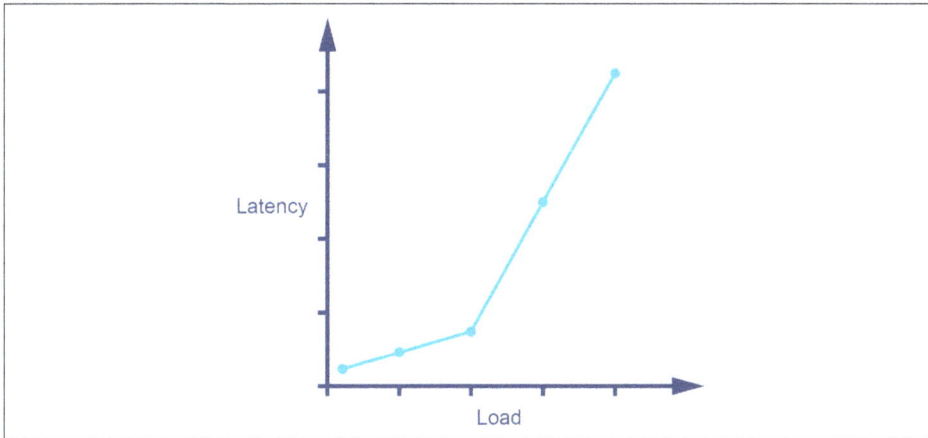

Figure 1-1. A performance elbow

By contrast, Figure 1-2 shows the much happier case of throughput scaling almost linearly as machines are added to a cluster. This is close to ideal behavior and is only likely to be achieved in extremely favorable circumstances—e.g., scaling a stateless protocol with no need for session affinity with a single server.

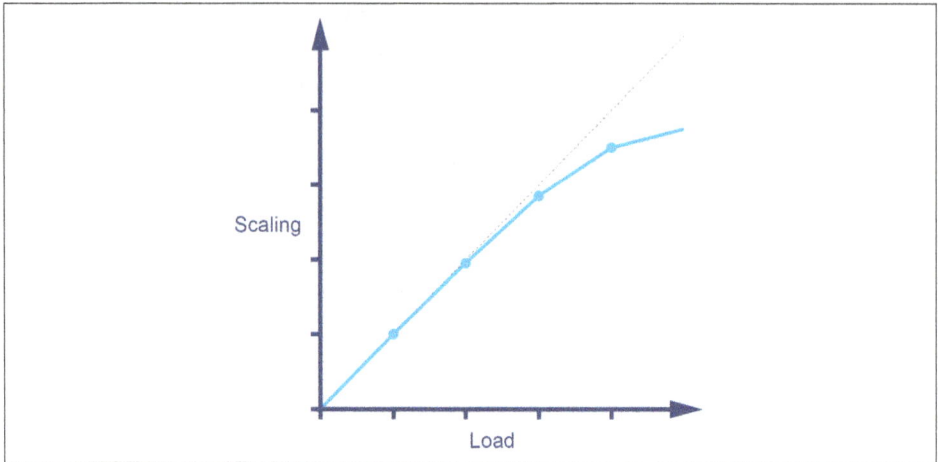

Figure 1-2. Near-linear scaling

In Chapter 13 we will meet Amdahl's law, named for the famous computer scientist (and "father of the mainframe") Gene Amdahl of IBM. Figure 1-3 shows a graphical representation of his fundamental constraint on scalability: the maximum possible speedup as a function of the number of processors devoted to the task.

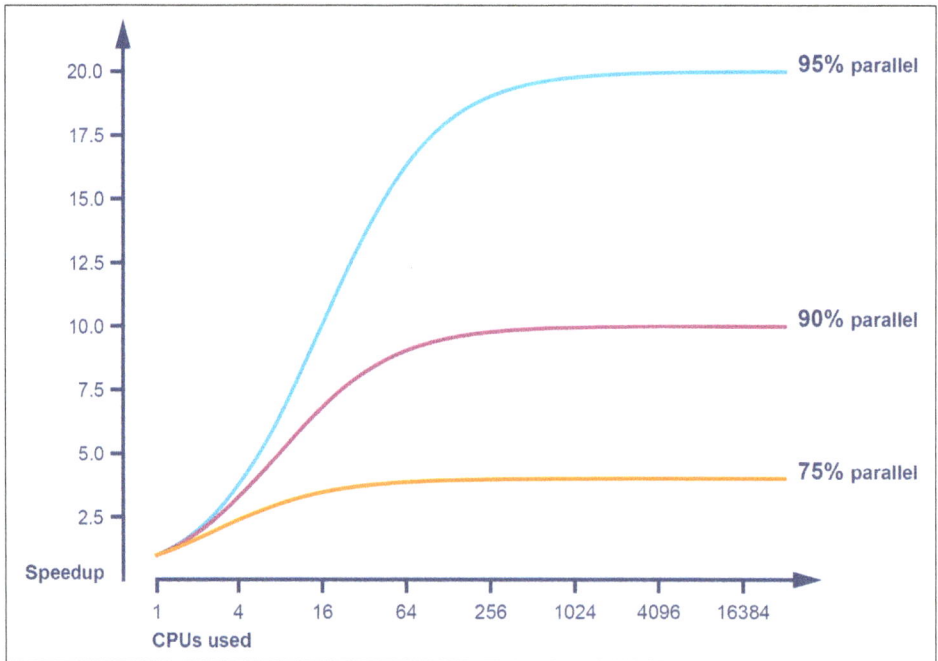

Figure 1-3. Amdahl's law

We display three cases: where the underlying task is 75%, 90%, and 95% paralleliza-ble. This clearly shows that whenever the workload has any piece at all that must be performed serially, linear scalability is impossible, and there are strict limits on how much scalability can be achieved. This justifies the commentary around Figure 1-2—even in the best cases, linear scalability is all but impossible to achieve.

The limits imposed by Amdahl's law are surprisingly restrictive. Note in particular that the x-axis of the graph is logarithmic, so even with an algorithm that is 95% parallelizable (and thus only 5% serial), 32 processors are needed for a factor-of-12 speedup. Even worse, no matter how many cores are used, the maximum speedup is only a factor of 20 for that algorithm. In practice, many algorithms are far more than 5% serial, so they have a more constrained maximum possible speedup.

Another common subject of performance graphs in software systems is memory utilization. As we will see in Chapter 4, the underlying technology in the JVM's garbage collection subsystem naturally gives rise to a "sawtooth" pattern of memory used for healthy applications that aren't under stress. We can see an example in Figure 1-4, which is a close-up of a screenshot from the JDK Mission Control tool (JMC) provided by Eclipse Adoptium.

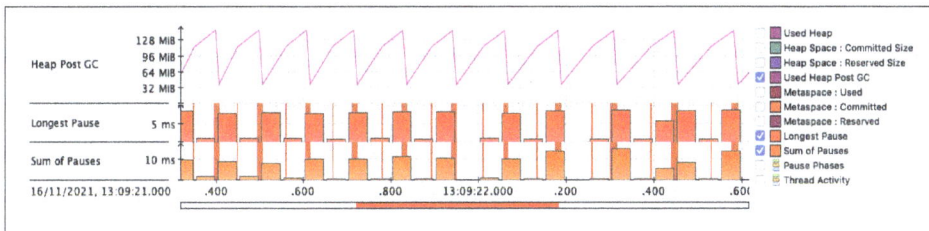

Figure 1-4. Healthy memory usage

One key performance metric for JVM is the allocation rate--effectively, how quickly it can create new objects (in bytes per second). We will have a great deal to say about this aspect of JVM performance in Chapters 4 and 5.

In Figure 1-5, we can see a zoomed-in view of allocation rate, also captured from JMC. This has been generated from a benchmark program that is deliberately stress-ing the JVM's memory subsystem—we have tried to make the JVM achieve 8 GiB/s of allocation, but as we can see, this is beyond the capability of the hardware, and instead the maximum allocation rate of the system is between 4 and 5 GiB/s.

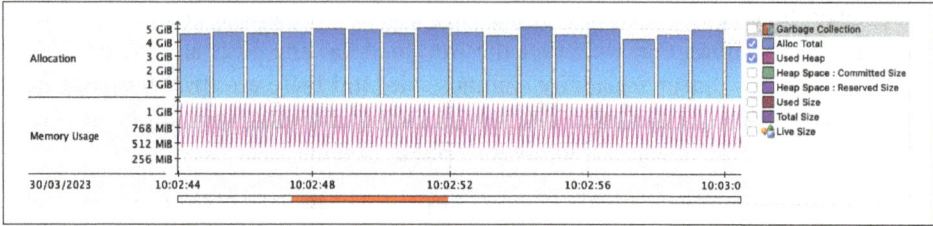

Figure 1-5. Sample problematic allocation rate

Note that tapped-out allocation is a different problem than the system having a resource leak. In that case, it is common for it to manifest in a manner like that shown in Figure 1-6, where an observable (in this case latency) slowly degrades as the load is ramped up, before hitting an inflection point where the system rapidly degrades.

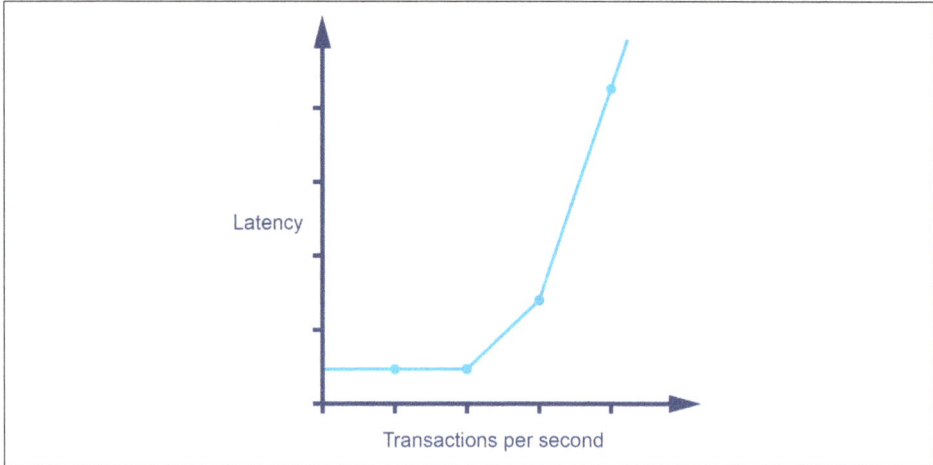

Figure 1-6. Degrading latency under higher load

Let's move on to discuss some extra things to consider when working with cloud systems.

Performance in Cloud Systems

Modern cloud systems are nearly always distributed systems in that they are composed of a cluster of nodes (JVM instances) interoperating via shared network resources. This means that, in addition to all the complexity of single-node systems, there is another level of complexity that must be addressed.

Operators of distributed systems have to think about things such as:

- How is work shared out among the nodes in the cluster?
- How do we roll out a new version of the software (or new config) to the cluster?
- What happens when a node leaves the cluster?
- What happens when a new node joins the cluster?
- What happens if the new node is misconfigured in some way?
- What happens if the new node behaves differently than the rest of the cluster in some way?
- What happens if there is a problem with the code that controls the cluster itself?
- What happens if there is a catastrophic failure of the entire cluster, or some infrastructure that it depends upon?
- What happens if a component in the infrastructure the cluster depends upon is a limited resource and becomes a bottleneck to scalability?

These concerns, which we will explore fully later in the book, have a major impact on how cloud systems behave. They affect the key performance observables such as throughput, latency, efficiency, and utilization.

Not only that, but there are two very important aspects—which differ from the single-JVM case—that may not be obvious at first sight to newcomers to cloud systems.

The first is that the unit of deployable code in the cloud is the *container* (we will have a great deal more to say about this later), rather than the application's JVM process (as it was in the days of big, bare-metal servers). It is also true that many possible performance impacts are caused by the internal behavior of a cluster, which may be opaque to the engineer.

We will discuss this in detail in Chapter 10 when we tackle the topic of observability in modern systems and how to implement solutions to this visibility problem.

The second is that the efficiency and utilization of how a service uses cloud providers has a direct effect on the cost of running that service. Inefficiencies and misconfigurations can show up in the cost base of a service far more directly. In fact, this is one way to think about the rise of cloud.

In the old days, teams would often own actual physical servers in dedicated areas (usually called *cages*) in datacenters. Purchasing these servers represented *capital expenditure*, and the servers were tracked as an asset.

When we use cloud providers, such as AWS or Azure, we are renting time on machines actually owned by companies such as Amazon or Microsoft. This is *operational expenditure*, and it is a cost (or liability). This shift means that the computational requirements of our systems are now much more open to scrutiny by the financial folks.

Overall, it is important to recognize that cloud systems fundamentally consist of clusters of processes (in our case, JVMs) that dynamically change over time. The clusters can grow or shrink in size, but even if they do not, over time the participating processes will change. This stands in sharp contrast to traditional host-based systems, where the processes forming a cluster are usually much more long-lived and belong to a known—and stable—collection of hosts.

Summary

In this chapter, we have started to discuss what Java performance is and is not. We have introduced the fundamental topics of empirical science and measurement, and the basic vocabulary and observables that a good performance exercise will use. We have introduced some common cases that are often seen within the results obtained from performance tests. Finally, we have introduced the very basics of the sorts of additional issues that can arise in cloud systems.

Let's move on and begin discussing some major aspects of performance testing as well as how to handle the numbers that are generated by those tests.

## CHAPTER 2

Performance Testing Methodology

Performance testing is undertaken for a variety of reasons. In this chapter, we will introduce the different types of performance test that a team may wish to execute and discuss some best practices for each subtype of testing.

Later in the chapter, we will discuss statistics—and some very important human factors—that are often neglected when considering performance problems.

Types of Performance Tests

Performance tests are frequently conducted for the wrong reasons, or conducted badly. The reasons for this vary widely but are often rooted in a failure to understand the nature of performance analysis and a belief that "doing something is better than doing nothing." As we will see several times throughout the book, this belief is often a dangerous half-truth at best.

One of the more common mistakes is to speak generally of "performance testing" without engaging with the specifics. In fact, there are many different types of large-scale performance tests that can be conducted on a system.

Good performance tests are quantitative. They ask questions that produce a numeric answer that can be handled as an experimental output and subjected to statistical analysis.

The types of performance tests we will discuss in this book usually have independent (but somewhat overlapping) goals. It is, therefore, important to understand the quantitative questions you are trying to answer before deciding what type of testing should be carried out.

This doesn't have to be that complex—simply writing down the questions the test is intended to answer can be enough. However, it is usual to consider why these tests are important for the application and confirming the reason with the application owner (or key customers).

Some of the most common test types, and an example question for each, are as follows:

Latency test
    What is the end-to-end transaction time?

Throughput test
    How many concurrent transactions can the current system capacity deal with?

Stress test
    What is the breaking point of the system?

Load test
    Can the system handle a specific load?

Endurance test
    What performance anomalies are discovered when the system is run for an extended period?

Capacity planning test
    Does the system scale as expected when additional resources are added?

Degradation
    What happens when the system is partially failed?

Let's look in more detail at each of these test types in turn.

Latency Test

Latency is one of the most common types of performance test because it is often a system observable of keen interest to management (and users): how long are our customers waiting for a transaction (or a page load)?

This can be a double-edged sword because the simplicity of the question (that a latency test seeks to answer) can cause teams to focus too much on latency. This, in turn, can cause the team to ignore the necessity of identifying quantitative questions for other types of performance tests.

> The goal of a latency tuning exercise is usually to directly improve the user experience or to meet a service-level agreement.

However, even in the simplest cases, a latency test has some subtleties that must be treated carefully. One of the most noticeable is that a simple mean (average) is not very useful as a measure of how well an application is reacting to requests. We will discuss this subject more fully in "Statistics for JVM Performance" on page 29 and explore additional measures.

Throughput Test

Throughput is probably the second most common quantity to be performance tested. It can even be thought of as dual to latency, in some senses.

For example, when we are conducting a latency test, it is important to state (and control) the concurrent transactions count when producing a distribution of latency results. Similarly, when we are conducting a throughput test, we must make sure to keep an eye on latency and check that it is not blowing up to unacceptable values as we ramp up.

The observed latency of a system should be stated at known and controlled throughput levels, and vice versa.

We determine the "maximum throughput" by noticing when the latency distribution suddenly changes—effectively a "breaking point" (also called an *inflection point*) of the system. The point of a stress test, as we will see in an upcoming section, is to locate such points and the load levels at which they occur.

A throughput test, on the other hand, is about measuring the observed maximum throughput before the system starts to degrade. Once again, these test types are discussed separately but are rarely truly independent in practice.

Stress Test

One way to think about a stress test is as a way to determine how much spare headroom the system has. The test typically proceeds by placing the system into a steady state of transactions—that is, a specified throughput level (often the current peak). The test then ramps up the concurrent transactions slowly, until the system observables start to degrade.

The value just before the observables started to degrade determines the maximum throughput achieved in a stress test.

Load Test

A load test differs from a throughput test (or a stress test) in that it is usually framed as a binary test: "Can the system handle this projected load or not?" Load tests are sometimes conducted in advance of expected business events—for example, the onboarding of a new customer or market that is expected to drive greatly increased traffic to the application.

Other examples of possible events that could warrant performing this type of test include advertising campaigns, social media events, and "viral content."

Endurance Test

Some problems manifest only over much longer periods of time (often measured in days). These include slow memory leaks, cache pollution, and memory fragmentation (especially for applications that may eventually suffer a GC concurrent mode failure; see Chapter 5 for more details).

To detect these types of issues, an endurance test (also known as a soak test) is the usual approach. These are run at average (or high) utilization, but within observed realistic loads for the system. During the test, resource levels are closely monitored to spot any breakdowns or exhaustions of resources.

This type of test is more common in low-latency systems, as it is very common that those systems will not be able to tolerate the length of a stop-the-world event caused by a full GC cycle (see Chapter 4 and subsequent chapters for more on stop-the-world events and related GC concepts).

Endurance tests are not performed as often as they perhaps should be, for the simple reason that they take a long time to run and can be very expensive—but there are no shortcuts. There is also the inherent difficulty of testing with realistic data or usage patterns over a long period. This can be one of the major reasons why teams end up "testing in production."

This type of test is also not always applicable to microservice or other architectures where a lot of code changes may be deployed in a short time.

Capacity Planning Test

Capacity planning tests bear many similarities to stress tests, but they are a distinct type of test. The role of a stress test is to find out what the current system will cope with, whereas a capacity planning test is more forward-looking and seeks to find out what load an upgraded system could handle.

For this reason, capacity planning tests are often carried out as part of a scheduled planning exercise rather than in response to a specific event or threat.

Degradation Test

Once upon a time, rigorous failover and recovery testing was really only practiced in the most highly regulated and scrutinized environments (including banks and financial institutions). However, as applications have migrated to the cloud, clustered deployments (e.g., based on Kubernetes) have become more common. One primary consequence of this is that more developers now need to be aware of the possible failure modes of clustered applications.

> A full discussion of all aspects of resilience and failover testing is outside the scope of this book. In Chapter 14, we will discuss some of the simpler effects that can be seen in cloud systems when a cluster partially fails or needs to recover.

In this section, the only type of resilience test we will discuss is the degradation test—this type of test is also known as a *partial failure* test.

The basic approach to this test is to see how the system behaves when a component or entire subsystem suddenly loses capacity while the system is running at simulated loads equivalent to usual production volumes. Examples could be application server clusters that suddenly lose members or network bandwidth that suddenly drops.

Key observables during a degradation test include the transaction latency distribution and throughput.

One particularly interesting subtype of partial failure test is known as the *Chaos Monkey* (*https://oreil.ly/TL_I2*). This is named after a project at Netflix that was undertaken to verify the robustness of its infrastructure.

The idea behind Chaos Monkey is that in a truly resilient architecture, the failure of a single component should not be able to cause a cascading failure or have a meaningful impact on the overall system.

Chaos Monkey forces system operators to confront this possibility by randomly killing off live processes in the production environment.

To successfully implement Chaos Monkey–type systems, an organization must have very high levels of system hygiene, service design, and operational excellence. Nevertheless, it is an area of interest and aspiration for an increasing number of companies and teams.

As we will see several times in this book, well-architected cloud systems are "designed for failure," in the sense that in a large enough deployment, some aspect of the system is broken at any given time. Perfectly working systems are an artifact of small system sizes, not the norm.

In addition, many systems are built with few assumptions about the particulars of hardware and infrastructure. These systems may also choose not to couple directly to specific features provided by their cloud vendor—this means that it is possible to run on top of multiple platforms for redundancy and failover reasons.

In this case, the software design accounts for, and encodes, these failure assumptions. As a result, coding for cloud can look very different from writing code to run on large upfront investments of static infrastructure—which are designed to "minimally fail."

Best Practices Primer

When deciding where to focus your effort in a performance tuning exercise, three golden rules can provide useful guidance:

- Identify what you care about and figure out how to measure it.
- Optimize what matters, not what is easy to optimize.
- Start by optimizing the largest contributions.

The second point has a converse, which is to remind yourself not to fall into the trap of attaching too much significance to whatever quantity you can easily measure. Not every observable is significant to a business, but it is sometimes tempting to report on an easy measure rather than the right measure.

To the third point, it is also easy to fall into the trap of optimizing small things simply for the sake of optimizing.

Top-Down Performance

One of the aspects of Java performance that many engineers miss at first sight is that large-scale benchmarking of Java applications is usually much easier than trying to get accurate numbers for small sections of code.

This is such a widely misunderstood point that, to deliberately deemphasize it, we do not discuss *microbenchmarking* in the main book text at all. Instead, it is discussed in Appendix A, a placement that more accurately reflects the utility of the technique for the majority of applications.

The approach of starting with the performance behavior of an entire application is usually called *top-down* performance.

To make the most of the top-down approach, a testing team needs a test environment, a clear understanding of what it needs to measure and optimize, and an understanding of how the performance exercise will fit into the overall software development lifecycle.

Creating a Test Environment

Setting up a test environment is one of the first tasks most performance testing teams will need to undertake. Wherever possible, this should be an exact duplicate of the production environment in all aspects.

> Some teams may be in a position where they are forced to forgo testing environments and simply measure in production using modern deployment and observability techniques. This is the subject of Chapter 10, but it is not recommended as an approach unless it's necessary.

This includes not only application servers (which should have the same number of CPUs, same version of the OS and Java runtime, etc.) but also web servers, databases, message queues, and so on. Any services (e.g., third-party network services that are not easy to replicate or do not have sufficient QA capacity to handle a production-equivalent load) will need to be mocked for a representative performance testing environment.

> Performance testing environments that are significantly different from the production deployments that they purport to represent are usually ineffective—they fail to produce results that have any usefulness or predictive power in the live environment.

For traditional (i.e., non-cloud-based) environments, a production-like performance testing environment is relatively straightforward to achieve in theory—the team simply buys as many machines as are in use in the production environment and then configures them in exactly the same way as production is configured.

Management is sometimes resistant to the additional infrastructure cost this represents. This is almost always a false economy, but sadly, many organizations fail to account correctly for the cost of outages. This can lead to a belief that the savings from not having an accurate performance testing environment are meaningful, as it fails to properly account for the risks introduced by having a QA environment that does not mirror production.

The advent of cloud technologies has changed this picture. More dynamic approaches to infrastructure management are now widespread. This includes on-demand and autoscaling infrastructure, as well as approaches such as *immutable infrastructure*, also referred to as treating server infrastructure as "livestock, not pets."

In theory, these trends make the construction of a performance testing environment that looks like production easier. However, there are subtleties here. For example:

- Having a process that allows changes to be made in a test environment first and then migrated to production
- Making sure that a test environment does not have some overlooked dependencies that depend upon production
- Ensuring that test environments have realistic authentication and authorization systems, not dummy components

Despite these concerns, the possibility of setting up a testing environment that can be turned off when not in use is a key advantage of cloud-based deployments. This can bring significant cost savings to the project, but it requires a proper process for starting up and shutting down the environment as scheduled.

Identifying Performance Requirements

The overall performance of a system is not solely determined by your application code. As we will discover throughout the rest of this book, the container, operating system, and hardware all have a role to play.

> In "A Simple System Model" on page 184, we will meet a simple system model that describes in more detail how the interaction between OS, hardware, JVM, and code impacts performance.

Therefore, the metrics that we will use to evaluate performance should not be thought about solely in terms of the code. Instead, we must consider systems as a whole and the observable quantities that are important to customers and management. These are usually referred to as performance *nonfunctional requirements* (NFRs) and are the key indicators that we want to optimize.

> One useful approach is that of service level objectives (SLOs), which we will discuss in Chapter 10.

Some performance goals are obvious:

- Reduce 95% percentile transaction time by 100 ms.
- Improve system so that 5x throughput on existing hardware is possible.
- Improve average response time by 30%.

Others may be less apparent:

- Reduce resource cost to serve the average customer by 50%.
- Ensure system is still within 25% of response targets, even when application clusters are degraded by 50%.
- Reduce customer "drop-off" rate by 25% by removing 10 ms of latency.

An open discussion with the stakeholders as to exactly what should be measured and what goals are to be achieved is essential. Ideally, this discussion should form part of the first kickoff meeting for any performance exercise.

Performance Testing as Part of the SDLC

Some companies and teams prefer to think of performance testing as an occasional, one-off activity. However, more sophisticated teams tend to make ongoing performance tests, and in particular, performance regression testing, an integral part of their software development lifecycle (SDLC).

This requires collaboration between developers and infrastructure teams to control which versions of code are present in the performance testing environment at any given time. It is also virtually impossible to implement without a dedicated testing environment.

Java-Specific Issues

Much of the science of performance analysis is applicable to any modern software system. However, the nature of the JVM is such that there are certain additional complications that the performance engineer should be aware of and consider carefully. These largely stem from the dynamic self-management capabilities of the JVM, such as the dynamic tuning of memory areas and JIT compilation.

For example, modern JVMs analyze which methods are being run to identify candidates for JIT compilation to optimized machine code. This means that if a method is not being JIT-compiled, then one of two things is true about the method:

- It is not being run frequently enough to warrant being compiled.
- The method is too large or complex to be analyzed for compilation.

The second condition is, by the way, much rarer than the first. In Chapter 6, we will discuss JIT compilation in detail and show some simple techniques for ensuring that the important methods of applications are targeted for JIT compilation by the JVM.

Having discussed some of the most common best practices for performance, let's now turn our attention to the pitfalls and antipatterns that teams can fall prey to.

Causes of Performance Antipatterns

An antipattern is an undesired behavior of a software project or team that is observed across a large number of projects.[1] The frequency of occurrence leads to the conclusion (or suspicion) that some underlying factor is responsible for creating the unwanted behavior. Some antipatterns may at first sight seem to be justified, with their nonideal aspects not immediately obvious. Others are the result of negative project practices slowly accreting over time.

A partial catalog of antipatterns can be found in Appendix B—where an example of the first kind would be something like *Distracted by Shiny*, whereas *Tuning by Folklore* is an example of the second kind.

In some cases, the behavior may be driven by social or team constraints, or by common misapplied management techniques, or by simple human (and developer) nature. By classifying and categorizing these unwanted features, we develop a *pattern language* for discussing them, and hopefully eliminating them from our projects.

Performance tuning should always be treated as a very objective process, with precise goals set early in the planning phase. This is easier said than done: when a team is under pressure or not operating under reasonable circumstances, this can simply fall by the wayside.

Many readers will have seen the situation where a new client is going live or a new feature is being launched, and an unexpected outage occurs—in user acceptance testing (UAT) if you are lucky but often in production. The team is then left scrambling to find and fix what has caused the bottleneck. This usually means performance testing has not been carried out, or the team "ninja" made an assumption and has now disappeared (ninjas are good at this).

A team that works in this way will likely fall victim to antipatterns more often than a team that follows good performance testing practices and has open and reasoned conversations. As with many development issues, it is often the human elements,

---

1 The term was popularized by the book *AntiPatterns: Refactoring Software, Architectures, and Projects in Crisis*, by William J. Brown, Raphael C. Malveau, Hays W. McCormick III, and Thomas J. Mowbray (New York: Wiley, 1998).

such as communication problems, rather than any technical aspect, that leads to an application having problems.

One interesting possibility for classification was provided in a blog post by Carey Flichel called "Why Developers Keep Making Bad Technology Choices" (*https://oreil.ly/62DPf*). The post specifically calls out five main reasons that cause developers to make bad choices. Let's look at each in turn.

Boredom

Most developers have experienced boredom in a role, and for some, this doesn't have to last very long before they seek a new challenge or role—either in the company or elsewhere. However, other opportunities may not be present in the organization, and moving somewhere else may not be possible.

It is likely many readers have come across a developer who is simply riding it out, perhaps even actively seeking an easier life. However, bored developers can harm a project in a number of ways.

For example, they might introduce code complexity that is not required, such as writing a sorting algorithm directly in code when a simple `Collections.sort()` would be sufficient. They might also express their boredom by looking to build components with technologies that are unknown or perhaps don't fit the use case just as an opportunity to use them—which leads us to the next section.

Résumé Padding

Occasionally the overuse of technology is not tied to boredom but rather represents the developer exploiting an opportunity to boost their experience with a particular technology on their résumé (or CV).

In this scenario, the developer is making an active attempt to increase their potential salary and marketability as they're about to re-enter the job market. It's unlikely that many people would get away with this inside a well-functioning team, but it can still be the root of a choice that takes a project down an unnecessary path.

The consequences of an unnecessary technology being added due to a developer's boredom or résumé padding can be far-reaching and very long-lived, lasting for many years after the original developer has left.

Social Pressure

Technical decisions are often at their worst when concerns are not voiced or discussed at the time choices are being made. This can manifest in a few ways; for example, perhaps a junior developer doesn't want to make a mistake in front of more senior members of their team, or perhaps a developer fears appearing to their peers as uninformed on a particular topic.

Another particularly toxic type of social pressure is for competitive teams, wanting to be seen as having high development velocity, to rush key decisions without fully exploring all the consequences.

Lack of Understanding

Developers may look to introduce new tools to help solve a problem because they are not aware of the full capability of their current tools. It is often tempting to turn to a new and exciting technology component because it is great at performing one specific task. However, introducing more technical complexity must be balanced with what the current tools can actually do.

For example, Hibernate is sometimes seen as the answer to simplifying translation between domain objects and databases. If the team has only limited understanding of Hibernate, developers can make assumptions about its suitability based on having seen it used in another project.

This lack of understanding can cause overcomplicated usage of Hibernate and unrecoverable production outages. By contrast, rewriting the entire data layer using simple JDBC calls allows the developer to stay in familiar territory.

One of the authors taught a Hibernate course that contained an attendee in exactly this position; they were trying to learn enough Hibernate to see if the application could be recovered but ended up having to rip out Hibernate over the course of a weekend—definitely not an enviable position.

Misunderstood/Nonexistent Problem

Developers may use a technology to solve a particular issue where the problem space itself has not been adequately investigated. Without having measured performance values, it is almost impossible to understand the success of a particular solution. Often, collating these performance metrics enables a better understanding of the problem.

To avoid antipatterns, it is important to ensure that communication about technical issues is open to all participants in the team and actively encouraged. Where things are unclear, gathering factual evidence and working on prototypes can help to steer team decisions. A technology may look attractive; however, if the prototype does not measure up, then the team can make a more informed decision.

To see how these underlying causes can lead to a variety of performance antipatterns, interested readers should consult Appendix B.

Statistics for JVM Performance

If performance analysis is truly an experimental science, then we will inevitably find ourselves dealing with distributions of results data. Statisticians and scientists know that results that stem from the real world are virtually never represented by clean, stand-out signals. We must deal with the world as we find it, rather than the overidealized state in which we would like to find it.

> In God we trust; all others must use data.[2]
>> —W. Edwards Deming (attr)

All measurements contain some amount of error, so repeated runs must be used to try to minimize the effect of errors in any individual run. The gold standard for Java performance was established in 2007 in the paper "Statistically Rigorous Java Performance Evaluation" (*https://oreil.ly/mjhzo*).[3] This contains the frequently repeated rule that thirty runs are necessary for reasonable statistical behavior in a highly dynamic software system, such as the JVM.

In the next section, we'll describe the two main types of error that a Java developer can expect to encounter when doing performance analysis.

Types of Error

Two main sources of error an engineer may encounter are:

Random error
    A measurement error or an unconnected factor affects results in an uncorrelated.

Systematic error
    An unaccounted factor affects measurement of the observable in a correlated way.

Specific words are associated with each type of error. For example, *accuracy* is used to describe the level of systematic error in a measurement; high accuracy corresponds to low systematic error. Similarly, *precision* is the term corresponding to random error; high precision is low random error.

The graphics in Figure 2-1 show the effect of these two types of error on a measurement. The extreme left image shows a clustering of shots (which represent our measurements) around the true result (the center of the target). These measurements have both high precision and high accuracy.

---

2 Mary Walton, *The Deming Management Method* (Mercury Books, 1989).

3 Andy Georges, Dries Buytaert, and Lieven Eeckhout. 2007. "Statistically Rigorous Java Performance Evaluation," *ACM SIGPLAN Notices*, vol. 42, iss. 10 (October 2007): 57–76.

The second image has a systematic effect (miscalibrated sights, perhaps?) that is causing all the shots to be off-target, so these measurements have high precision but low accuracy. The third image shows shots basically on target but loosely clustered around the center, so low precision but high accuracy. The final image shows no clear pattern, a result of having both low precision and low accuracy.

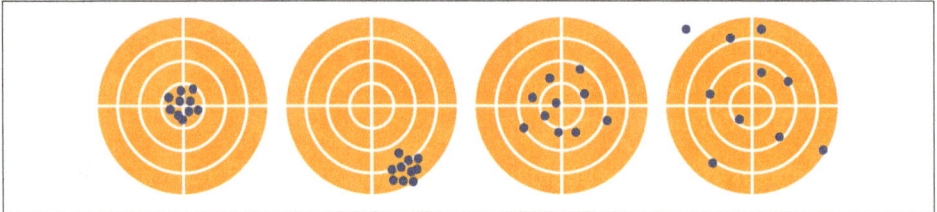

Figure 2-1. Different types of error

Let's move on to explore these types of error in more detail, starting with random error.

Random error

Random errors are hopefully familiar to most people—they are a very well-trodden path. However, they still deserve a mention here, as any handling of observed or experimental data needs to contend with them to some degree.

> The discussion assumes readers are familiar with basic statistical handling of normally distributed measurements (mean, mode, standard deviation, etc.); readers who aren't should consult a basic textbook, such as the *Handbook of Biological Statistics* (*http://biostathandbook.com*).[4]

Random errors are caused by unknown or unpredictable changes in the environment. In general scientific usage, these changes can occur in either the measuring instrument or the environment, but for software, we assume that our measuring harness is reliable, so the source of random error can only be the operating environment.

---

4 John H. McDonald, *Handbook of Biological Statistics*, 3rd ed. (Baltimore, MD: Sparky House Publishing, 2014).

Random error is usually considered to obey a Gaussian (aka normal) distribution. A couple of typical examples of Gaussian distributions are shown in Figure 2-2.

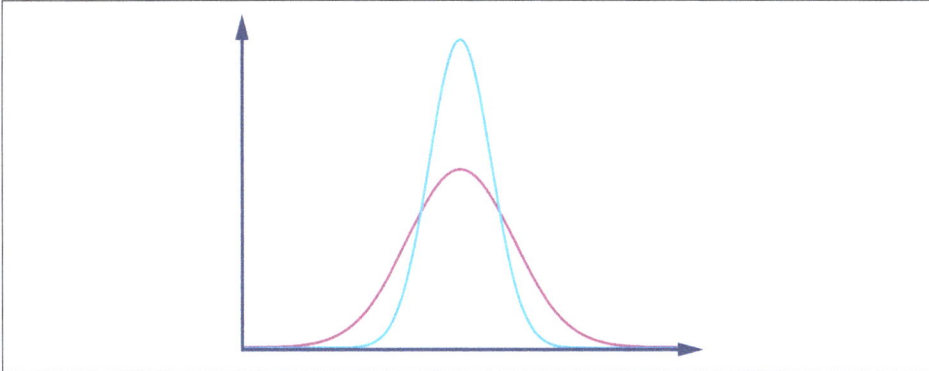

Figure 2-2. A Gaussian distribution (aka normal distribution or bell curve)

The distribution is a good model for the case where an error is equally likely to make a positive or negative contribution to an observable. However, as we will see in the section on non-normal statistics, the situation for JVM measurements is a little more complicated.

Systematic error

As an example of systematic error, consider a performance test running against a group of backend Java web services that send and receive JSON. This type of test is very common when it is problematic to directly use the application frontend for load testing.

Figure 2-3 was generated from the Apache JMeter load-generation tool. In it, there are actually two systematic effects at work. The first is the linear pattern observed in the topmost line (the outlier service), which represents slow exhaustion of some limited server resource.

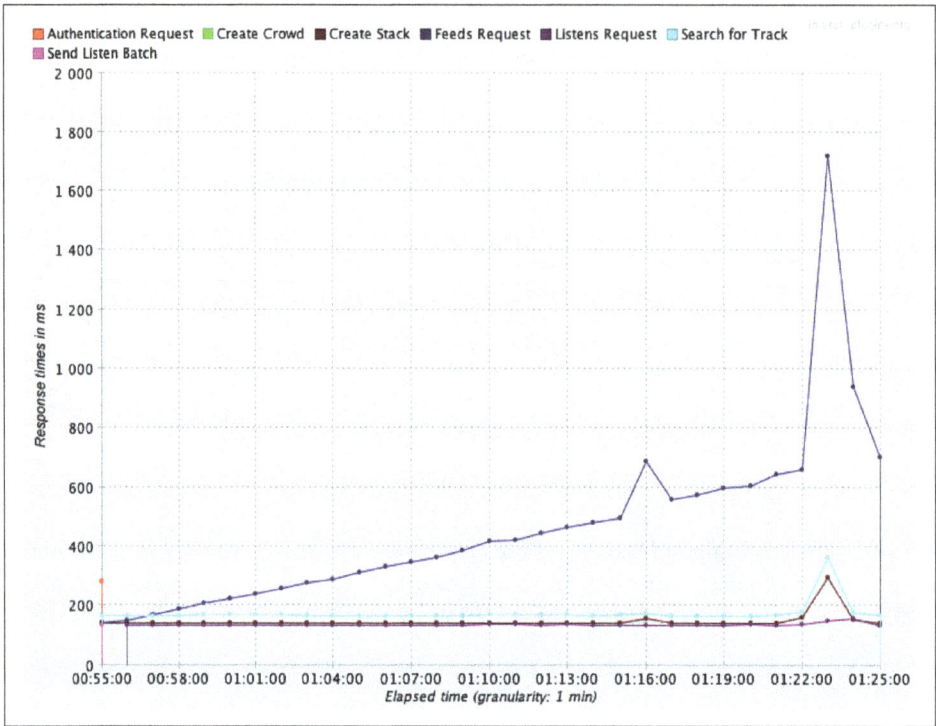

Figure 2-3. Systematic error

This type of pattern is often associated with a memory leak or some other resource being used and not released by a thread during request handling, and it represents a candidate for investigation—this looks like it could be a genuine problem.

Further analysis would be needed to confirm the type of resource that was being affected; we can't just conclude that it's a memory leak.

The second effect that should be noticed is the consistency of the majority of the other services at around the 180 ms level. This is suspicious, as the services are doing very different amounts of work in response to a request. So why are the results so consistent?

The answer is that while the services under test are located in London, this load test was conducted from Mumbai, India. The observed response time includes the irreducible round-trip network latency from Mumbai to London. This is in the range of 120–150 ms, so it accounts for the vast majority of the observed time for the services other than the outlier.

This large, systematic effect is drowning out the differences in the actual response time (as the services are actually responding in much less than 120 ms). This is an example of a systematic error that does not represent a problem with our application.

Instead, this error stems from a problem in our test setup not duplicating production, so the good news is that this artifact completely disappeared (as expected) when the test was rerun from London.

We've met some examples of sources of error and mentioned some notorious pitfalls, so let's move on to discuss an aspect of JVM performance measurement that requires some special care and attention to detail.

Non-Normal Statistics

Statistics based on the normal distribution do not require much mathematical sophistication. For this reason, the standard approach to statistics that is typically taught at precollege or undergraduate level focuses heavily on the analysis of normally distributed data.

Students are taught to calculate the mean and the standard deviation (or variance), and sometimes higher moments, such as skew and kurtosis. However, these techniques have a serious drawback, in that the results can easily become distorted if the distribution has even relatively few far-flung outlying points.

In Java performance, the outliers represent slow transactions and unhappy customers. We need to pay special attention to these points and avoid techniques that dilute the importance of outliers.

In Figure 2-4 we can see a more realistic curve for the likely distribution of method (or transaction) times. It is clearly not a normal distribution.

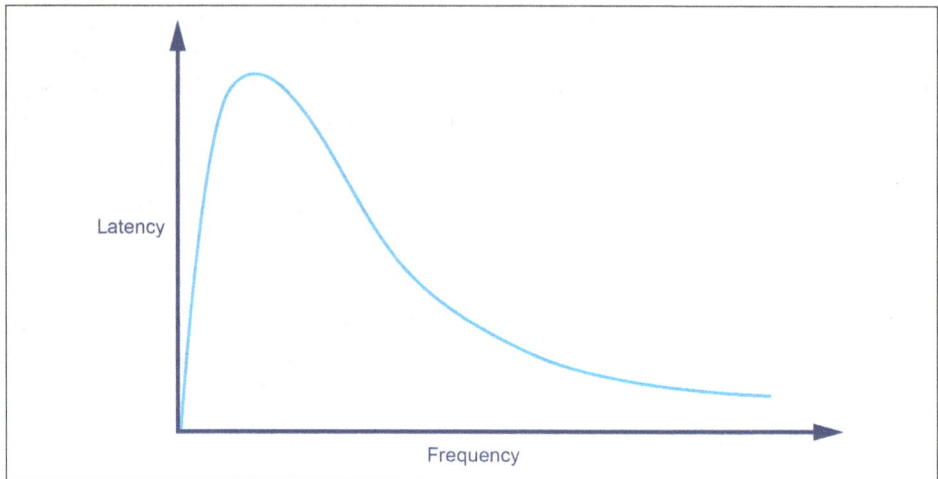

Figure 2-4. A more realistic view of the distribution of transaction times

The shape of the distribution in Figure 2-4 shows something that we know intuitively about the JVM: it has "hot paths" where all the relevant code is already JIT-compiled, there are no GC cycles, and so on. These represent a best-case scenario (albeit a common one); there simply are no calls that are "a bit faster" due to random effects.

This violates a fundamental assumption of Gaussian statistics and forces us to consider distributions that are non-normal.

> For distributions that are non-normal, many "basic rules" of normally distributed statistics are violated. In particular, standard deviation/variance and other higher moments are basically useless.

To consider it from another viewpoint: unless a large number of customers are already complaining, it is unlikely that improving the average response time is a useful performance goal. For sure, doing so will improve the experience for everyone, but it is far more usual for a few disgruntled customers to be the cause of a latency tuning exercise. This implies that the outlier events are likely to be of more interest than the experience of the majority who are receiving satisfactory service.

One technique that is very useful for handling the non-normal, "long-tail" distributions the JVM produces is to use a modified scheme of percentiles. Remember that a distribution is a whole collection of points—a shape of data, and is not well-represented by a single number.

Instead of computing just the mean, which tries to express the whole distribution in a single result, we can use a sampling of the distribution at intervals. When used for normally distributed data, the samples are usually taken at regular intervals. However, a small adaptation allows the technique to be used more effectively for JVM statistics.

The modification is to use a sampling that takes into account the long-tail distribution by starting from the mean, then the 90th percentile, and then moving out logarithmically, as shown in the following method timing results. This means that we're sampling according to a pattern that better corresponds to the shape of the data:

```
50.0% level was 23 ns
90.0% level was 30 ns
99.0% level was 43 ns
99.9% level was 164 ns
99.99% level was 248 ns
99.999% level was 3,458 ns
99.9999% level was 17,463 ns
```

The samples show us that while the average time was 23 ns to execute a getter method, for 1 request in 1,000, the time was an order of magnitude worse, and for 1 request in 100,000, it was *two* orders of magnitude worse than average.

Long-tail distributions can also be referred to as *high dynamic range* (HDR) distributions. The dynamic range of an observable is usually defined as the maximum recorded value divided by the minimum (assuming the latter is nonzero).

Logarithmic percentiles are a useful simple tool for understanding the long tail. However, for more sophisticated analysis, we can use a public domain library for handling datasets with high dynamic range. The library, called HdrHistogram, is available from GitHub (*https://oreil.ly/6Ax3R*). It was originally created by Gil Tene (Azul Systems), with additional work by Mike Barker and other contributors.

A histogram is a way of summarizing data by using a finite set of ranges (called *buckets*) and displaying how often data falls into each bucket.

HdrHistogram is also available on Maven Central. At the time of writing, the current version is 2.1.12, and you can add it to your projects by adding this dependency stanza to *pom.xml*:

```xml
<dependency>
    <groupId>org.hdrhistogram</groupId>
    <artifactId>HdrHistogram</artifactId>
    <version>2.1.12</version>
</dependency>
```

Let's look at a simple example using HdrHistogram. This example takes in a file of numbers and computes the HdrHistogram for the difference between successive results:

```java
public class BenchmarkWithHdrHistogram {
    private static final long NORMALIZER = 1_000_000;

    private static final Histogram HISTOGRAM
            = new Histogram(TimeUnit.MINUTES.toMicros(1), 2);

    public static void main(String[] args) throws Exception {
        final List<String> values = Files.readAllLines(Paths.get(args[0]));
        double last = 0;
        for (final String tVal : values) {
            double parsed = Double.parseDouble(tVal);
            double gcInterval = parsed - last;
            last = parsed;
            HISTOGRAM.recordValue((long)(gcInterval * NORMALIZER));
        }
        HISTOGRAM.outputPercentileDistribution(System.out, 1000.0);
    }
}
```

The output shows the times between successive garbage collections. As we'll see in Chapters 4 and 5, GC does not occur at regular intervals, and understanding the distribution of how frequently it occurs could be useful. Here's what the histogram plotter produces for a sample GC log:

```
Value     Percentile TotalCount 1/(1-Percentile)

   14.02 0.000000000000          1            1.00
 1245.18 0.100000000000         37            1.11
 1949.70 0.200000000000         82            1.25
 1966.08 0.300000000000        126            1.43
 1982.46 0.400000000000        157            1.67

...

28180.48 0.996484375000        368          284.44
28180.48 0.996875000000        368          320.00
28180.48 0.997265625000        368          365.71
36438.02 0.997656250000        369          426.67
36438.02 1.000000000000        369
#[Mean    =      2715.12, StdDeviation   =      2875.87]
#[Max     =     36438.02, Total count    =          369]
#[Buckets =           19, SubBuckets     =          256]
```

The raw output of the formatter is rather hard to analyze, but fortunately, the HdrHistogram project includes an online formatter (*https://oreil.ly/gMwqt*) that can be used to generate visual histograms from the raw output.

For this example, it produces output like that shown in Figure 2-5.

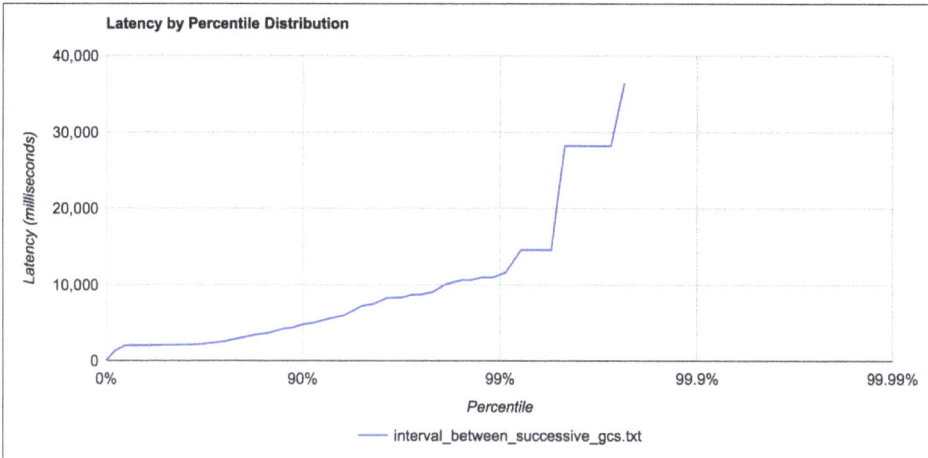

Figure 2-5. Example HdrHistogram visualization

For many observables that we wish to measure in Java performance tuning, the statistics are often highly non-normal, and HdrHistogram can be a very useful tool in helping to understand and visualize the shape of the data.

The tool can also help with detecting and understanding *coordinated omission*. This is a term that describes the phenomenon in which the measuring system inadvertently coordinates with the system being measured in a way that either incorrectly measures outliers or causes some requests to be skipped and not sent.[5]

Interpretation of Statistics

Empirical data and observed results do not exist in a vacuum, and it is quite common that one of the hardest jobs lies in interpreting the results we obtain from measuring our applications.

> No matter what the problem is, it's always a people problem.
>
> —Gerald Weinberg (attr)

Quite a few different problems are associated with interpretation. Let's start by taking a quick look at one notorious issue that frequently accompanies systematic error— spurious correlation.

---

5 For more on this, see Ivan Prisyazhnyy, "On Coordinated Omission," Scylla, April 22, 2021, *https://oreil.ly/VoW98*.

Spurious Correlation

One of the most famous aphorisms about statistics is "correlation does not imply causation"—that is, just because two variables appear to behave similarly does not imply that there is an underlying connection between them.

This is a very important concept for a performance engineer to grasp and warrants a bit of unpacking. Wikipedia enumerates four different options (*https://oreil.ly/wOjt1*). For any two correlated events, A and B, there are these possible relationships:

- A causes B (direct causation).
- B causes A (reverse causation).
- A and B are both caused by C (common causation)
- There is no connection between A and B; the correlation is a coincidence.

The first two cases are relatively straightforward. The third case, common causation, is the situation when two variables are linked, but we draw an incorrect causal link. That is, it's a true correlation, not a spurious one, but that doesn't mean we can infer a causal relationship.

For example, in healthcare, breastfeeding babies in infancy correlates with higher IQ scores later in childhood. This is well-evidenced, but in this case, there's a third factor that is causal and drives the correlation—essentially, that higher rates of breastfeeding tend to occur with higher social class, which in turn leads to more time spent on encouraging a child's mental development.

In the most extreme examples of the fourth case, if a practitioner looks hard enough, then a correlation can be found between entirely unrelated measurements (*https://oreil.ly/nY8Kb*). For example, in Figure 2-6 we can see that consumption of chicken in the US is well correlated with total import of crude oil.[6]

---

6 The spurious correlations in this section come from Tyler Vigen's site and are reused here with permission under CC BY 4.0. If you enjoy them, a book with many more amusing examples is available from his website.

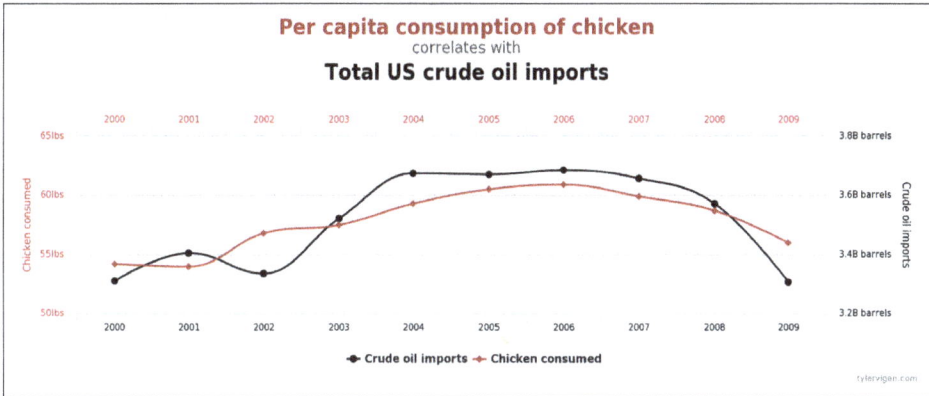

Figure 2-6. A completely spurious correlation (Vigen)

These numbers are clearly not causally related; there is no factor that drives both the import of crude oil and the eating of chicken. However, it isn't the absurd and ridiculous correlations that the practitioner needs to be wary of.

In Figure 2-7, we see the revenue generated by video arcades correlated to the number of computer science PhDs awarded. It isn't too much of a stretch to imagine a sociological study that claimed a link between these observables, perhaps arguing that "stressed doctoral students were finding relaxation with a few hours of video games." These types of claim are depressingly common, despite no such common factor actually existing.

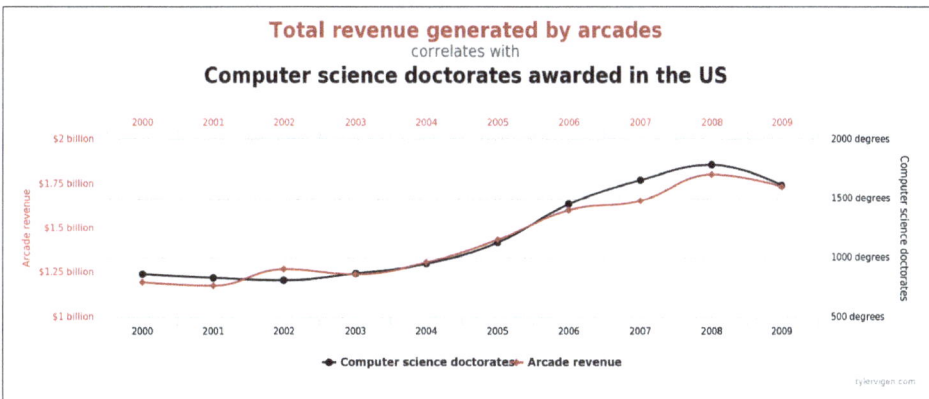

Figure 2-7. A less spurious correlation? (Vigen)

In the realm of the JVM and performance analysis, we need to be especially careful not to attribute a causal relationship between measurements based solely on correlation and that the connection "seems plausible."

The first principle is that you must not fool yourself—and you are the easiest person to fool.[7]

—Richard Feynman

In Figure 2-8, we show an example memory allocation rate for a real Java application. This example is for a reasonably well-performing application.

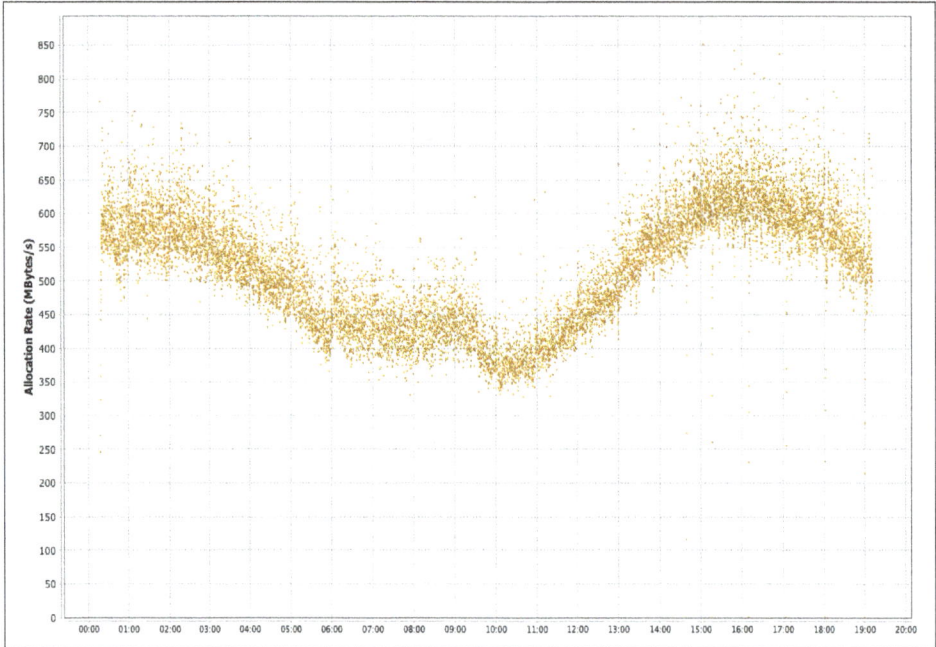

Figure 2-8. Example allocation rate

The interpretation of the allocation data is relatively straightforward, as there is a clear signal present. Over the time period covered (almost a day), allocation rates were basically stable between 350 and 700 MB per second. There is a downward trend starting approximately 5 hours after the JVM started up, and a clear minimum between 9 and 10 hours, after which the allocation rate starts to rise again.

These types of trends in observables are very common, as the allocation rate will usually reflect the amount of work an application is actually doing, and this will vary widely depending on the time of day. However, when we are interpreting real observables, the picture can rapidly become more complicated.

---

7 Richard Feynman and Ralph Leighton, *Surely You're Joking, Mr. Feynman!* (W.W. Norton, 1985).

The Hat/Elephant Problem

This can lead to what is sometimes called the "hat/elephant" problem, after a passage in *The Little Prince* by Antoine de Saint-Exupéry. In the book, the narrator describes drawing, at age six, a picture of a boa constrictor that has eaten an elephant. However, as the view is external, the picture just resembles (at least to the ignorant eyes of the adults in the story) a slightly shapeless hat.

The metaphor stands as an admonition to the reader to have some imagination and to think more deeply about what you are really seeing, rather than just accepting a shallow explanation at face value.

The problem, as applied to software, is illustrated by Figure 2-9. All we can initially see is a complex histogram of HTTP request-response times. However, just like the narrator of the book, if we can imagine or analyze a bit more, we can see that the complex picture is actually made up of several fairly simple pieces.

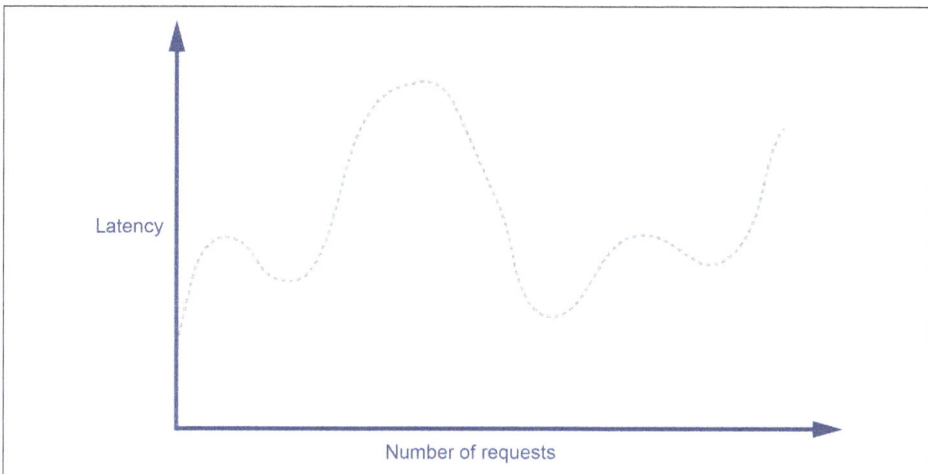

Figure 2-9. Hat or elephant eaten by a boa?

The key to decoding the response histogram is to realize that "web application responses" is a very general category, including successful requests (so-called 2xx responses), client errors (4xx, including the infamous 404 error), and server errors (5xx, especially 500 Internal Server Error).

Each type of response has a different characteristic distribution for response times. If a client makes a request for a URL that has no mapping (a 404), then the web server can immediately reply with a response. This means that the histogram for only client error responses looks more like Figure 2-10.

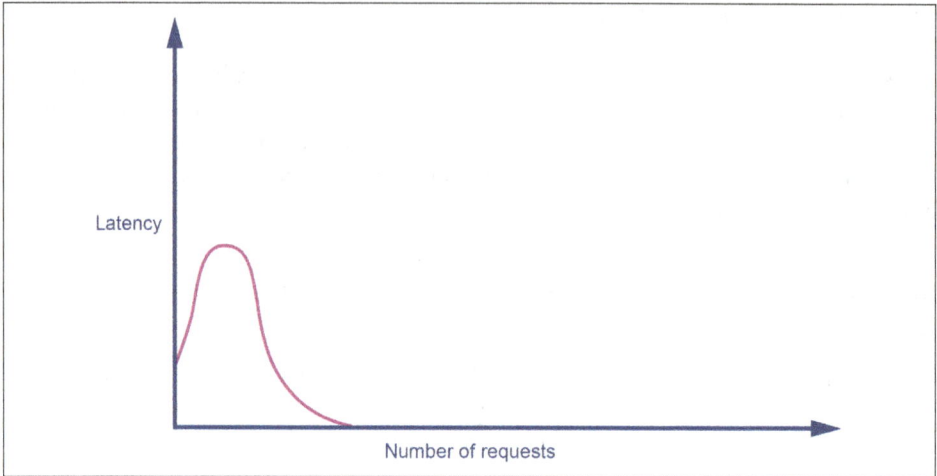

Figure 2-10. Client errors

By contrast, server errors often occur after a large amount of processing time has been expended (for example, due to backend resources being under stress or timing out). So, the histogram for server error responses might look like Figure 2-11.

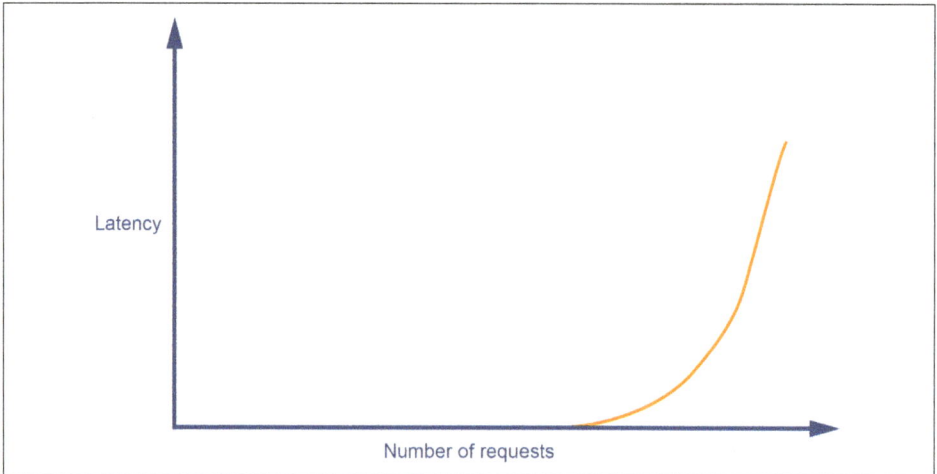

Figure 2-11. Server errors

The successful requests will have a long-tail distribution, but in reality, we can expect the response distribution to be "multimodal" and have several local maxima. An example is shown in Figure 2-12 and represents the possibility that there could be two common execution paths through the application with quite different response times.

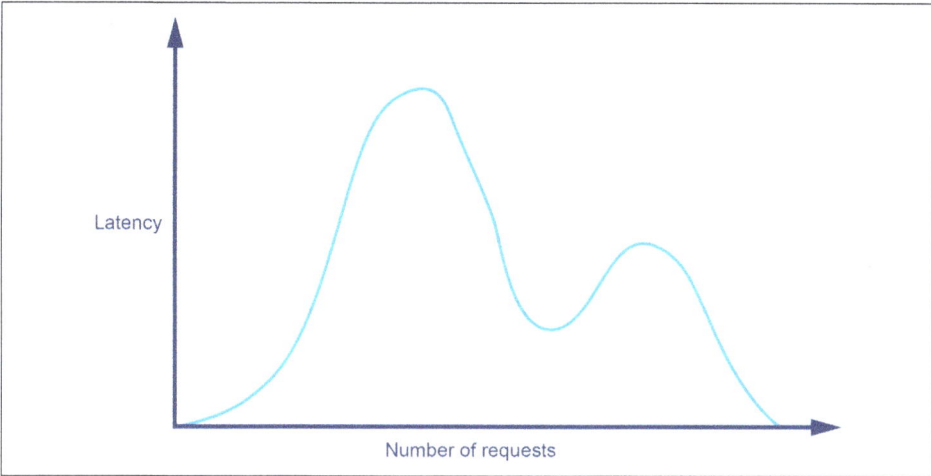

Figure 2-12. Successful requests

Combining these different types of responses into a single graph results in the structure shown in Figure 2-13. We have rederived our original "hat" shape from the separate histograms.

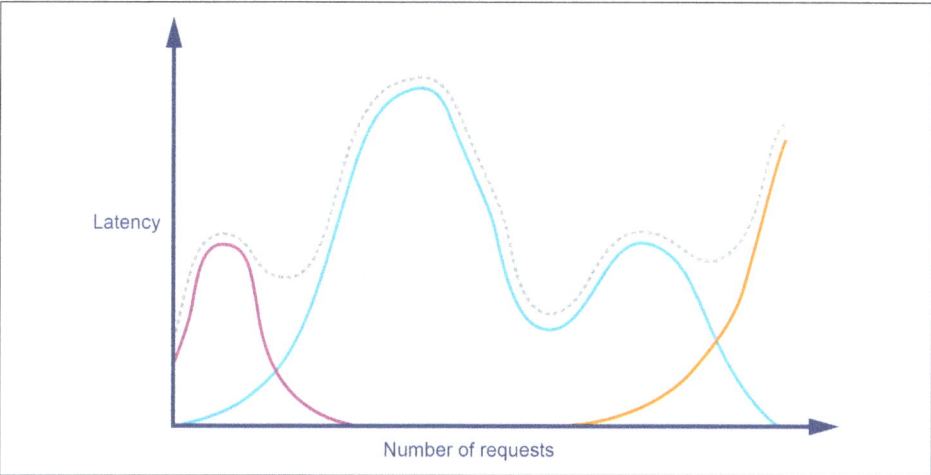

Figure 2-13. Hat or elephant revisited

The concept of breaking down a general observable into more meaningful subpopulations is a very useful one. It shows that we need to make sure that we understand our data and domain well enough before trying to infer conclusions from our results. We may well want to further break down our data into smaller sets; for example, the successful requests may have very different distributions for requests that are predominantly read, as opposed to requests that are updates or uploads.

The engineering team at PayPal has written extensively about its use of statistics and analysis; they have a blog (*https://oreil.ly/CHgkJ*) that contains excellent resources. In particular, the piece "Statistics for Software" (*https://oreil.ly/ZLK_v*) by Mahmoud Hashemi is a great introduction to their methodologies and includes a version of the hat/elephant problem discussed earlier.[8]

Also worth mentioning is the "Datasaurus Dozen"—a collection of datasets that have the same basic statistics but wildly different appearances.[9]

Cognitive Biases and Performance Testing

Humans can be bad at forming accurate opinions quickly—even when faced with a problem where they can draw upon past experiences and similar situations.

A cognitive bias is a psychological effect that causes the human brain to draw incorrect conclusions. It is especially problematic because the person exhibiting the bias is usually unaware of it and may believe they are being rational.

Many of the antipatterns we observe in performance analysis (such as those in Appendix B, which you might want to read in conjunction with this section) are caused, in whole or in part, by one or more cognitive biases that are, in turn, based on unconscious assumptions.

For example, with the *Blame Donkey* antipattern, if a component has caused several recent outages, the team may be biased to expect that same component to be the cause of any new performance problem. Any data that's analyzed may be more likely to be considered credible if it confirms the idea that the Blame Donkey component is responsible.

The antipattern combines aspects of the biases known as confirmation bias and recency bias (a tendency to assume that whatever has been happening recently will keep happening).

> A single component in Java can behave differently from application to application depending on how it is optimized at runtime. To remove any pre-existing bias, it is important to look at the application as a whole.

---

8 Mahmoud Hashemi whote this article when working for PayPal, but this is now attributed to the Paypal Tech Blog Team.

9 Justin Matejka and George Fitzmaurice, "Same Stats, Different Graphs: Generating Datasets with Varied Appearance and Identical Statistics through Simulated Annealing," *ACM SIGCHI Conference on Human Factors in Computing Systems 2017*, Denver (2017).

Biases can be complementary or dual to each other. For example, some developers may be biased to assume that the problem is not software-related at all, and the cause must be the infrastructure the software is running on; this is common in the *Works for Me* antipattern, characterized by statements like: "This worked fine in UAT, so there must be a problem with the production kit." The converse is to assume that every problem must be caused by software, because that's the part of the system the developer knows about and can directly affect.

Let's meet some of the most common biases that every performance engineer should look out for.

> Knowing where the trap is—that's the first step in evading it.[10]
> —Duke Leto Atreides I

By recognizing these biases in ourselves, and others, we increase the chance of being able to do sound performance analysis and solve the problems in our systems.

Reductionist Thinking

The reductionist thinking cognitive bias is based on an analytical approach that presupposes that if you break a system into small enough pieces, you can understand it by understanding its constituent parts. Understanding each part means reducing the chance of incorrect assumptions being made.

The major problem with this view is simple to explain—in complex systems, it just isn't true. Nontrivial software (or physical) systems almost always display emergent behavior, where the whole is greater than a simple summation of its parts would indicate.

Confirmation Bias

Confirmation bias can lead to significant problems when it comes to performance testing or attempting to look at an application subjectively. A confirmation bias is introduced, usually not intentionally, when a poor test set is selected or results from the test are not analyzed in a statistically sound way. Confirmation bias is quite hard to counter, because there are often strong motivational or emotional factors at play (such as someone in the team trying to prove a point).

Consider an antipattern such as *Distracted by Shiny*, where a team member is looking to bring in the latest and greatest NoSQL database. They run some tests against data that isn't like production data, because representing the full schema is too complicated for evaluation purposes.

---

10 Frank Herbert, *Dune* (Chilton Books, 1965).

They quickly prove that on a test set the NoSQL database produces superior access times on their local machine. The developer has already told everyone this would be the case, and on seeing the results, they proceed with a full implementation. There are several antipatterns at work here, all leading to new, unproved assumptions in the new library stack.

Fog of War (Action Bias)

The fog of war bias usually manifests itself during outages or situations where the system is not performing as expected and the team is under pressure. Some common causes include:

- Changes to infrastructure that the system runs on, perhaps without notification or realizing there would be an impact
- Changes to libraries that the system is dependent on
- A strange bug or race condition that manifests itself, but only on busy days

In a well-maintained application with sufficient observability tooling, these should generate clear signals that will lead the support team to the cause of the problem.

However, too many applications have not tested failure scenarios and lack appropriate tooling. Under these circumstances even experienced engineers can fall into the trap of needing to feel that they're doing something to resolve the outage and mistaking motion for velocity—the "fog of war" descends.

At this time, many of the human elements discussed in this chapter can come into play if participants are not systematic about their approach to the problem.

For example, an antipattern such as *Blame Donkey* can shortcut a full investigation and lead the production team down a particular path of investigation—often missing the bigger picture. Similarly, the team may be tempted to break the system down into its constituent parts and look through the code at a low level without first establishing in which subsystem the problem truly resides.

Risk Bias

Humans are naturally risk averse and resistant to change. Mostly this is because people have seen examples of how change can cause things to go wrong—this leads them to attempt to avoid that risk. This can be incredibly frustrating when taking small, calculated risks could move the product forward. Much of this risk aversion arises from teams that are reluctant to make changes that might modify the performance profile of the application.

We can reduce this risk bias significantly by having a robust set of unit tests and production regression tests. The performance regression tests are a great place to link in the system's nonfunctional requirements and ensure that the concerns the NFRs represent are reflected in the regression tests.

However, if either of these is not sufficiently trusted by the team, change becomes extremely difficult, and the risk factor is not controlled. This bias often manifests in a failure to learn from application problems (including service outages) and implement appropriate mitigation.

Summary

When you are evaluating performance results, it is essential to handle the data appropriately and avoid falling into unscientific and subjective thinking. This includes avoiding the statistical pitfalls of relying upon Gaussian models when they are not appropriate.

In this chapter, we have met some different types of performance tests, testing best practices, and human problems that are native to performance analysis.

In the next chapter, we're going to move on to an overview of the JVM, introducing the basic subsystems, the lifecycle of a "classic" Java application, and a first look at monitoring and tooling.

## CHAPTER 3

Overview of the JVM

There is no doubt that Java is one of the largest technology platforms on the planet—the best available estimate is of over 10+ million developers working with Java.

The design of the JVM is high level, with the aim of removing complexity for developers. Key aspects, such as garbage collection and execution optimization are kept under the control of the JVM on behalf of developers. The fact that Java is consciously aimed at mainstream developers leads to a situation in which many developers do not need to know about the low-level intricacies of the platform they work with daily. As a result, developers may not meet these internal aspects very frequently—but only when an issue arises, such as a customer complaining about a performance problem.

For developers who are interested in performance, however, it is important to understand the basics of the JVM technology stack. Understanding JVM technology enables developers to write better software and provides the theoretical background required for investigating performance-related issues.

This chapter introduces how the JVM executes Java to provide a basis for deeper exploration of these topics later in the book. In particular, Chapter 6 has an in-depth treatment of bytecode, which is complementary to the discussion here.

We suggest that you read through this chapter then come back to it for a second pass after you have read Chapter 6.

Interpreting and Classloading

According to the specification that defines the Java virtual machine (usually called the VM spec), the JVM is a stack-based interpreted machine. This means that rather than having registers (like a physical hardware CPU), it uses an execution stack of partial results and performs calculations by operating on the top value (or values) of that stack.

If you're not familiar with how interpreters work, then you can think of the basic behavior of the JVM interpreter as essentially "a `switch` inside a `while` loop." The interpreter processes each opcode of the program independently of the last and uses the evaluation stack to hold the results of computations and as intermediate results.

> As we will see when we delve into the internals of the Oracle/OpenJDK VM (HotSpot), the situation for real production-grade Java interpreters is more complex, but *switch-inside-while* using a stack interpreter is an acceptable mental model for the moment.

When we launch our application using the `java HelloWorld` command, the operating system starts the virtual machine process (the `java` binary). This sets up the Java virtual environment and initializes the interpreter that will actually execute the user code in the `HelloWorld.class` file.

The entry point into the application will be the `main()` method of `HelloWorld.class`. To hand over control to this class, it must be loaded by the virtual machine before execution can begin.

To achieve this, the Java class loading mechanism is used. When a new Java process is initializing, a chain of class loaders is used. The initial loader is known as the Bootstrap class loader (historically also known as the "Primordial class loader"), and it loads classes in the core Java runtime. The main point of the Bootstrap class loader is to get a minimal set of classes (which includes essentials such as `java.lang.Object`, `Class`, and `Classloader`) loaded to allow other class loaders to bring up the rest of the system.

At this point, it is also instructive to discuss a little bit of how the Java Platform Module System (sometimes referred to as JPMS) has changed the picture of application startup somewhat. First of all, from Java 9 onward, all JVMs are modular--there is no "compatibility" or "classic" mode that restores the Java 8 monolithic JVM runtime.

This means that during startup a module graph is always constructed—even if the application itself is nonmodular. This must be a directed acyclic graph (DAG), and it is a fatal startup error if the application's module metadata attempts to construct a module graph that contains a cycle.

The module graph has various advantages, including:

- Only required modules are loaded.
- Inter-module metadata can be confirmed to be good at startup time.

The module graph has a main module, which is where the entrypoint class lives. If the application has not yet been fully modularized, then it will have both a module-path and a classpath, and the application code may be in the UNNAMED module.

> Full details of the modules system are outside the scope of this book. An expanded treatment can be found in *Java in a Nutshell*, 8th Edition by Benjamin J. Evans, Jason Clark, and David Flanagan (O'Reilly) or a more in-depth reference, such as *Java 9 Modularity* by Sander Mak and Paul Bakker (O'Reilly).

In practice, the work of the Bootstrap class loader involves loading java.base and some other supporting modules (including some perhaps-surprising entries—e.g., java.security.sasl and java.datatransfer).

Java models class loaders as objects within its own runtime and type system, so there needs to be some way to bring an initial set of classes into existence. Otherwise, there would be a circularity problem in defining what a class loader is.

The Bootstrap class loader does not verify the classes it loads (largely to improve startup performance), and it relies on the boot classpath being secure. Anything loaded by the Bootstrap class loader is granted full security permissions, so this group of modules is kept as restricted as possible.

> Legacy versions of Java up to and including 8 used a monolithic runtime, and the Bootstrap class loader loaded the contents of rt.jar.

The rest of the base system (i.e., the equivalent of the rest of the old rt.jar used in version 8 and earlier) is loaded by the *Platform class loader*, which is available via the method ClassLoader::getPlatformClassLoader. It has the Bootstrap class loader as its parent, as the old Extension class loader has been removed.

In the new modular implementations of Java, far less code is required to bootstrap a Java process, and accordingly, as much JDK code (now represented as modules) as possible has been moved out of the scope of the bootstrap loader and into the platform loader instead.

Finally, the Application class loader is created; it is responsible for loading user classes from the defined classpath. Some texts, unfortunately, refer to this as the "System" class loader. This term should be avoided, for the simple reason that it doesn't load the system classes (the Bootstrap and Platform class loaders do). The Application class loader is encountered extremely frequently, and it has the Platform loader as its parent.

Java loads in dependencies on new classes when they are first encountered during the execution of the program. If a class loader fails to find a class, the behavior is usually to delegate the lookup to the parent. If the chain of lookups reaches the Bootstrap class loader and it isn't found, a `ClassNotFoundException` will be thrown. It is important that developers use a build process that effectively compiles with the exact same classpath that will be used in production, as this helps to mitigate this potential issue.

Normally, Java loads a class only once, and a `Class` object is created to represent the class in the runtime environment. However, it is important to realize that under some circumstances the same class can be loaded twice by different class loaders. As a result, a class in the system is identified by the class loader used to load it as well as the fully qualified class name (which includes the package name).

> Some execution contexts, such as application servers (e.g., Tomcat or JBoss EAP) by design display this behavior when multiple tenant applications are present in the server. This enables different tenants to have different versions of the classes they need.

It is also the case that some tools (e.g., Java agents) can potentially reload and retransform classes as part of bytecode weaving--and such tools are often used in monitoring and observability.

Executing Bytecode

It is important to appreciate that Java source code goes through a significant number of transformations before execution. The first is the compilation step using the Java compiler `javac`, often invoked as part of a larger build process.

The job of `javac` is to convert Java code into `.class` files that contain bytecode. It achieves this by doing a fairly straightforward translation of the Java source code, as shown in Figure 3-1. The diagram clearly shows that the creation of class files is not the whole story—and much of the JVM's power comes from what happens at runtime.

Accordingly, very few optimizations are done during compilation by `javac`, and the resulting bytecode is still quite readable and recognizable as Java code when viewed in a disassembly tool, such as the standard `javap`.

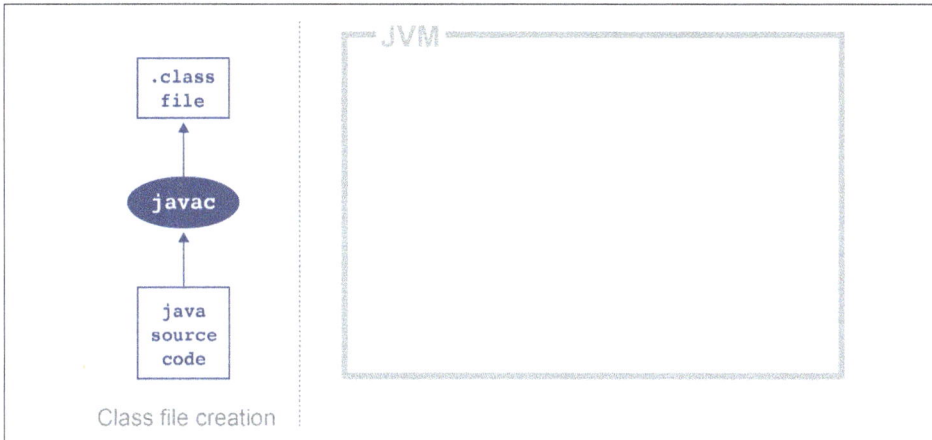

Figure 3-1. Java class file compilation

Bytecode is an *intermediate representation* that is not tied to a specific machine architecture. Decoupling from the machine architecture provides portability, meaning already developed (or compiled) software can run on any platform supported by the JVM and provides an abstraction from the Java language. This provides our first important insight into the way the JVM executes code.

The Java language and the Java virtual machine are now independent to a degree, so the J in JVM is potentially a little misleading, as the JVM can execute any JVM language that can produce a valid class file. In fact, Figure 3-1 could just as easily show the Kotlin compiler `kotlinc` generating bytecode for execution on the JVM.

Regardless of the source code compiler used, the resulting class file has a very well-defined structure specified by the VM spec (Table 3-1). Any class that is loaded by the JVM will be verified to conform to the expected format before being allowed to run.

Table 3-1. Anatomy of a class file

Component	Description
Magic number	`0xCAFEBABE`
Version of class file format	The minor and major versions of the class file
Constant pool	The pool of constants for the class
Access flags	Whether the class is abstract, static, and so on
This class	The name of the current class

Component	Description
Superclass	The name of the superclass
Interfaces	Any interfaces in the class
Fields	Any fields in the class
Methods	Any methods in the class
Attributes	Any attributes of the class (e.g., name of the source file)

Every class file starts with the magic number 0xCAFEBABE, the first 4 bytes in hexadecimal serving to denote conformance to the class file format. The following 4 bytes represent the minor and major versions used to compile the class file, and these are checked to ensure that the version of the JVM is not of a lower version than the one used to compile the class file. The major and minor version are checked by the class loader to ensure compatibility; if these are not compatible, an UnsupportedClassVer sionError will be thrown at runtime, indicating the runtime is a lower version than the compiled class file.

> Magic numbers provide a way for Unix environments to identify the type of a file (whereas Windows will typically use the file extension). For this reason, they are difficult to change once decided upon. Unfortunately, this means that Java is stuck using the rather embarrassing and sexist 0xCAFEBABE for the foreseeable future.

The constant pool holds constant values in code: for example, names of classes, interfaces, and fields. When the JVM executes code, the constant pool table is used to refer to values rather than having to rely on the precise layout of memory structures at runtime.

Access flags are used to determine the modifiers applied to the class. The first part of the flag block identifies general properties, such as whether a class is public, followed by whether it is final and thus cannot be subclassed. The flags also determine whether the class file represents an interface or an abstract class. The final part of the flag block indicates whether the class file represents a synthetic class (i.e., one that is not present in source code), an annotation type, or an enum.

The this class, superclass, and interface entries are indexes into the constant pool to identify the type hierarchy belonging to the class. Fields and methods define a signature-like structure, including the modifiers that apply to the field or method. A set of attributes is then used to represent structured items for more complicated and non-fixed-size structures. For example, methods use the Code attribute to represent the bytecode associated with that particular method.

Figure 3-2 provides a mnemonic for remembering the structure.

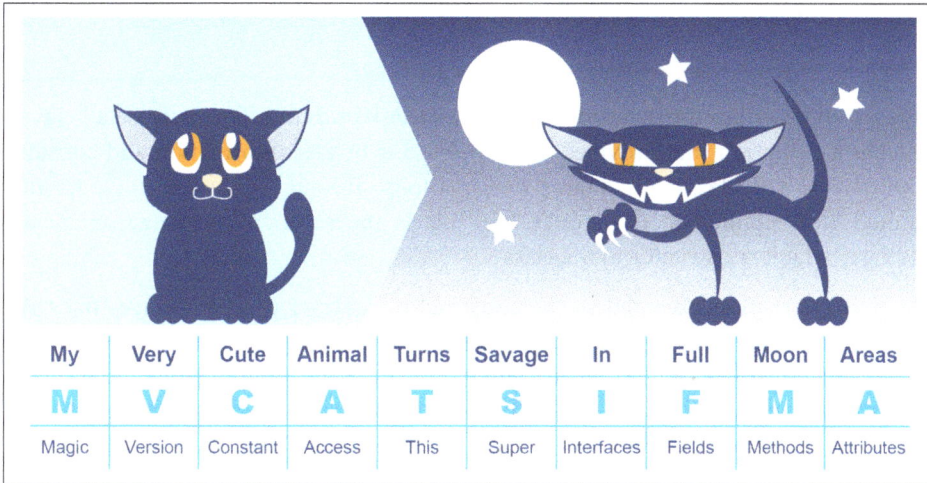

My	Very	Cute	Animal	Turns	Savage	In	Full	Moon	Areas
M	**V**	**C**	**A**	**T**	**S**	**I**	**F**	**M**	**A**
Magic	Version	Constant	Access	This	Super	Interfaces	Fields	Methods	Attributes

Figure 3-2. Mnemonic for class file structure

In this very simple code example, it is possible to observe the effect of running `javac`:

```java
public class HelloWorld {
    public static void main(String[] args) {
        for (int i = 0; i < 10; i++) {
            System.out.println("Hello World");
        }
    }
}
```

Java ships with a class file disassembler called `javap`, allowing inspection of *.class* files. Taking the *HelloWorld* class file and running `javap -c HelloWorld` gives the following output:

```
public class HelloWorld {
  public HelloWorld();
    Code:
       0: aload_0
       1: invokespecial #1     // Method java/lang/Object."<init>":()V
       4: return

  public static void main(java.lang.String[]);
    Code:
       0: iconst_0
       1: istore_1
       2: iload_1
       3: bipush        10
       5: if_icmpge     22
       8: getstatic     #2     // Field java/lang/System.out ...
      11: ldc           #3     // String Hello World
      13: invokevirtual #4     // Method java/io/PrintStream.println ...
      16: iinc          1, 1
```

```
19: goto       2
22: return
    }
```

This layout describes the bytecode for the file *HelloWorld.class*. For more detail, javap also has a -v option that provides the full class file header information and constant pool details. The class file contains two methods, although only the single main() method was supplied in the source file; this is the result of javac automatically adding a default constructor to the class.

The first instruction executed in the constructor is aload_0, which places the this reference onto the first position in the stack. The invokespecial command is then called, which invokes an instance method that has specific handling for calling super-constructors and creating objects. In the default constructor, the invoke matches the default constructor for Object, as an override was not supplied.

> Opcodes in the JVM (*https://oreil.ly/t2HDn*) are concise and represent the type, the operation, and the interaction among local variables, the constant pool, and the stack. See Chapter 6 for more details.

Moving on to the main() method, iconst_0 pushes the integer constant 0 onto the evaluation stack. istore_1 stores this constant value into the local variable at offset 1 (represented as i in the loop). Local variable offsets start at 0, but for instance methods, the 0th entry is always this. The variable at offset 1 is then loaded back onto the stack, and the constant 10 is pushed for comparison using if_icmpge ("if integer compare greater or equal"). The test succeeds only if the current integer is >= 10.

For the first 10 iterations, this comparison test fails, so we continue to instruction 8. Here the static method from System.out is resolved, followed by the loading of the "Hello World" string from the constant pool. The next invoke, invokevirtual, invokes an instance method based on the class. The integer is then incremented, and goto is called to loop back to instruction 2.

This process continues until the if_icmpge comparison eventually succeeds (when the loop variable is >= 10); on that iteration of the loop, control passes to instruction 22, and the method returns.

Introducing HotSpot

In April 1999, Sun introduced HotSpot—one of the biggest-ever changes (in terms of performance) to the dominant Java implementation. HotSpot is a virtual machine that has evolved to enable performance that is comparable to (or better than) languages such as C and C++ (see Figure 3-3). To explain how this is possible, let's delve a little deeper into the design of languages intended for application development.

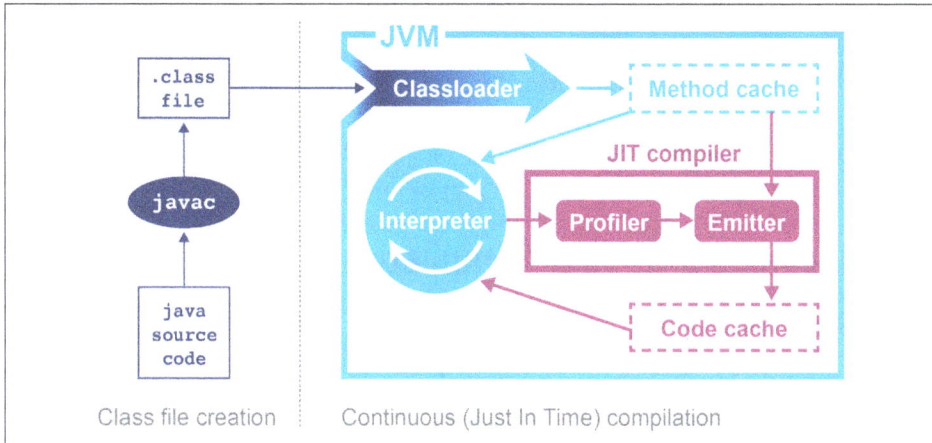

Figure 3-3. The HotSpot JVM

Language and platform design frequently involves making decisions and tradeoffs between desired capabilities. In this case, the division is between languages that stay "close to the metal" and rely on ideas such as "zero-cost abstractions," and languages that favor developer productivity and "getting things done" over strict low-level control.

> In general, C++ implementations obey the zero-overhead principle: What you don't use, you don't pay for. And further: What you do use, you couldn't hand code any better.[1]
>
> —Bjarne Stroustrup

The zero-overhead principle sounds great in theory, but it requires all users of the language to deal with the low-level reality of how operating systems and computers actually work. This is a significant extra cognitive burden that is placed upon developers who may not care about raw performance as a primary goal.

Not only that, but it also requires the source code to be compiled to platform-specific machine code at build time—usually called *ahead-of-time* (AOT) compilation. This is because alternative execution models such as interpreters, virtual machines, and portability layers all are most definitely not zero-overhead.

---

1 Bjarne Stroustrup, "Abstraction and the C++ Machine Model," *Lecture Notes in Computer Science*, vol. 3605 (Springer, 2005).

The phrase "what you do use, you couldn't hand code any better" also has a sting in its tail. It implies a number of things, but most important for our purposes is that a developer is not able to produce better code than an automated system (such as a compiler).

Java has never subscribed to the zero-overhead abstraction philosophy. Instead, the approach taken by the HotSpot virtual machine is to analyze the runtime behavior of your program and intelligently apply optimizations where they will benefit performance the most. The goal of the HotSpot VM is to allow you to write idiomatic Java and follow good design principles rather than contort your program to fit the JVM.

Introducing Just-in-Time Compilation

Java programs begin their execution in the bytecode interpreter, where instructions are performed on a virtualized stack machine. This abstraction from the CPU gives the benefit of class file portability, but to get maximum performance, your program must make optimal use of its native features.

HotSpot achieves this by compiling units of your program from interpreted bytecode into native code, which then executes directly, without requiring the overhead of the abstractions of the interpreter. The units of compilation in the HotSpot VM are the method and the loop. This is known as *just-in-time* (JIT) compilation.

JIT compilation works by monitoring the application while it is running in interpreted mode and observing the parts of code that are most frequently executed. During this analysis process, programmatic trace information is captured that allows for more sophisticated optimization. Once execution of a particular method passes a threshold, the profiler will look to compile and optimize that particular section of code.

There are many advantages to the JIT approach to compilation, but one of the main ones is that it bases compiler optimization decisions on trace information that is collected while methods are being interpreted. This information enables HotSpot to make more informed optimizations if the method is eligible for compilation.

Some JIT compilers also have the capability to re-JIT if a better optimization becomes apparent later on during execution. This includes some of HotSpot's compilers.

Not only that, but HotSpot has had hundreds of engineering years (or more) of development attributed to it, and new optimizations and benefits are added with almost every new release. This means that all Java applications benefit from the latest HotSpot performance optimizations in the VM without even needing to be recompiled.

After being translated from Java source to bytecode and now going through another step of (JIT) compilation, the code actually being executed has changed very significantly from the source code as written. This is a key insight, and it will drive our approach to dealing with performance-related investigations. JIT-compiled code executing on the JVM may well look nothing like the original Java source code.

The general picture is that languages like C++ and Rust tend to have more predictable performance but at the cost of forcing a lot of low-level complexity onto the user.

Note also that "more predictable" does not necessarily mean "better." AOT compilers produce code that may have to run across a broad class of processors—and usually are not able to assume that specific processor features are available.

Environments that use profile-guided optimization (PGO), such as Java, have the potential to use runtime information in ways that are simply impossible to most AOT platforms. This can offer improvements to performance, such as dynamic inlining and optimizing away virtual calls. HotSpot can even detect the precise CPU type it is running on at VM startup and can use this information to enable optimizations designed for specific processor features if available.

The technique of detecting precise processor capabilities is known as *JVM intrinsics* and is not to be confused with the intrinsic locks introduced by the `synchronized` keyword.

A full discussion of PGO and JIT compilation can be found in Chapter 6.

The sophisticated approach that HotSpot takes is a great benefit to the majority of ordinary developers, but this tradeoff (to abandon zero-overhead abstractions) means that in the specific case of high-performance Java applications, the developer must be very careful to avoid "common sense" reasoning and overly simplistic mental models of how Java applications actually execute.

Once again, analyzing the performance of small sections of Java code (*microbenchmarks*) is usually much harder than analyzing entire applications, and is a very specialized task that the majority of developers should not undertake.

HotSpot's compilation subsystem is one of the two most important subsystems that the virtual machine provides. The other is automatic memory management, which has been one of the major selling points of Java since the early years.

JVM Memory Management

In languages such as C, C++, and Objective-C the programmer is responsible for managing the allocation and release of memory. The benefits of managing memory and lifetime of objects yourself are more deterministic performance and the ability to tie resource lifetime to the creation and deletion of objects. However, these benefits come at a huge cost—for correctness, developers must be able to accurately account for memory.

Unfortunately, decades of practical experience showed that many developers have a poor understanding of patterns for memory management. Later versions of C++ and Objective-C have improved this somewhat by using smart pointer idioms in the standard library. However, at the time Java was created, poor memory management was a major cause of application errors. This led to concern among developers and managers about the amount of time spent dealing with language features rather than delivering value for the business.

Java looked to help resolve the problem by introducing automatically managed heap memory using a process known as *garbage collection* (GC). Simply put, garbage collection is a nondeterministic process that triggers the recovery and reuse of no-longer-needed memory when the JVM requires more memory for allocation.

GC comes at a cost: when it runs, it traditionally *stopped the world*, which means while GC is in progress, the application pauses. Usually these pause times are incredibly short, but as an application is put under pressure, these times can increase.

Having said that, the JVM's garbage collection in 2024 is best in class and is far more sophisticated than the introductory algorithm that is often taught in computer science undergraduate courses. For example, stopping the world is much less necessary and intrusive in modern algorithms, as we will see later.

Removing the concern of memory management from the developer provides the benefits of improving the correctness of an application. Garbage collection impacts performance and is an important subsystem in the JVM. The impact has the potential to be both positive and negative to the running application.

Garbage collection is a major topic within Java performance optimization, so we will devote Chapters 4 and 5 to the details of Java GC.

Threading and the Java Memory Model

One of the major advances that Java brought in with its first version was built-in support for multithreaded programming. The Java platform allows the developer to create new threads of execution. For example, in Java 8 syntax:

```
Thread t = new Thread(() -> {System.out.println("Hello World!");});
t.start();
```

Not only that, but basically all production JVMs are multithreaded—and this means that all Java programs are inherently multithreaded, as they execute as part of a JVM process.

This fact produces additional, irreducible complexity in the behavior of Java programs, and it makes the work of the performance analyst harder. However, it allows the JVM to take advantage of all available cores, which provides all sorts of performance benefits to the Java developer.

The relationship between Java's conception of a thread (an "application thread") and the operating system's view of a thread (a "platform thread") has an interesting history. In the very earliest days of the platform, a sharp distinction was made between the two concepts, and application threads were *remapped* or *multiplexed* onto a pool of platform threads—e.g., in the Solaris $M:N$, or the Linux *green threads* models.

However, this approach proved not to provide an acceptable performance profile and added needless complexity. As a result, in most mainstream JVM implementations, this model was replaced with a simpler one—each Java application thread corresponding precisely to a dedicated platform thread.

This is not the end of the story, however.

In the 20+ years since the "app thread == platform thread" transition, applications have grown and scaled massively—and so has the number of threads (or, more generally, *execution contexts*) that an application might want to create. This has led to the "thread bottleneck" problem, and solving it has been the focus of a major research project within OpenJDK (Project Loom).

The result is *virtual threads*, a new form of thread available only in Java 21+, which can be used efficiently for certain tasks—especially those performing network I/O.

Programmers must explicitly choose to create a thread as virtual—otherwise they are platform threads and retain the same behavior as before (so the semantics of all existing Java programs are preserved when run on a JVM with virtual thread capability).

It is safe to assume that every platform thread (or any thread, before Java 21) is backed by a unique OS thread that is created when the start() method is called on the corresponding Thread object.

Virtual threads are Java's take on an idea that can be found in various other modern languages—for example, Go programmers may regard a Java virtual thread as being broadly similar to a goroutine. We will discuss virtual threads in more detail in Chapter 13.

We should also briefly discuss Java's approach to handling data in a multithreaded program. It dates from the late 1990s and has these fundamental design principles:

- All threads in a Java process share a single, common garbage-collected heap.
- Any object created by one thread can be accessed by any other thread that has a reference to the object.
- Objects are mutable by default; that is, the values held in object fields can be changed unless the programmer explicitly uses the final keyword to mark them as immutable.

The Java Memory Model (JMM) is a formal model of memory that explains how different threads of execution see the changing values held in objects. That is, if threads A and B both have references to object obj, and thread A alters it, what happens to the value observed in thread B?

This seemingly simple question is actually more complicated than it seems, because the operating system scheduler (which we will meet in Chapter 7) can forcibly evict platform threads from CPU cores. This can lead to another thread starting to execute and accessing an object before the original thread had finished processing it, and potentially seeing the object in a prior or even invalid state.

The only defense the core of Java provides against this potential object damage during concurrent code execution is the mutual exclusion lock, and this can be very complex to use in real applications. Chapter 13 contains a detailed look at how the JMM works and the practicalities of working with threads and locks.

Monitoring and Tooling for the JVM

The JVM is a mature execution platform, and it provides a number of technology alternatives for instrumentation, monitoring, and observability of running applications. The main technologies available for these types of tools for JVM applications are:

- Java Management Extensions (JMX)
- Java agents
- The JVM Tool Interface (JVMTI)
- The Serviceability Agent (SA)

JMX is a general-purpose technology for controlling and monitoring JVMs and the applications running on them. It provides the ability to change parameters and call methods in a general way from a client application. A full treatment of how this is implemented is, unfortunately, outside the scope of this book. However, JMX (and its associated network transport, *Remote Method Invocation* or RMI) is a fundamental aspect of the management capabilities of the JVM.

A Java agent is a tooling component that uses the interfaces in `java.lang.instrument` to modify the bytecode of methods as classes are loaded. The modification of bytecode allows instrumentation logic, such as method timing or distributed tracing (see Chapter 10 for more details), to be added to any application, even one that has not been written with any support for those concerns.

This is an extremely powerful technique, and installing an agent changes the standard application lifecycle that we met in the last section. To be installed, an agent must be packaged as a JAR and provided via a startup flag to the JVM:

```
-javaagent:<path-to-agent-jar>=<options>
```

The agent JAR must contain a manifest file, `META-INF/MANIFEST.MF`, and it must include the attribute `Premain-Class`.

This attribute contains the name of the agent class, which must implement a public static `premain()` method that acts as the registration hook for the Java agent. This method will run on the main application thread *before* the `main()` method of the application (hence the name). Note that the premain method must exit, or the main application will not start.

Bytecode transformation is the usual intent of an agent, and this is done by creating and registering bytecode transformers—objects that implement the `ClassFileTransformer` interface.

However, a Java agent is just Java code, so it can do anything that any other Java program can, i.e., it can contain arbitrary code to execute. This flexibility means that, for example, an agent can start additional threads that can persist for the entire life of the application, and can collect data for sending out of the application and into an external monitoring system.

We will have a little more to say about JMX and agents in Chapter 11, where we discuss their use in cloud observability tools.

If the Java instrumentation API is not sufficient, then the JVMTI may be used instead. This is a native interface of the JVM, so agents that use it must be written in a native compiled language—essentially, C or C++. It can be thought of as a communication interface that allows a native agent to monitor and be informed of events by the JVM. To install a native agent, provide a slightly different flag:

```
-agentlib:<agent-lib-name>=<options>
```

or:

```
-agentpath:<path-to-agent>=<options>
```

The requirement that JVMTI agents be written in native code means that these agents can be more difficult to write and debug. Programming errors in JVMTI agents can damage running applications and even crash the JVM.

Therefore, where possible, it is usually preferable to write a Java agent over JVMTI code. Agents are much easier to write, but some information is not available through the Java API, and JVMTI may be the only possibility available to access that data.

The final approach is the Serviceability Agent. This is a set of APIs and tools that can expose both Java objects and HotSpot data structures.

The SA does not require any code to be run in the target VM. Instead, the HotSpot SA uses primitives like symbol lookup and reading of process memory to implement debugging capability. The SA has the ability to debug live Java processes as well as core files (also called *crash dump files*).

One tool that should be introduced at this point is VisualVM, which is a graphical tool based on the NetBeans platform (*https://oreil.ly/CjWqa*). It used to ship as part of the JDK and was previously distributed in Oracle JDK versions 6–8 and in GraalVM versions 19–23.0.

However, it has since been moved out of the main distribution, so developers will have to download the binary separately from the VisualVM website (*https://oreil.ly/Z4w6h*). After downloading, you will have to ensure that the jvisualvm binary is added to your path, or you may get an obsolete version from an old Java version.

jvisualvm is a replacement for the now obsolete jconsole tool from earlier Java versions. If you are still using jconsole, you should move to VisualVM (there is a compatibility plug-in to allow jconsole plug-ins to run inside VisualVM).

When VisualVM is started for the first time, it will calibrate the machine it is running on, so there should be no other applications running that might affect the performance calibration.

When the desktop application is started for the first time, a screen similar to that shown in Figure 3-4 is displayed (after a short calibration pause).

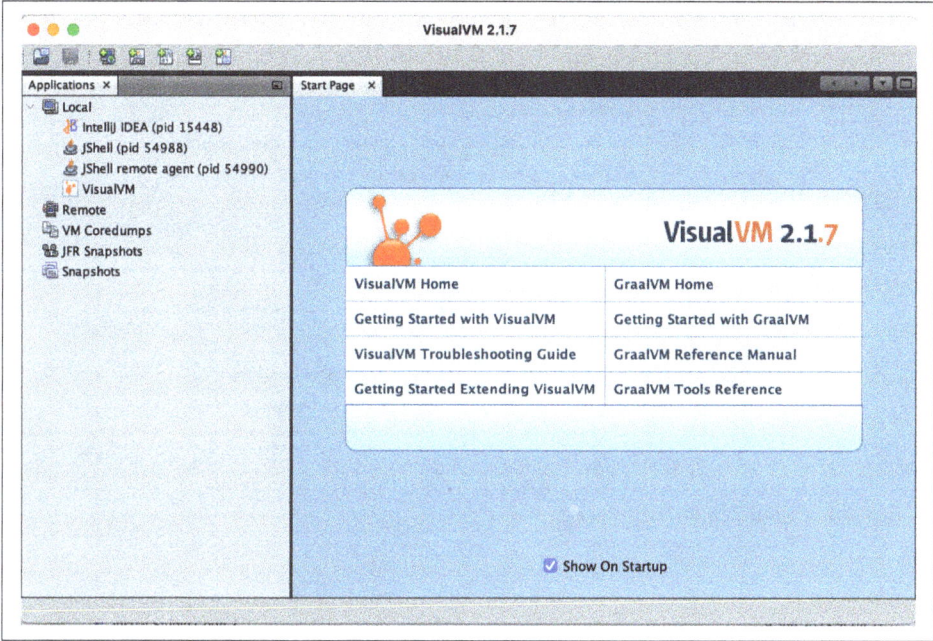

Figure 3-4. VisualVM startup screen

On the lefthand side are a choice of Local and Remote JVMs as well as snapshots and dump files. Note that VisualVM is, itself, a Java application.

Selecting a JVM from this sidebar gives the default view shown in Figure 3-5.

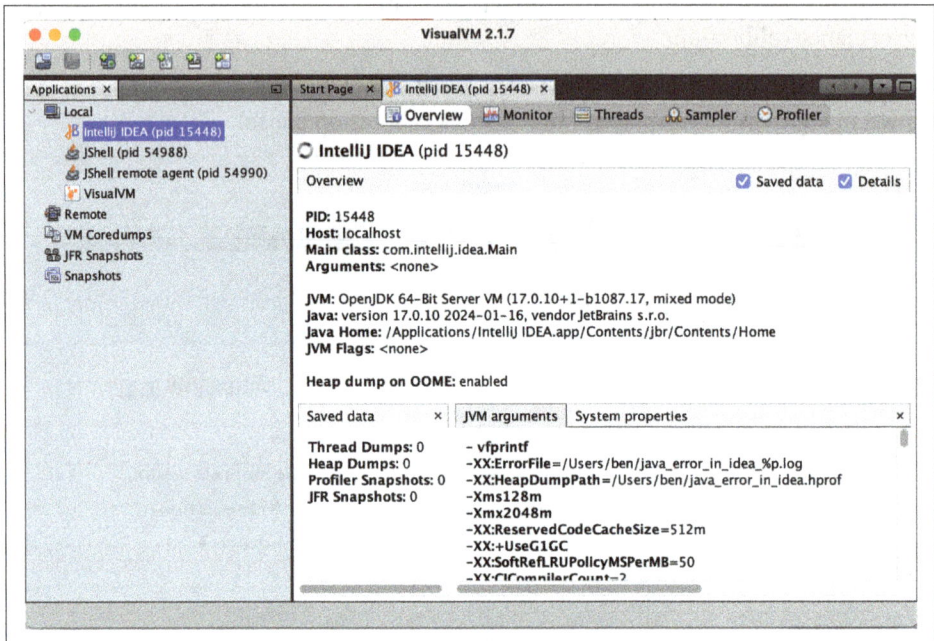

Figure 3-5. VisualVM default view

The most familiar view of VisualVM is the Monitor screen, which is similar to that shown in Figure 3-6.

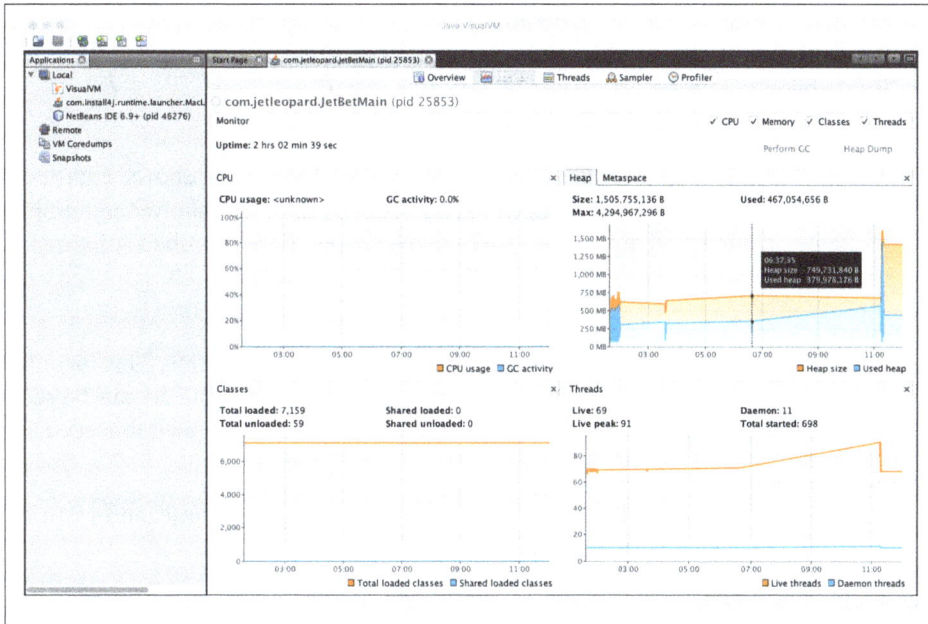

Figure 3-6. VisualVM Monitor screen

VisualVM is used for live monitoring of a running process, and it uses the JVM's *attach mechanism.* This works slightly differently depending on whether the process is local or remote.

Local processes are fairly straightforward. VisualVM lists them down the lefthand side of the screen. Double-clicking on one of them causes it to appear as a new tab in the righthand pane.

To connect to a remote process, the remote side must accept inbound connections (over JMX). For standard Java processes, this means `jstatd` must be running on the remote host (see the manual page for `jstatd` for more details).

> Many application servers and execution containers provide an equivalent capability to `jstatd` directly in the server. Such processes do not need a separate `jstatd` process so long as they are capable of port-forwarding JMX and RMI traffic.

To connect to a remote process, enter the hostname and a display name that will be used on the tab. The default port to connect to is 1099, but this can be changed easily.

Out of the box, VisualVM presents the user with four tabs:

Overview
> Provides a summary of information about your Java process. This includes the full flags that were passed in and all system properties. It also displays the exact Java version executing.

Monitor
> This is the tab most similar to the legacy `jconsole` view. It shows high-level telemetry for the JVM, including CPU and heap usage. It also shows the number of classes loaded and unloaded, and an overview of the numbers of threads running.

Threads
> Each thread in the running application is displayed with a timeline. This includes both application threads and VM threads. The state of each thread can be seen with a small amount of history. Thread dumps can also be generated if needed.

Sampler and Profiler
> In these two tabs, simplified sampling of CPU and memory utilization can be accessed. This will be discussed more fully in Chapter 12.

The plug-in architecture of VisualVM allows additional tools to be easily added to the core platform to augment the core functionality. These include plug-ins that allow interaction with JMX consoles and bridging to legacy JConsole, and a very useful garbage collection plug-in, VisualGC.

Java Implementations, Distributions, and Releases

In this section, we will briefly discuss the landscape of Java implementations and distributions as well as the Java release cycle.

This is an area that changes a lot over time—so this description is correct at the time of writing only. Since then, for example, vendors may have entered (or exited) the business of making a Java distribution, or the release cycle may have changed. Caveat lector!

Many developers may only be familiar with the Java binaries produced by Oracle (Oracle JDK). However, as of 2024, we have quite a complex landscape, and it's important to understand the basic components of what makes up "Java."

First, there's the source code that will be built into a binary. The source code required to build a Java implementation comes in two parts:

- Virtual machine source code
- Class library source code

The OpenJDK project, which can be found at the OpenJDK website (*https://openjdk.org*), is the project to develop the open source reference implementation of Java—which is licensed under the GNU Public License version 2, with Classpath Exemption (GPLv2+CE) (*https://oreil.ly/5TgST*). The project is led and supported by Oracle—which provides a majority of the engineers who work on the OpenJDK codebase.

The critical point to understand about OpenJDK is that it provides *source code only*. This is true both for the VM (HotSpot) and for the class libraries.

The combination of HotSpot and the OpenJDK class libraries forms the basis of the vast majority of Java distributions used in today's production environments (including Oracle's). However, there are several other Java VMs that we will meet—and discuss briefly in this book—including Eclipse OpenJ9 and GraalVM. These VMs can also be combined with the OpenJDK class libraries to produce a complete Java implementation.

However, source code, by itself, is not all that useful to developers—it needs to be built into a binary distribution, tested, and optionally certified.

This is somewhat similar to the situation with Linux—the source code exists and is freely available, but in practice, virtually no one except those folks developing the next version work directly with source. Instead, developers consume a binary Linux distribution.

In the Java world there are a number of vendors who make distributions available, just as there are for Linux. Let's meet the vendors and take a quick look at their various offerings.

Choosing a Distribution

Developers and architects should consider carefully their choice of JVM vendor. Some large organizations—notably X (formerly Twitter) and Alibaba—even choose to maintain their own private (or semi-public) builds of OpenJDK, although the engineering effort required for this is beyond the reach of many companies.

With this in mind, the main factors that organizations typically care about are:

- Do I have to pay money to use this in production?
- How can I get any bugs I discover fixed?
- How do I get security patches?

To take these in turn:

A binary that has been built from OpenJDK source (which is GPLv2+CE-licensed) is free to use in production. This includes all binaries from Eclipse Adoptium, Red Hat, Amazon, and Microsoft, as well as binaries from lesser-known suppliers such as BellSoft. Some, but not all, of Oracle's binaries also fall into this category.

Next up, to get a bug fixed in OpenJDK, the discoverer may do one of two things: either buy a support contract and get the vendor to fix it, or ask an OpenJDK author to file a bug against the OpenJDK repo and then hope (or ask nicely) that someone fixes it for you. Or there's always the inevitable third option that all open source software provides—fix it yourself and then submit a patch.

The final point—about security updates—is slightly more subtle. First off, note that almost all changes to Java start off as commits to a public OpenJDK repository on GitHub. The exception to this is certain security fixes that have not yet been publicly disclosed.

When a fix is released and made public, there is a process by which the patch flows back into the various OpenJDK repos. The vendors will then be able to take that source code fix and build and release a binary that contains it. However, there are some subtleties to this process, which is one reason why most Java shops prefer to remain on a long-term support (or LTS) version—we will have more to say about this in the section about Java versions.

Now that we've discussed the main criteria for choosing a distribution, let's meet some of the main offerings available:

Oracle
> Oracle's Java (Oracle JDK is perhaps the most widely known implementation. It is essentially the OpenJDK codebase, relicensed under Oracle's proprietary licenses with a few extremely minor differences (such as the inclusion of some additional components that are not available under an open source license). Oracle achieves this by having all contributors to OpenJDK sign a license agreement that permits dual licensing of their contribution to both the GPLv2+CE of OpenJDK and Oracle's proprietary license.[2]

Eclipse Adoptium
> This community-led project started life as AdoptOpenJDK, changing its name when it transitioned into the Eclipse Foundation. The members of the Adoptium project (from companies such as Red Hat, Google, Microsoft, and Azul) consist mostly of build and test engineers rather than development engineers (who

---

2 The latter has changed multiple times, so linking to the currently latest version might not be helpful—it could be out of date by the time you read this.

implement new features and fix bugs). This is by design—many of Adoptium's member companies also make major contributions to upstream OpenJDK development, but they do so under their own company names rather than Adoptium. The Adoptium project takes the OpenJDK source and builds fully tested binaries on multiple platforms. As a community project, Adoptium does not offer paid support, although member companies may choose to do so—for example, Red Hat does for some operating systems.

Red Hat

Red Hat is one of the the longest standing non-Oracle producers of Java binaries—as well as the second largest contributor to OpenJDK (behind Oracle). It produces builds and provides support for its operating systems—RHEL and Fedora—and Windows (for historical reasons). Red Hat also releases freely available container images based on its Universal Base Image (UBI) Linux system.

Amazon Corretto

Corretto is Amazon's distribution of OpenJDK, and it is intended to run primarily on AWS cloud infrastructure. Amazon also provides builds for Mac, Windows, and Linux to provide a consistent developer experience and encourage developers to use their builds across all environments.

Microsoft OpenJDK

Microsoft has been producing binaries since May 2021 (OpenJDK 11.0.11) for Mac, Windows, and Linux. Just as for AWS, Microsoft's distribution is largely intended to provide an easy on-ramp for developers who will be deploying on their Azure cloud infrastructure.

Azul Systems

Zulu is a free OpenJDK implementation provided by Azul Systems--which also offers paid support for its OpenJDK binaries. Azul also offers a high-performance proprietary JVM called "Azul Platform Prime" (previously known as Zing). Prime is not an OpenJDK distribution.

GraalVM

GraalVM is a relatively new addition to this list. Originally a research project at Oracle Labs, it has graduated to a fully productionized Java implementation (and much more too). GraalVM can operate in dynamic VM mode and includes an OpenJDK-based runtime—augmented with a JIT compiler that is written in Java. However, GraalVM is also capable of *native compilation* of Java—essentially AOT compilation. We will have more to say on this subject later in the book.

OpenJ9

OpenJ9 started life as IBM's proprietary JVM (when it was just called J9) but was made open source in 2017 partway through its life (just like HotSpot). It is now built on top of an Eclipse open runtime project (OMR). It is fully compliant with

Java certification. IBM Semeru Runtimes are zero-cost runtimes built with the OpenJDK class libraries and the Eclipse OpenJ9 JVM (which is Eclipse-licensed).

Android

Google's Android project is sometimes thought of as being "based on Java." However, the picture is actually a little more complicated. Android uses a cross compiler to convert class files to a different (*.dex*) file format. These *.dex* files are then executed by the Android Runtime (ART), which is not a JVM. In fact, Google now recommends the Kotlin language over Java for developing Android apps. As this technology stack is so far from the other examples, we won't consider Android any further in this book.

Note that this list is not intended to be comprehensive—there are other distributions available as well.

The vast majority of the rest of this book focuses on the technology found in HotSpot. This means the material applies equally to Oracle's Java and the distributions provided by Adoptium, Red Hat, Amazon, Microsoft, Azul Zulu, and all other OpenJDK-derived JVMs.

We also include some material related to Eclipse Open J9. This is intended to provide an awareness of alternatives rather than a definitive guide. Some readers may wish to explore these technologies more deeply, and they are encouraged to proceed by setting performance goals, and then measuring and comparing, in the usual manner.

Finally, before we discuss the Java release cycle, a word about the performance characteristics of the various OpenJDK distributions.

Teams occasionally ask questions about performance because they believe that certain distributions include different JIT or GC components that are not available in other OpenJDK-based distributions.

Let's clear that up right now: all the OpenJDK distributions build from the same source, so there are no functional differences in the like-for-like versions—this is helped by the extremely robust test suite run on OpenJDK builds across all distributions.

In addition, there should be *no* systematic performance-related differences between the various HotSpot-based implementations when comparing like-for-like versions and build flag configurations. The only minor exception to this is that Oracle does not ship the Shenandoah garbage collector developed by Red Hat and Amazon and instead promotes its own ZGC collector.

Some vendors choose very specific build flag combinations that are highly specific to their cloud environments, and some research indicates that these combinations *may* help for some subset of workloads, but this is far from clear-cut.

Once in a while, social media excitedly reports that significant performance differences have been found between some of the distributions. However, carrying out such tests in a sufficiently controlled environment is notoriously difficult—so any results should be treated with healthy skepticism unless they can be independently verified as statistically rigorous.

The Java Release Cycle

We can now complete the picture by briefly discussing the Java release cycle.

New feature development happens in the open—at a collection of GitHub repositories. Small to medium features and bug fixes are accepted as pull requests directly against the main branch in the main OpenJDK repository (*https://oreil.ly/t-tNB*). Larger features and major projects are frequently developed in forked repos and then migrated into mainline when ready.

Every six months, a new release of Java is cut from whatever is in main. Features that "miss the train" must wait for the next release—the six-month cadence and strict timescale has been maintained since September 2017. These releases are known as "feature releases," and they are run by Oracle, in its role as steward of Java.

Oracle ceases to work on any given feature release as soon as the next feature release appears. However, an OpenJDK member of suitable standing and capability can offer to continue running the release after Oracle steps down. To date, this has only happened for certain releases—in practice Java 8, 11, 17, and 21, which are known as *update releases*.

The significance of these releases is that they match Oracle's long-term support release concept. Technically, this is purely a construct of Oracle's sales process—whereby Oracle customers who do not want to upgrade Java every six months have certain stable versions that Oracle will support them on.

In practice, the Java ecosystem has overwhelmingly rejected the official Oracle dogma of "upgrade your JDK every six months"—project teams and engineering managers simply have no appetite for it. Instead, teams upgrade from one LTS version to the next, and the update release projects (8u, 11u, 17u, and 21u) remain active, delivering security patches and a small number of bug fixes and backports. Oracle and the community work together to keep all these maintained code streams secure.

This is the final piece we need to answer the question of how to pick a Java distribution. If you want a zero-cost Java distribution that receives security patches and has a nonzero chance of security (and possibly bug) fixes, select your choice of OpenJDK vendor and stick to the LTS versions.

Any of: Adoptium, Red Hat, Amazon, and Microsoft is a fine choice—and so are some of the others. Depending on how and where you're deploying your software (e.g., applications deploying in AWS may prefer Amazon's Corretto distribution), you may have a reason to pick one of those over the others.

For a more in-depth guide to the various options and some of the licensing complexities, you can consult Java Is Still Free (*https://oreil.ly/rtvjM*). This document was written by the Java Champions (*https://oreil.ly/qzTMd*), an independent body of Java experts and leaders.

Summary

In this chapter, we have taken a quick tour through the overall anatomy of the JVM, including: compilation of bytecode, interpretation, JIT compilation to native code, memory management, threading, the lifecycle of a Java process monitoring, and finally, how Java is built and distributed.

It has been possible to touch on only some of the most important subjects, and virtually every topic mentioned here has a rich, full story behind it that will reward further investigation.

In Chapter 4, we will begin our journey into garbage collection, starting with the basic concepts of mark-and-sweep and diving into the specifics, including some of the internal details of how HotSpot implements GC.

Understanding Garbage Collection

In this chapter, we will be introducing the garbage collection subsystems of the JVM. We will approach this by starting with an overview of the basic theory of *mark and sweep* (also known as *tracing garbage collection*). Then, we'll look at the low-level features of the HotSpot runtime and how it represents Java objects at runtime.

In the second half of the chapter, we'll talk about the key concepts of allocation and lifetime before discussing two key techniques that HotSpot uses to help with allocation. Then we'll bring together all the topics we've met and introduce the simplest of HotSpot's production collectors, the *parallel collectors*, and explain some of the details that make them useful for many production workloads.

Garbage collection is a huge subject, so we can cover only some introductory material in this chapter. In Chapter 5 we will cover a selection of more advanced topics.

Let's begin by noting that the Java environment has several iconic or defining features, and garbage collection is one of the most immediately recognizable.

The essence of Java's garbage collection is that rather than requiring the programmer to understand the precise lifetime of every object in the system, the runtime should keep track of objects on the programmer's behalf and automatically get rid of objects that are no longer required. The automatically reclaimed memory can then be wiped and reused.

However, when the platform was first released, there was considerable hostility to GC. This was fueled by the fact that Java deliberately provided no language-level way to control the behavior of the collector (and continues not to, even in modern versions).

The System.gc() method exists but is basically useless for any practical purpose.[1]

This meant that, in the early days, there was a certain amount of frustration over Java's functionality—compounded by the not-great performance of Java's GC. This fed into perceptions of the platform as a whole, and even today, you may encounter people who still assume, incorrectly, that Java GC is a problem. The truth is that, these days, Java's GC is incredibly fast (best in class) and entirely suitable for the vast majority of production workloads.

In fact, the early vision of mandatory, non-user-controllable GC has been more than vindicated, and these days very few application developers would attempt to defend the opinion that memory should be managed by hand. Even modern takes on systems programming languages (e.g., Rust and Go) regard memory management as the proper domain of the compiler and runtime, respectively, rather than the programmer.[2]

There are two basic rules of garbage collection that all implementations strive to adhere to:

- No live object must ever be collected.
- Algorithms must collect all garbage.

Of these two rules, the first is by far the more important. Collecting a live object could lead to segmentation faults or (even worse) silent corruption of program data. Java's GC algorithms need to be sure that they will never collect an object the program is still using.

If a GC algorithm consistently fails to collect some garbage, then the worst case is that, over time, the application will run out of memory and eventually crash. This is a terrible outcome, but even this is better than the alternative of collecting live objects and causing memory corruption.

However, having said this, the second rule has quite a lot of flexibility.

---

1 There is also the Unsafe class and its capabilities, which we will discuss in Chapter 13, along with the reasons why they should not be used.

2 In anything other than exceptional circumstances.

For example, the generational algorithms we will meet later in this chapter often leave older objects in the heap for a long time, until a full GC cycle is triggered. In addition, in the next chapter, we will meet algorithms that avoid collecting areas of memory that have not yet accumulated enough garbage.

Overall, the idea of the programmer surrendering some low-level control in exchange for not having to account for every low-level detail by hand is the essence of Java's managed approach and expresses James Gosling's conception of Java as a blue-collar language for getting things done.

Introducing Mark and Sweep

Most Java programmers, if pressed, can recall that Java's GC relies on an algorithm called *mark and sweep*, but most also struggle to recall any details as to how the process actually operates.

In this section we will introduce a basic form of the algorithm and show how it can be used to reclaim heap memory automatically. This is deliberately simplified and is only intended to introduce a few basic concepts—it is not representative of how production JVMs actually carry out GC (we'll meet those later).

This introductory form of the mark-and-sweep algorithm uses an allocated object list to hold a pointer to each object that has been allocated but not yet reclaimed. The overall GC algorithm can then be expressed as:

1. Loop through the allocated list, clearing the mark bit.
2. Starting from any pointers into the heap, find all the objects you can.
3. Set a mark bit on each object reached.
4. Loop through the allocated list, and for each object whose mark bit hasn't been set:

    a. Reclaim the memory in the heap and place it back on the free list.

    b. Remove the object from the allocated list.

The live objects are usually located depth-first, and the resulting graph of objects is called the *live object graph*. It is sometimes also called the *transitive closure of reachable objects*, and an example can be seen in Figure 4-1. Conversely, unreachable objects are sometimes referred to as *dead*.

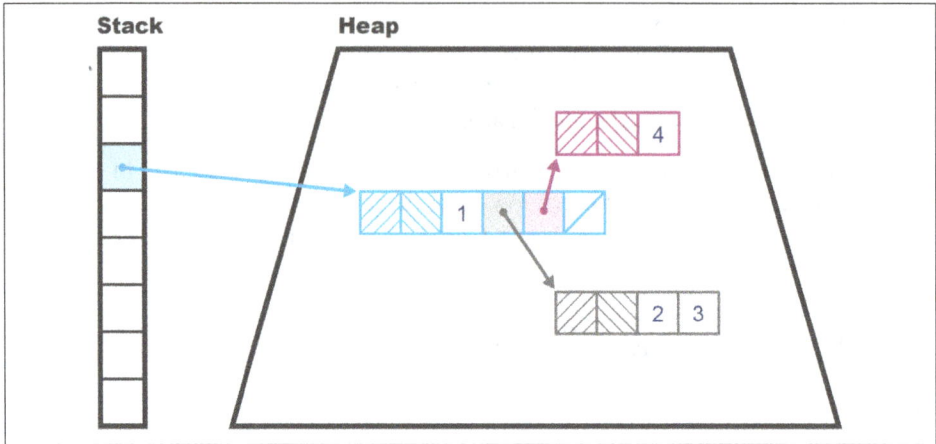

Figure 4-1. Simple view of memory layout

The state of the heap can be hard to visualize, but fortunately there are some simple tools to help us. One of the simplest is the `jmap -histo` command-line tool. This shows the number of bytes allocated per type, and the number of instances that are collectively responsible for that memory usage. It produces output like the following:

```
num     #instances       #bytes  class name
------------------------------------------------
  1:        20839      14983608  [B
  2:       118743      12370760  [C
  3:        14528       9385360  [I
  4:          282       6461584  [D
  5:       115231       3687392  java.util.HashMap$Node
  6:       102237       2453688  java.lang.String
  7:        68388       2188416  java.util.Hashtable$Entry
  8:         8708       1764328  [Ljava.util.HashMap$Node;
  9:        39047       1561880  jdk.nashorn.internal.runtime.CompiledFunction
 10:        23688       1516032  com.mysql.jdbc.Co...$BooleanConnectionProperty
 11:        24217       1356152  jdk.nashorn.internal.runtime.ScriptFunction
 12:        27344       1301896  [Ljava.lang.Object;
 13:        10040       1107896  java.lang.Class
 14:        44090       1058160  java.util.LinkedList$Node
 15:        29375        940000  java.util.LinkedList
 16:        25944        830208  jdk.nashorn.interna...FinalScriptFunctionData
 17:           20        655680  [Lscala.concurrent.forkjoin.ForkJoinTask;
 18:        19943        638176  java.util.concurrent.ConcurrentHashMap$Node
 19:          730        614744  [Ljava.util.Hashtable$Entry;
 20:        24022        578560  [Ljava.lang.Class;
```

This shows a snapshot of the heap (and there are other, more complex and powerful tools such as Eclipse MAT available), but we may want to carry out live analysis instead.

In this case, we can use GUI tools such as the Sampling tab of VisualVM (introduced in Chapter 3) or the VisualGC plug-in to VisualVM. These tools provide a real-time view, which can be useful for a quick sense of how the heap is changing.

However, in general, the moment-to-moment view of the heap is not sufficient for accurate analysis. Instead, we should use a tool like JDK Flight Recorder (JFR) or GC logs for better insight into questions such as, "How big is my heap? How is it changing? Do I have a leak?"

Garbage Collection Glossary

The jargon used to describe GC algorithms is sometimes a bit confusing (and the meaning of some of the terms has changed over time). For the sake of clarity, we include a basic glossary of how we use specific terms:

Stop-the-world (STW)
> The GC cycle requires all application threads to be paused while garbage is collected. This prevents application code from invalidating the GC thread's view of the state of the heap. This is the usual case for simple GC algorithms.

Concurrent
> GC threads can run while application threads are running. This is more difficult to achieve, and more expensive in terms of computation expended. HotSpot's default collector (since Java 9) is *Garbage First* (G1), and it has some concurrent aspects, as we will see.

Parallel
> Multiple threads (and multiple cores) are used to execute garbage collection.

Exact
> An exact GC scheme has enough type information about the state of the heap to ensure that all garbage can be collected on a single cycle. More loosely, an exact scheme has the property that it can always tell the difference between a field that is an `int` and one that's an object reference.

Conservative
> A conservative scheme lacks the information of an exact scheme. As a result, conservative schemes frequently fritter away resources and are typically far less efficient due to their fundamental ignorance of the type system they purport to represent.

Moving
> In a moving collector, objects can be relocated in memory. This means that they do not have stable addresses. Environments that (unlike Java) provide direct access to raw pointers are not a natural fit for moving collectors.

Compacting

At the end of the collection cycle, allocated memory (i.e., surviving objects) is arranged as a single contiguous region (usually at the start of the region), and a pointer indicates the start of empty space that is available for objects to be written into. A compacting collector will avoid memory fragmentation.

Evacuating

At the end of the collection cycle, the collected region is totally empty, and all live objects have been moved (evacuated) to another region of memory. A good evacuating collector will avoid memory fragmentation.

In most other languages and environments, the same terms are used—but be careful, as some environments do things such as transpose the meaning of "concurrent" and "parallel," or refer to "moving" as "copying."

The term "concurrent" is also best understood as being a sliding scale rather than a binary state. Depending on the collector in use, more or less of the work of a collection can be performed concurrently with application threads.

Introducing the HotSpot Runtime

In addition to the general GC terminology, HotSpot introduces terms that are more specific to the implementation. To obtain a full understanding of how garbage collection works on this JVM, we need to get a grip on some of the details of HotSpot's internals.

For what follows, it will be very helpful to remember that Java has only two sorts of value:

- Primitive types (`byte`, `int`, etc.)
- Object references

Many Java programmers loosely talk about *objects*, but for our purposes it is important to remember that, unlike C++, Java has no general address dereference mechanism and can only use an *offset operator* (the `.` operator) to access fields and call methods on *object references*.

Also keep in mind that Java's method call semantics are purely call-by-value, although for object references, this means that the value copied is the address of the object in the heap.

Representing Objects at Runtime

HotSpot represents Java objects at runtime via a structure called an *oop*. This is short for *ordinary object pointer*, and it is a genuine pointer in the C sense. These pointers can be placed in local variables of reference type, where they point from the stack frame of the Java method into the memory area comprising the Java heap.

One important fact to remember is that HotSpot does not use system calls to manage the Java heap. As we will see in Chapter 5, HotSpot manages the heap size from user space code, so we can use simple observables to determine whether the GC subsystem is causing some types of performance problems.

There are several different data structures that comprise the family of oops, and the sort that represent instances of a Java class are called *instanceOops*, or *arrayOops* if they represent an array. The general rule is that anything in the Java heap must have an object header.

Accordingly, the memory layout of an instanceOop starts with two machine words of header present on every object (arrayOops have these, and an additional 32 bits of header—the array's length). The *mark word* is the first of these and is a pointer that points at instance-specific metadata. Next is the *klass word*, which points at class-wide metadata.

The klass word is used to locate the klass metatdata (or klass), which is held outside of the main part of the Java heap (but not outside the C heap of the JVM process). As they exist outside the Java heap, the klasses do not require an object header.

> The *k* at the start of "klass" is used to help disambiguate the VM-level klass from an instanceOop representing the Java `Class<?>` object—they are not the same thing.

In Figure 4-2, we can see the difference for a simple case—on the top left an `Entry` object similar to the `Map.Entry` that we might use in a `HashMap`, and on the top right, the `Entry.class` object (e.g., obtained via `getClass()`). Both of these Java objects have klasses, which are shown below the dotted line:

```
record Entry<K,V> (int hash, K key, V value, Entry<K,V> next) {}
```

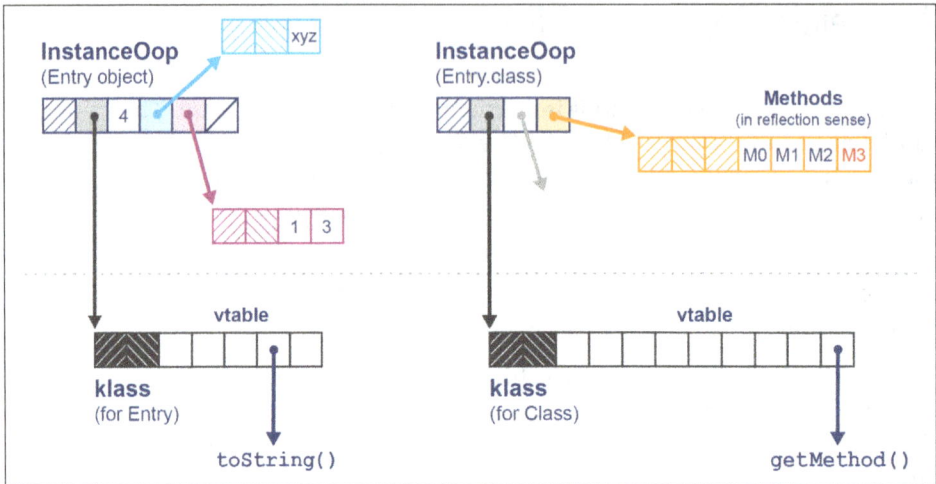

Figure 4-2. Klass and Class objects

Fundamentally, the klass contains the virtual function table (or *vtable*) for the class, whereas the Class object contains (among other things) an array of references to Method objects for use in reflective invocation. We will have more to say on this subject in Chapter 6, when we discuss JIT compilation.

Oops are usually machine words, so 32 bits on a legacy 32-bit machine, and 64 bits on a modern processor. However, this has the potential to waste a possibly significant amount of memory. To help mitigate this, HotSpot provides a technique called *compressed oops*. If the option:

```
-XX:+UseCompressedOops
```

is set (and it is the default for 64-bit heaps), then the following oops in the heap will be compressed:

- The klass word of every object in the heap
- Instance fields of reference type
- Every element of an array of objects

This means that, in general, a HotSpot object header consists of:

- Mark word at full native size
- Klass word (possibly compressed)
- 32 bits indicating the length if the object is an array
- A 32-bit gap (if required by alignment rules)

The instance fields of the object then follow immediately after the header. The memory layout for compressed oops can be seen in Figure 4-3.

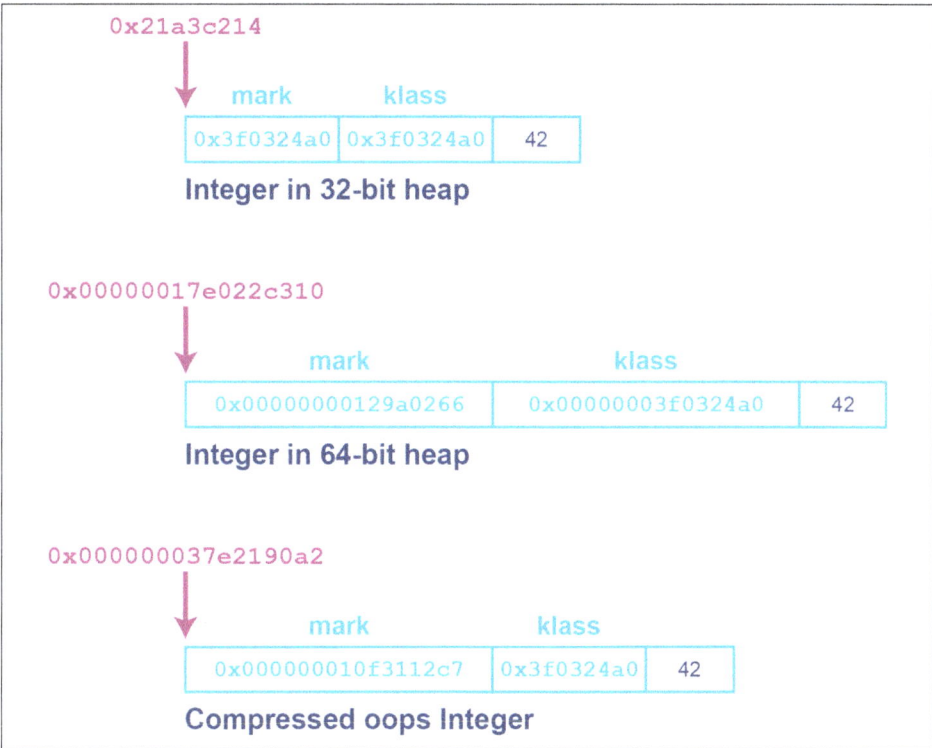

Figure 4-3. Compressed oops

In the past, some extremely latency-sensitive applications could occasionally see improvements by switching off the compressed oops feature—at the cost of increased heap size (typically an increase of 10%–50%). However, the class of applications for which this would yield measurable performance benefits is very small. For most modern applications, this would be a classic example of the antipattern known as *Fiddling with Switches* (see Appendix B for a full description).

As we remember from basic Java, arrays are objects. This means that the JVM's arrays are represented as oops as well. This is why arrays have a third word of metadata as well as the usual mark and klass words—the array's length. This also explains why array indices in Java are limited to 32-bit values, as the first versions of Java were purely for 32-bit architectures.

The use of additional metadata to carry an array's length alleviates a whole class of problems present in C and C++, where not knowing the length of the array means that additional parameters must be passed to functions.

The managed environment of the JVM does not allow a Java reference to point anywhere but at an oop (or null). This means that at a low level:

- A Java value is a bit pattern corresponding either to a primitive value or to the address of an oop (a Java reference).
- Any Java reference considered as a pointer refers to the start of an object in the main part of the Java heap.
- Addresses that are the targets of Java references contain a mark word followed by a klass word as the next machine word.
- A klass and an instance of Class<?> are different (as the former lives in the metadata area of the heap), and a klass cannot be placed into a Java variable.

HotSpot defines a hierarchy of oops in .hpp files that are kept in src/hotspot/share/oops in the main branch OpenJDK source tree.

The basic overall inheritance hierarchy for oops looks like this (as of Java 22):

```
oop (abstract base)
  instanceOop (instance objects)
    stackChunkOop
  arrayOop (array abstract base)
    objArrayOop (array object)
    objArrayOop (array of primitives)
```

This use of oop structures to represent objects at runtime, with one pointer to house class-level metadata and another to house instance metadata, is not peculiar to HotSpot—many other JVMs and other execution environments use a related mechanism.

GC Roots

Articles and blog posts about HotSpot frequently refer to *GC roots*. These are "anchor points" for memory, essentially known pointers that originate from outside a memory pool of interest and point into it. They are *external* pointers as opposed to *internal* pointers, which originate inside the memory pool and point to another memory location within the memory pool.

We saw an example of a GC root in Figure 4-1. However, as we will see, there are other sorts of GC root, including:

- Stack frames
- Java Native Interface (JNI)
- Registers[3]
- Code roots (from the JVM code cache)
- Globals
- Class metadata from loaded classes

If this definition seems rather complex, then the simplest example of a GC root is a local variable of reference type that will always point to an object in the heap (provided it is not null).

In the next section, we'll take a closer look at two of the most important characteristics that drive the garbage collection behavior of any Java or JVM workload. A good understanding of these characteristics is essential for any developer who wants to really grasp the factors that drive Java GC (which is one of the key overall drivers for Java performance).

Allocation and Lifetime

The two primary drivers of the garbage collection behavior of a Java application are:

- Allocation rate
- Object lifetime

The allocation rate is the amount of memory used by newly created objects over some time period (usually measured in MB/s). This is not exposed by the JVM directly by default but is a relatively easy observable to estimate, and tools such as JFR can provide it (although there are potential performance implications for doing so, as we will discuss later in the book).

By contrast, the object lifetime is normally a lot harder to measure (or even estimate). In fact, one of the major arguments against using manual memory management is the complexity involved in truly understanding object lifetimes for a real application. As a result, object lifetime is, if anything, even more fundamental than allocation rate.

> Garbage collection can also be thought of as "memory reclamation and reuse." The ability to use the same physical piece of memory over and over again, because objects are short-lived, is a key assumption of garbage collection techniques.

---

3 This could occur in JIT-compiled code when an object reference has been *hoisted* into a register.

The idea that objects are created, they exist for a time, and then the memory used to store their state can be reclaimed is essential; without it, garbage collection would not work at all. As we will see in Chapter 5, there are a number of different tradeoffs that garbage collectors must balance—and some of the most important of these tradeoffs are driven by lifetime and allocation concerns.

Weak Generational Hypothesis

One key part of the JVM's memory management relies upon an observed runtime effect of software systems, the weak generational hypothesis (WGH):

> The distribution of object lifetimes on the JVM and similar software systems is bimodal—with the vast majority of objects being very short-lived and a secondary population having a much longer life expectancy.

This can be seen graphically in Figure 4-4.

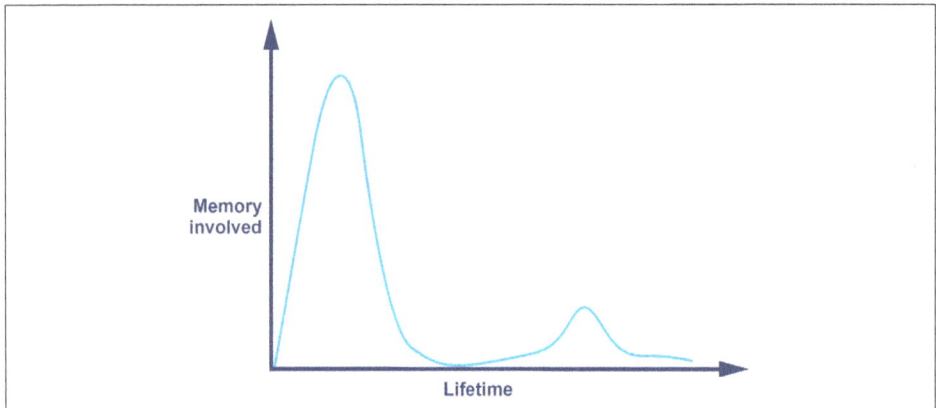

Figure 4-4. Weak generational hypothesis

This hypothesis, which is really an experimentally observed and validated rule about the behavior of object-oriented workloads, leads to an obvious conclusion. That is, garbage-collected heaps should be structured in such a way as to allow short-lived objects to be easily and quickly collected, and for long-lived objects to be separated from short-lived objects.

This implies that the heap should have two separate areas—a short-lived area and a long-lived area—and that they should be collected separately in *young* and *full* collections, respectively.

One key technique is to use a mark-and-sweep collection on the recently created objects area—which is usually called *Eden*. During sweeping, the collector uses an evacuation phase to move any surviving objects to the long-lived space. Then the entire Eden space can be reclaimed at once.

We can see an image of this in Figure 4-5.

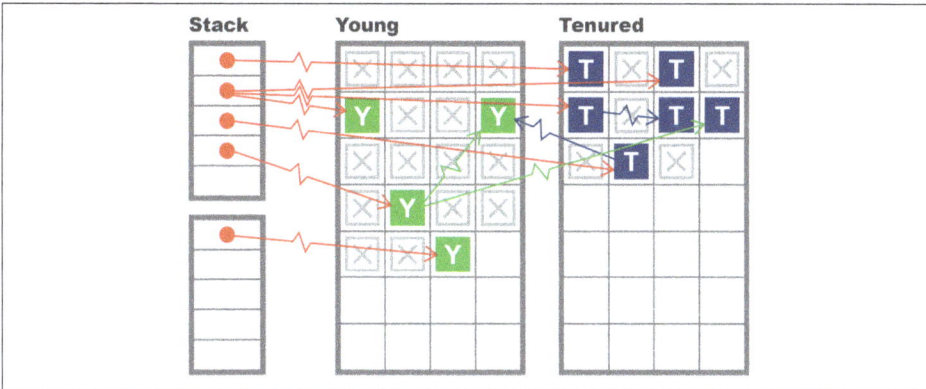

Figure 4-5. Simple generational heap

Note that one of the main consequences of using a generational heap is that it costs nothing at all to collect a dead object—there's simply no bookkeeping to do for it, as we care only about the live objects.

HotSpot uses several mechanisms to try to take advantage of the weak generational hypothesis and to improve on this picture of a generational heap. We'll meet some of them as we explore the capabilities of a real collector in the next two sections.

Production GC Techniques in HotSpot

In this section, we will build on the theory we've met so far and introduce some techniques that will allow us, in the next section, to understand how the simplest production GCs in HotSpot work. Let's start with one of the most important techniques used to improve allocation performance.

Thread-Local Allocation

Eden is the region of the heap where most objects are created, and very short-lived objects (those with lifetimes less than the remaining time to the next GC cycle) will never be located anywhere else. For this reason, it is a critical region to manage efficiently, because if the WGH holds, then a great many of our objects can be collected at zero cost.

For improved allocation efficiency, HotSpot partitions Eden into buffers and hands out individual regions of Eden for application threads to use as allocation regions for new objects. The advantage of this approach is that each thread knows that it does not have to consider the possibility that other threads are allocating within that buffer. These regions are called *thread-local allocation buffers* (TLABs).

HotSpot dynamically sizes the TLABs that it gives to application threads, so if a thread is burning through memory, it can be given larger TLABs to reduce the overhead in providing buffers to the thread.

The exclusive control that an application thread has over its TLABs means that allocation is O(1) for JVM threads. This is because when a thread creates a new object, storage is allocated for the object, and the thread-local pointer is updated to the next free memory address. In terms of C code, this is a simple pointer bump—that is, one additional instruction to move the "next free" pointer onward.

This behavior can be seen in Figure 4-6, where each application thread holds a separate buffer to allocate new objects.

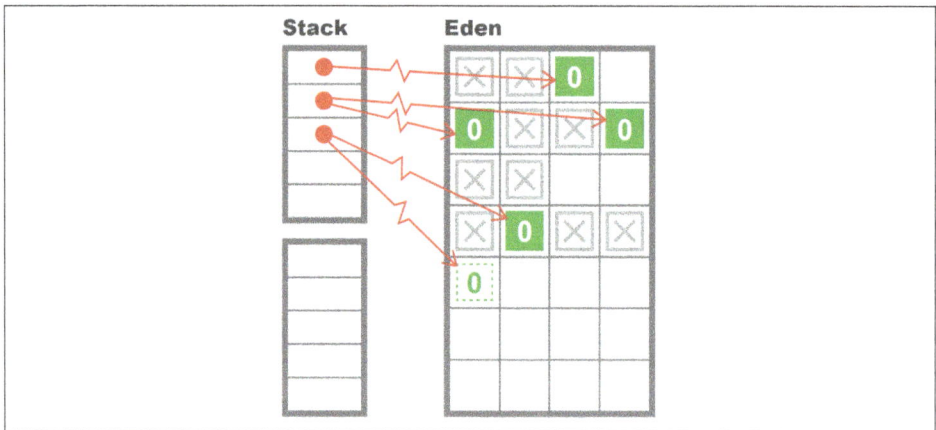

Figure 4-6. Thread-local allocation

If an application thread fills its current TLAB, then the JVM provides a pointer to a new area of Eden, i.e., a new TLAB. This means that a young GC will occur when the JVM has no more TLABs to hand out.

Hemispheric Collection

One particular special case of the evacuating collector is worth noting. Sometimes referred to as a *hemispheric evacuating collector*, this type of collector uses two (usually equal-sized) spaces. The central idea is to use the spaces as temporary holding areas for objects that are not actually long-lived. This prevents short-lived objects from cluttering up the tenured generation and reduces the frequency of full GCs.

The spaces have a couple of basic properties:

- When the collector is collecting the currently live hemisphere, objects are moved in a compacting fashion to the other hemisphere, and the collected hemisphere is emptied for reuse.

- One-half of the space is kept completely empty at all times.

This approach does, of course, use twice as much memory as can actually be held within the hemispheric part of the collector. This is somewhat wasteful, but it is often a useful technique if the size of the spaces is not excessive. HotSpot uses this hemispheric approach in combination with the Eden space to provide a collector for the young generation.

The hemispheric part of HotSpot's young heap is referred to as the *survivor spaces*. As we can see from the view of VisualGC shown in Figure 4-7, the survivor spaces are normally relatively small as compared to Eden, and the role of the survivor spaces swaps with each young generational collection.

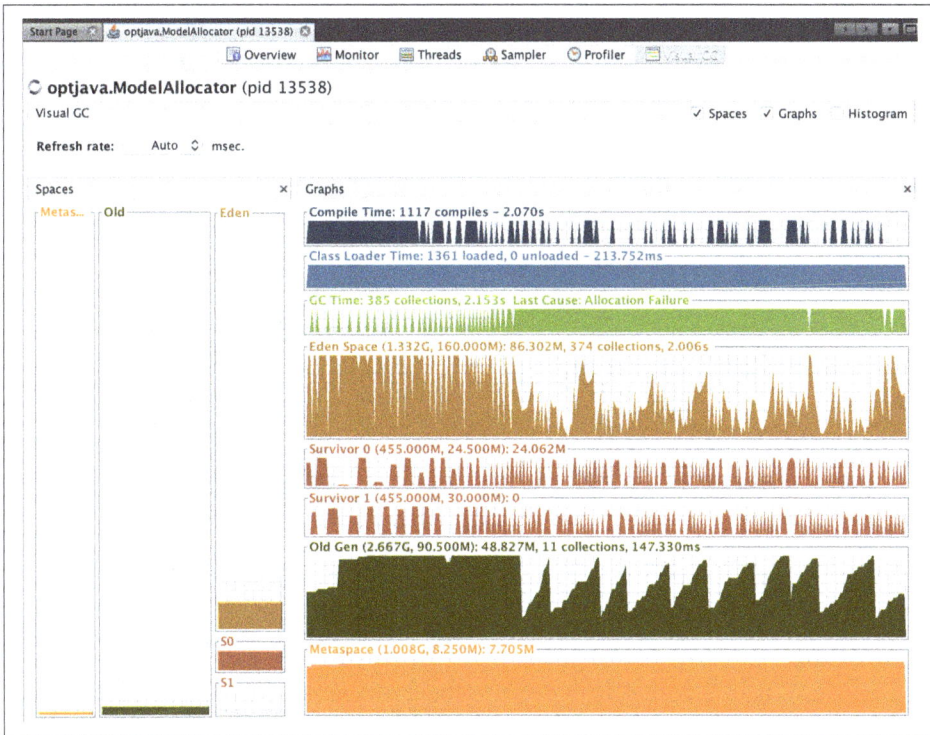

Figure 4-7. The VisualGC plug-in

The VisualGC plug-in for VisualVM is a very useful initial GC debugging tool. As we will discuss in Chapter 5, the GC logs contain far more useful information and allow a much deeper analysis of GC than is possible from the moment-to-moment JMX data that VisualGC uses. However, when starting a new analysis, it is often helpful to simply eyeball the application's memory usage.

Using VisualGC, it is possible to see some aggregate effects of garbage collection, such as objects being relocated in the heap and the cycling between survivor spaces that happens at each young collection.

The "Classic" HotSpot Heap

Let's bring it all together and describe the basic aspects of the HotSpot heap:

- It tracks the "generational count" of each object (the number of garbage collections that the object has survived so far).
- With the exception of large objects, it creates new objects in the "Eden" space (also called the "nursery") and expects to move surviving objects to one of two survivor spaces.
- It maintains a separate area of memory (the "old" or "tenured" generation) to hold objects that are deemed to have survived long enough that they are likely to be long-lived.

This approach leads to the view shown in simplified form in Figure 4-8, where objects that have survived a certain number of garbage collection cycles are promoted to the tenured generation. Note the contiguous nature of the regions, as shown in the diagram.

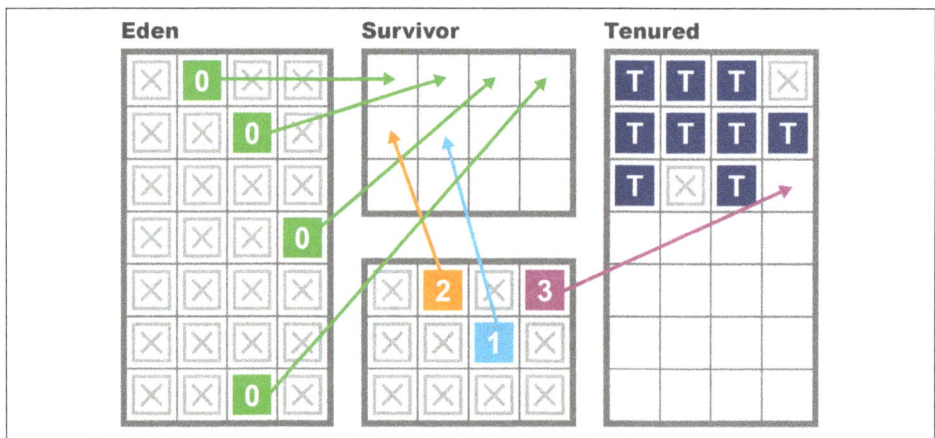

Figure 4-8. HotSpot's heap

Dividing memory into different regions for purposes of generational collection has some additional consequences in terms of how HotSpot implements a mark-and-sweep collection. One important technique involves keeping track of pointers that point into the young generation from outside. This saves the GC cycle from having to traverse the entire object graph to determine the young objects that are still live.

"There are relatively few references from old to young objects" is sometimes cited as a secondary part of the weak generational hypothesis.

To facilitate this process, HotSpot maintains a structure called a *card table* to help record which old-generation objects could potentially point at young objects. The card table is essentially an array of bytes managed by the JVM. Each element of the array corresponds to a 512-byte area of old-generation space.

Later on, we'll meet *remembered sets*, which are a more sophisticated version of the card table.

The central idea is that when a field of reference type on an old object, o, is modified, the card table entry for the card containing the oop corresponding to o is marked as *dirty*. HotSpot achieves this with a simple *write barrier* when updating reference fields. It essentially boils down to this bit of code being executed after the field store:

```
cards[*oop >> 9] = 0;
```

Note that the dirty value for the card is 0, and the right-shift by 9 bits gives the size of the card table as 512 bytes.

Finally, we should note that this description of the heap in terms of contiguous young and old areas is a historic one—this is the way that Java's collectors have traditionally managed memory. Modern collectors, such as G1, do not require contiguous storage of the generations—instead, they have *regions* that still belong to generations but do not need to be colocated with each other.

We will have much more to say about these *regional collectors*, as we will see in "G1" on page 114. For now, the classic view of the HotSpot heap provides an excellent way to move beyond the simplest, most basic view of tracing garbage collection, and a first step to understanding the realities of production collectors.

Recall that unlike C/C++ and similar environments, Java does not use the operating system to manage dynamic memory. Instead, the JVM allocates (or reserves) memory up front, when the JVM process starts, and manages a single, contiguous memory pool from user space.

As we have seen, this pool of memory is made up of different regions with dedicated purposes, and the address that an object resides at will very often change over time as the collector relocates objects, which are normally created in Eden. Collectors that perform relocation are known as "evacuating" collectors, as mentioned in "Garbage Collection Glossary" on page 79.

Many, but not all, of the collectors that HotSpot ships with are evacuating—let's meet some simple examples in the next section.

The Parallel Collectors

In Java 8 and earlier versions, the default collectors for the JVM are the parallel collectors. These are fully STW for both young and full collections, and they are optimized for throughput. After stopping all application threads, the parallel collectors use all available CPU cores to collect memory as quickly as possible.

The available parallel collectors are:

Parallel GC
> The simplest collector for the young generation

ParNew
> A slight variation of Parallel GC that is used with the deprecated Concurrent Mark Sweep collector

ParallelOld
> The parallel collector for the old (aka tenured) generation

The parallel collectors are, in some ways, similar to each other—they are designed to use multiple threads to identify live objects as quickly as possible and to do minimal bookkeeping.

> From Java 17 onward, the Concurrent Mark Sweep (CMS) collector has been removed, and there is only one parallel GC, with the young and old parallel collections being what make up the Parallel GC.

There are some differences between the different collections, so let's take a closer look.

Young Parallel Collections

The most common type of collection is a young generational collection. This usually occurs when a thread tries to allocate an object into Eden but doesn't have enough space in its TLAB, and the JVM can't allocate a fresh TLAB for the thread. When this occurs, the JVM has no choice other than to stop all the application threads—because if one thread is unable to allocate, then very soon every thread will be unable.

> Threads can also allocate outside of TLABs (e.g., for large blocks of memory). The desired case is when the rate of non-TLAB allocation is low, for several reasons, e.g., too many allocations of short-lived large objects will force additional full GCs, which are more expensive than young collections.

Once all application threads are stopped, HotSpot looks at the young generation (which is defined as Eden and the currently nonempty survivor space) and identifies all objects that are not garbage. This will utilize the GC roots (and the card table to identify GC roots coming from the old generation) as starting points for a parallel marking scan.

The Parallel GC collector then evacuates all of the surviving objects into the currently empty survivor space (and increments their generational count as they are relocated). Finally, Eden and the just-evacuated survivor space are marked as empty, reusable space, and the application threads are started so the process of handing out TLABs to application threads can begin again. This process is shown in Figures 4-9 and 4-10.

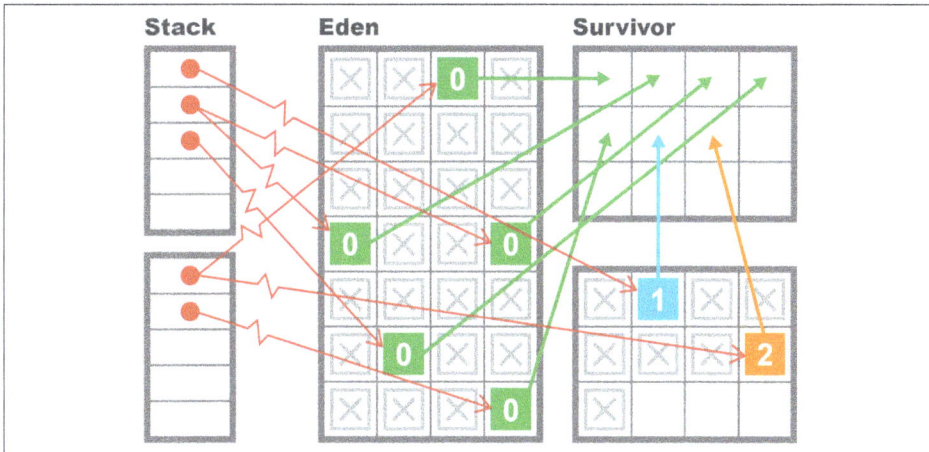

Figure 4-9. Collecting the young generation

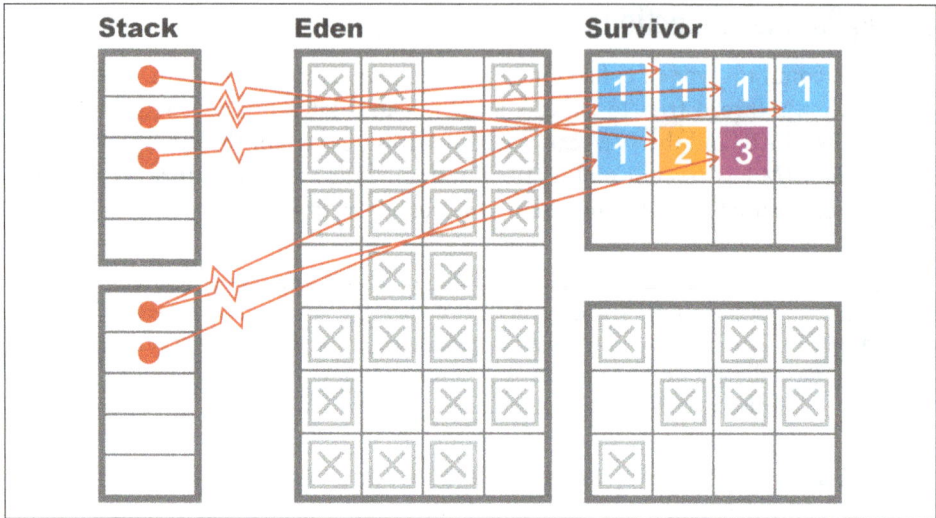

Figure 4-10. Evacuating the young generation

This approach attempts to take full advantage of the weak generational hypothesis by touching only live objects. It also wants to be as efficient as possible and run using all cores as much as possible to shorten the STW pause time.

Old Parallel Collections

The ParallelOld collector was the default collector for the old generation up until Java 8, and for some applications that care primarily about sustained throughput performance, it can still outperform G1.[4]

As we'll see in the next chapter, the default for Java 11+ is the G1 collector.

It has some strong similarities to Parallel GC but also some fundamental differences. In particular, Parallel GC is a hemispheric evacuating collector, whereas ParallelOld is a compacting collector with only a single continuous memory space.

This means that as the old generation has no other space to be evacuated to, the parallel collector attempts to relocate objects within the old generation to reclaim space

---

4 This is especially true for Java 8 applications but less so for Java 11, and by Java 17 it is very difficult to find any workload where Parallel outperforms G1. You have to measure your performance before changing GC algorithm.

that may have been left by old objects dying. Thus, the collector can potentially be very efficient in its use of memory, and it will not suffer from memory fragmentation.

This results in a very efficient memory layout at the cost of using a potentially large amount of CPU during full GC cycles. We saw the evacuating approach in Figures 9 and 10, and the difference between this approach and in-place compaction can be seen in Figure 4-11.

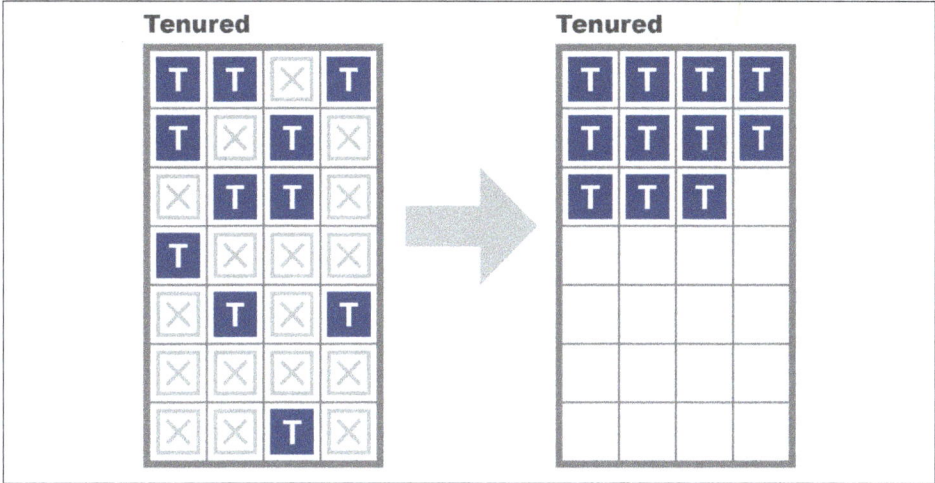

Figure 4-11. Evacuating collection

The behavior of the two memory spaces is radically different, as they are serving different purposes. The purpose of the young collections is to deal with the short-lived objects, so the occupancy of the young space is changing radically with allocation and clearance at GC events.

By contrast, the old space does not change as obviously. Occasional large objects will be created directly in tenured, but apart from that, the space will only change at collections—either by objects being promoted from the young generation, or by a full rescan and rearrangement at an old or full collection.

Serial and SerialOld

The Serial and SerialOld collectors are included in this section largely as a cautionary tale.

They operate similarly to the Parallel GC and ParallelOld collectors, but with one important difference—they use only a single CPU core to perform GC. To be absolutely explicit about this—they are not concurrent collectors and are still fully STW.

On multicore systems, the use of these collectors is obviously wrong—as all but one of the CPUs sits idle while a single core performs STW GC. This leads to vastly increased pause times for no benefit, so these collectors should not be used without a conscious choice (see "Containers and GC" on page 232 for an important subtlety).

Limitations of Parallel Collectors

The parallel collectors deal with the entire contents of a generation at once and try to collect as efficiently as possible. However, this design has some drawbacks. First, they are fully stop-the-world. This is not usually an issue for young collections, as the weak generational hypothesis means that very few objects should survive.

> The design of the young parallel collectors is such that dead objects are never touched, so the length of the marking phase is proportional to the (small) number of surviving objects.

This basic design, coupled with the usually small size of the young regions of the heap, means that the pause time of young collections is very short for most workloads. A typical pause time for a young collection on a modern 2 GB JVM (with default sizing) might well be just a few milliseconds—and may even by submillisecond.

However, collecting the old generation is often a very different story. For one thing, the old generation is by default seven times the size of the young generation. This fact alone will make the expected STW length of a full collection much longer than for a young collection.

Another key fact is that the marking time is proportional to the number of live objects in a region. Old objects may be long-lived, so a potentially larger number of old objects may survive a full collection.

This behavior also explains a key weakness of ParallelOld collection--the STW time will scale roughly linearly with the size of the heap. As heap sizes continue to increase, ParallelOld starts to scale badly in terms of pause time.

Newcomers to GC theory sometimes entertain private theories that minor modifications to mark-and-sweep algorithms might help to alleviate STW pauses. However, this is not the case.

Garbage collection has been a very well-studied research area of computer science for over 40 years, and production collectors are complex, with many tradeoffs. It is extremely unlikely that any such "can't you just…" tweak will yield any generally applicable improvement.

As we will see in Chapter 5, mostly concurrent collectors do exist, and they can run with greatly reduced pause times. However, they are not a panacea, and several fundamental difficulties with garbage collection remain.

As an example, let's consider TLAB allocation. This provides a great boost to allocation performance but is of no help to collection cycles. To see why, consider this code:

```java
public static void main(String[] args) {
    int[] anInt = new int[1];
    anInt[0] = 42;
    Runnable r = () -> {
        anInt[0]++;
        System.out.println("Changed: "+ anInt[0]);
    };
    new Thread(r).start();
}
```

The variable `anInt` is an array object containing a single `int`. It is allocated from a TLAB held by the main thread but immediately afterward is passed to a new thread. To put it another way, the key property of TLABs—that they are private to a single thread—is true only at the point of allocation. This property can be violated as soon as objects have been allocated.

The Java environment's ability to trivially create new threads is a fundamental, and extremely powerful, part of the platform. However, it complicates the picture for garbage collection considerably, as new threads imply execution stacks, each frame of which is a source of GC roots.

The Role of Allocation

Java's garbage collection process is most commonly triggered when memory allocation is requested but there is not enough free memory on hand to provide the required amount. This means that GC cycles do not occur on a fixed or predictable schedule but purely on an as-needed basis.

This is one of the most critical aspects of garbage collection: it is not deterministic and does not occur at a regular cadence.[5] Instead, a GC cycle is triggered when one or more of the heap's memory spaces are essentially full, and further object creation would not be possible. This means, in the language of Chapter 10, that GC behavior is represented as events, and needs to be aggregated to produce metrics.

---

5 Some Java GCs have ways to configure *periodic GCs*, which are time-based—*do a GC at least every N (milli)seconds if not otherwise triggered*. This feature may appear superficially attractive, but in practice it is rarely useful and can be a source of performance problems as developers try to "outthink the GC."

The as-needed nature of GC events makes them hard to process using traditional time series analysis methods. The lack of regularity between GC events is an aspect that most time series libraries cannot easily accommodate.

When an STW GC occurs, all application threads are paused (as they cannot create any more objects, and no substantial piece of Java code can run for very long without producing new objects). The JVM takes over all of the cores to perform GC and reclaims memory before restarting the application threads.

To better understand why allocation is so critical, let's consider the following highly simplified case study. The heap parameters are set up as shown, and we assume that they do not change over time. Of course, a real application would normally have a dynamically resizing heap, but this example serves as a simple illustration:

Heap area	Size
Overall	2 GB
Old generation	1.5 GB
Young generation	500 MB
Eden	400 MB
SS1	50 MB
SS2	50 MB

After the application has reached its steady state, the following GC metrics are observed:

Metric	Values
Allocation rate:	100 MB/s
Young GC time:	2 ms
Full GC time:	100 ms
Object lifetime:	200 ms

This shows that Eden will fill in 4 seconds, so at steady state, a young GC will occur every 4 seconds. Eden has filled, so GC is triggered. Most of the objects in Eden are dead, but any object that is still alive will be evacuated to a survivor space (S1, for the sake of discussion). In this simple model, any objects that were created in the last 200 ms have not had time to die, so they will survive. So, we have:

GC0 @ 4 s   20 MB Eden → SS1 (20 MB)

After another 4 seconds, Eden refills and will need to be evacuated (to SS2 this time). However, in this simplified model, no objects that were promoted into SS1 by GC0 survive—their lifetime is only 200 ms, and another 4 s has elapsed, so all of the objects allocated prior to GC0 are now dead. We now have:

GC1　@ 8.002 s　20 MB Eden → SS2 (20 MB)

Another way of saying this is that after GC1, the contents of SS2 consist solely of objects newly arrived from Eden, and no object in SS2 has a generational age > 1. Continuing for one more collection, the pattern should become clear:

GC2　@ 12.004 s　20 MB Eden → SS1 (20 MB)

This idealized, simple model leads to a situation where no objects ever become eligible for promotion to the old generation, and the space remains empty throughout the run. This is, of course, very unrealistic.

Instead, the weak generational hypothesis indicates that object lifetimes will be a distribution, and due to the uncertainty of this distribution, some objects will end up surviving to reach tenured.

Let's look at a very simple simulator for this allocation scenario. It allocates objects, most of which are very short-lived but some of which have a considerably longer life span. It has a couple of parameters that define the allocation: x and y, which between them, define the size of each object; the allocation rate (mbPerSec); the lifetime of a short-lived object (shortLivedMS) and the number of threads that the application should simulate (nThreads). The default values are here:

```java
public class ModelAllocator implements Runnable {
    private volatile boolean shutdown = false;

    private double chanceOfLongLived = 0.02;
    private int multiplierForLongLived = 20;
    private int x = 1024;
    private int y = 1024;
    private int mbPerSec = 50;
    private int shortLivedMs = 100;
    private int nThreads = 8;
    private Executor exec = Executors.newFixedThreadPool(nThreads);
```

Omitting main() and any other startup/parameter-setting code, the rest of the ModelAllocator looks like this:

```java
public void run() {
    final int mainSleep = (int) (1000.0 / mbPerSec);

    while (!shutdown) {
```

```
                for (int i = 0; i < mbPerSec; i++) {
                    ModelObjectAllocation to =
                        new ModelObjectAllocation(x, y, lifetime());
                    exec.execute(to);
                    try {
                        Thread.sleep(mainSleep);
                    } catch (InterruptedException ex) {
                        shutdown = true;
                    }
                }
            }
        }

        // Simple function to model weak generational hypothesis
        // Returns the expected lifetime of an object - usually this
        // is very short, but there is a small chance of an object
        // being "long-lived"
        public int lifetime() {
            if (Math.random() < chanceOfLongLived) {
                return multiplierForLongLived * shortLivedMs;
            }

            return shortLivedMs;
        }
    }
```

The allocator main runner is combined with a simple mock object used to represent
the object allocation performed by the application:

```
public class ModelObjectAllocation implements Runnable {
    private final int[][] allocated;
    private final int lifeTime;

    public ModelObjectAllocation(final int x, final int y, final int liveFor) {
        allocated = new int[x][y];
        lifeTime = liveFor;
    }

    @Override
    public void run() {
        try {
            Thread.sleep(lifeTime);
            System.err.println(System.currentTimeMillis() +": "
                + allocated.length);
        } catch (InterruptedException ex) {
        }
    }
}
```

When seen in VisualVM, this will display the simple sawtooth pattern often observed
in the memory behavior of Java applications that are making efficient use of the heap.
This pattern can be seen in Figure 4-12.

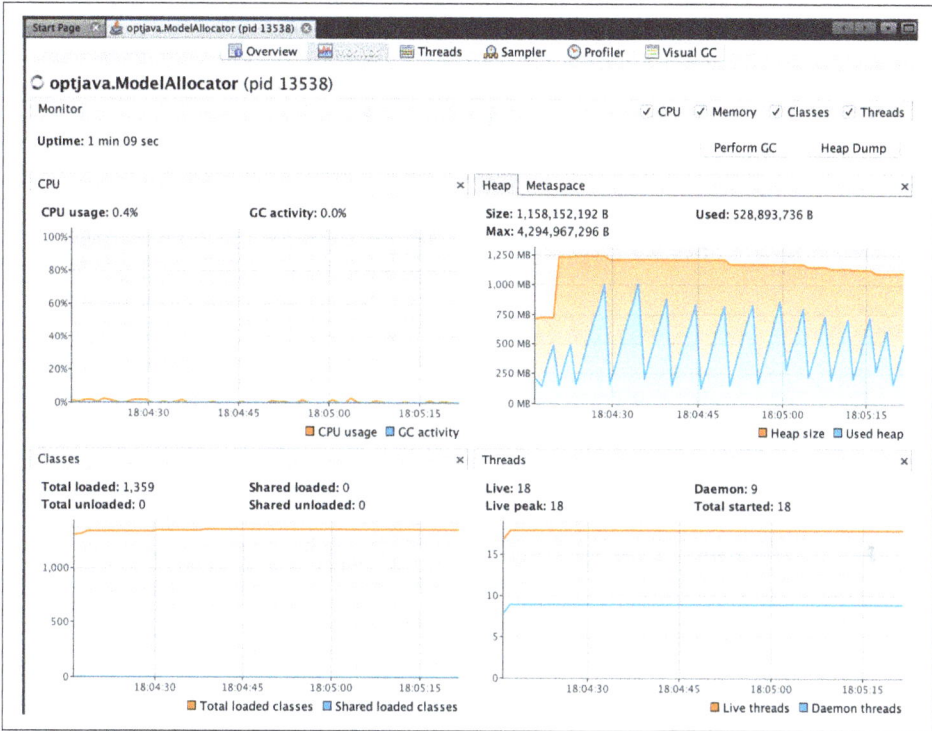

Figure 4-12. Simple sawtooth pattern

The interested reader can download the allocation and lifetime simulator referenced in this chapter and set parameters to see the effects of allocation rates and percentages of long-lived objects.

> Amazon provides its HyperAlloc tool, part of the Heapothesys project (*https://oreil.ly/N5xzt*). This benchmarking tool is "a synthetic workload which simulates fundamental application characteristics that affect garbage collector latency."

To finish this discussion of allocation, we want to shift focus to a very common aspect of allocation behavior. In the real world, allocation rates can be highly changeable and "bursty." Consider the following scenario for an application with a steady-state behavior as previously described:

2 s	Steady-state allocation	100 MB/s
1 s	Burst/spike allocation	1 GB/s
100 s	Back to steady-state	100 MB/s

The initial steady-state execution has allocated 200 MB in Eden. In the absence of long-lived objects, all of this memory has a lifetime of 100 ms. Next, the allocation spike kicks in. This allocates the other 200 MB of Eden space in just 200 ms, and of this, 100 MB is under the 100 ms age threshold. The size of the surviving cohort is larger than the survivor space, so the JVM has no option but to promote these objects directly into tenured. So we have:

GC0   @ 2.2 s   100 MB Eden → Tenured (100 MB)

The sharp increase in allocation rate has produced 100 MB of surviving objects, although note that in this model all of the "survivors" are, in fact, short-lived and will very quickly become dead objects cluttering up the tenured generation. They will not be reclaimed until a full collection occurs.

Continuing for a few more collections, the pattern becomes clear:

GC1   @ 2.602 s   200 MB Eden → Tenured (300 MB)

GC2   @ 3.004 s   200 MB Eden → Tenured (500 MB)

GC3   @ 7.006 s   20 MB Eden → SS1 (20 MB) [+ Tenured (500 MB)]

Notice that, as discussed, the garbage collector runs as needed, and not at regular intervals. The bigger the allocation rate, the more frequent are GCs. If the allocation rate is too high, then objects will end up being forced to be promoted early.

This phenomenon is called *premature promotion*; it is one of the most important indirect effects of garbage collection and a starting point for many tuning exercises, as we will see in the next chapter.

Summary

The subject of garbage collection has been a lively topic of discussion within the Java community since the platform's inception. In this chapter, we have introduced the key concepts that performance engineers need to understand to work effectively with the JVM's GC subsystem:

- Mark-and-sweep collection
- HotSpot's internal runtime representation for objects
- The weak generational hypothesis
- Practicalities of HotSpot's memory subsystems

- The parallel and serial collectors
- Allocation and the central role it plays

In the next chapter, we will discuss topics in modern GC—including concurrent collectors and HotSpot's default collector (G1) as well as less-common alternatives, such as Shenandoah and ZGC.

Several of the concepts we met in this chapter—especially allocation and specific effects such as premature promotion—will be of particular significance to the upcoming chapter, and it may be helpful to refer back to this material frequently.

## CHAPTER 5

Advanced Garbage Collection

In the last chapter, we introduced the basic theory of Java garbage collection and the conceptually simplest production collector (Parallel). From that starting point, we will move forward to introduce some of the theory of modern Java garbage collectors. After that, we will introduce the default garbage collector (G1) used by HotSpot (and GraalVM).

In general, for most workloads, G1 will be sufficient. However, there are a number of scenarios where the unavoidable tradeoffs that GC represents will guide the engineer's choice of collector. So, we will also consider some more rarely seen collectors. These are:

- Shenandoah
- Z Garbage Collector (ZGC)
- Balanced
- Legacy HotSpot collectors

Note that not all of these collectors are used in the HotSpot virtual machine—the Balanced collector we will be discussing is a collector from Eclipse OpenJ9.

Tradeoffs and Pluggable Collectors

One aspect of the Java platform that beginners don't always immediately recognize is that while Java has a garbage collector, the language and VM specifications do not say how GC should be implemented. In fact, there have been Java implementations (e.g., Epsilon, which you'll meet later, and Lego Mindstorms) that didn't implement any kind of GC at all![1]

---

1 Such a system is very difficult to program in, as every object that's created has to be reused, and any object that goes out of scope effectively leaks memory.

Within the Oracle/OpenJDK environment, the GC subsystem is treated as a pluggable subsystem. This means that the same Java program can execute with different garbage collectors without changing the semantics of the program, although the performance of the program may vary considerably based on which collector is in use.

The primary reason for having pluggable collectors is that GC is a very general computing technique. In particular, the same algorithm may not be appropriate for every workload. As a result, GC algorithms often represent a compromise or tradeoff between competing concerns.

> There is no single general-purpose GC algorithm that can optimize for all GC concerns simultaneously.

The main concerns that developers often need to consider when choosing a garbage collector include:

- Application STW pause time (aka pause length or duration)
- Throughput (as a percentage of GC time to application runtime)
- Pause frequency (how often the collector needs to stop the application)
- Reclamation efficiency (how much garbage can be collected by a single GC)
- Pause consistency (are all pauses roughly the same length?)

Of these, pause time often attracts a disproportionate amount of attention. While important for many applications, it should not be considered in isolation.

> For many workloads, pause time is not an effective or useful performance characteristic.

Let's consider a highly parallel batch-processing application. It is likely to be much more concerned with application throughput rather than pause length (or GC-induced application latency). This is because for many batch jobs, pause times of even tens of seconds are not really relevant, provided the application throughput is high and the job can finish within the defined work window. This means that a GC algorithm that favors CPU efficiency of GC and throughput is greatly preferred to an algorithm that is low-pause at any cost.

However, it's important to know that throughput is more subtle than it first appears. The definition we've given is a standard one, but it is possible that optimizing for a low proportion of time in GC might end up being at the expense of application throughput. That would do more harm than good.

For example, suppose an application is performing badly for whatever reason—perhaps an external factor. It will generate less garbage, but only because less work is being done. If there's less garbage, the GC has less work to do, so the proportion of time spent in GC will be lower—but that doesn't mean the application is doing better.

A second consideration involves compaction, which is a property that many of Java's collectors have, such as the ParallelOld collector we met in Chapter 4.[2] Compaction tends to leave related objects close together, and if they are closer together, reading them is more efficient, because they are more likely to already be in the right cache line.

Applications spend a lot of time allocating and reading memory, so spending time making that faster can be a good investment, even at the expense of a bit more time spent in GC—as always, we must measure and not guess.

The performance engineer should also note that there are a number of other tradeoffs and concerns that are sometimes important when considering the choice of collector.

With Oracle/OpenJDK, as of version 21, four collectors are provided. We have already met the parallel (aka throughput) collectors, and they are the easiest to understand from a theoretical and algorithmic point of view. In this chapter, we will meet the other mainstream collector (G1) and explain how it differs from Parallel GC.

Later in the chapter, starting with "Shenandoah" on page 122, we will meet some other collectors that are also available. Please note that not all of them are recommended for production use across all workloads, and some are now deprecated.

Let's get underway by discussing some fundamentals of concurrent garbage collection.

Concurrent GC Theory

As we discussed in the last chapter, nondeterminism in GC is directly caused by allocation behavior, and many of the systems that Java is used for exhibit highly variable allocation. Worse still, garbage collectors intended for general-purpose use have no domain knowledge with which to improve the determinism of their pauses.

---

2 Evacuating collectors also get compaction essentially "for free."

In specialized systems, such as graphics or animation display systems, there is often a fixed frame rate, which provides a regular, fixed opportunity for GC to be performed. Java does not provide any mechanism for the application to provide such information to the GC, as the philosophy of the platform is that the GC should be a managed subsystem.

GC is not aware of the details of the application, only the graph of the live objects in the heap. This only adds to the nondeterminism inherent in Java GC.

> The minor disadvantage of this arrangement is the delay of the computation proper; its major disadvantage is the unpredictability of these garbage collecting interludes.[3]
>
> —Dijkstra et al.

The starting point for modern GC theory is to try to address Dijkstra's insight that the nondeterministic nature of STW pauses (both in duration and in frequency) is the major annoyance of using GC techniques.

One approach is to use a collector that is concurrent (or at least partially or mostly concurrent) to reduce pause time by doing some of the work needed for collection while the application threads are running. This inevitably reduces the processing power available for the actual work of the application, as well as complicating the code needed to perform collection.

Before discussing concurrent collectors, though, there is an important piece of Java GC terminology and technology that we need to address, as it is essential to understanding the nature and behavior of modern garbage collectors.

JVM Safepoints

To carry out an STW garbage collection, such as those performed by HotSpot's parallel collectors, all application threads must be stopped. This seems almost a tautology, but until now, we have not discussed exactly *how* the JVM achieves this.

The JVM is not actually a completely preemptive multithreading environment—this is something of an open secret in the Java world.

This does not mean that it is purely a cooperative environment—quite the opposite. The operating system can still preempt (remove a thread from a core) at any time.

---

3 Edsger Dijkstra, Leslie Lamport, A. J. Martin, C. S. Scholten, and E. F. M. Steffens, "On-the-Fly Garbage Collection: An Exercise in Cooperation," *Communications of the ACM* 21 (1978): 966–975.

This is done, for example, when a thread has exhausted its timeslice or put itself into a `wait()`.

As well as this core OS functionality, the JVM also needs to perform coordinated actions. To facilitate this, the runtime requires each application thread to have special execution points, called *safepoints*, where the thread's internal data structures are in a known-good state. At these times, the thread is able to be suspended for coordinated actions.

> We can see the effects of safepoints in STW GC (the classic example) and thread synchronization, but there are others as well.

To understand the point of safepoints, consider the case of a fully STW garbage collector, such as Parallel. For this to run, it requires a stable object graph. This means that all application threads must be paused.

There is no way for a GC thread (which executes in user space) to demand that the OS enforces this requirement on an application thread, so the application threads (which are executing as part of the JVM process) must cooperate to achieve this.

There are two primary rules that govern the JVM's approach to safepointing:

- The JVM cannot force a thread into the safepoint state.
- The JVM can prevent a thread from leaving the safepoint state.

This means that the implementation of the JVM interpreter must contain code to yield at a barrier if safepointing is required. For JIT-compiled methods, equivalent barriers must be inserted into the generated machine code. The general case for reaching safepoints, then, looks like this:

1. The JVM sets a global "time to safepoint" flag.
2. Individual application threads poll and see that the flag has been set.
3. They pause and wait to be woken up again.

When this flag is set, all app threads must stop. Threads that stop quickly must wait for slower stoppers (and this time may not be fully accounted for in the pause time statistics).

Normal app threads use this polling mechanism. They will always check in between executing any two bytecodes in the interpreter.[4] In compiled code, the most common cases where the JIT compiler has inserted a poll for safepoints are exiting a compiled method and when a loop branches backward (e.g., to the top of the loop).

It is possible for a thread to take a long time to safepoint, and even theoretically to never stop (but this is essentially a pathological case that must be deliberately provoked).

> The idea that all threads must be fully stopped before the STW phase can commence is similar to the use of latches, such as that implemented by `CountDownLatch` in the `java.util.concurrent` library.

Some specific cases of safepoint conditions are worth mentioning here.

A thread is automatically at a safepoint if it:

- Is blocked on a monitor
- Is executing JNI code

A thread is *not* necessarily at a safepoint if it:

- Is partway through executing a bytecode (interpreted mode)
- Has been interrupted by the OS
- Is in JITed code and not at an explicit safepoint

You will meet the safepointing mechanism again later, as it is a critical piece of the internal workings of the JVM.

Let's move on to discuss a classic piece of computer science theory that is fundamental to understanding concurrent garbage collection.

Tri-Color Marking

Dijkstra and Lamport's 1978 paper describing their *tri-color marking* algorithm was a landmark for both correctness proofs of concurrent algorithms and GC, and the basic algorithm it describes remains an important part of garbage collection theory.

The algorithm works by maintaining a set of gray nodes, which are nodes that have been discovered but not yet fully processed. The algorithm runs as follows:

---

4 In recent versions of the JVM, "thread-local handshake polling" has been added, which changes the picture somewhat, but this is still a reasonable mental model for devs who are new to the area.

- GC roots are colored gray.
- All other nodes (objects) are colored white.
- A marking thread chooses a random gray node.
- If the node has no white child nodes, the marking thread colors the node black.
- Otherwise, the marking thread moves to a white child node and colors it gray.
- This process is repeated until there are no gray nodes left.
- All black objects have been proven to be reachable and must remain alive.
- White nodes are eligible for collection and correspond to objects that are no longer reachable.

There are some complications, but this is the basic form of the algorithm. An example is shown in Figure 5-1.

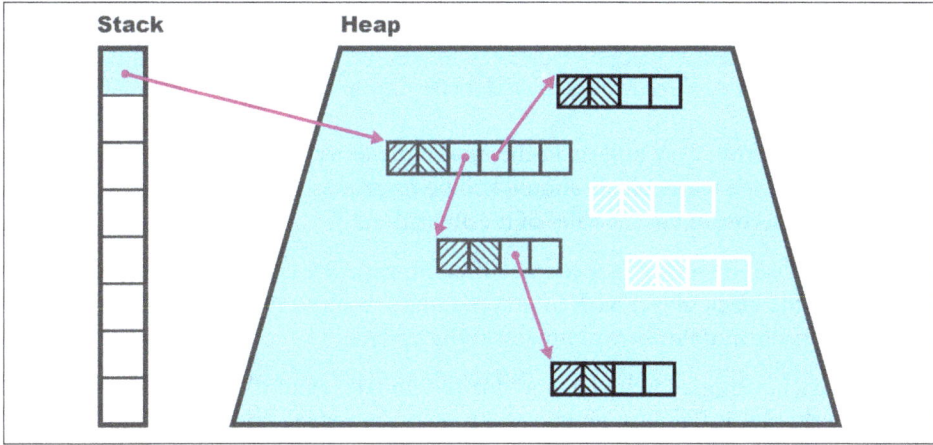

Figure 5-1. Tri-color marking

Concurrent collection also frequently uses a technique called *snapshot at the beginning* (SATB). This means that the collector regards objects as live if they were reachable at the start of the collection cycle or have been allocated since. This adds some minor wrinkles to the algorithm, such as mutator threads needing to create new objects in the black state if a collection is running and in the white state if no collection is in progress.

The tri-color marking algorithm needs to be combined with a small amount of additional work to ensure the changes introduced by the running application threads do not cause live objects to be collected. This is because in a concurrent collector, application (mutator) threads are changing the object graph, while marking threads are executing the tri-color algorithm.

Consider the situation where an object has already been colored black by a marking thread, and then is updated to point at a white object by a mutator thread. This is the situation shown in Figure 5-2.

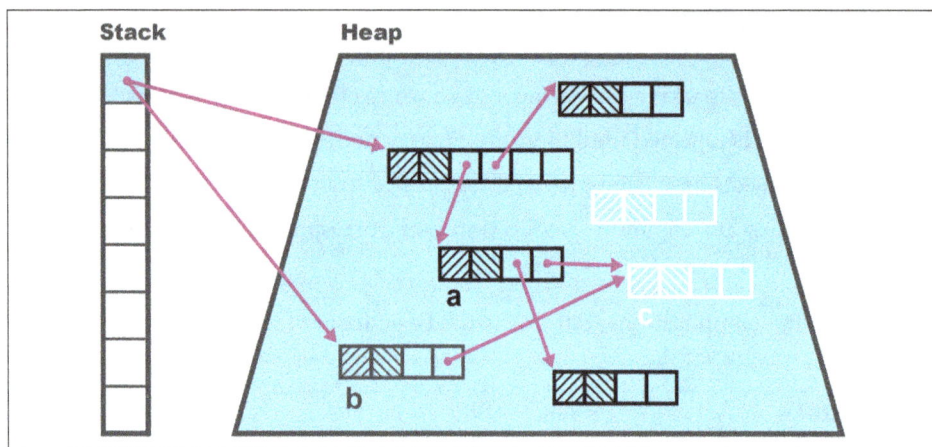

Figure 5-2. A mutator thread could invalidate tri-color marking

If all references from gray objects to the new white object are now deleted, we have a situation where the white object should still be reachable but will be deleted, as it will not be found, according to the rules of the algorithm.

This problem can be solved in a couple different ways. We could, for example, change the color of the black object back to gray, adding it back to the set of nodes that need processing as the mutator thread processes the update.

That approach, using a "write barrier" for the update, would have the nice algorithmic property that it would maintain the *tri-color invariant* throughout the whole of the marking cycle.

> Tri-color invariant: no black object node may hold a reference to a white object node during concurrent marking.

However, this comes at a cost—it destroys a property ("monotonicity") needed for a simple proof that the marking algorithm terminates.

An alternative approach is to keep a queue of all changes that could potentially violate the invariant, and then have a secondary "fixup" phase that runs after the main phase has finished. This fixup must, of necessity, be a STW phase, but in practice, it is usually very short.

The modern general purpose collector, G1, uses the second approach (known as a *remark phase*)—we will discuss this in more detail when we meet it in "G1" on page 114.[5] First, let's talk about other important techniques for concurrent garbage collection.

Forwarding Pointers

In this section, we'll discuss the use of *forwarding pointers*. These are also known as *Brooks pointers* after their inventor, Rodney Brooks.[6] This technique, in its simplest form, uses an additional word of memory per object to indicate whether the object has been relocated during a previous phase of garbage collection and to give the location of the new version of the object's contents.

The resulting heap layout (as used by early versions of the Shenandoah collector, for example) for its object pointers (oops) can be seen in Figure 5-3. Note that if the object has not been relocated, then the Brooks pointer simply points at the start of the object header.

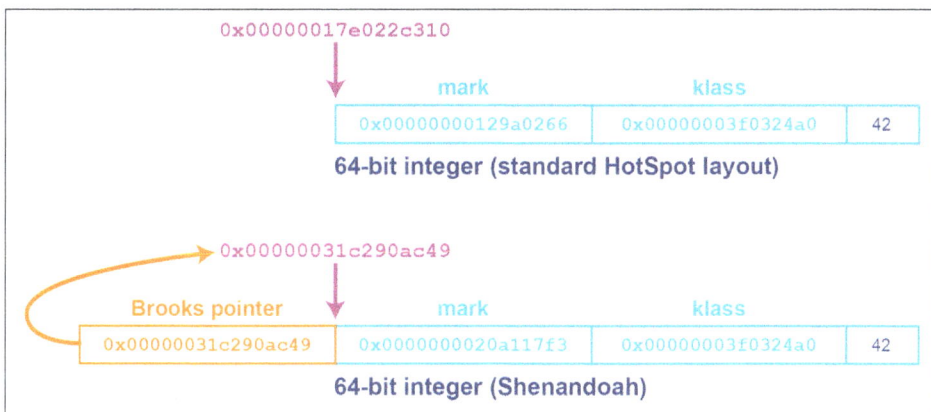

Figure 5-3. *The Brooks pointer*

The Brooks pointer mechanism relies upon the availability of hardware compare-and-swap (CAS) operations to provide atomic updates of the forwarding address.

---

5 In practice, G1 performs most of this work concurrently and does not need to add to the Remark STW time.

6 Rodney Brooks, "Trading Data Space for Reduced Time and Code Space in Real-Time Garbage Collection on Stock Hardware," in LFP'84, *Proceedings of the 1984 ACM Symposium on LISP and Functional Programming* (New York: ACM, 1984): 256–262.

During a concurrent marking phase, the collector threads trace through the heap and mark any live objects. If an object reference points to an oop that has a forwarding pointer, then the reference is updated to point directly at the new oop location. This can be seen in Figure 5-4.

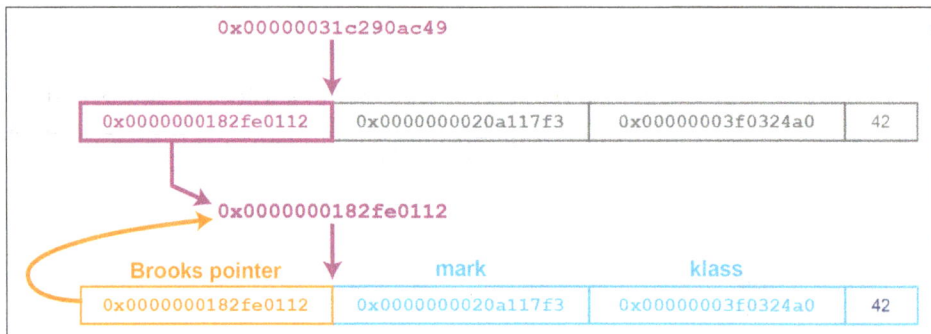

Figure 5-4. Updating the forwarding pointer

This can be a useful technique, but its obvious downside is that it requires an extra word of memory per object. For example, this increases the heap space required for an `Integer` object from 20 to 28 bytes. This can represent a significant additional overhead.

This technique is used by Shenandoah and other advanced collectors—we will have more to say about the practical usage of it later, including ways to mitigate the increased memory requirements.

Let's move on to meet our next major topic—the G1 collector that is the default for the HotSpot virtual machine for versions of Java newer than 8.

G1

G1 (the "Garbage First" collector) is a very different style of collector than the parallel collectors. It was first introduced in a highly experimental and unstable form in Java 6, but was extensively rewritten throughout the lifetime of Java 7, and it became stable and production-ready with the release of Java 8u40.

> We do not recommend using G1 with any version of Java prior to 8u40, regardless of the type of workload being considered.

G1 was originally intended to be a replacement low-pause collector that superseded the Concurrent Mark Sweep (CMS) collector (which is no longer supported). It was designed to be a collector that was:

- Much easier to tune than CMS
- Less susceptible to premature promotion
- Capable of better scaling behavior (especially pause time) on big heaps
- Able to greatly reduce the need to fall back to full STW collections

However, over time, G1 evolved into being thought of as more of a general-purpose collector. It became the default collector in Java 9, taking over from the parallel collectors. G1 has continued to improve over subsequent Java releases—it is greatly improved in Java 11, and better still in Java 17 and 21.

One of the most important concepts in G1 is that of *pause goals*. These allow the developer to specify the desired maximum amount of time that the application should pause on each garbage collection cycle.

Note that this is expressed as a goal, and there is no guarantee that the application will be able to meet it. If this value is set too low, then the GC subsystem will be unable to meet the goal.

The default value for pause goals is 200 ms—but in practice, pauses are usually much less than this, so the default value is usually fine for most applications with typical heap sizes. For applications with very large heaps (tens or hundreds of gigabytes), the pause goal may need to be adjusted.

Garbage collection is driven by allocation, which can be highly unpredictable for many Java applications. This can limit or destroy G1's ability to meet pause goals.

Another major difference that the design of the G1 collector has is that it rethinks the notion of generations as we have met them so far. Specifically, unlike the parallel collectors, G1 does not have dedicated, contiguous memory spaces per generation, and instead introduces *regions*.

G1 Heap Layout and Regions

The G1 heap is based upon the concept of fixed-sized regions that make up a generation. These are areas that are by default 1 MB in size (but are larger on bigger heaps). The use of regions allows for noncontiguous generations and makes it possible to have a collector that does not need to collect all garbage on each run (*incremental collection*).

> The overall G1 heap is still contiguous in memory—it's just that the memory that makes up each generation no longer has to be.

The region-based layout of the G1 heap can be seen in Figure 5-5.

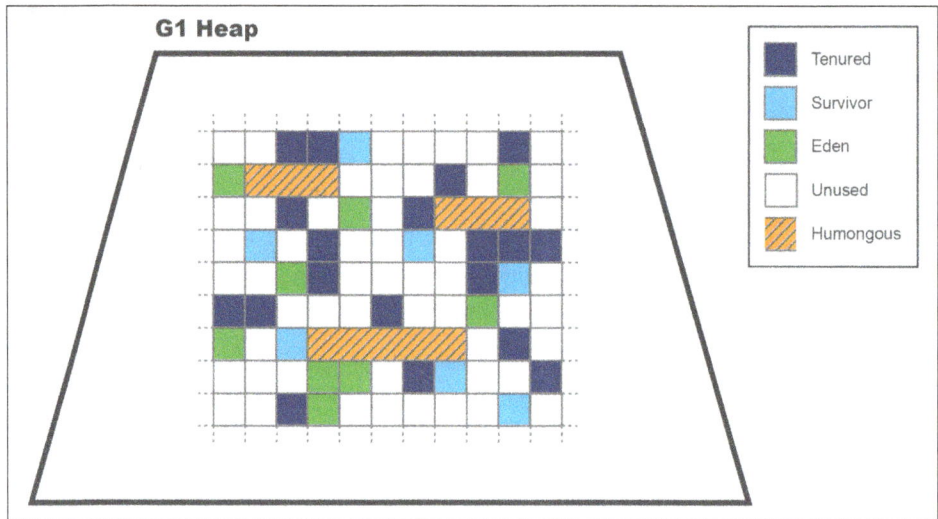

Figure 5-5. G1 regions

As you can see, G1 still has a concept of a young generation made up of Eden and survivor regions.

As of Java 21, G1's algorithm allows regions of a power of 2 MB—so 1, 2, 4 ... MB, with the max size being 512 MB. By default, it expects between 2,048 and 4,095 regions in the heap and will adjust the region size to achieve this.

To calculate the region size, we compute this value:

```
<Heap size> / 2048
```

and then round it down to the nearest permitted region size value. Then the number of regions can be calculated:

```
Number of regions = <Heap size> / <region size>
```

As usual, we can change the value of the region size by applying a configuration option, but in practice this is rarely necessary.

If an application creates an object that occupies more space than half a region size, then it is considered a *humongous object*.

These objects are directly allocated in special *humongous regions*, which are free, contiguous regions that are immediately made part of the tenured generation (rather than Eden). The typical case for this is large arrays (as arrays are objects in Java).

G1 Collections

G1 has two kinds of collections:

Young GC (aka G1New)
    The regions to be collected include only young regions.

Mixed GC (aka G1Old)
    The collection set contains both young and old regions.

A young collection is a STW collection seeking to reclaim as much heap as fast as possible. It does so by completely evacuating regions so they can immediately be reused.

While warming up, the collector keeps track of the statistics of how many "typical" regions can be collected per GC run. If enough memory can be collected to balance the new objects that have been allocated since the last GC, then the collector is not losing ground to allocation, and G1New collections will continue. This means that pause times can be controlled, as long as the collector can stay ahead of the allocation rate.

A mixed collection is a mostly concurrent collection used when the number of old objects has risen sufficiently that a young collection is no longer sufficient to reclaim enough memory to balance allocation. At this point, it is worth expending extra effort to reclaim old objects and increase the number of free regions.

The point when a mixed collection will start is known as the *Initiating Heap Occupancy Percent* (IHOP) threshold. G1 automatically determines IHOP based on earlier application behavior. The default initial value is 45% (but this can be changed with a config switch), and the application will adjust up or down adaptively.

This gives us a reasonable high-level picture of the collector, i.e., that G1:

- Is a regional, generational collector
- Is an evacuating collector
- Provides "statistical compaction"
- Uses a concurrent marking phase (for mixed collections)

The concepts of TLAB allocation, evacuation to survivor space, and promoting to tenured are broadly similar to the other HotSpot GCs you've already met.

However, G1 mixed collections are a little more complex than the collections we've already discussed, so let's take a closer look.

G1 Mixed Collections

One of the most often overlooked aspects of G1 is, bizarrely, its great strength. Specifically, G1 mixed collections mostly run concurrently with application threads. By default, some of the available cores (at least one) will perform the concurrent phases of G1, and the other half will continue to execute application code.

> The exact formula for `ConcGCThreads`—the number of cores used for concurrent GC—is a little complicated (*https://oreil.ly/L7_RM*):
>
> ```
> max(1, (ParallelGCThreads + 2) / 4)
> ```
>
> where `ParallelGCThreads` is usually the number of cores, at least on small machines.

This has two main consequences:

- Application throughput is reduced while a mixed collection is running.
- It is possible for the application to need to perform a young GC while a concurrent collection is underway.

Note that in the case where a young GC needs to run during a mixed collection, it will typically take longer to complete than normal, as the young GC will have only a reduced number of cores to work with.

G1Old has four phases:

1. Concurrent Start (includes a STW G1New)
2. Concurrent Mark
3. Remark (STW)
4. Cleanup (STW)

The Concurrent Mark phase typically takes much longer than the others. This means that for most of its run time, G1Old runs alongside application threads. However, for three phases (Concurrent Start, Remark, and Cleanup), all application threads must be stopped. The overall effect (as compared to ParallelOld) should be to replace a single long STW pause with three STW pauses, which are usually very short.

The purpose of the Concurrent Start phase is to provide a stable set of starting points for GC that are within each region; these are the GC roots for the purposes of the collection cycle. After the initial marking has concluded, the Concurrent Mark phase commences. This essentially runs a form of the tri-color marking algorithm on the heap, keeping track of any changes that might later require fixup.

After the Concurrent Mark, G1Old must fix up its records to avoid violating the first rule of garbage collectors—collecting an object that is still alive. This is the Remark phase, and a substantial amount of work has been done to remove tasks from this STW phase and move them into the Concurrent Mark phase.[7]

The Cleanup phase is mostly STW and comprises accounting tasks that identify regions that are now completely free and ready to be reused (e.g., as Eden regions).

Remembered Sets

Recall that when we met the ParallelOld collector, the heuristic "few references from old to young objects" was discussed, in "Weak Generational Hypothesis" on page 86. HotSpot uses a mechanism called card tables to help take advantage of this phenomenon in the parallel (and also CMS) collectors.

The G1 collector has a related feature to help with region tracking. The *Remembered Sets* (usually just called *RSets*) are per-region entries that track outside references that point into a heap region.

This means that instead of tracing through the entire heap for references that point into a region, G1 just needs to examine the RSets and then scan those regions for references.

Figure 5-6 shows how the RSets are used to implement G1's approach to dividing up the work of GC between allocator and collector.

---

7 At the time of writing (August 2024), the main potential timesink in Remark is the processing of weak references, as this could result in unbounded marking activity.

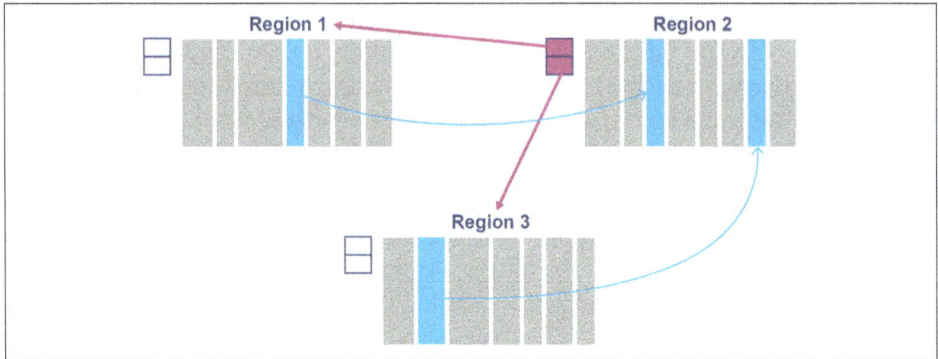

Figure 5-6. Remembered Sets

RSets (and also card tables in Parallel) is a technique that can contribute to a GC problem called *floating garbage*. This is an issue caused when objects that are otherwise dead are kept alive by references from dead objects outside the current collection set. That is, on a global mark they can be seen to be dead, but a more limited local marking may incorrectly report them as alive, depending on the root set used. RSets could cause increased floating garbage due to scanning pointers from dead objects within the region.

During the Cleanup phase of a mixed collection, G1 performs RSet "scrubbing." This is a process that looks at the RSets of regions that pointed into evacuated regions and updates references to objects that have been moved to other regions.

Full Collections

A full GC is an STW collection similar to the full collections we have already met in the parallel collectors.

A full GC cleans the entire heap—both young and tenured spaces (old gen). It also compacts the objects in the humongous regions in place—they are not included in normal evacuation phases to reduce copying overhead.

Full GCs can be caused in several ways—one of them is via fragmentation of the humongous regions. If this occurs, then allocation of humongous objects can fail, even though there is enough free memory to satisfy the allocation request (because the free space is not in a contiguous block).

Another possibility is that if the Concurrent Mark phase during a mixed collection is not able to finish before the application has allocated all available heap memory, then G1 will have no choice but to perform a full GC—this is sometimes called a *concurrent mode failure*.

Normally, the IHOP threshold is set dynamically so that this does not happen; however, if the application's allocation profile changes, the predicted value (based on past behavior) might be wrong.

To avoid this type of full GC, the obvious thing to do is to start a concurrent marking phase earlier—this will usually happen adaptively, but for some workloads, a different IHOP threshold may need to be set manually with a config switch.

JVM Config Flags for G1

If you're still running Java 8, then the switch that you need to enable G1 is:

```
+XX:UseG1GC
```

For modern versions of Java, no switch is needed—but be careful when running in containers. If your container only has a single visible core, then G1 will not be able to run concurrently (as there is only core) and will fall back to the serial collector. This is unlikely to be what you want.

As we mentioned earlier, G1 is based around *pause goals*. The switch that controls this core behavior of the collector is:

```
-XX:MaxGCPauseMillis=200
```

In other words, the default pause time goal is 200 ms. In practice, if your heap size is single-digit numbers of gigabytes, then the collector will probably never get anywhere near this value—and your STW times will be a lot lower.

If concurrent mode failures are causing too-frequent full GCs, then it is possible to adjust the IHOP threshold. The first thing to try is to ask the JVM to reduce the threshold for when to start mixed collections. This is done by increasing the buffer size used in IHOP calculation:

```
-XX:G1ReservePercent=10
```

It is also possible to disable the adaptive calculation of IHOP by setting it manually, although this is not recommended for most applications and should be attempted only if the adaptive approach has been unsuccessful. This is done using a pair of switches:

```
-XX:-G1UseAdaptiveIHOP
-XX:InitiatingHeapOccupancyPercent=45
```

In some circumstances, you may want to keep the adaptive behavior, but just change the initial value of IHOP. In this case, you would only set -XX:InitiatingHeapOccu pancyPercent=n.

One other option that may also be of use is the option of changing the region size, overriding the default algorithm:

```
-XX:G1HeapRegionSize=<n>m
```

Note that <n> must be a power of 2, between 1 and 512, as before, and must indicate a value in megabytes. The m suffix is mandatory, and if it is omitted, there may be unexpected results.

G1 has improved greatly since its introduction, and it is a superb general-purpose collector. However, it is not the only collector available for HotSpot—others exist, although they are usually suitable only for specific workloads.

Let's move on to discuss Shenandoah, the first of these alternative collectors.

Shenandoah

An alternative to G1 is the *Shenandoah* collector. It was created by Red Hat within the OpenJDK project and was made available as an experimental collector in Java 12. It was productionized in Java 15, and is a fully supported collector in Java 17 and 21.[8]

> Red Hat has also backported Shenandoah to Java 8 and 11 for its downstream OpenJDK distributions.

Shenandoah's goal is to bring down pause times on large (meaning tens or hundreds of gigabytes) heaps. There is no such thing as a free lunch, however, so Shenandoah potentially uses significantly more CPU resources than G1 to achieve this goal.

Shenandoah's approach to achieving low latency on large heaps is to perform concurrent compaction. The resulting phases of collection in Shenandoah are:

1. Init Mark (STW)
2. Concurrent Mark
3. Final Mark (STW)
4. Concurrent Cleanup
5. Concurrent Evacuation
6. Init Update Refs (STW)
7. Concurrent Update Refs
8. Final Update Refs (STW)
9. Concurrent Cleanup

These phases may initially seem similar to those seen in G1, and some similar approaches (e.g., SATB) are used by Shenandoah. However, there are some fundamental differences.

---

8 Oracle does not ship Shenandoah, but it is available in all other OpenJDK builds.

Concurrent Evacuation

Let's take a look at how the GC threads (which are running concurrently with app threads) perform evacuation. To make things a bit easier to understand, we'll talk about the original version of Shenandoah, which was implemented using forwarding pointers:

1. Copy the object into a TLAB (speculatively).

2. Use a CAS operation to update the forwarding pointer to point at the speculative copy.

3. If this succeeds, then the compaction thread won the race, and all future accesses to this version of the object will be via the Brooks pointer.

4. If it fails, the compaction thread lost. It undoes the speculative copy and follows the Brooks pointer left by the winning thread.

As Shenandoah is a concurrent collector, while a collection cycle is running, more garbage is being created by the application threads. Therefore, collection has to be able to keep up with the production of new garbage; otherwise the application will suffer a concurrent mode failure.

JVM Config Flags for Shenandoah

Shenandoah can be activated with the following switch:

```
-XX:+UseShenandoahGC
```

A comparison of Shenandoah's pause times as compared to other collectors can be seen in Figure 5-7.

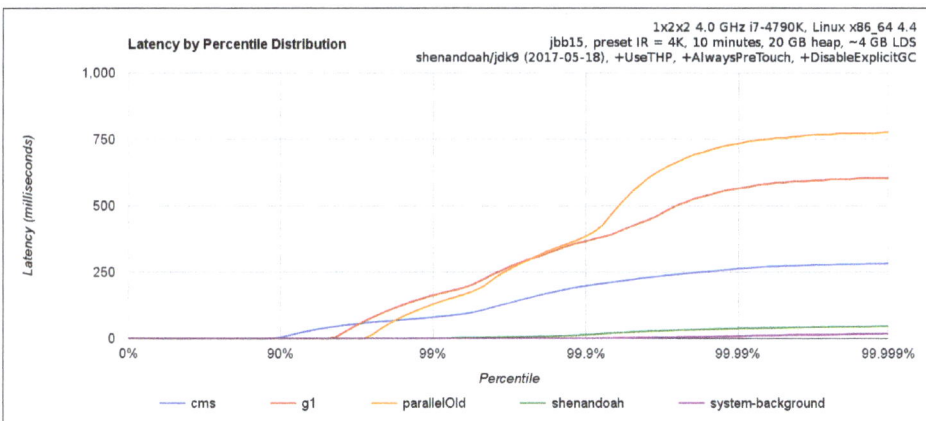

Figure 5-7. Shenandoah compared to other collectors (Shipilëv)

Compared to G1 and collectors such as Parallel, it is not anticipated that Shenandoah will require any special configuration by most users.

Shenandoah's Evolution

Shenandoah's design has evolved over time, and the current implementation is quite different from the original version. One area in which we see this is in the use of Brooks pointers. The original design of Shenandoah used the classical version of Brooks pointers, with the extra word of header at negative offset.

However, it is possible to use a trick to avoid consuming the additional word of memory. To see how the trick works, notice that the use of a forwarding pointer has two aspects:

- It indicates that this version of the object may be invalid.
- It indicates the address at which the valid version of the object can be found.

It turns out to be possible to use a specific combination of bits in the mark word—a combination previously unused by HotSpot—to indicate that the object is invalid. In other words, we can directly indicate on the mark word that the object has been forwarded.

The contents of the rest of the storage for this object no longer matters—as the correct version of the object can be found by following the forwarding pointer. This means that some of the object's memory can be used to store the forwarding pointer, so the extra word of memory in the object header is no longer needed.

This trick could be implemented on the original version of Shenandoah, but it was not found to be an acceptable performance tradeoff at the time. However, this changed with the arrival of a technique known as *loaded-reference barriers* in HotSpot with Java 13.[9] This opened the way for a new version of Shenandoah that shipped with Java 13 and contained these improvements.[10]

Further improvements were made in subsequent releases, such as:

- Java 14: Self-fixing barriers
- Java 14: Concurrent class unloading
- Java 15: Concurrent reference processing
- Java 17: Concurrent thread-stack processing

---

9 Shenandoah GC in JDK 13, Part 1 (*https://oreil.ly/BY66L*).

10 Shenandoah GC in JDK 13, Part 2 (*https://oreil.ly/X92lH*).

The end result is that the Java 17 version of Shenandoah is production-ready, as are Red Hat's backports. However, it's worth being reminded that it is not considered a general-purpose collector—it is intended for use on large heaps only.

One other note of caution is that, at the time of writing, Shenandoah is not a generational collector. Attempts are under way to add this feature, but it is not yet available.[11]

Let's move on to meet the next alternative collector for HotSpot—ZGC.

ZGC

Oracle has also been working on a collector that serves a similar purpose to Shenandoah, known as ZGC. The intent is to deliver a collector in which all GC operations that scale with the size of the heap or the size of metaspace are moved out of safepoints (i.e., STW phases) and into concurrent phases.

> The major user-visible goal for ZGC is to meet the user expectation that time spent inside of GC safepoints does not exceed one millisecond on heaps up to 1 TB (although ZGC can handle heap sizes up to 16 TB).

ZGC was first introduced as an experimental collector for Linux/x64 in Java 11 and has evolved significantly from that initial starting point. It is now a fully supported collector in Java 17 and 21, across a range of operating systems.

In theoretical terms, we can say that ZGC is:

- Concurrent
- Region-based
- Compacting
- Aware of non-uniform memory access (NUMA)
- Using colored pointers
- Using load barriers

This means that it is somewhat similar to G1 and Shenandoah in some aspects—for example, ZGC is a concurrent, region-based collector.

Not only this, but some of the key technologies and techniques (e.g., concurrent reference and thread-stack processing) that Shenandoah relies upon were initially

---

11 JEP 404: Generational Shenandoah (Experimental) (*https://openjdk.org/jeps/404*).

implemented by the ZGC team and then utilized by both collectors. ZGC also uses a version of remembered sets (similar to G1).

However, in other respects, ZGC is quite different from the other collectors.

For example, one other important implementation detail is that ZGC does not use Brooks pointers but instead utilizes *colored pointers*.

This technique stores additional metadata about object lifecycle in the object pointer/oop itself. The metadata describes such things as whether the object is known to be alive and whether the address is correct (i.e., if this is the canonical copy of the object). This oop layout can be seen in Figure 5-8.

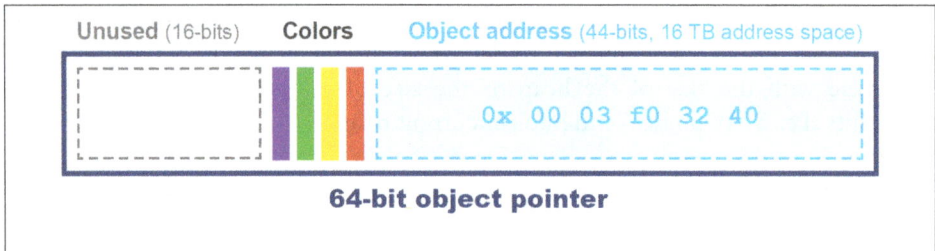

Figure 5-8. ZGC colored pointers

When a load barrier is encountered, the GC thread will check the colored pointer and ensure it is the expected value before proceeding.

> For ZGC there are no compressed oops—so the colored pointer is always 64 bits. This provides for 44 bits of heap addressing, which is sufficient for heaps up to 16 TB in size.

Standard ZGC uses multimapping, so each physical page of memory is referred to by multiple virtual pages. This can lead to misleading numbers—the traditional RSS number can over-report heap usage when using ZGC by as much as 3x, compared to the accurate PSS figure.

ZGC can be enabled with this switch:

```
-XX:+UseZGC
```

It is a major goal of ZGC to avoid requiring users to tune the collector.

For example, ZGC has no IHOP (in the sense of G1) but instead uses a cost model to decide when to start a collection. As another example, the number of threads used for GC is also a dynamic property of ZGC—including being able to change the size of the GC thread pool during a collection.

ZGC has been widely used for production workloads for several years now, but until now, there has always been a potential issue with it—it has not been a generational collector.

Java 21 introduced a new version of ZGC, known as *Generational ZGC*. Nongenerational ZGC is the older version of ZGC—and as you might expect from the name, it doesn't take advantage of generations to optimize its runtime characteristics.

Nongenerational collectors are more susceptible to allocation stalls, as they cannot perform a quick young GC to reclaim space. Adding generations to ZGC is, therefore, a useful step forward, as it helps to reduce the impact of a highly variable allocation rate.

Generational ZGC uses the terms *minor* and *major* for its collections—minor collections affect only the young objects, whereas major collections run over the entire heap. In this way, they are similar to the young and mixed collections of G1.

As noted in the previous section, nongenerational ZGC uses multimapped memory, which can cause over-reporting of memory usage. Generational ZGC avoids this by using explicit code in the memory barriers instead.

Generational ZGC also uses a different approach to colored pointers--it uses 12 color bits instead of 4, as you can see in Figure 5-9.

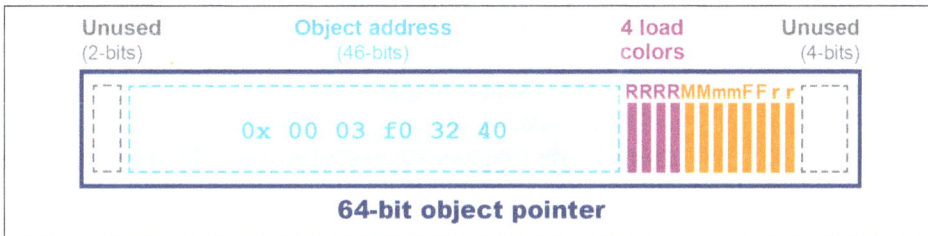

| Unused (2-bits) | Object address (46-bits) | 4 load colors | Unused (4-bits) |

0x 00 03 f0 32 40   RRRRMMmmFFrr

64-bit object pointer

Figure 5-9. Generational ZGC colored pointers

We should also note that the references stored on the JVM stack are implemented as *colorless pointers*, and the GC algorithm needs to translate these into colored pointers before they can be used in the heap.

This is a significant increase in complexity over the version used by nongenerational ZGC; however, it does open the door to some interesting optimizations, and the long-term intent is for Generational ZGC to completely replace the nongenerational version.

> More detail of how Generational ZGC is implemented can be found in JEP 439 (*https://openjdk.org/jeps/439*).

Generational ZGC is enabled with these command-line options:

```
-XX:+UseZGC -XX:+ZGenerational
```

Current users of the older version are encouraged to transition to use the newer Generational version of ZGC.

Let's move on to meet the final collector that we will discuss in this chapter—the Balanced collector of the OpenJ9 JVM.

Balanced (Eclipse OpenJ9)

The Eclipse open source foundation maintains a JVM called OpenJ9. This was historically a proprietary JVM produced by IBM, but it was made open source several years ago. The VM has several different collectors that can be switched on, including a high-throughput collector similar to the parallel collector HotSpot defaults to.

In this section, however, we will discuss the Balanced collector. It is a region-based collector available on 64-bit JVMs and designed for heaps in excess of 4 GB. Its primary design goals are to:

- Improve scaling of pause times on large Java heaps.
- Minimize worst-case pause times.
- Utilize awareness of NUMA performance.

To achieve the first goal, the heap is split into a number of regions, which are managed and collected independently. Like G1, the Balanced collector wants to manage at most 2,048 regions, so it will choose a region size to achieve this. The region size is a power of 2, as for G1, but Balanced will permit regions as small as 512 KB.

As we would expect from a generational region-based collector, each region has an associated age, with age-zero regions (Eden) used for allocation of new objects. When the Eden space is full, a collection must be performed. The IBM term for this is a *partial garbage collection* (PGC).

A PGC is an STW operation that collects all Eden regions and may additionally choose to collect regions with a higher age, if the collector determines that they are worth collecting. In this manner, PGCs are similar to G1's mixed collections.

> Once a PGC is complete, the age of regions containing the surviving objects is increased by 1. These are sometimes referred to as *generational regions*.

Another benefit, as compared to other OpenJ9 GC policies, is that class unloading can be performed incrementally. Balanced can collect class loaders that are part of the current collection set during a PGC. This is in contrast to other OpenJ9 collectors, where class loaders could be collected only during a global collection.

One downside is that because a PGC only has visibility of the regions it has chosen to collect, this type of collection can suffer from floating garbage. To resolve this problem, Balanced employs a *global mark phase* (GMP). This is a partially concurrent operation that scans the entire Java heap, marking dead objects for collection. Once a GMP completes, the following PGC acts on this data. Thus, the amount of floating garbage in the heap is bounded by the number of objects that died since the last GMP started.

The final type of GC operation that Balanced carried out is *global garbage collection* (GGC). This is a full STW collection that compacts the heap. It is similar to the full collections that would be triggered in HotSpot by a concurrent mode failure.

OpenJ9 Object Headers

The basic OpenJ9 object header is a *class slot*, the size of which is 64 bits, or 32 bits when compressed references is enabled.

> Compressed references is the default for heaps smaller than 57 GB and is similar to HotSpot's compressed oops technique.

However, the header may have additional slots, depending on the type of object:

- Synchronized objects will have monitor slots.
- Objects put into internal JVM structures will have hashed slots.

In addition, the monitor and hashed slots are not necessarily adjacent to the object header—they may be stored anywhere in the object, taking advantage of otherwise wasted space due to alignment. OpenJ9's object layout can be seen in Figure 5-10.

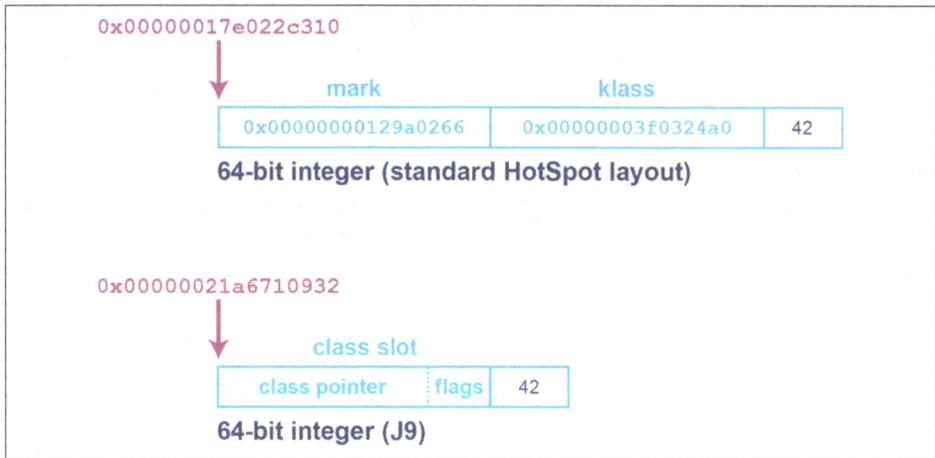

Figure 5-10. OpenJ9 object layout

The highest 24 (or 56) bits of the class slot are a pointer to the class structure, which is off-heap, similarly to Java's Metaspace. The lower 8 bits are flags that are used for various purposes depending on the GC policy in use.

Large Arrays in Balanced

Allocating large arrays in Java is a common trigger for compacting collections, as enough contiguous space must be found to satisfy the allocation. We saw one aspect of this in the discussion of G1, where humongous object allocation results in fragmentation and insufficient space for a large allocation—resulting in a concurrent mode failure.

For a region-based collector, it is entirely possible to allocate an array object in Java that exceeds the size of a single region. To address this, Balanced uses an alternate representation for large arrays that allows them to be allocated in discontiguous chunks. This representation is known as *arraylets*, and this is the only circumstance under which heap objects can span regions.

The arraylet representation is invisible to user Java code, and instead is handled transparently by the JVM. The allocator will represent a large array as a central object, called the *spine*, and a set of array *leaves*. The leaves contain the actual entries of the array and are pointed to by entries of the spine. This enables entries to be read with only the additional overhead of a single indirection. An example can be seen in Figure 5-11.

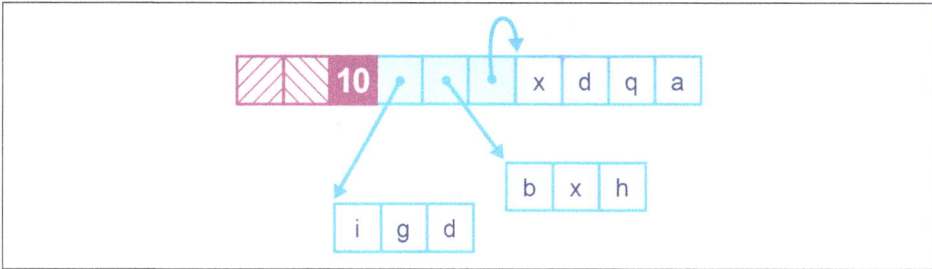

Figure 5-11. Arraylets in OpenJ9

> The arraylet representation is potentially visible through JNI APIs (although not from regular Java), so the programmer should be aware that when porting JNI code from another JVM, the spine and leaf representation may need to be taken into account.

Performing partial GCs on regions reduces average pause time, although overall time spent performing GC operations may be higher due to the overhead of maintaining information about the regions of a spine and its leaves. Crucially, the likelihood of requiring a global STW collection or compaction (the worst case for pause times) is greatly reduced, with this typically occurring as a last resort when the heap is full.

There is an overhead to managing regions and discontiguous large arrays, and thus, Balanced is suited to applications where avoiding large pauses is more important than outright throughput.

NUMA and Balanced

Non-uniform memory access is a memory architecture used in multiprocessor systems, typically medium to large servers. Such a system involves a concept of distance between memory and a processor, with processors and memory arranged into nodes. A processor on a given node may access memory from any node, but access time is significantly faster for local memory (that is, memory belonging to the same node).

For JVMs that are executing across multiple NUMA nodes, the Balanced collector can split the Java heap across them. Application threads are arranged such that they favor execution on a particular node, and object allocations favor regions in memory local to that node. A schematic view of this arrangement can be seen in Figure 5-12.

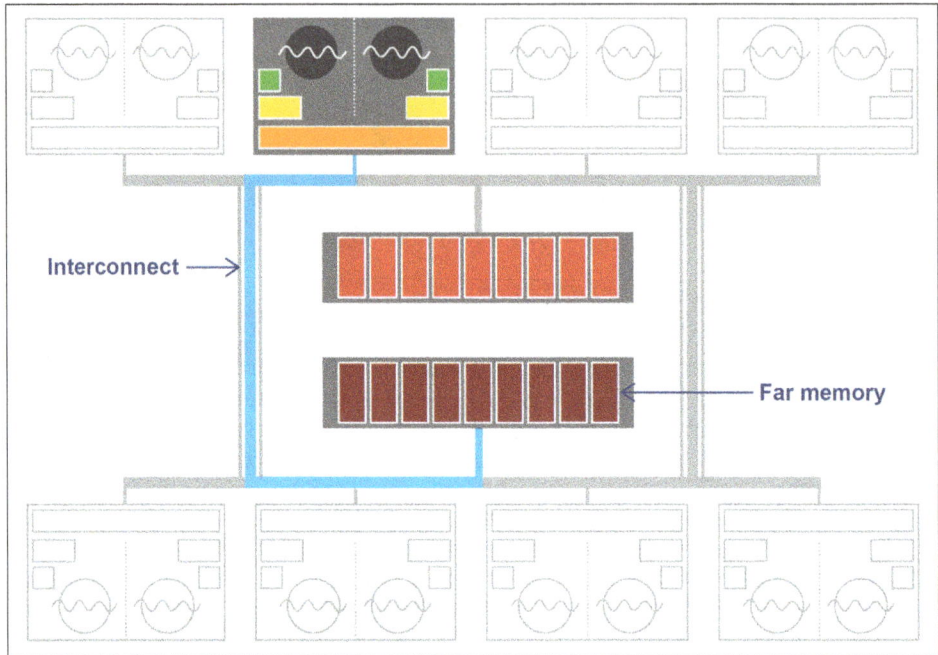

Figure 5-12. Non-uniform memory access

In addition, a partial garbage collection will attempt to move objects closer (in terms of memory distance) to the objects and threads that refer to them. This means the memory referenced by a thread is more likely to be local, improving performance. This process is invisible to the application.

Niche HotSpot Collectors

In earlier versions of HotSpot, various other collectors were available. Most of them have been removed, but as of Java 21, two niche collectors still exist. We mention them for completeness here, but neither is recommended for production use.

CMS

The Concurrent Mark Sweep (CMS) collector was designed to be an extremely low-pause collector for the tenured (aka old generation) space only. It was paired with a slightly modified parallel collector for collecting the young generation—called ParNew rather than Parallel GC.

It is present in Java 8 and 11, but it was deprecated in Java 9, and is no longer available as of Java 14.[12] In practice, for Java 8, CMS still outperforms G1 for certain workloads that require a low-pause GC. However, G1 improved very significantly between Java 8 and 11. As a result, the workloads for which CMS is the best choice are much rarer for Java 11—and, of course, the collector is not available at all for Java 17 or 21.

The CMS collector is activated with the following flag:

```
-XX:+UseConcMarkSweepGC
```

CMS has a broadly similar phase structure to a G1 mixed collection in terms of its GC duty cycles. So, an important question is: what happens if Eden fills up while CMS is running?

The answer is, unsurprisingly, that because application threads cannot continue, they pause, and a (STW) young GC runs while CMS is running. This young GC run will usually take longer than in the case of the parallel collectors, because it has only half the cores available for young generation GC (the other half of the cores are running CMS).

Under normal circumstances, the young collection promotes only a small number of objects to tenured, and the CMS old collection completes normally, freeing up space in tenured. The application then returns to normal processing, with all cores released for application threads.

However, consider the case of a very high allocation rate, perhaps with premature promotion. This can potentially cause a situation in which the young collection has too many objects to promote for the available space in tenured.

This is a form of concurrent mode failure, and the JVM has no choice at this point but to fall back to a collection using ParallelOld, which is fully STW. Effectively, the allocation pressure was so high that CMS did not have time to finish processing the old generation before all the "headroom" space to accommodate newly promoted objects filled up.

To avoid frequent concurrent mode failures, CMS needs to start a collection cycle before tenured is completely full. This is similar to the IHOP behavior of G1 that we met in "Concurrent Evacuation" on page 123.

---

12 The Java Enhancement Process has 3 steps involved in removing a feature: deprecated, deprecated for removal and removed. Features can stay at the first two levels for as many releases as they need to, and some features may be deprecated without any realistic expectation that they will ever be removed.

Epsilon

The Epsilon collector is not a legacy collector. However, it is included here because it *must not be used in production under any circumstances*. While CMS, if encountered within your environment, should be flagged as high risk and marked for immediate analysis and removal, Epsilon is slightly different.

Epsilon is an experimental collector designed for testing purposes only. It is a *zero-effort* collector. This means it makes no effort to actually collect any garbage. Every byte of heap memory that is allocated while running under Epsilon is effectively a memory leak. It cannot be reclaimed and will eventually cause the JVM (probably very quickly) to run out of memory and crash.

> Develop a GC that only handles memory allocation, but does not implement any actual memory reclamation mechanism. Once available Java heap is exhausted, perform the orderly JVM shutdown.
>
> —JEP 318: Epsilon: A No-Op Garbage Collector (*https://openjdk.java.net/jeps/318*)

Such a "collector" can be useful for the following purposes:

- Performance testing and microbenchmarks
- Regression testing
- Testing low/zero-allocation Java application or library code

In particular, Java Microbenchmark Harness (JMH tests would benefit from the ability to confidently exclude any GC events from disrupting performance numbers. Memory allocation regression tests, ensuring that changed code does not greatly alter allocation behavior, would also become easy to do. Developers could write tests that run with an Epsilon configuration that accepts only a bounded number of allocations and then fails on any further allocation due to heap exhaustion.

Finally, the proposed VM-GC interface would also benefit from having Epsilon as a minimal test case for the interface itself.

Summary

Garbage collection is a truly fundamental aspect of Java performance analysis and tuning. Java's rich landscape of garbage collectors is a great strength of the platform, but it can be intimidating for the newcomer, especially given the scarcity of documentation that considers the tradeoffs and performance consequences of each choice.

In this chapter, we have outlined the decisions that face performance engineers and the tradeoffs they must make when deciding on an appropriate collector to use for their applications. We have discussed some of the underlying theory and met a range of modern GC algorithms that implement these ideas.

In the next chapter, we will put some of this theory to work and introduce logging, monitoring, and tooling as a way to bring some scientific rigor to our discussion of performance-tuning garbage collection.

## CHAPTER 6

Code Execution on the JVM

The two main services that any JVM provides are memory management and an easy-to-use container for execution of application code. We covered garbage collection in some depth in Chapters 4 and 5, and in this chapter we turn to code execution.

> Recall that the Java virtual machine specification, usually referred to as the VM spec, describes how a conforming Java implementation needs to behave.

The VM spec defines execution of Java bytecode in terms of an interpreter. However, broadly speaking, interpreted environments have unfavorable performance as compared to programming environments that execute machine code directly. Most production-grade modern Java environments solve this problem by providing dynamic compilation capability.

As we discussed in Chapter 3, this ability is otherwise known as *just-in-time compilation*, or just *JIT compilation*. It is a mechanism by which the JVM keeps track of which methods are being executed to determine whether individual methods are eligible for compilation to directly executable code.

In this chapter, we start by laying out the basic lifecycle of a Java application, as it typically happens today. Then, we provide a brief overview of bytecode interpretation and why HotSpot is different from other interpreters that you may be familiar with.

We then turn to the basic concepts of JIT compilation and profile-guided optimization. We discuss the code cache and then introduce the basics of HotSpot's compilation subsystem.

Toward the end of the chapter, we discuss recent changes in the Java platform driven by a rethinking of how execution of Java programs should be handled. These developments have largely been prompted by the shift to cloud-deployed applications and the need to address the concerns of this new deployment environment.

Lifecycle of a Traditional Java Application

Let's start by diving a little deeper into what actually happens when you type: `java HelloWorld` on a Unix-like system (such as Linux or Mac; similar remarks apply to Windows).

At a low level, standard process execution occurs to set up the JVM, which is a single process. The shell locates the JVM binary (e.g., possibly in `$JAVA_HOME/bin/java`) and starts a process corresponding to that binary, passing the arguments (including the entrypoint class name).

The newly started process analyzes the command-line flags and prepares for VM initialization, which will be customized via the flags (for heap size, GC, etc.). At this time the process probes the machine it is running on and examines various system parameters, such as how many CPU cores the machine has, how much memory, and what precise set of CPU instructions are available.

This very detailed information is used to customize and optimize how the JVM configures itself. For example, the JVM will use the number of cores to determine how many threads to use when garbage collection runs and to size the *common pool* of threads.

> The auto-probing and self-configuring behavior of the JVM is important to be aware of, as it affects how Java applications behave in containers. We will cover this further in Chapter 8.

One key early step is to reserve an area of userspace memory (from the operating system, aka C, heap) equal to `Xmx` (or the default value) for the Java heap--the area where all Java objects will be stored. Another vital step is to initialize a repository to store Java classes and associated metadata in (known as *Metaspace* in HotSpot).

Then the VM itself is created, usually via the function `JNI_CreateJavaVM`, on a new thread for HotSpot. The VM's own threads—such as the GC threads and the threads that perform JIT compilation—also need to be started up.

As discussed earlier, the bootstrapping classes are prepared and then initialized. The first bytecodes are run and first objects are created as soon as classes are loaded—e.g., in the class initializer (`static {}` blocks aka `clinit` methods) for the bootstrapping classes.

The significance of this is that the JVM's basic functions—such as JIT compilation and GC—are running from very early in the lifecycle of the application. As the VM starts up, there may be some GC and JIT activity even before control reaches the entrypoint class. Once it does, then further classloading will happen as the application begins to execute and needs to run code from classes that are not present in the class metadata cache.

For most typical production applications, therefore, the startup phase is characterized by a spike in classloading, JIT, and GC activity while the application reaches a steady state. Once this has occurred, the amount of JIT and classloading usually drops sharply because:

- The entire "world" of classes that the application needs has been loaded.
- The set of methods that are called often have already been converted to machine code by the JIT compiler.

However, it is important to recognize that "steady state" does not mean "zero change." It is perfectly normal for applications to experience further classloading and JIT activity—such as *deoptimization* and *reoptimization*. This can be caused when a rarely executed code path is encountered and causes a new class to be loaded.

One other important special case of the startup-steady-state model is sometimes referred to as "two-phase classloading." This occurs in applications that use Spring and other similar dependency injection techniques.

In this case, the core framework classes are loaded first. After that, the framework examines the main application code and config to determine a graph of objects that need to be instantiated to activate the application. This triggers a second phase of classloading where the application code and its other dependencies are loaded.

The case of GC behavior is a little bit different. In an application that is not suffering any particular performance problem, the pattern of GC is also likely to change when the steady state is reached—but GC events will still occur.

This is because in Java applications (apart from a very few pathological use cases), objects are created, are alive for some time, and then are automatically collected—this is the entire point of automatic memory management. However, the pattern of steady state GC may well look very different to that of the startup phase.

The overall impression that you should be building up from this description is one of a highly dynamic runtime. Applications that are deployed on it display the runtime characteristics of a well-defined startup phase, followed by a steady state where small (but usually nonzero) amounts of change occur. The community has adopted the term *dynamic VM mode* for this traditional Java application lifecycle.

However, with the rise of Cloud Native Java, there has been increased interest in new operational and deployment modes for Java applications that are better suited to containers and the cloud, and that deviate from dynamic VM mode in various ways.

We will discuss these recent developments later in the chapter, but first we need to discuss the basics of how code is executed on the JVM.

Overview of Bytecode Interpretation

As we saw briefly in "Executing Bytecode" on page 52, the JVM interpreter operates as a stack machine. This means that, unlike with physical CPUs, there are no registers used as immediate holding areas for computation. Instead, all values to be operated on are placed on an *evaluation stack*, and the stack machine instructions work by transforming the value(s) at the top of the stack.

The JVM provides three primary areas to hold data:

- The *evaluation stack*, which is local to a particular method
- *Local variables* to temporarily store results (also local to methods)
- The *object heap*, which is shared between methods and between threads

A series of VM operations that use the evaluation stack to perform computation can be seen in Figures 6-1 through 6-5, as a form of pseudocode that should be instantly recognizable to Java programmers.

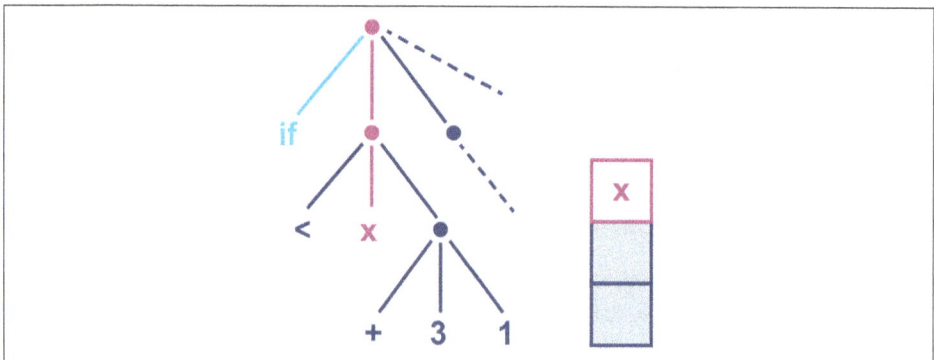

Figure 6-1. Initial interpretation state

The interpreter must now compute the righthand subtree to determine a value to compare with the contents of x.

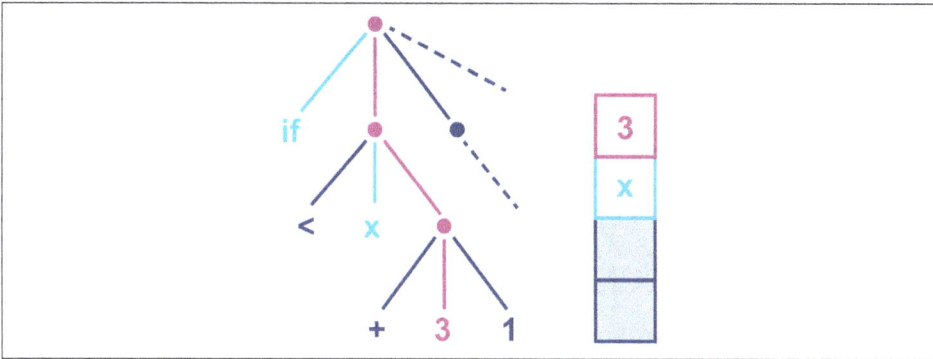

Figure 6-2. Subtree evaluation

The first value of the next subtree, an int constant 3, is loaded onto the stack.

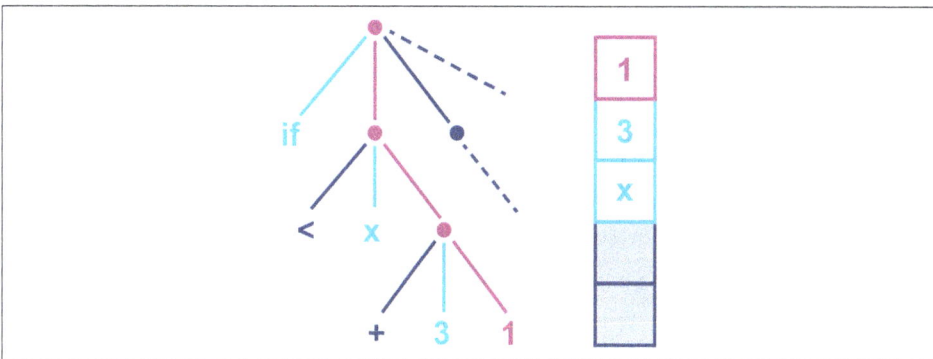

Figure 6-3. Subtree evaluation (Step 2)

Now another int value, 1, is also loaded onto the stack. In a real JVM, these values will either have been loaded from the constants area of the class file or will use a "shortcut form" for common, small constants.

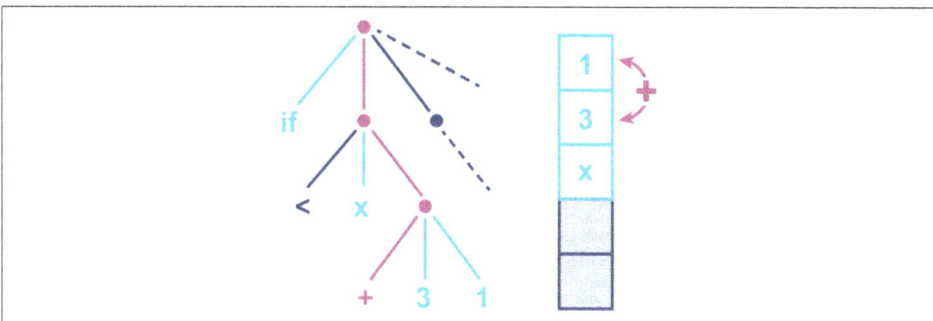

Figure 6-4. Subtree evaluation (Step 3)

At this point, the addition operation acts on the top two elements of the stack, removes them, and replaces them with the result of adding the two numbers together.

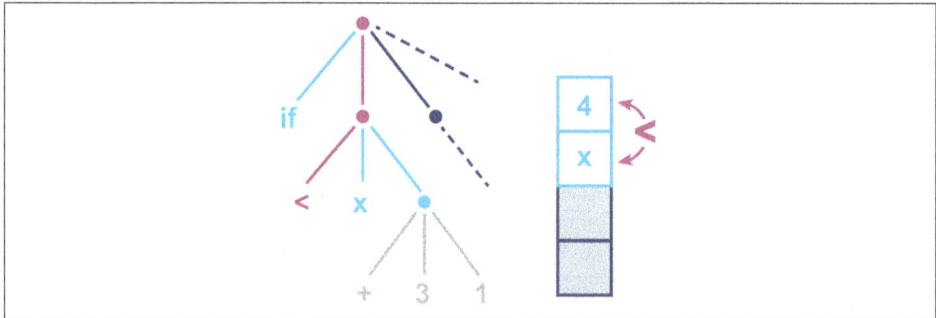

Figure 6-5. Final subtree evaluation

The resulting value is now available for comparison with the value contained in x, which has remained on the evaluation stack throughout the entire process of evaluating the other subtree.

Introduction to JVM Bytecode

In the case of the JVM, each stack machine operation code (opcode) is represented by one byte, hence the name *bytecode*. Accordingly, opcodes run from 0 to 255, of which roughly 200 are in use as of Java 23.

Bytecode instructions are typed, in the sense that iadd and dadd expect to find the correct primitive types (two int and two double values, respectively) at the top two positions of the stack.

Many bytecode instructions come in "families," with as many as one instruction for each primitive type and one for object references.

For example, within the store family, specific instructions have specific meanings: dstore means "store the top of stack into a local variable of type double," whereas astore means "store the top of stack into a local variable of reference type." In both cases, the type of the local variable must match the type of the incoming value.

As Java was designed to be highly portable, the JVM specification was designed to be able to run the same bytecode without modification on both *big-endian* and *little-endian* hardware architectures. As a result, JVM bytecode has to make a decision about which endianness convention to follow (with the understanding that hardware with the opposite convention must handle the difference in software).

Bytecode is big-endian, so the most significant byte of any multi-byte sequence comes first.

Some opcode families, such as load, have *shortcut forms*. This allows the argument to be omitted, which saves the cost of the argument bytes in the class file. In particular, aload_0 puts the current object (i.e., this) on the top of the stack. As that is such a common operation, this results in a considerable savings in class file size.

However, as Java classes are typically fairly compact, this design decision was probably more important in the early days of the platform, when class files—often applets—would be downloaded over a 14.4 Kbps modem.

Since Java 1.0, only one new bytecode opcode (invokedynamic) has been introduced, and two (jsr and ret) have been deprecated.

The use of shortcut forms and type-specific instructions greatly inflates the number of opcodes that are needed, as several are used to represent the same conceptual operation. The number of assigned opcodes is thus much larger than the number of basic operations that bytecode represents, and bytecode is actually conceptually very simple.

Let's meet some of the main bytecode categories, arranged by opcode family. Note that in the tables that follow, c1 indicates a two-byte constant pool index, whereas i1 indicates a local variable in the current method. The parentheses indicate that the family has some opcodes that are shortcut forms.

The first category we'll meet is the *load and store* category, depicted in Table 6-1. This category comprises the opcodes that move data on and off the stack—for example, by loading it from the constant pool or by storing the top of the stack into a field of an object in the heap.

Table 6-1. Load and store category

Family name	Arguments	Description
load	(i1)	Loads value from local variable i1 onto the stack
store	(i1)	Stores top of stack into local variable i1
ldc	c1	Loads value from CP#c1 onto the stack
const		Loads simple constant value onto the stack

Family name	Arguments	Description
pop		Discards value on top of stack
dup		Duplicates value on top of stack
getfield	c1	Loads value from field indicated by CP#c1 in object on top of stack onto the stack
putfield	c1	Stores value from top of stack into field indicated by CP#c1
getstatic	c1	Loads value from static field indicated by CP#c1 onto the stack
putstatic	c1	Stores value from top of stack into static field indicated by CP#c1

The difference between ldc and const should be made clear. The ldc bytecode loads a constant from the constant pool of the current class. This holds strings, primitive constants, class literals, and other (internal) constants needed for the program to run.[1]

The const opcodes, on the other hand, take no parameters and are concerned with loading a finite number of true constants, such as aconst_null, dconst_0, and iconst_m1 (the latter of which loads -1 as an int).

The next category, the *arithmetic bytecodes*, apply only to primitive types, and none of them take arguments, as they represent purely stack-based operations. This simple category is shown in Table 6-2.

Table 6-2. Arithmetic category

Family name	Description
add	Adds two values from top of stack
sub	Subtracts two values from top of stack
div	Divides two values from top of stack
mul	Multiplies two values from top of stack
(cast)	Casts value at top of stack to a different primitive type
neg	Negates value at top of stack
rem	Computes remainder (integer division) of top two values on stack

In Table 6-3, we can see the *flow control* category. This category represents the bytecode-level representation of the looping and branching constructs of source-level languages. For example, Java's for, if, while, and switch statements will all be transformed into flow control opcodes after source code compilation.

---

1 Recent versions of the JVM also permit more exotic constants to support modern advanced VM techniques.

Table 6-3. Flow control category

Family name	Arguments	Description
if	(i1)	Branch to the location indicated by the argument if the condition is true
goto	i1	Unconditional branch to the supplied offset
return		Returns from the current method to caller, passing back the value on top of the stack (if any)
tableswitch		Jump to a location specified in a jump table, using a label as the jump index
lookupswitch		Jump to a location specified in a jump table, using a key for the jump index

A detailed description of how tableswitch and lookupswitch operate is outside the scope of this book. You can refer to the latest Java virtual machine specification (*https://oreil.ly/_4_H5*) for more details.

The flow control category seems very small, but the true count of flow control opcodes is surprisingly large. This is due to there being a large number of members of the if opcode family. We met the if_icmpge opcode (*if-integer-compare-greater-or-equal*) in the javap example back in Chapter 3, but there are many others that represent different variations of the Java if statement.

The deprecated jsr and ret bytecodes (which have not been output by javac since Java 6) are also part of this family. They are no longer legal for modern versions of the platform so have not been included in this table.

One of the most important categories of opcodes is shown in Table 6-4. This is the *method invocation* category, the only mechanism that the Java program allows to transfer control to a new method. That is, the platform completely separates the concepts of local flow control (i.e., within a method) and transfer of control to another method.

Table 6-4. Method invocation category

Opcode name	Arguments	Description
invokevirtual	c1	Invokes the method found at CP#c1 via virtual dispatch
invokespecial	c1	Invokes the method found at CP#c1 via "special" (i.e., exact) dispatch
invokeinterface	c1, count, 0	Invokes the interface method found at CP#c1 using interface offset lookup
invokestatic	c1	Invokes the static method found at CP#c1
invokedynamic	c1, 0, 0	Dynamically looks up which method to invoke and executes it

The JVM's design—and use of explicit *method call* opcodes—means that there is no equivalent of a `call` operation as found in machine code.

Instead, JVM bytecode uses some specialist terminology; we speak of a *call site*, which is a place within a method (the caller) where another method (the callee) is called. Not only that, but in the case of a nonstatic method call, there is always some object that we resolve the method upon. This object is known as the *receiver object*, and its runtime type is referred to as the *receiver type*.

> Calls to static methods are always turned into `invokestatic` and have no receiver object.

Java programmers who are new to looking at the VM level may be surprised to learn that method calls on Java objects are actually transformed into one of three possible bytecodes (`invokevirtual`, `invokespecial`, or `invokeinterface`), depending on the context of the call.

> It can be a very useful exercise to write some Java code and see what circumstances produce each possibility, by disassembling a simple Java class with `javap`.

Instance method calls are normally turned into `invokevirtual` instructions, except when the static type of a receiver object is only known to be an interface type. In this case, the call is instead represented by an `invokeinterface` opcode. Finally, in the cases (e.g., private methods or superclass calls) where the exact method for dispatch is known at compile time, an `invokespecial` instruction is produced.

This raises the question of how `invokedynamic` enters the picture. The short answer is that there is no direct language-level access to `invokedynamic` in Java, even as of version 23.

In fact, when `invokedynamic` was added to the runtime in Java 7, there was no way at all to force `javac` to emit the new bytecode. In this old version of Java, the invoke dynamic technology had only been added to support long-term experimentation and non-Java dynamic languages (especially JRuby).

However, from Java 8 onward, `invokedynamic` has become a crucial part of the Java language, and it is used to provide support for advanced language features. Let's take a look at a simple example from Java 8 lambdas:

```
public class LambdaExample {
    private static final String HELLO = "Hello";

    public static void main(String[] args) throws Exception {
        Runnable r = () -> System.out.println(HELLO);
        Thread t = new Thread(r);
        t.start();
        t.join();
    }
}
```

This trivial usage of a lambda expression produces bytecode as shown:

```
public static void main(java.lang.String[]) throws java.lang.Exception;
  Code:
    0: invokedynamic #2,  0  // InvokeDynamic #0:run:()Ljava/lang/Runnable;
    5: astore_1
    6: new            #3     // class java/lang/Thread
    9: dup
   10: aload_1
   11: invokespecial #4      // Method java/lang/Thread.
                      //          "<init>":(Ljava/lang/Runnable;)V
   14: astore_2
   15: aload_2
   16: invokevirtual #5      // Method java/lang/Thread.start:()V
   19: aload_2
   20: invokevirtual #6      // Method java/lang/Thread.join:()V
   23: return
```

Even if we know nothing else about it, the form of the invokedynamic instruction indicates that some method is being called, and the return value of that call is placed upon the stack.

Digging further into the bytecode we discover that, unsurprisingly, this value is the object reference corresponding to the lambda expression. It is created by a platform factory method that is being called by the invokedynamic instruction. This invocation makes reference to extended entries in the constant pool of the class to support the dynamic runtime nature of the call.

This is perhaps the most obvious use case of invokedynamic for Java programmers, but it is not the only one. This opcode is extensively used by non-Java languages on the JVM, such as Kotlin, JRuby, and Scala, and increasingly by Java frameworks as well. We will meet some related aspects of invokedynamic later in the book.

The final category of opcodes we'll consider are the *platform opcodes*. They are shown in Table 6-5, and comprise operations such as allocating new heap storage and manipulating the intrinsic locks (the monitors used by synchronization) on individual objects.

Table 6-5. Platform opcodes category

Opcode name	Arguments	Description
new	c1	Allocates space for an object of type found at CP#c1
newarray	prim	Allocates space for a primitive array of type prim
anewarray	c1	Allocates space for an object array of type found at CP#c1
arraylength		Replaces array on top of stack with its length
monitorenter		Locks monitor of object on top of stack
monitorexit		Unlocks monitor of object on top of stack

For newarray and anewarray the length of the array being allocated needs to be on top of the stack when the opcode executes.

In the catalog of bytecodes, there is a clear difference between "coarse" and "fine-grained" bytecodes, in terms of the complexity required to implement each opcode.

For example, arithmetic operations will be very fine-grained and are implemented in pure assembly in HotSpot. By contrast, coarse operations (e.g., operations requiring constant pool lookups, especially method dispatch) will need to call back into the HotSpot VM.

Along with the semantics of individual bytecodes, we should also say a word about safepoints in interpreted code. In Chapter 5 we met the concept of a JVM safepoint, as a point where the JVM needs to perform some housekeeping and requires a consistent internal state. This includes the object graph (which is, of course, being altered by the running application threads in a very general way).

To achieve this consistent state, all application threads must be stopped to prevent them from mutating the shared heap for the duration of the JVM's housekeeping. How is this done?

The solution is to recall that every JVM application thread is a true OS thread.[2] Not only that, but for threads executing interpreted methods, when an opcode is about to be dispatched the application thread is definitely running JVM interpreter code, not user code. The heap should, therefore, be in a consistent state, and the application thread can be stopped.

Therefore, "in between bytecodes" is an ideal time to stop an application thread, and it is one of the simplest examples of a safepoint.[3]

---

2 At least in mainstream server JVMs.

3 Modern versions of HotSpot may not need to check in between every bytecode, due to advances such as thread-local handshakes, but it remains a useful mental model for developers new to JVM internals.

The situation for JIT-compiled methods is more complex, but essentially equivalent barriers must be inserted into the generated machine code by the JIT compiler.

Simple Interpreters

As mentioned in Chapter 3, the simplest interpreter can be thought of as a `switch` statement inside a `while` loop. Let's look at a simple example of this type of interpreter, written in Java, that can execute a small subset of JVM bytecode.[4]

The `execMethod()` method of the interpreter interprets a single method of bytecode. Just enough opcodes have been implemented (some of them with dummy implementations) to allow integer math and "Hello World" to run.

A full implementation capable of handling even a very simple program would require complex operations, such as constant pool lookup, to have been implemented and work properly. However, even with only some very bare bones available, the basic structure of the interpreter is clear:

```java
public EvalValue execMethod(final byte[] instr) {
    if (instr == null || instr.length == 0)
        return null;

    EvaluationStack eval = new EvaluationStack();

    int current = 0;
    LOOP:
    while (true) {
        byte b = instr[current++];
        Opcode op = table[b & 0xff];
        if (op == null) {
            System.err.println("Unrecognized opcode byte: " + (b & 0xff));
            System.exit(1);
        }
        byte num = op.numParams();
        switch (op) {
            case IADD:
                eval.iadd();
                break;
            case ICONST_0:
                eval.iconst(0);
                break;
// ...
            case IRETURN:
                return eval.pop();
            case ISTORE:
                istore(instr[current++]);
```

---

4 This code is based on version 0.1.1 of ocelotvm (*https://oreil.ly/NZ_5R*)—a partial implementation of a JVM interpreter designed for teaching.

```
            break;
        case ISUB:
            eval.isub();
            break;
        // Dummy implementation
        case ALOAD:
        case ALOAD_0:
        case ASTORE:
        case GETSTATIC:
        case INVOKEVIRTUAL:
        case LDC:
            System.out.print("Executing " + op + " with param bytes: ");
            for (int i = current; i < current + num; i++) {
                System.out.print(instr[i] + " ");
            }
            current += num;
            System.out.println();
            break;
        case RETURN:
            return null;
        default:
            System.err.println("Saw " + op + " : can't happen. Exit.");
            System.exit(1);
        }
    }
}
```

Bytecodes are read one at a time from the method and are dispatched based on the code. In the case of opcodes with parameters, these are read from the stream as well, to ensure that the read position remains correct.

Temporary values are evaluated on the `EvaluationStack`, which is a local variable in `execMethod()`. The arithmetic opcodes operate on this stack to perform the calculation of integer math.

Method invocation is not implemented in the simplest version of the interpreter—but if it were, then it would proceed by looking up a method in the constant pool, finding the bytecode corresponding to the method to be invoked, and then recursively calling `execMethod()`.

HotSpot-Specific Details

HotSpot is a production-quality JVM with extensive advanced features designed to enable fast execution, even in interpreted mode. Rather than the simple style that we met in the simple interpreter example, HotSpot is a *template interpreter*, which generates the interpreter dynamically each time it is started up.

This is significantly more complex to understand and makes reading even the interpreter source code a challenge for the newcomer. HotSpot also uses a relatively large amount of assembly language to implement the simple VM operations (such as arithmetic) and exploits the native platform stack frame layout for further performance gains.

Also potentially surprising is that HotSpot defines and uses JVM-specific (aka private) bytecodes that do not appear in the VM spec. These are used to allow HotSpot to differentiate common hot cases from the more general use case of a particular opcode.

This is designed to help deal with a surprising number of edge cases. For example, a `final` method cannot be overridden, so the developer might think an `invokespecial` opcode would be emitted by `javac` when such a method is called.

However, the Java Language Specification has something to say about this case:

> Changing a method that is declared `final` to no longer be declared `final` does not break compatibility with pre-existing binaries.
> —JLS 13.4.17

Consider a piece of Java code such as:

```java
public class A {
    public final void fMethod() {
        // ... do something
    }
}

public class CallA {
    public void otherMethod(A obj) {
        obj.fMethod();
    }
}
```

Now, suppose `javac` compiled calls to `final` methods into `invokespecial`. The bytecode for `CallA::otherMethod` would look something like this:

```
public void otherMethod()
  Code:
    0: aload_1
    1: invokespecial #4          // Method A.fMethod:()V
    4: return
```

Now, suppose the code for A changes so that `fMethod()` is made nonfinal. It can now be overridden in a subclass; we'll call it B. Now suppose that an instance of B is passed to `otherMethod()`. From the bytecode, the `invokespecial` instruction will be executed, and the wrong implementation of the method will be called.

This is a violation of the rules of Java's object orientation. Strictly speaking, it violates the *Liskov substitution principle* (named for Barbara Liskov, one of the pioneers of object-oriented programming), which, simply stated, says that an instance of a subclass can be used anywhere that an instance of a superclass is expected. This principle is also the *L* in the famous SOLID principles of software engineering.

For this reason, calls to `final` methods must be compiled into `invokevirtual` instructions. However, because the JVM knows that such methods cannot be overriden, the HotSpot interpreter has a private bytecode that is used exclusively for dispatching `final` methods. The private bytecode approach in HotSpot is a performance optimiziation enabling a compile time statically bound function call. Without this, a dynamic call at runtime would be required to determine the correct function call.

To give another example, the language specification says that an object that is subject to finalization must register with the finalization subsystem (*https://oreil.ly/mpKY4*). This registration must occur immediately after the supercall to the `Object` constructor `Object::<init>` has completed. In the case of JVMTI and other potential rewritings of the bytecode, this code location may become obscured. To ensure strict conformance, HotSpot has a private bytecode that marks the return from the original `Object` constructor.

A list of the opcodes can be found in *hotspot/src/share/vm/interpreter/bytecodes.cpp*, and the HotSpot-specific special cases are listed there as "JVM bytecodes."

With a basic understanding of how the JVM interprets bytecode, let's move on to look at how it utilizes JIT compilation.

JIT Compilation in HotSpot

Just-in-time compilation is a general technique whereby programs are converted (usually from some convenient intermediate format) into highly optimized machine code at runtime. HotSpot and other mainstream production-grade JVMs rely heavily on this approach.

To be efficient, the technique uses runtime information to guide the optimization process. This is known as *profile-guided optimization* (PGO), and we'll turn to this subject next.

Profile-Guided Optimization

In its simplest form, PGO gathers information about your program at runtime and builds a profile that can be used to determine which parts of your program are used frequently and would benefit most from optimization—which in HotSpot means JIT compilation.

The JIT subsystem shares VM resources with your running program, so the cost of this profiling and any optimizations performed needs to be balanced against the expected performance gains over the process lifetime.

The cost of compiling bytecode to native code is paid at runtime and consumes resources (CPU cycles, memory) that could otherwise be dedicated to executing your program. Therefore, JIT compilation is performed sparingly, and the VM collects statistics about your program (looking for "hot spots") to know where best to optimize.

Recall the overall architecture that was shown back in Figure 3-3: the profiling subsystem is keeping track of which methods are running. If a method crosses a threshold that makes it eligible for compilation, then the emitter subsystem fires up a compilation thread to convert the bytecode into machine code.

The design of modern versions of `javac` is intended to produce "dumb bytecode." It performs only very limited optimizations, and instead provides a representation of the program that is easy for the JIT compiler to understand.

In Chapter 3, we introduced the problem of JVM warmup—which we now understand to be a result of PGO. This period of unstable performance when the application starts up has frequently led Java developers to ask questions such as, "Can't we save the compiled code to disk and use it the next time the application starts up?" or "Isn't it very wasteful to rerun optimization and compilation decisions every time we run the application?"

The problem is that these questions contain some assumptions about the nature of running application code. Let's look at an example from the financial industry to illustrate the problem.

US unemployment figures are released once a month. This *nonfarm payroll* (NFP) day produces traffic in trading systems that is highly unusual and not normally seen throughout the rest of the month.

If optimizations had been saved from another day and run on NFP day, they would not be as effective as freshly calculated optimizations. This would have the end result of making a trading system that uses precomputed optimizations actually less competitive than an application using PGO.

PGO is not a one-way street, and compilation decisions can be adjusted at runtime based on a drop in runtime performance caused by a change in profile. However, with projects like GraalVM and Leyden as seen in Chapter 15, the answer in the Java ecosystem to "Should we ahead-of-time compile or use PGO?" is more complex to answer. We will revisit this discussion as we look at newer technologies later.

This behavior, where application performance varies significantly between different runs of the application, is very common and represents the kind of domain information that an environment like Java is supposed to protect the developer from.

For this reason, HotSpot does not attempt to save any profiling information for application code and instead discards it when the VM shuts down, so the profile must be built again from scratch each time.

In the next section, we'll dig a little deeper into the mechanics of how HotSpot implements JIT compilation, building on the discussion of object layout that we introduced in Chapter 4.

Klass Words, Vtables, and Pointer Swizzling

Let's start by recalling that HotSpot is a multithreaded C++ application. This might seem a simplistic statement, but it is worth remembering that as a consequence, every executing Java program is actually always part of a multithreaded application from the operating system's point of view. Even single-threaded Java apps are always executing alongside VM threads.

One of the most important groups of threads within HotSpot are the threads that comprise the JIT compilation subsystem. This includes profiling threads that detect when a method is eligible for compilation and the compiler threads themselves that generate the actual machine code.

The method-scoped nature of HotSpot's JIT compilation uses the virtual function tables (vtables) as a key part of the implementation.

The overall picture is that when compilation is indicated by the emitter subsystem, the method is placed on a compiler thread, which compiles in the background. The overall process can be seen in Figure 6-6.

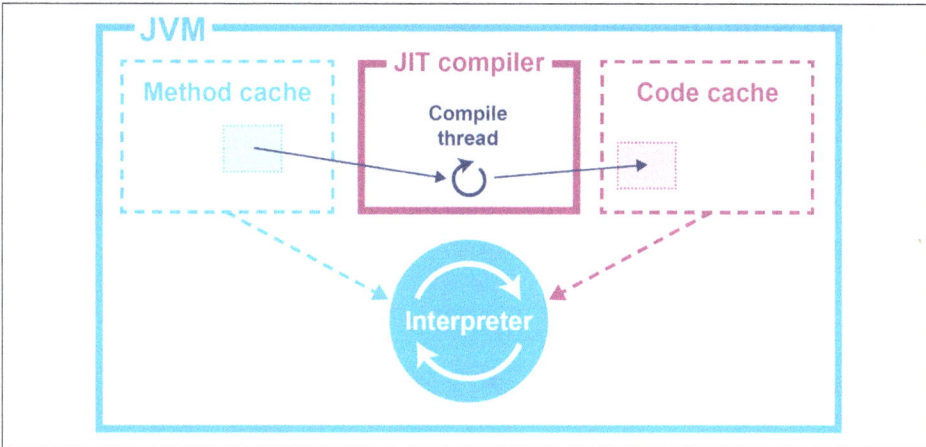

Figure 6-6. Simple compilation of a single method

When the optimized machine code is available, the entry in the vtable of the relevant klass is updated to point at the new compiled code.

> The vtable pointer updating is given the slightly strange name of *pointer swizzling*.

This means that any new calls to the method will get the compiled form, whereas threads that are currently executing the interpreted form will finish the current invocation in interpreted mode but will pick up the new compiled form on the next call.

You should also know that the basic unit of compilation in HotSpot is a whole method, so all the bytecode corresponding to a single method is compiled into native code at once. However, HotSpot also supports compilation of a hot loop using a technique called *on-stack replacement* (OSR).

OSR is used to help the case where a method is not called frequently enough to be compiled but contains a loop that would be eligible for compilation if the loop body was a method in its own right.

When considering machine optimized code, it is important that the HotSpot optimizations are available on a given architecture to achieve the benefits. OpenJDK HotSpot has been widely ported to many different architectures, with x86, x86-64, and ARM being the primary targets. SPARC, Power, MIPS, and S390 are also supported to varying degrees. Oracle officially supports Linux, macOS, and Windows as operating systems, but there are open source projects to natively support a much wider selection, including BSDs and embedded systems.

Compilers Within HotSpot

The HotSpot JVM actually has not one but two JIT compilers in it. These are properly known as C1 and C2, but they are sometimes referred to as the client compiler and the server compiler, respectively. Historically, C1 was used for GUI apps and other "client" programs, whereas C2 was used for long-running "server" applications. Modern Java apps generally blur this distinction, and HotSpot has changed to take advantage of the new landscape.

A compiled code unit is known as an *nmethod* (short for native method).

The general approach that both compilers take is to rely on a key measurement to trigger compilation: the number of times a method is invoked, or the *invocation count*. Once this counter hits a certain threshold, the VM is notified and will consider queuing the method for compilation.

The compilation process proceeds by first creating an internal representation of the method. Next, optimizations are applied that take into account profiling information that has been collected during the interpreted phase. However, the internal representation of the code that C1 and C2 produce is quite different. C1 is designed to be simpler and have shorter compile times than C2. The tradeoff is that, as a result, C1 does not optimize as fully as C2.

One technique that is common to both is *single static assignment*. This essentially converts the program to a form where no reassignment of variables occurs. In Java programming terms, the program is effectively rewritten to contain only `final` variables.

Historically, the JVM required the developer to choose between the C1 and C2 compilers at appliction startup time. However, since Java 6, the JVM has supported a mode called *tiered compilation*, which is the default for modern applications.

This is often loosely explained as running in interpreted mode until the simple C1 compiled form is available, then switching to using that compiled code while C2 completes more advanced optimizations.

However, this description is not completely accurate. From the *advancedThresholdPolicy.hpp* source file, we can see that within the VM there are five possible levels of execution:

- Level 0: interpreter
- Level 1: C1 with full optimization (no profiling)

- Level 2: C1 with invocation and backedge counters
- Level 3: C1 with full profiling
- Level 4: C2

We can also see in Table 6-6 that not every level is utilized by each compilation approach.

Table 6-6. Compilation pathways

Pathway	Description
0-3-4	Interpreter, C1 with full profiling, C2
0-2-3-4	Interpreter, C2 busy so quick-compile C1, then full-compile C1, then C2
0-3-1	Trivial method
0-4	No tiered compilation (straight to C2)

In the case of the trivial method, the method starts off interpreted as usual but then C1 (with full profiling) is able to determine the method to be trivial. This means that it is clear that the C2 compiler would produce no better code than C1, so compilation terminates.

As noted, tiered compilation has been the default for some time now, and it is not normally necessary to adjust its operation during performance tuning. However, an awareness of its operation is still sometimes useful, as it can complicate the observed behavior of compiled methods and potentially mislead the unwary performance engineer.

The Code Cache

JIT-compiled code is stored in a memory region called the *code cache*. This area also stores other native code belonging to the VM itself, such as parts of the interpreter.

The code cache has a fixed maximum size that is set at VM startup. It cannot expand past this limit, so it is possible for it to fill up. At this point, no further JIT compilations are possible, and any remaining uncompiled code will execute only in the interpreter. This will have an impact on performance and can result in the application being significantly less performant than the potential maximum.

Internally, the code cache is implemented as a heap containing an unallocated region and a linked list of freed blocks. Each time native code is removed, its block is added to the free list. A process called the *sweeper* is responsible for recycling blocks.

When a new native method is to be stored, the free list is searched for a block large enough to store the compiled code. If none is found, then, subject to the code cache having sufficient free space, a new block will be created from the unallocated space.

Native code can be removed from the code cache when:

- It is de-optimized (an assumption underpinning a speculative optimization turned out to be false).
- It is replaced with another compiled version (in the case of tiered compilation).
- The class containing the method is unloaded.

You can control the maximum size of the code cache using the VM switch:

```
-XX:ReservedCodeCacheSize=<n>
```

Note that with tiered compilation enabled, more methods will reach the lower compilation thresholds of the C1 client compiler. To account for this, the default maximum size is larger to hold these additional compiled methods.

In Java 8 on Linux x86-64 the default maximum sizes for the code cache are:

```
251658240 (240MB) when tiered compilation is enabled (-XX:+TieredCompilation)
 50331648  (48MB) when tiered compilation is disabled (-XX:-TieredCompilation)
```

A single code cache can become fragmented—for example if many of the intermediate compilations from the C1 compiler are removed after they are replaced by C2 compilations. This can lead to the unallocated region being used up and all the free space residing in the free list.

The code cache allocator will have to traverse the linked list until it finds a block big enough to hold the native code of a new compilation. In turn, the sweeper will also have to do more work to scan for blocks that can be recycled to the free list.

In the end, any garbage collection scheme that does not relocate memory blocks will be subject to fragmentation, and the code cache is not an exception.

Without a compaction scheme, the code cache can fragment, and this can cause compilation to stop — it is just another form of cache exhaustion, after all. In Java 9, JEP 197 introduced the Segmented Code Cache, which aims to address the challenges of a single code cache. Tiered compilation has increased the amount of compiled code by approximately 200-400%. The code cache segmentation groups by compiled code types, closely tied to lifetime, helping to prevent the fragmentation effects and associated sweeps and collections.

This grouping has a locality benefit, improving access times. The groups of the Segmented Code Cache are:

- *Non-method code heap*, which contains non method compilations that will last in the code cache for the duration of the application. The size can be configured using -XX:NonMethodCodeHeapSize.
- *Profiled code heap*, which contains lightly opimized compiled code, which tends to have a short lifetime. The size can be configured using -XX:ProfiledCodeHeap Size.
- *Non-profiled code heap*, which contains fully optimized, non-profiled methods, which tend to have a long lifetime. The size can be configured using -XX:Non ProfiledCodeHeapSize.

> These sizes are fixed, and adjusting them can have unexpected consequences if not fully tested with your application.

Logging JIT Compilation

One important JVM switch that all performance engineers should know about is:

```
-XX:+PrintCompilation
```

This will cause a log of compilation events to be produced on STDOUT and will allow the engineer to get a basic understanding of what is being compiled.

For example, if the caching example from Example 7-1 is invoked like this:

```
java -XX:+PrintCompilation optjava.Caching 2>/dev/null
```

Then the resulting log (under Java 21) will look something like this:

```
50   1  3   java.lang.Object::<init> (1 bytes)
55   2  3   java.lang.String::hashCode (60 bytes)
55   3  3   jdk.internal.util.ArraysSupport::signedHashCode (37 bytes)
56   5  3   java.util.ImmutableCollections$SetN::probe (56 bytes)
56   6  3   java.lang.Math::floorMod (20 bytes)
56   4  3   jdk.internal.util.ArraysSupport::vectorizedHashCode (158 bytes)
58   7  3   java.lang.StringLatin1::hashCode (52 bytes)
58   8  3   java.lang.String::equals (56 bytes)
58   9  3   java.lang.StringLatin1::equals (36 bytes)
58  11  4   java.lang.Object::<init> (1 bytes)
59  10  3   java.util.Objects::equals (23 bytes)
59  12  3   java.lang.module.ModuleDescriptor$Exports::<init> (20 bytes)
59   1  3   java.lang.Object::<init> (1 bytes)    made not entrant
59  13  3   java.util.Objects::requireNonNull (14 bytes)
```

```
59  16  3  java.util.Set::of (4 bytes)
59  14  3  java.util.AbstractCollection::<init> (5 bytes)
60  15  3  java.util.ImmutableCollections$AbstractImmutableCollection::<init> ↵
(5 bytes)
60  17  3  java.lang.module.ModuleDescriptor::modsHashCode (43 bytes)
60  18  3  java.util.Set::of (68 bytes)
61  19  3  java.lang.String::coder (15 bytes)
61  21  3  java.lang.String::length (11 bytes)
61  20  1  java.lang.module.ModuleDescriptor::name (5 bytes)
62  22  3  java.lang.String::isLatin1 (19 bytes)
62  23  1  java.lang.module.ModuleReference::descriptor (5 bytes)
65  24  3  java.lang.String::charAt (25 bytes)
66  25  3  java.lang.StringLatin1::charAt (15 bytes)
...
```

Note that as the vast majority of the JRE standard libraries are written in Java, they will be eligible for JIT compilation alongside application code. We should, therefore, not be surprised to see so many nonapplication methods present in the compiled code.

> The exact set of methods that are compiled may vary slightly from run to run, even on a very simple benchmark. This is a side effect of the dynamic nature of PGO and should not be of concern.

The `PrintCompilation` output is formatted in a relatively simple way. First comes the time at which a method was compiled (in milliseconds since VM start). Next is a number that indicates the order in which the method was compiled in this run. Some of the other fields are:

n

Method is native

s

Method is synchronized

!

Method has exception handlers

%

Method was compiled via on-stack replacement

The level of detail available from `PrintCompilation` is somewhat limited. To access more detailed information about the decisions made by the HotSpot JIT compilers, we can use:

```
-XX:+LogCompilation
```

This is a diagnostic option we must unlock using an additional flag:

```
-XX:+UnlockDiagnosticVMOptions
```

This instructs the VM to output a logfile containing XML tags representing information about the queuing and optimization of bytecode into native code. The LogCompilation flag can be verbose and generate hundreds of megabytes of XML output.

However, as we will see in the next chapter, the open source JITWatch tool can parse this file and present the information in a more easily digestible format.

Other VMs, such as IBM's J9 with the Testarossa JIT, can also be made to log JIT compiler information, but there is no standard format for JIT logging, so developers must learn to interpret each log format or use appropriate tooling.

Simple JIT Tuning

When undertaking a code tuning exercise, it is relatively easy to ensure that the application is taking advantage of JIT compilation.

The general principle of simple JIT compilation tuning: "Any method that wants to compile should be given the resources to do so." To achieve this aim, follow this checklist:

1. First run the app with the PrintCompilation switch on.
2. Collect the logs that indicate which methods are compiled.
3. Now increase the size of the code cache via ReservedCodeCacheSize.
4. Rerun the application.
5. Look at the set of compiled methods with the enlarged cache.

The performance engineer will need to take into account the nondeterminism inherent in the JIT compilation. Keeping this in mind, a couple of obvious tells can easily be observed:

- Is the set of compiled methods larger in a meaningful way when the cache size is increased?
- Are all methods that are important to the primary transaction paths being compiled?

If the number of compiled methods does not increase (indicating that the code cache is not being fully utilized) as the cache size is increased, then provided the load pattern is representative, the JIT compiler is not short of resources.

At this point, it should be straightforward to confirm that all the methods that are part of the transaction hot paths appear in the compilation logs. If not, then the next step is to determine the root cause—why these methods are not compiling.

Effectively, this strategy is making sure that JIT compilation never shuts off by ensuring the JVM never runs out of code cache space. We will meet more sophisticated techniques later in the book, but this simple JIT tuning approach can help provide performance boosts for a surprising number of applications.

Evolving Java Program Execution

At the start of this chapter, we introduced the typical lifecycle stages of a Java application. A graphical depiction of this process can be seen in Figure 6-7.

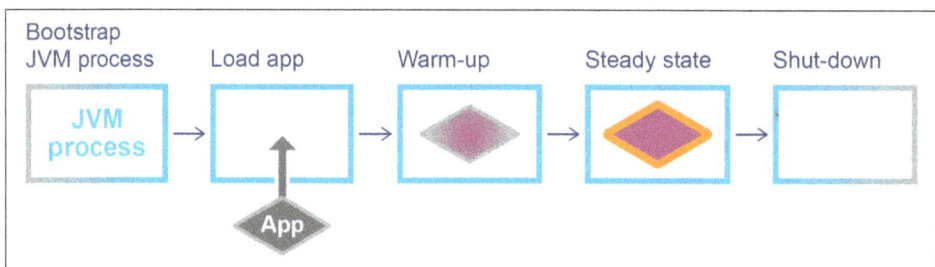

Figure 6-7. Simple lifecycle of a Java application

This represents the standard mental model for the overall lifecycle of Java applications and has been for as long as Java has had JIT compilation. However, it does have certain drawbacks—the major one being that execution time can be slower while the application transitions into steady state (i.e., "JVM warm-up").

This transition time can easily run into the tens of seconds after application start. For long-running applications, this is not usually a problem—a process that is running continuously for hours (or days or weeks) receives far more benefit from the JIT compiled code than the one-off effort expended to create it at startup.

In the cloud native world, however, processes may be much shorter-lived. This raises several questions:

- Under what circumstances is the amortized cost of Java startup and JIT actually worth it?

- What could be done to make Java applications start up faster and avoid those costs?

- Are too many resources (especially memory) being used to provide dynamic capabilities that are not actually needed by many cloud native workloads?

To set the scene, let's first talk about AOT compilation and then move on to discuss one of the most popular modern frameworks that has been designed with these questions in mind—Quarkus.

Ahead-of-Time (AOT) Compilation

If you have experience programming in languages such as C and C++, you will be familiar with AOT compilation (you may have just called it "compilation"). This is the process whereby an external program (the compiler) takes human-readable program source and outputs directly executable machine code.

Compiling your source code ahead of time means you have only a single opportunity to take advantage of any potential optimizations.

You will most likely want to produce an executable targeted to the platform and processor architecture you intend to run it on. These closely targeted binaries will be able to take advantage of any processor-specific features that can speed up your program.

However, in most cases, the executable is produced without knowledge of the specific platform that it will be executed upon. This means that AOT compilation must make conservative choices about which processor features are likely to be available. If the code is compiled with the assumption that certain features are available, and they turn out not to be, then the binary will not run at all.

This leads to a situation where AOT-compiled binaries usually do not take full advantage of the CPU's capabilities, and potential performance enhancements are left on the table.

The sophisticated JIT present in HotSpot does not suffer from these limitations. As we discussed at the start of this chapter, when HotSpot starts up, it probes the CPU to see exactly what instructions are available. With this information, the JVM can decide to enable processor-specific optimizations (referred to as *compiler intrinsics*) to tailor JIT compilation to the actual runtime environment in use. This is one of the mechanisms that means that Java applications can often get a performance boost just by upgrading the JVM they run on—without even recompiling the code.

New compiler intrinsics, and other enhancements, are developed all the time, and it is very common for applications to see noticeable gains, such as when upgrading the major version of the JVM used in production.

In general, Java applications have traditionally not been AOT-compiled.[5] There are a number of reasons for this, but chief among them is that the JVM is actually a very dynamic execution environment—which stands in contrast to the view of many developers that Java is a "static" language.

One particular problem that native compilation of Java applications runs into is how to handle *reflection*. Reflection is a dynamic, runtime mechanism that is very widely used in Java—many common frameworks and developer tools (such as debuggers and code browsers) rely upon reflection to implement their capabilities.

Fundamentally, Java applications can use reflection to load classes and to invoke methods whose names are unknown at compile time. This is an extremely powerful capability, and it can be used to implement very open and dynamic systems, but it can (and does) come into conflict with the more encapsulated systems that are desirable for AOT compilation and other cloud native techniques.

A full discussion of reflection and related dynamic techniques can be found in the second edition of *The Well-Grounded Java Developer* by Benjamin J. Evans et al. (Manning, 2022).

Any AOT scheme for Java must eventually confront the fact that reflection and other dynamic techniques are everywhere in the ecosystem. We will have more to say about this subject when we discuss GraalVM later in this chapter.

Finally, we should note that AOT compilation is a *mechanism*, but what application owners and SREs actually care about is the performance of their applications—i.e., *outcomes*. It is a common error of technologists to confuse the two, especially when the former represents a fascinating intellectual challenge.

Let's move on to meet Quarkus, an increasingly popular modern application development framework that focuses on cloud native deployment and can leverage, but does not require, AOT compilation.

Quarkus

Quarkus (*https://quarkus.io*) is a well-established Java framework that has been developed by Red Hat and the community.[6] It is designed to be used in a cloud native environment, including microservices and serverless apps, and as such, it is optimized for fast startup and developer productivity.

---

5 There are exceptions to this, including the iOS App Store, which only permitted AOT-compiled Java apps, as the App Store rules forbid techniques such as JIT compilation.

6 Quarkus also supports Kotlin in core (and Scala via a community-supported Quarkiverse extension).

Quarkus describes itself as a "Kubernetes Native Java stack tailored for OpenJDK HotSpot and GraalVM, crafted from the best of breed Java libraries and standards." It implements standards such as the Jakarta EE and MicroProfile APIs as well as supporting emerging standards like OpenTelemetry.[7]

One of the mechanisms Quarkus uses for this is to introduce a new phase to the lifecycle of a Java application: the *build phase*. The aim of the build phase is to perform as much of the work that would normally be done at application startup as possible—effectively shifting computation from runtime to compilation time.

For example, dependency injection in Quarkus is based on ArC—a CDI-based dependency injection library that has been designed to fit the lifecycle of Quarkus applications.[8]

Quarkus also moves ("shifts left") operations like classpath annotation scanning from runtime to build time. For this to work, we need to declare all dependencies at build time—Quarkus provides an indexing capability called Jandex to handle this, and a bytecode generation library (Gizmo) to reduce or remove the need for reflection.

This shift of computation makes sense in the cloud native world that we live in because of how applications are deployed these days, i.e., containers. In a container, new dependencies do not show up at runtime because container deployments are immutable. Furthermore, the shifting of code is actually beneficial to the C2 JIT because it leads to generation of Java code that is less dynamic, which makes C2's job easier.

In production, Quarkus is capable of running in two modes: a dynamic VM mode that uses the HotSpot JVM in a traditional manner, and a *native mode* that uses an AOT capability provided by the GraalVM native image compiler (which we will discuss later in this chapter).

Developers sometimes assume that native mode is necessary to achieve fast startup of Quarkus applications. However, a surprising amount of startup computation can be shifted to build time—including such things as building the application's object dependency graph. For example, starting a REST service in Java and responding to a request on a traditional stack is approximately 4.3 seconds, Quarkus + JIT is 0.943 seconds, and native compilation is 0.016 seconds.[9]

The aggressive use of build-time shifting wherever possible means that Quarkus applications in dynamic VM mode typically start much faster than traditional Java systems. Native mode can provide some extra performance benefit, but exactly how

---

7 Jakarta EE is the successor to the Java EE standard, which was transferred to the Eclipse Foundation in 2017.

8 ArC implements the CDI Lite specification.

9 Data from *https://quarkus.io*.

much depends on the details of the application. Many teams find the startup and peak performance of Quarkus in dynamic VM mode to be excellent and do not feel the need to add the extra complexity required to build native-mode applications.

These two phases can be seen in Figure 6-8.

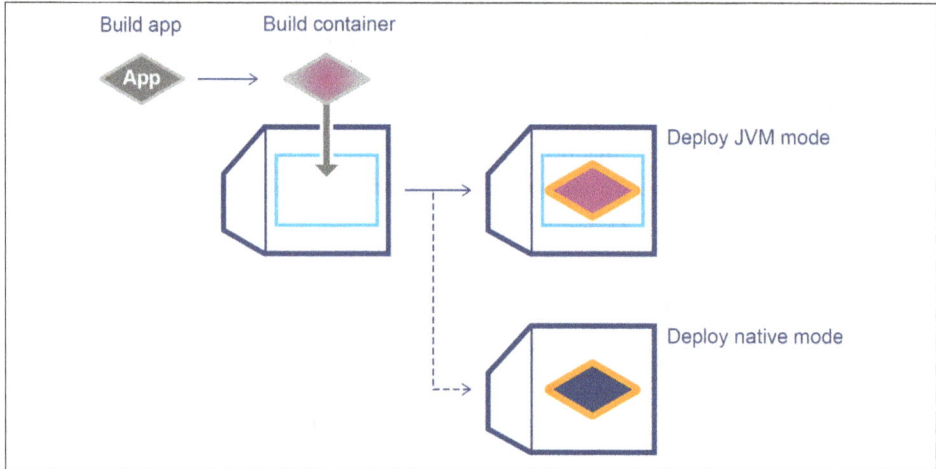

Figure 6-8. Quarkus build and deploy

Quarkus emphasizes developer productivity, and many teams have adopted Quarkus based primarily on the developer experience it provides.

For example, Quarkus provides a development mode, which can be as simple as running `./mvnw quarkus:dev` for a local application. This starts Quarkus with *live reload* and background compilation. This means that when you modify your Java files and/or resource files (including the configuration property file) and refresh your browser, your changes will automatically take effect.

The Quarkus framework enables both imperative and reactive styles of application development, which means that it can be easily adopted by teams migrating over from purely imperative models, such as Spring Boot. When an application requires high scalability, Quarkus also provides the capability to use reactive (i.e., nonblocking) programming.

With the flexibility provided by the choice of imperative and reactive programming styles, as well as both dynamic VM and native modes, it is perhaps not surprising that Quarkus is being adopted by an increasing number of organizations and teams.

GraalVM

GraalVM (*https://www.graalvm.org*) describes itself as "a high-performance JDK designed to accelerate the execution of applications written in Java and other JVM languages."

Oracle developed GraalVM in its research division before shipping it as a product and currently provides two distinct distributions of the technology: Oracle GraalVM Community Edition (CE) and Oracle GraalVM Enterprise Edition (EE). The community edition is open source, but the enterprise edition is proprietary software that requires a paid license from Oracle to deploy in production.

GraalVM includes Truffle, a language implementation framework written in Java, to build interpreters for multiple programming languages, which then run on GraalVM.

Truffle is a fascinating technology, but perhaps more interesting for our purposes is the native image functionality. This is a key feature of GraalVM, implemented via the Graal compiler—a JIT compiler that is written in Java and can also operate as an AOT compiler.[10]

GraalVM's native image has been steadily maturing for a number of years, and it is now deployed by an increasing number of teams who want to deploy Java applications but want to minimize startup time as much as possible.

One important caveat is that native image needs to know at build time the reflectively accessed program elements. It attempts to determine this automatically, by performing a static analysis that detects calls to the Reflection API. If the analysis fails, or the reflective code path is too complex, then the application's build script must manually specify the elements that will be reflectively accessed at run time.

Quarkus can leverage GraalVM's native image capabilities (*https://oreil.ly/ktROy*) to produce native executables. Many developers and teams find that using Quarkus in native mode is easier than standalone GraalVM.

This is for several reasons, but the primary one is that compiling to native with Quarkus is much easier than building directly from scratch using GraalVM, because Quarkus has already done the heavy lifting of making the libraries work in native mode. Without framework help, getting production-quality builds from GraalVM can be challenging.

Red Hat recommends using the downstream Mandrel distribution of GraalVM CE, which is specifically tailored to working with Quarkus applications.

---

10 The Graal compiler works by essentially "compiling itself" to produce a native library that can be shipped as a JIT compiler for GraalVM.

Summary

The JVM's initial code execution environment is the bytecode interpreter. We have explored the basics of the interpreter, as a working knowledge of bytecode is essential for a proper understanding of JVM code execution. The basic theory of JIT compilation has also been introduced.

However, for most performance work, the behavior of JIT-compiled code is far more important than any aspect of the interpreter. For many applications, the simple tuning of the code cache shown in this chapter will be sufficient. Applications that are particularly performance-sensitive may require a deeper exploration of JIT behavior.

We have also discussed some initial aspects of specifically cloud native behavior, as it relates to the lifecycle of cloud-deployed Java applications.

In the next chapter, we will begin our journey into the deployment aspects that modern, cloud native Java applications require. The first building block of this will be a review of the relevant aspects of hardware and operating systems, which are still the bottom layer of application stacks.

## CHAPTER 7

Hardware and Operating Systems

Why should Java developers care about hardware?

For many years the computer industry has been driven by Moore's law, a hypothesis made by Intel founder Gordon Moore about long-term trends in processor capability. The law (really an observation or extrapolation) can be framed in a variety of ways, but one of the most usual is:

> The number of transistors on a mass-produced chip roughly doubles every 18 months.
>
> —Moore's law (informally)

This phenomenon represents an exponential increase in computer power over time. It was originally cited in 1965, so represents an incredible long-term trend, unparalleled in the history of computation. The effects of Moore's law have been transformative in many (if not most) areas of the modern world. The death of Moore's law has been repeatedly proclaimed for decades now. However, there are very good reasons to suppose that, for all practical purposes, this incredible progress in chip technology has (finally) come to an end:

> Transistors can only get so small and, eventually, the more permanent laws of physics get in the way. Already transistors can be measured on an atomic scale, with the smallest ones commercially available only 3 nanometers wide, barely wider than a strand of human DNA (2.5nm). While there's still room to make them smaller (in 2021, IBM announced the successful creation of 2-nanometer chips), such progress has become prohibitively expensive and slow, putting reliable gains into question. And there's still the physical limitation in that wires can't be thinner than atoms, at least not with our current understanding of material physics.
>
> — Audrey Woods, "The Death of Moore's Law: What it means and what might fill the gap going forward" (*https://oreil.ly/dU1Us*)

Hardware has become increasingly complex to make good use of the "transistor budget" available in modern computers. The software platforms that run on that hardware have also increased in complexity to exploit the new capabilities. More horsepower is available, but engineers have to do more work in software to harness it, so the performance delivered is diminished by this overhead.

Software applications now pervade (nearly) every aspect of global society. And that software is becoming increasingly complex, as application developers take advantage of the performance available.

Or, to put it another way:

> Software is eating the world.
>
> —Marc Andreessen

As we will see, Java has been a beneficiary of the increasing amount of computer power. The design of the language and runtime has been well suited (or lucky) to use this trend in processor capability, as we have discussed in previous chapters. However, the truly performance-conscious Java programmer needs to understand the principles and technology that underpin the platform to best use the available resources.

This is particularly pertinent because, as we will see in later chapters, the development of cloud native applications has somewhat changed the performance landscape. But before turning to those subjects, let's take a quick look at modern hardware and operating systems, as an understanding of those subjects will help with everything that follows.

Introduction to Modern Hardware

Many university courses on hardware architectures still teach a simple-to-understand, classical view of hardware. This abstracted logical view of hardware focuses on a simple register-based machine, with arithmetic, logic, and load and store operations. Since the 1990s, the world of the application developer has, to a large extent, revolved around the Intel x86/x64 architecture (and more recently the rise of the ARM chip).

However, this is an area of technology that has undergone radical change. The simple mental model of a processor's operation is now incorrect, and intuitive reasoning based on it is liable to lead to utterly wrong conclusions.

To help address this, in this chapter, we will discuss several of these advances in CPU technology. We will start with the behavior of memory, as this is by far the most important to a modern Java developer.

Memory

As Moore's law advanced, the exponentially increasing number of transistors was initially used for faster and faster clock speed. The reasons for this are obvious: faster clock speed means more instructions completed per second. Accordingly, the speed of processors has advanced hugely, and the 2+ GHz processors that we have today are hundreds of times faster than the original 4.77 MHz chips found in the first IBM PC.

However, the increasing clock speeds uncovered another problem—faster chips require a faster stream of data to act upon. As Figure 7-1 shows,[1] over time, main memory could not keep up with the demands of the processor core for fresh data.

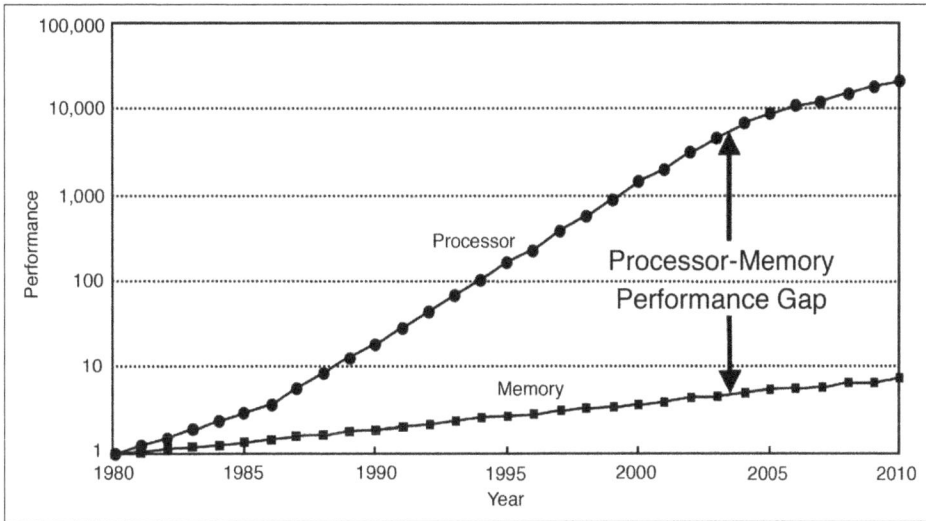

Figure 7-1. Gap between processor and memory performance capabilities (Hennessy and Patterson, 2011)

This results in a problem: if the CPU is waiting for data, then faster cycles don't help, as the CPU will just have to idle until the required data arrives.

---

1 John L. Hennessy and David A. Patterson, *Computer Architecture: A Quantitative Approach*, 5th ed. (Burlington, MA: Morgan Kaufmann, 2011).

Memory Caches

To solve this problem, CPU caches were introduced. These are memory areas on the CPU that are slower than CPU registers but faster than main memory. The idea is for the CPU to fill the cache with copies of often-accessed memory locations rather than constantly having to re-address main memory.

Modern CPUs have several layers of cache, with the most-often-accessed caches being located close to the processing core. The cache closest to the CPU is usually called *L1* (for "level 1 cache"), with the next being referred to as *L2*, and so on. Different processor architectures have a varying number and configuration of caches, but a common choice is for each execution core to have a dedicated, private L1 and L2 cache, and an L3 cache that is shared across some or all of the cores. The effect of these caches in speeding up access times is shown in Figure 7-2.[2]

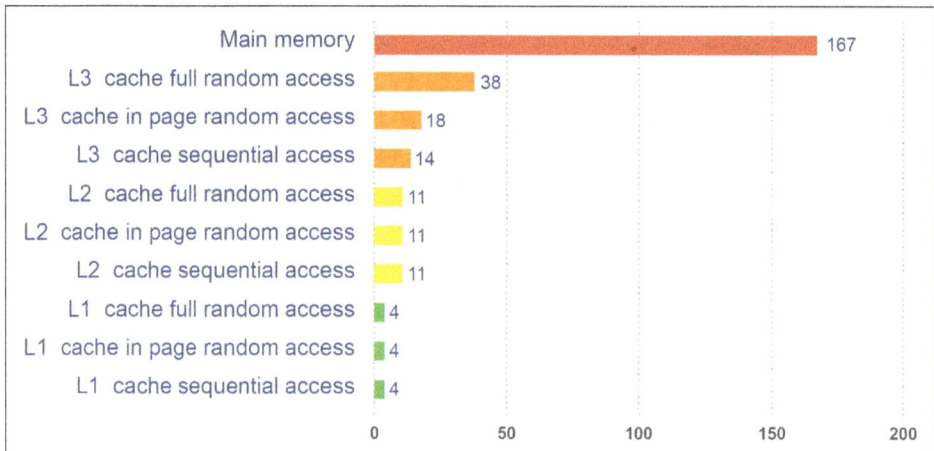

Figure 7-2. Access times for various types of memory

This approach to cache architecture improves access times and helps keep the core fully stocked with data to operate on. Due to the clock speed versus access time gap, more transistor budget is devoted to caches on a modern CPU.

The resulting design can be seen in Figure 7-3. This shows the L1 and L2 caches (private to each CPU core) and a shared L3 cache that is common to all cores on the CPU. Main memory is accessed over the Northbridge component, and it is traversing this bus that causes the large drop-off in access time to main memory.

---

2 Access times shown in terms of number of clock cycles per operation; data provided by Google.

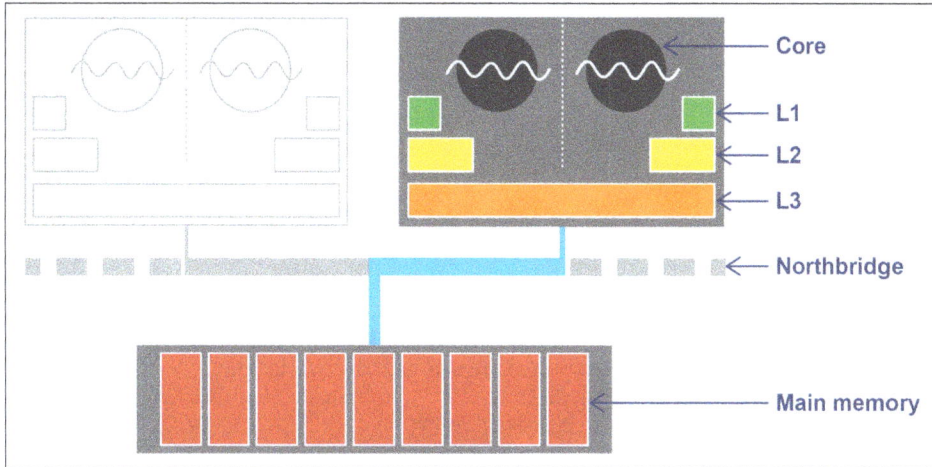

Figure 7-3. Overall CPU and memory architecture

Although the addition of a caching architecture hugely improves processor throughput, it introduces a new set of problems. These problems include determining how memory is fetched into and written back from the cache. The solutions to this problem are usually referred to as *cache consistency protocols*.

> There are other problems that crop up when this type of caching is applied in a parallel processing environment, as we will see later in this book.

At the lowest level, a protocol called MESI (and its variants) is commonly found on a wide range of processors. It defines four states for any line in a cache. Each line (usually 64 bytes) is:

- Modified (but not yet flushed to main memory)
- Exclusive (present only in this cache, but does match main memory)
- Shared (may also be present in other caches; matches main memory)
- Invalid (may not be used; will be dropped as soon as practical)

The idea of the protocol is that multiple processors can simultaneously be in the Shared state. However, if a processor transitions to any of the other valid states (Exclusive or Modified), then this will force all the other processors into the Invalid state. This is shown in Table 7-1, where Y indicates a permitted transition and - represents a transition that is not permitted.

Table 7-1. MESI allowable states between processors

	M	E	S	I
M	-	-	-	Y
E	-	-	-	Y
S	-	-	Y	Y
I	Y	Y	Y	Y

The protocol works by broadcasting the intention of a processor to change state. An electrical signal is sent across the shared memory bus, and the other processors are made aware. The full logic for the state transitions is shown in Figure 7-4.

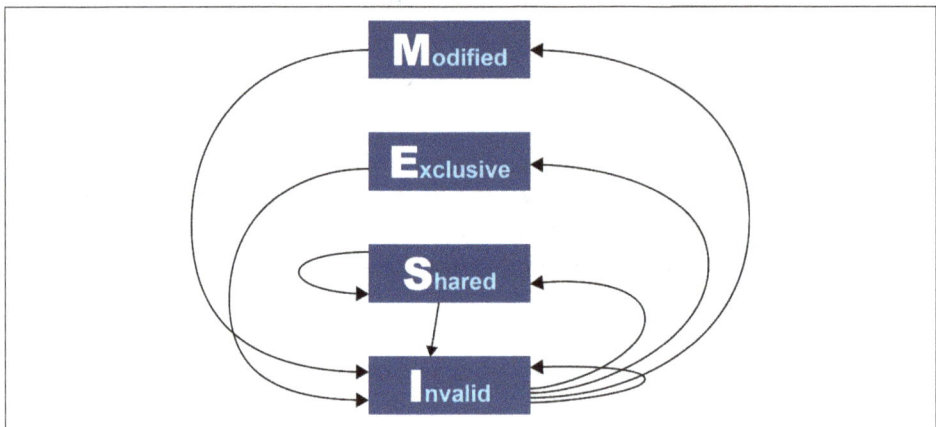

Figure 7-4. MESI state transition diagram

Originally, processors wrote every cache operation directly into main memory. This was called *write-through* behavior, but it was and is very inefficient, and it required a large amount of bandwidth to memory. More recent processors also implement *write-back* behavior, where traffic back to main memory is significantly reduced by processors writing only modified (dirty) cache blocks to memory when the cache blocks are replaced.

The overall effect of caching technology is to greatly increase the speed at which data can be written to, or read from, memory. This is expressed in terms of the bandwidth to memory. The *burst rate*, or theoretical maximum, is based on several factors:

- Clock frequency of memory
- Width of the memory bus (usually 64 bits)
- Number of interfaces (usually two in modern machines)

This is multiplied by two in the case of DDR RAM (DDR stands for "double data rate" as it communicates on both edges of a clock signal).

Applying the formula to 2024 commodity hardware gives a theoretical maximum write speed of 17+ GB/s per core, with overall system bandwidth of 70–90 GB/s.[3] In practice, of course, this could be limited by many other factors in the system. As it stands, this gives a modestly useful value to allow us to see how close the hardware and software can get.

Let's write some simple code to exercise the cache hardware, as seen in Example 7-1.

Example 7-1. Caching example

```java
public class Caching {

    private final int ARR_SIZE = 2 * 1024 * 1024;
    private final int[] testData = new int[ARR_SIZE];

    private void run() {
        System.err.println("Start: "+ System.currentTimeMillis());
        for (int i = 0; i < 15_000; i++) {
            touchEveryLine();
            touchEveryItem();
        }
        System.err.println("Warmup finished: "+ System.currentTimeMillis());
        System.err.println("Item     Line");
        for (int i = 0; i < 100; i++) {
            long t0 = System.nanoTime();
            touchEveryLine();
            long t1 = System.nanoTime();
            touchEveryItem();
            long t2 = System.nanoTime();
            long elItem = t2 - t1;
            long elLine = t1 - t0;
            double diff = elItem - elLine;
            System.err.println(elItem + " " + elLine +" "+  (100 * diff / elLine));
        }
    }

    private void touchEveryItem() {
        for (int i = 0; i < testData.length; i++)
            testData[i]++;
    }

    private void touchEveryLine() {
        for (int i = 0; i < testData.length; i += 16)
            testData[i]++;
```

---

3 According to documentation for the Intel Core i9-13900K Processor (*https://oreil.ly/xOBYg*).

```
    }

    public static void main(String[] args) {
        Caching c = new Caching();
        c.run();
    }
}
```

Intuitively, `touchEveryItem()` does 16 times as much work as `touchEveryLine()`, as 16 times as many data items must be updated. However, the point of this simple example is to show how badly intuition can lead us astray when dealing with JVM performance. Let's look at some sample output from the `Caching` class, as shown in Figure 7-5.

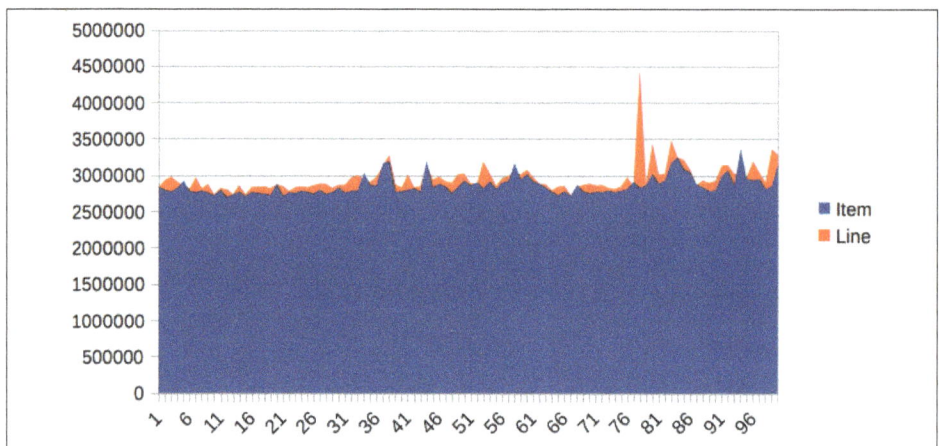

Figure 7-5. Time (ns) elapsed for caching example

The graph shows 100 runs of each function and is intended to show several different effects. First, notice that the results for both functions are remarkably similar in terms of time taken, so the intuitive expectation of "16 times as much work" is clearly false.

Instead, the dominant effect of this code is to exercise the memory bus by transferring the contents of the array from main memory into the cache to be operated on by `touchEveryItem()` and `touchEveryLine()`.

In terms of the statistics of the numbers, although the results are reasonably consistent, there are individual outliers that are 30%–35% different from the median value.

Overall, we can see that each iteration of the simple memory function takes around 3 milliseconds (2.86 ms on average) to traverse a 100 MB chunk of memory, giving an effective memory bandwidth of just under 3.5 GB/s. This is less than the theoretical maximum, but is still a reasonable number. Designing for theoretical limits can be a recipe for disappointment (or disaster). Empirical numbers are useful for baselines and planning purposes. Results that are significantly different—i.e., orders of magnitude—from theoretical limits might be considered unreasonable and warrant further exploration.

> Modern CPUs have a hardware prefetcher that can detect predictable patterns in data access (usually just a regular "stride" through the data). In this example, we're taking advantage of that fact to get closer to a realistic maximum for memory access bandwidth.

One of the key themes in Java performance is the sensitivity of applications to object allocation rates. We will return to this point several times, but this simple example gives us a basic yardstick for the upper limit of allocation rates.

Modern Processor Features

Hardware engineers sometimes refer to the new features that have become possible as a result of Moore's law as "spending the transistor budget." Memory caches are the most obvious use of the growing number of transistors, but other techniques have also appeared over the years.

Translation Lookaside Buffer

One very important use of hardware caching is the translation lookaside buffer (TLB), a hardware cache for the *page tables* that map virtual memory locations (which are the ones seen by application code) to hardware locations. This greatly speeds up a very frequent operation—access to the physical address underlying a virtual address.

> We have already met the TLAB feature of HotSpot's GC in Chapter 4, and some texts refer to a TLAB as a TLB, which can be confusing as the two concepts are not related. Always check which feature is being discussed when you see TLB mentioned.

Without the TLB, all virtual address lookups would take 16 cycles, even if the page table was held in the L1 cache. The resulting performance would be unacceptable, so the TLB is basically essential for all modern chips.

Branch Prediction and Speculative Execution

One of the advanced processor tricks that appears on modern processors is branch prediction. This is used to prevent the processor from having to wait to evaluate a value needed for a conditional branch. Modern processors have multistage instruction pipelines. This means that the execution of a single CPU cycle is broken down into a number of separate stages. There can be several instructions in flight (at different stages of execution) at once.

In this model a conditional branch is problematic, because until the condition is evaluated, it isn't known what the next instruction after the branch will be. This can cause the processor to stall for a number of cycles (in practice, up to 20), as it effectively empties the multistage pipeline behind the branch.

> Speculative execution was, famously, the cause of major security problems (including Meltdown and Spectre (*https://spectreattack.com*)) that were discovered to affect very large numbers of CPUs in early 2018.

To avoid this, the processor can dedicate transistors to building up a heuristic to decide which branch is more likely to be taken. Using this guess, the CPU fills the pipeline based on a gamble. If it works, then the CPU carries on as though nothing had happened. If it's wrong, then the partially executed instructions are dumped, and the CPU has to pay the penalty of emptying the pipeline.

Hardware Memory Models

The core question about memory that must be answered in a multicore system is "How can multiple different CPUs access the same memory location consistently?"

The answer to this question is highly hardware-dependent, but in general, javac, the JIT compiler, and the CPU are all allowed to make changes to the order in which code executes. This is subject to the provision that any changes don't affect the outcome as observed by the current thread.

For example, suppose we have a piece of code like this:

```
myInt = otherInt;
intChanged = true;
```

There is no code between the two assignments, so the executing thread doesn't need to care about what order they happen in, and thus the environment is at liberty to change the order of instructions.

However, this could mean that in another thread that has visibility of these data items, the order could change, and the value of myInt read by the other thread could be the old value, despite intChanged being seen to be true.

This type of reordering (stores moved after stores) is not possible on x86 chips, but as Table 7-2 shows, there are other architectures where it can, and does, happen.

Table 7-2. Hardware memory support

	ARMv7	POWER	SPARC	x86	AMD64	zSeries
Loads moved after loads	Y	Y	-	-	-	-
Loads moved after stores	Y	Y	-	-	-	-
Stores moved after stores	Y	Y	-	-	-	-
Stores moved after loads	Y	Y	Y	Y	Y	Y
Atomic moved with loads	Y	Y	-	-	-	-
Atomic moved with stores	Y	Y	-	-	-	-
Incoherent instructions	Y	Y	Y	Y	-	Y

In the Java environment, the Java Memory Model (JMM) is explicitly designed to be a weak model to take into account the differences in consistency of memory access between processor types. Correct use of locks and volatile access is a major part of ensuring that multithreaded code works properly. This is a very important topic that we will return to in Chapter 13.

A trend in recent years has been for software developers to seek greater understanding of the workings of hardware to derive better performance. The term *mechanical sympathy* has been coined to describe this approach, especially as applied to the low-latency and high-performance spaces.

> The name "mechanical sympathy" comes from the great racing driver Jackie Stewart, who was a three times world Formula 1 champion. He believed the best drivers had enough understanding of how a machine worked so they could work in harmony with it.
>
> —Martin Thompson

It can be seen in recent research into lock-free algorithms and data structures, which we will meet in Chapter 13.

Operating Systems

The point of an operating system is to control access to resources that must be shared between multiple executing processes. All resources are finite, and all processes are greedy, so the need for a central system to arbitrate and meter access is essential. Among these scarce resources, the two most important are usually memory and CPU time.

Virtual addressing via the memory management unit (MMU) and its page tables is the key feature that enables access control of memory and prevents one process from damaging the memory areas owned by another.

The TLBs that we met earlier in the chapter are a hardware feature that improves lookup times to physical memory. The use of the buffers improves performance for software's access time to memory. However, the MMU is usually too low level for developers to measure.

Instead, let's take a closer look at the OS process scheduler, as this controls access to the CPU and is a far more user-visible piece of the operating system kernel.

The Scheduler

The job of the process scheduler is to manage access to the CPU cores (and to respond to interrupts). On a modern system there are almost always more platform threads that can run simultaneously, so this CPU contention requires an access control mechanism to resolve it.

> In this section, we are explicitly talking about the OS-level platform threads. Java 21+ virtual threads do not follow this model—instead, it would be the *carrier threads* that virtual threads are multiplexed onto, which obey this model. See Chapter 13 for more details.

This access control uses a queue known as the *run queue* as a waiting area for the *platform threads* that are eligible to run but must wait their turn for the CPU. The overall lifecycle of a platform thread is shown in Figure 7-6.

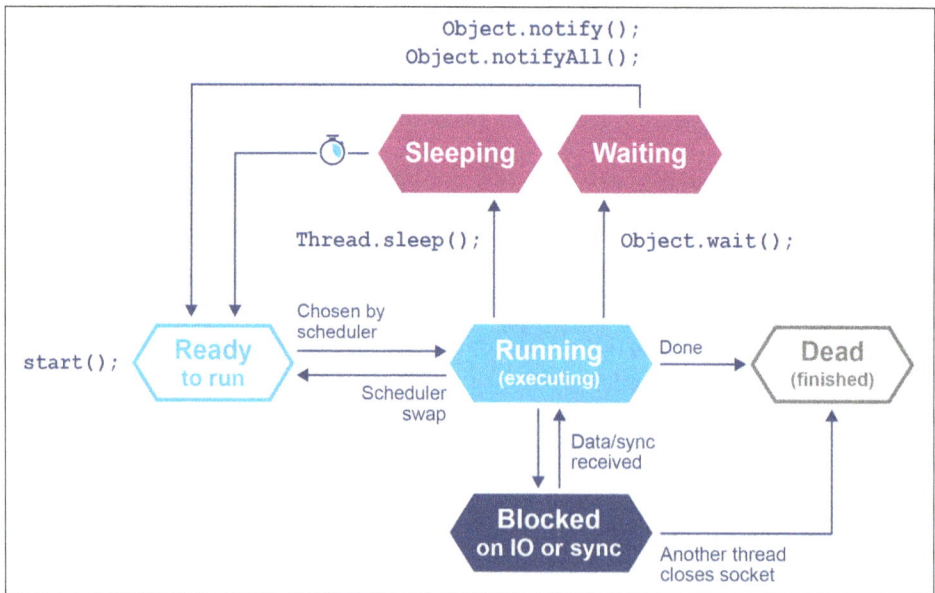

Figure 7-6. Thread lifecycle

In this relatively simple view, the OS scheduler moves platform threads on and off the single core in the system. At the end of the time quantum (often 10 ms or 100 ms in older operating systems), the scheduler moves the thread to the back of the run queue to wait until it reaches the front of the queue and is eligible to run again.

If a thread wants to voluntarily give up its time quantum, it can do so either for a fixed amount of time (via `sleep()`) or until a condition is met (using `wait()`). Finally, a thread can also block on I/O or a software lock.

When you are meeting this model for the first time, it may help to think about a machine that has only a single execution core. Real hardware is, of course, more complex, and virtually any modern machine will have multiple cores, which allows for true simultaneous execution of multiple execution paths. This means that reasoning about execution in a true multiprocessing environment is very complex and counterintuitive.

An often-overlooked feature of operating systems is that, by their nature, they introduce periods of time when code of interest is not running on the CPU. A process that has completed its time quantum will not get back on the CPU until it arrives at the front of the run queue again. Combined with the fact that CPU is a scarce resource, this means that code is waiting more often than it is running.

This means that the statistics we want to generate from processes that we actually want to observe are affected by the behavior of other processes on the systems. This "jitter" and the overhead of scheduling is a primary cause of noise in observed results. We discussed the statistical properties and handling of real results in Chapter 2 and observed this in `Caching.java`.

One of the easiest ways to see the action and behavior of a scheduler is to try to observe the overhead imposed by the OS to achieve scheduling. The following code executes 1,000 separate 1 ms sleeps. Each of these sleeps will involve the thread being sent to the back of the run queue and having to wait for a new time quantum. So, the total elapsed time of the code gives us some idea of the overhead of scheduling for a typical process:

```
long start = System.currentTimeMillis();
for (int i = 0; i < 1_000; i++) {
    Thread.sleep(1);
}
long end = System.currentTimeMillis();
System.out.println("Millis elapsed: " + (end - start) / 1000.0);
```

Running this code will cause wildly divergent results, depending on the operating system. Most Unixes will report roughly 10%–20% overhead. Earlier versions of Windows had notoriously bad schedulers, with some versions of Windows XP reporting up to 180% overhead for scheduling (so that 1,000 sleeps of 1 ms would take 2.8 s).

There are even reports that some proprietary OS vendors have inserted code into their releases to detect benchmarking runs and cheat the metrics.

Now that we understand the scheduling quantum and the impact that has on process thread execution, let's delve a little deeper into how the JVM typically calls into the operating system when required.

The JVM and the Operating System

The JVM provides a portable execution environment that is independent of the operating system by providing a common interface to Java code. However, for some fundamental services, such as thread scheduling (or even something as mundane as getting the time from the system clock), the underlying operating system must be accessed.

This capability is provided by native methods, which are denoted by the keyword `native`. They are written in C but are accessible as ordinary Java methods. This interface is referred to as the Java Native Interface (JNI). For example, `java.lang.Object` declares multiple nonprivate native methods; all these methods deal with relatively low-level platform concerns.

Let's look at a more straightforward and familiar example: getting the system time.

Consider the `os::javaTimeMillis()` function. This is the (system-specific) code responsible for implementing the Java `System.currentTimeMillis()` static method. The code that does the actual work is implemented in C++ but is accessed from Java via a "bridge" of C code. Let's look at how this code is actually called in HotSpot.

As you can see in Figure 7-7, the native `System.currentTimeMillis()` method is mapped to the JVM entry point method `JVM_CurrentTimeMillis()`. This mapping is achieved via the JNI `Java_java_lang_System_registerNatives()` mechanism contained in `java/lang/System.c`.

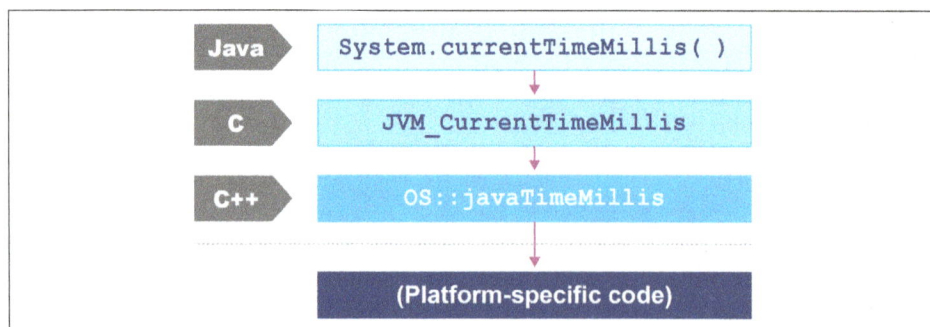

Figure 7-7. The HotSpot calling stack

`JVM_CurrentTimeMillis()` is a call to the VM entry point method. This presents as a C function but is really a C++ function exported with a C calling convention. The call boils down to the call `os::javaTimeMillis()` wrapped in a couple of OpenJDK macros.

This method is defined in the `os` namespace and is operating system dependent. Definitions for this method are provided by the OS-specific subdirectories of source code within OpenJDK. This provides a simple demonstration of how the platform-independent parts of Java can call into services that are provided by the underlying operating system and hardware.

Let's look at a related subject, which is what happens when the scheduler needs to change which threads are currently executing.

Context Switches

A *context switch* is the process by which the OS scheduler removes a currently running platform thread and replaces it with another. There are several different types of context switch, but broadly speaking, they all involve swapping the executing instructions and the stack state of the thread.

A context switch can be a costly operation, whether between user threads or from user mode into kernel mode (sometimes called a *mode switch*). The latter case is particularly important, because a user thread may need to swap into kernel mode to perform some function partway through its time slice. However, this switch will force instruction and other caches to be emptied, as the memory areas accessed by the user space code will not normally have anything in common with the kernel.

A context switch into kernel mode will invalidate the TLBs and potentially other caches. When the call returns, these caches will have to be refilled, so the effect of a kernel mode switch persists even after control has returned to user space. This causes the true cost of a system call to be masked.[4]

For example, Figure 7-8 highlights the cost of an inter-process communication (IPC) call—it's made in user mode but requires a switch to kernel mode. After the switch happens (represented as a "syscall exception," but note that this is not a Java exception, but an interrupt), then performance drops and only slowly recovers as the cache refills.

---

4 Livio Soares and Michael Stumm, "FlexSC: Flexible System Call Scheduling with Exception-Less System Calls," in OSDI'10, *Proceedings of the 9th USENIX Conference on Operating Systems Design and Implementation* (Berkeley, CA: USENIX Association, 2010): 33–46.

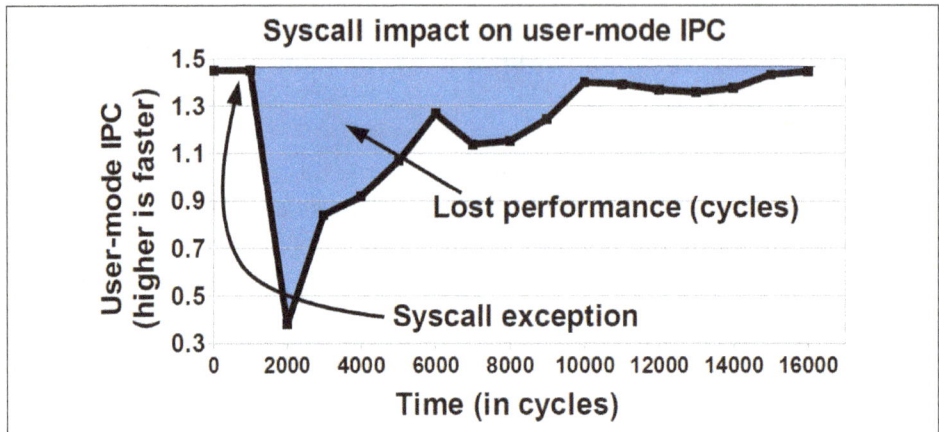

Figure 7-8. Impact of a system call (Soares and Stumm, 2010)

To mitigate this when possible, Linux provides a mechanism known as the *virtual dynamic shared object* (vDSO). This is a memory area in user space that is used to speed up syscalls that do not really require kernel privileges. It achieves this speed increase by not actually performing a context switch into kernel mode. Let's look at an example to see how this works with a real syscall.

For example, a very common Unix system call is `gettimeofday()`. This returns the "wallclock time" as understood by the operating system. Behind the scenes, it is actually just reading a kernel data structure to obtain the system clock time. As this is side-effect free, it does not need privileged access.

If we can use the vDSO to arrange for this data structure to be mapped into the address space of the user process, then there's no need to perform the switch to kernel mode. As a result, the refill penalty shown in Figure 7-7 does not have to be paid.

Given how often most Java applications need to access timing data, this is a welcome performance boost. The vDSO mechanism generalizes this example slightly and can be a useful technique, even if it is available only on Linux.

A Simple System Model

In this section, we cover a simple model for describing basic sources of possible performance problems. The model is expressed in terms of operating system observables of fundamental subsystems and can be directly related back to the outputs of standard Unix command-line tools.

This may seem too low level or antiquated by the standards of modern cloud applications, but the point is to establish a foundational model that we can then use with the sources of data (e.g., observability data) that we will actually use to diagnose problems.

The model is based on a simple conception of a Java application running on a Unix or Unix-like operating system. Figure 7-9 shows the basic components of the model, which consist of:

- The hardware and operating system the application runs on
- The JVM (or container) the application runs in
- The application code itself
- Any external systems the application calls
- The incoming request traffic that is arriving at the application

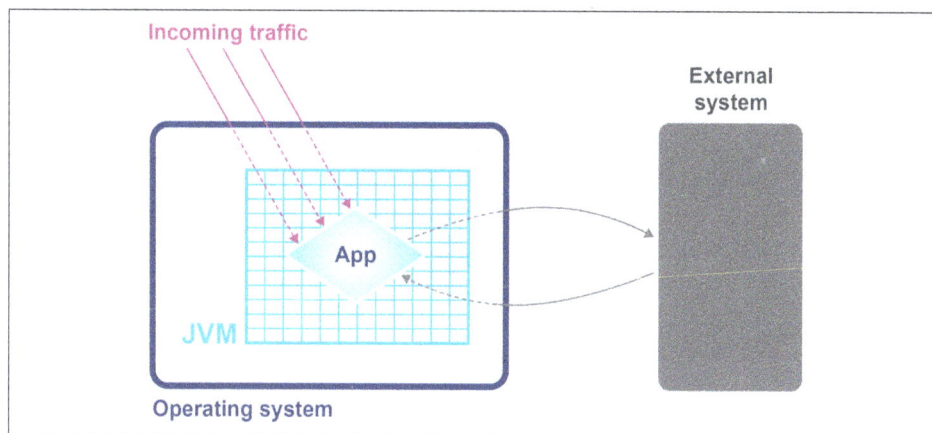

Figure 7-9. Simple system model

Any of these aspects of a system can be responsible for a performance bottleneck. Some simple diagnostic techniques can be used to narrow down or isolate particular parts of the system as potential culprits for performance issues.

In fact, one definition for a well-performing application is that efficient use is being made of system resources. This includes CPU usage, memory, and network or I/O bandwidth.

> If an application is causing one or more resource limits to be hit, then the result will be a performance problem.

The first step in any performance diagnosis is to recognize which resource limit is being hit. We cannot tune performance without dealing with the resource shortage—either by increasing the available resources or the efficiency of use.

It is also worth noting that the operating system itself should not normally be a major contributing factor to system utilization—the role of an operating system is to manage resources on behalf of user processes, not to consume them itself.

The only real exception to this rule is when resources are so scarce that the OS is having difficulty allocating anywhere near enough to satisfy user requirements. For most modern server-class hardware, the only time this should occur is when I/O (or occasionally memory) requirements greatly exceed capability.

Utilizing the CPU

A key metric for application performance is CPU utilization. CPU cycles are quite often the most critical resource needed by an application, so efficient use of them is essential for good performance. CPU-bound applications should be aiming for as close to 100% usage as possible during periods of high load, although this is difficult to achieve in practice due to other dependencies of your application. Looking at your process at a high level helps to reveal constraints on your application.

> When you are analyzing application performance, the system must be under enough load to exercise it. The behavior of an idle application is usually meaningless for performance work.

Three basic tools that every performance engineer should be aware of are vmstat, ifstat, and iostat.

vmstat
: Reports statistics on virtual memory, including information about sizing, IO, and accessing

ifstat
: Provides statistics on the network interface and would be used as a starting point to debug network-level process interaction

`iostat`

Monitors input/output on devices and would be used to identify any device interactions causing an issue

On Linux and other Unixes, these command-line tools provide immediate and often very useful insight into the current state of the virtual memory and I/O subsystems, respectively.

The tools only provide numbers at the level of the entire host, but this is frequently enough to point the way to more detailed diagnostic approaches. Let's look at how to use `vmstat` as an example:

```
$ vmstat 1
 r  b swpd   free    buff  cache    si   so  bi  bo   in   cs us sy  id wa st
 2  0    0 759860 248412 2572248     0    0   0  80   63  127  8  0  92  0  0
 2  0    0 759002 248412 2572248     0    0   0   0   55  103 12  0  88  0  0
 1  0    0 758854 248412 2572248     0    0   0  80   57  116  5  1  94  0  0
 3  0    0 758604 248412 2572248     0    0   0  14   65  142 10  0  90  0  0
 2  0    0 758932 248412 2572248     0    0   0  96   52  100  8  0  92  0  0
 2  0    0 759860 248412 2572248     0    0   0   0   60  112  3  0  97  0  0
```

The parameter 1 following `vmstat` indicates that we want `vmstat` to provide ongoing output at a frequency of 1 sample per second (until interrupted via Ctrl-C) rather than a single snapshot. New output lines are printed every second, which enables a performance engineer to leave this output running (or capture it into a log) while an initial performance test is performed.

The output of `vmstat` is relatively easy to understand and contains a large amount of useful information, divided into sections:

1. The first two columns show the number of runnable (`r`) and blocked (`b`) processes.

2. In the memory section, the amount of swapped and free memory is shown, followed by the memory used as buffer and as cache.

3. The swap section shows the memory swapped in from and out to disk (`si` and `so`). Modern server-class machines should not normally experience very much swap activity.

4. The block in and block out counts (`bi` and `bo`) show the number of 512-byte blocks that have been received from and sent to a block (I/O) device.

5. In the system section, the number of interrupts (`in`) and the number of context switches per second (`cs`) are displayed.

6. The CPU section contains a number of directly relevant metrics, expressed as percentages of CPU time. In order, they are user time (`us`), kernel time (`sy`, for

"system time"), idle time (id), waiting time (wa), and "stolen time" (st, for virtual machines).

Over the course of the remainder of this book, we will meet many other, more sophisticated tools. However, it is important not to neglect the basic tools at our disposal. Complex tools may have behaviors that can mislead us, whereas the simple tools that operate close to processes and the operating system can convey clear, uncluttered views of how our systems are actually behaving.

Let's consider an example. In "The JVM and the Operating System" on page 182, we discussed the impact of a context switch, and we saw the potential impact of a full context switch to kernel space in Figure 7-7. However, whether between user threads or into kernel space, context switches introduce unavoidable wastage of CPU resources.

A well-tuned program should be making maximum possible use of its resources, especially CPU. For workloads that are primarily dependent on computation ("CPU-bound" problems), the aim is to achieve close to 100% utilization of CPU for userland work.

To put it another way, if we observe that the CPU utilization is not approaching 100% user time, then the next obvious question is, "Why not?" What is causing the program to fail to achieve that? Are involuntary context switches caused by locks the problem? Is it due to blocking caused by I/O contention?

The vmstat tool can, on most operating systems (especially Linux), show the number of context switches occurring, so a vmstat 1 run allows the analyst to see the real-time effect of context switching. A process that is failing to achieve 100% userland CPU usage and is also displaying a high context switch rate is likely to be blocked on I/O, experiencing thread lock contention, or is written in such a way that it is causing unnecessary context switches.

However, vmstat output is not enough to fully disambiguate these cases on its own— vmstat can only help indicate I/O problems, as it provides only a crude view of I/O operations. More detailed diagnosis would be possible with tools like JMC (on the desktop) or Java Flight Recorder (or commercial profiling tools). See Chapters 10, 11, and 12 for more details.

Garbage Collection

As we saw in Chapter 4, in the HotSpot JVM (by far the most commonly used JVM), memory is allocated at startup and managed from within user space. That means that system calls (such as sbrk()) are not needed to allocate memory. In turn, this means that kernel-switching activity for garbage collection is quite minimal.

Thus, if a system is exhibiting high levels of system CPU usage, then it is definitely not spending a significant amount of its time in GC, as GC activity burns user space CPU cycles and does not impact kernel space utilization.

On the other hand, if a JVM process is using 100% (or close to that) of CPU in user space, then garbage collection could be the culprit. When analyzing a performance problem, if simple tools (such as `vmstat`) show consistent 100% CPU usage but with almost all cycles being consumed by user space, then we should ask, "Is it the JVM or user code that is responsible for this utilization?"

In many cases, high user space utilization by the JVM is caused by the GC subsystem, so a useful rule is to check the GC log and see how often new entries are being added to it.

Garbage collection logging in the JVM is incredibly cheap, to the point that even the most accurate measurements of the overall cost cannot reliably distinguish it from random background noise. GC logging is also incredibly useful as a source of data for analytics. It is therefore imperative that GC logs be enabled for all JVM processes, especially in production.

We would encourage the reader to consult with their operations staff and confirm whether GC logging is on in production. Observability tools, such as those we will discuss in Chapters 10 and 11, do report some GC metrics, but these are aggregated data and the detail of individual GC events has been lost—and some of it can be very important for diagnosis.

I/O

File I/O has traditionally been one of the murkier aspects of overall system performance. Partly, this comes from its closer relationship with messy physical hardware, with engineers making quips about "spinning rust," but it is also because I/O lacks abstractions as clean as we see elsewhere in operating systems.

In the case of memory, the elegance of virtual memory as a separation mechanism works well. However, I/O has no comparable abstraction that provides suitable isolation for the application developer.

Fortunately, while most Java programs involve some simple I/O, the class of applications that heavily use the I/O subsystems is relatively small, and in particular, most applications do not simultaneously try to saturate I/O at the same time as either CPU or memory.

Not only that, but established operational practice has led to a culture in which production engineers are already aware of the limitations of I/O and actively monitor processes for heavy I/O usage.

For the performance analyst/engineer, it suffices to have an awareness of the I/O behavior of our applications. Tools such as `iostat` (and even `vmstat`) have the basic counters (e.g., blocks in or out), which are often all we need for basic diagnosis, especially if we make the assumption that only one I/O-intensive application is present per host.

Note that in virtualized environments (basically all cloud applications), I/O-intensive applications can give rise to what is known as the "noisy neighbor" problem—where one container has high requirements for things such as bandwidth or disk I/O and negatively affects the performance of other users running on the same underlying physical machine.

The performance engineer should pay particular attention to this possibility, as it may be difficult to detect directly.

Mechanical Sympathy

Mechanical sympathy is the idea that having an appreciation of the hardware is invaluable for those cases where we need to squeeze out extra performance.

> You don't have to be an engineer to be a racing driver, but you do have to have mechanical sympathy.
>
> —Jackie Stewart (attr)

The phrase was originally coined by Martin Thompson as a direct reference to Jackie Stewart and his car. However, as well as the extreme cases, it is also useful to have a baseline understanding of the concerns outlined in this chapter when dealing with production problems and looking at improving the overall performance of your application.

For many Java developers, mechanical sympathy is a concern that is possible to ignore. This is because the JVM provides a level of abstraction away from the hardware to unburden the developer from a wide range of performance concerns. However, developers can use Java and the JVM quite successfully in the high-performance and low-latency space, by gaining an understanding of the JVM and the interaction it has with hardware. One important point to note is that the JVM actually makes reasoning about performance and mechanical sympathy harder, as there is more to consider.

Whether mechanical sympathy is important to your project or not will depend upon the application's business goals and service-level agreements.

Let's consider an example: the behavior of cache lines.

Earlier in this chapter, we discussed the benefit of processor caching. The use of cache lines enables the fetching of blocks of memory. In a multithreaded environment, cache lines can cause a problem when you have two threads attempting to read or write to a variable located on the same cache line, resulting in a race condition. The first thread will invalidate the cache line on the second thread, causing it to be reread from memory. Once the second thread has performed the operation, it will then invalidate the cache line in the first. This ping-pong behavior results in a drop-off in performance known as *false sharing*—but how can this be fixed?

Mechanical sympathy would suggest that first we need to understand that this is happening, and only after that, determine how to resolve it. In Java, the layout of fields in an object is not guaranteed, meaning it is easy to end up with variables sharing a cache line. One way to get around this would be to add padding around the variables to force them onto a different cache line.

Summary

Processor design and modern hardware have changed enormously. Driven by Moore's law and by engineering limitations (notably the relatively slow speed of memory), advances in processor design have become somewhat esoteric. The cache miss rate has become the most obvious leading indicator of how performant an application is.

In the Java space, the design of the JVM allows it to use additional processor cores even for single-threaded application code. This means that Java applications have received significant performance advantages from hardware trends, compared to other environments.

As Moore's law fades, attention will turn once again to the relative performance of software. Performance-minded engineers need to understand at least the basic points of modern hardware and operating systems to ensure that they can make the most of their hardware and not fight against it.

In the next chapter, we will move from the consideration of a single host and its hardware and operating system, and begin to consider the highly virtualized/containerized environments that increasingly represent the environments where Java applications are deployed.

## CHAPTER 8

Components of the Cloud Stack

Reasoning about Java performance on a single machine is difficult—there are many variables arising from the JVM subsystems and the underlying hardware. Prior to this chapter, we have explored and discussed how to approach these challenges. We've discussed some aspects of JVM internals, diagnostics, and operating system performance tools and how they help to interrogate a running process. Going further, mechanical sympathy—understanding the interaction between the JVM and hardware—allows us to address high-performance concerns on a single JVM.

In this chapter, we are going to break the single JVM model and look at platforms supporting a horizontal deployment model for Java processes. You will see how platforms hosting Java processes have significantly shifted. Specifically, cloud native environments have altered the landscape and, with that, the categorization of topics that architects and performance engineers need to understand.

In particular, in addition to the key questions highlighted in "A Taxonomy for Performance" on page 7, there are situations where developers working in cloud-based platforms will also need to consider:

- Optimization for cost
- Optimization for reliability
- Scaling horizontally

In other words, optimizing for cost, reliability, and elastic scale (managing performance across multiple instances of running Java processes) will be key factors in complementing the classic taxonomy for performance.

In this chapter, you will learn an overview of some of the key cloud native building blocks and associated standards. You will also learn about Java standards relevant to building cloud native applications. We will cover a primer on virtualization, containers, and images.

We will then cover networking, as there are some major differences that influence the way that you will need to consider designing for cloud native. Finally, we will introduce the Fighting Animals repository, which we will use in subsequent chapters to practically acquaint you with new concepts.

Java Standards for the Cloud Stack

Frameworks in Java extend the core Java libraries offered in the JDK to assist in solving real-world problems. This assists developers in solving common problems on common deployment targets and platforms. Distributed platforms based on microservices-based architectures have become more prevalent. It is important to consider not just a single framework but also the available standards that apply to distributed deployment methodologies.

Standards create portability across a range of cloud native Java products including Quarkus, Helidon, and Open Liberty.[1]

Of particular importance are these two open standards:

- Jakarta EE (*https://jakarta.ee*), which we mentioned in Chapter 6, provides a series of Enterprise Java standards and is widely adopted, but a full treatment of it is outside the scope of this book.
- MicroProfile (*https://microprofile.io*) is a standard for distributed systems on a cloud native platform, and as of version 6.1, effectively decomposes Jakarta EE 10 into a set of related, but independent, standardized components.

In particular, MicroProfile provides a set of vendor-neutral standards that support microservice based-architectures and distributed system best practice. It is of particular interest to Java developers and architects because it provides standardization for libraries for building twelve-factor apps (*https://12factor.net*). Without standards, it is easy to end up in a situation where developers build their own solution or potentially get locked into a particular framework.

> The Eclipse Foundation is the home of both the MicroProfile and Jakarta EE working groups. These working groups are responsible for defining enterprise Java and microservices standards, respectively. Eclipse also hosts the Adoptium community build of OpenJDK.

---

1 Some popular frameworks, such as Spring, have not historically participated in standardization efforts.

Figure 8-1 describes the standards covered in MicroProfile 6.1 and demonstrates the key aspects you must consider when building applications in cloud native environments. As trends evolve to different patterns for building microservices-based architectures, Jakarta EE and MicroProfile will adapt and likely add new standards.

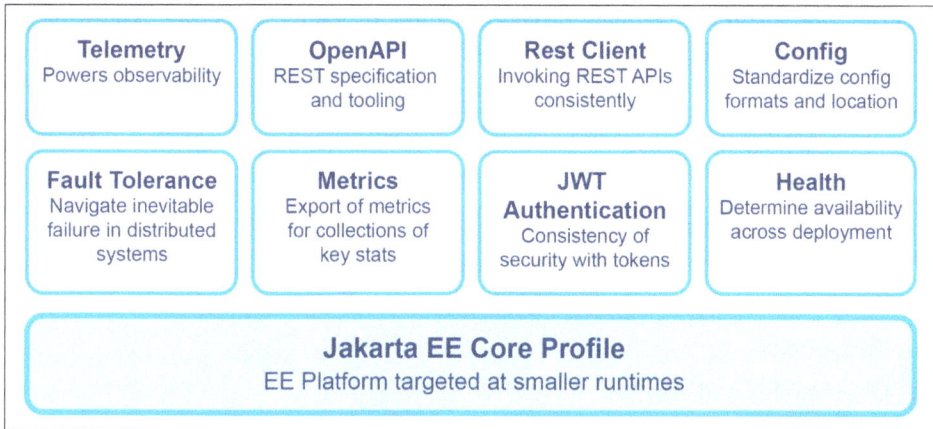

| **Telemetry** | **OpenAPI** | **Rest Client** | **Config** |
| Powers observability | REST specification and tooling | Invoking REST APIs consistently | Standardize config formats and location |

| **Fault Tolerance** | **Metrics** | **JWT Authentication** | **Health** |
| Navigate inevitable failure in distributed systems | Export of metrics for collections of key stats | Consistency of security with tokens | Determine availability across deployment |

Jakarta EE Core Profile
EE Platform targeted at smaller runtimes

Figure 8-1. Structure of the MicroProfile standard

Standards in Java are useful, but we also need to find a strategy to address vendor neutrality and portability in the platforms we target. Open source software has a long tradition of using open foundations to address these aspects of the software landscape.

Cloud Native Computing Foundation

The Cloud Native Computing Foundation (CNCF) is a vendor-neutral open source software foundation dedicated to making cloud native computing universal.

> Cloud native technologies empower organizations to build and run scalable applications in modern, dynamic environments such as public, private, and hybrid clouds. Containers, service meshes, microservices, immutable infrastructure, and declarative APIs exemplify this approach.
>
> —CNCF Charter

As vendor neutrality and portability is a significant architecture concern, it should not be a surprise that several CNCF projects are extremely important in the delivery of cloud native applications.

Compute platforms are not tied to a specific language stack, so advice given in the remainder of this chapter will expand beyond the scope of Java.

When building systems composed of multiple services, it is likely that you will need to revisit where and how certain components are deployed to meet evolving nonfunctional requirements. This is where CNCF is critical, hosting critical projects with different benefits to help meet business and nonfunctional requirements.

Figuring out which of the many projects to apply to your specific use case is tough. The CNCF Landscape (*https://landscape.cncf.io*) is an interactive map that attempts to categorize most of the projects and product offerings in the cloud native space. The CNCF Landscape is organized into multiple categories covering a range of concerns. Five of the key categories are:

- Application definition and deployment
- Orchestration and management
- Runtime
- Provisioning
- Observability and analysis

Within each of these categories in the CNCF Landscape, you will find the individual CNCF projects, the statistics of the project, and where the ownership of each project resides.

Note that the formats and standards for container images themselves are not part of the CNCF and are maintained by a separate standards initiative, the Open Container Initiative (OCI) (*https://opencontainers.org*). Although vendor neutral, projects on the CNCF Landscape include "for profit" projects. CNCF open source projects have different levels of maturity, which assists in developers and architects considering various technologies in their cloud native deployments:

Sandbox
Early innovative projects are at an early stage of development and may not yet be at production standard.

Incubating
The project is ready for production and has been demonstrated by active adoption. The project has adequate governance and maintenance, community, engineering principle, security, and ecosystem. It should meet the criteria of the incubating template (*https://oreil.ly/PbrIF*).

Graduated
The project has a proven track record of production usage in multiple industries and projects. It should meet the criteria of the graduation template (*https://oreil.ly/yLkPN*).

Architects frequently use the CNCF landscape. It is used as a mechanism to identify technologies in a specific problem area, discover the merits of the project, and for focusing proof of concepts and spikes of functionality.

Three CNCF projects are critically important to cloud native Java developers and performance engineers.

Kubernetes

Kubernetes (often shortened to K8s) is an open source container-orchestration system. It uses a cluster of compute nodes (hosts) to enable system operators and DevOps teams to deploy, scale, and coordinate distributed applications across the cluster. Kubernetes became a graduated project in CNCF in 2018.

In Chapter 9 you will learn about deploying Java applications using containers and Kubernetes.

Prometheus

Prometheus is a metrics format and time series database that is used to store metrics data. It was accepted to the CNCF in May 2016 as an incubating project and achieved graduated status in August 2018.

It is widely deployed among Kubernetes applications and has benefited from significant first-mover advantage, although the metrics landscape is evolving rapidly. You will learn more about Prometheus in Chapters 10 and 11.

OpenTelemetry

OpenTelemetry (OTel) is a set of standards, formats, and libraries that handles the collection, aggregation, and transport of observability data from applications into an observability system.

OTel (*https://oreil.ly/S2mhd*) is a CNCF project, and the technical development of the project takes place on GitHub (*https://github.com/open-telemetry*).

OTel is explicitly a cross-platform technology and is not Java-specific, although Java is a mature implementation of the standards. This means that there are a lot of different projects written in (and for) multiple programming languages.

OTel is currently an incubating project at CNCF, but it is seeing explosive growth and is already being used in production by many organizations. We will revisit OTel in depth in Chapter 11.

Underpinning the aforementioned technologies is the model for how things are deployed, so let's look at the importance of virtualization in the cloud native stack.

Virtualization

Before we can address the topic of virtualization, we first need to address the broader question—what is *cloud*? You will often hear the quip, *"Cloud is just someone else's computer,"* but there is more to it than that. The following helps provide a working definition:

> The simplest definition of cloud is a data centre that's full of identical hardware that no-one ever touches except to unpack it on day one and throw it away when it fails; in between, every deployment, update, investigation, and management process is automated.
>
> —Mary Branscombe (*https://oreil.ly/pfG-e*)

When your infrastructure is in the cloud, your capacity is commoditized and ready to run, available across a series of diverse application use cases. Access is not typically provided directly to the infrastructure and hardware. Instead, there needs to be control, management, and clear separation of the customer's runtime from both the infrastructure and potentially other customers.

For Java developers and performance engineers, this is our first tradeoff related to the move to cloud.

Access to the underlying operating system and hardware is available only at significant cost; typically you will have only limited insight into the physical platform, if at all. Perhaps surprisingly, virtualization techniques were originally developed in IBM mainframe environments as early as the 1970s. However, it was not until recently that x86 architectures were capable of supporting "true" virtualization.

> The traditional sysadmin techniques of "SSH into a box and have a look around" are not normally available in cloud environments— much more, arm's-length management techniques have become the standard approach.

Virtualization is typically defined by the following three conditions:

- Programs running on a virtualized OS should behave essentially the same as when running on bare metal.[2]

---

2 We will use "bare metal" to refer to running software directly on a host with a single operating system and no virtualization.

- A component, known as a *hypervisor*, must mediate all access to hardware resources.
- The overhead of the virtualization must be as small as possible and not a significant fraction of execution time.

In a traditional, unvirtualized system, the OS kernel runs in a special, privileged mode (hence the need to switch into kernel mode). This gives the OS direct access to hardware—this is the situation when working locally on your developer laptop, for example.

However, in a virtualized system, direct access to hardware by a guest OS is prohibited. Figure 8-2 outlines the structure, with the host operating system of the commoditized cloud infrastructure forming the base layer of the infrastructure. The `Feline` and `Mustelid` components are typical REST microservices that we will introduce later in the chapter.

The next layer is the hypervisor, which acts a layer of indirection between the operating system and the guest operating system. As a developer, you can deploy freely to the guest operating system, potentially using containers—we will discuss this option shortly.

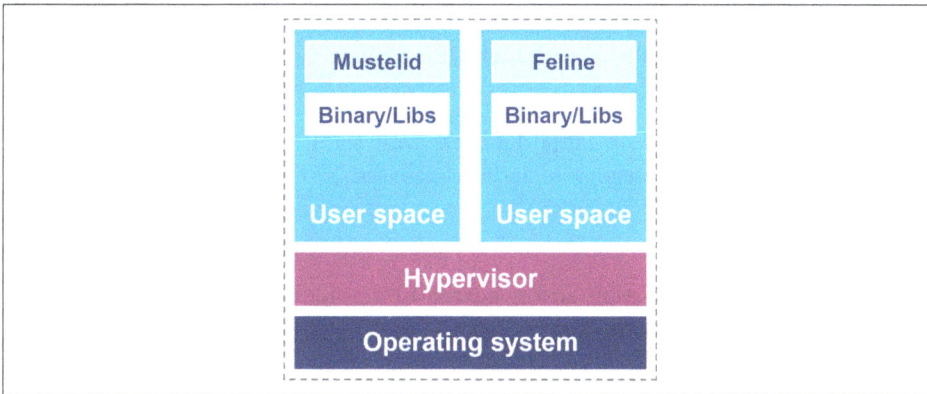

Figure 8-2. Virtualization stack

The hypervisor is at the core of virtualization, and it could be easy to look at it and remember tales of slow virtualized environments. The extensive use of virtual machines and hypervisors in the cloud has driven significant research and improvement to the overhead of hypervisors.

When moving to public cloud, your target platform will typically be a virtual machine packaged with the hypervisor. This will have an overall impact on performance that is, at least partly, out of your control—although public cloud providers do offer different options for the virtual machines available to you. Choosing the right virtual machines will become a factor for certain types of workload that run on public cloud.

Let's explore some of the virtual machines offered by cloud providers and what decisions you have as an architect and developer.

Choosing the Right Virtual Machines

Public cloud providers offer different types of virtual machines that are designed to suit different types of workload profile.

Amazon EC2 (*https://oreil.ly/FBJOg*) has a huge number of possible options for VM configuration depending on your use case. AWS also offers bare metal servers in addition to virtual machines; the following are some EC2 options available for running workloads:

General purpose
> The starting point for applications; however, within general purpose, there is a wide range of compute options. For example, in the M7g series, you can choose from a medium VM with a single vCPU and 4 GB of memory to the m7gd.metal, a bare metal machine with 64 CPU and 256 GB of memory.

Compute optimized
> Offer support for workloads with high CPU load.

Memory optimized
> Setup for workloads with large data sets with significant in-memory read and write profiles. This category includes databases, in-memory caching, and data analytics.

Accelerated computing
> Uses hardware acceleration and is geared to graphics, intense calculations, and generative AI applications.

Storage optimized
> Designed for read and write operations on local storage. This type of instance is focused on transactional databases and Apache Spark–style workloads.

High-performance computing
> Workloads are focused on complex simulations and deep learning–style workloads.

Azure (*https://oreil.ly/RNTDZ*) provides a wide range of options, from D-series used for general-purpose compute to L-series used for storage-optimized virtual machines.

Google Cloud (*https://oreil.ly/E9s_g*) has a similar set, including workloads focused on general purpose, ultra-high memory, compute-intensive, and demanding application workloads that require GPUs.

As part of designing your applications on cloud, generally the best approach is to start with general-purpose VMs and build from there. Instance types are often sized in powers of 2, so moving to bigger VMs is a cost tradeoff in situations where you just need a 5% extra CPU. Instance families provide a consistent ratio of CPU/memory/network throughput/storage (if they have it) across the instance sizes in that family. This can be a helpful starting point for picking an instance type.

Remember the lessons from earlier in the book—take small steps and measure whether adjusting VMs provides the type of performance benefit versus cost tradeoff that you are looking for.

In Chapter 9, you will explore how to further mix and match VMs within your application deployments, as part of the challenge will boil down to scheduling and deploying cloud-based applications. Orchestration platforms like Kubernetes provide the ability to mix and match VMs, so you can potentially run one specialized pool of nodes while other nodes focus on general-purpose use cases.

Virtualization Considerations

When designing cloud applications, optimize for cost, reliability, and scalability by choosing the right VM for your use case. For example, in situations where you are (or expect to be) CPU-intensive, this impact should be measured and confirmed as part of a performance test conducted in a production-like environment.

> One additional benefit of running in cloud is that creating ephemeral environments for testing is simpler. We will revisit this concept in Chapter 9.

Another option is to run a "best of both worlds" platform. In this model, some processes run on public cloud and some processes on bare metal. This provides the possibility of optimizing certain workloads that need burst scale and reliability, but also allows for performance and consideration of mechanical sympathy on core processing.

We will explore this further in "Container Orchestration" on page 215, when we look at orchestration systems and placement of processes, but Red Hat's OpenShift ("hybrid cloud") technology is a good example of this approach.

Now that you have an understanding of VMs, let's take a closer look at the building blocks for cloud native deployments, images, and containers.

Images and Containers

When Java arrived in the late 90s, it promised the hope of a great future of portability with its mantra of *"Write once, run everywhere,"* meaning any operating system and machine capable of running a Java virtual machine can run your code. This was an extremely audacious ambition, and the abstraction was not always perfect, especially in the early days.

Nevertheless, as with so many other aspects of modern software, Java served as the conduit by which advanced ideas truly entered the mainstream.

> Big ideas such as virtual machines, dynamic self-management, JIT compilation and garbage collection are now part of the general landscape of programming languages.
>
> —Benjamin J. Evans, "Java is a '90s Kid" in *97 Things Every Java Programmer Should Know*

The technology landscape continues to shift, and there has been an explosion in programming languages and platforms targeted at big data, artificial intelligence, cloud native routing, and network-level products. To support this array of complex technologies, the industry has had to react to deploying software on various operating systems, environments, and with a more diverse set of dependencies.

Portability is a design goal of cloud native applications, although it has appeared not in the portability of Java bytecode but at a slightly higher level—the *container image*. A container image (or just *image*) is an archive file that can be used to create an application process (or group of them) running under the control of an orchestration or container management system.

Let's dive deeper into image structure.

Image Structure

Just as in traditional Unix environments, the executable file on disk is the "frozen" representation of the program. At startup, this is converted into an active application process by executing the program. The image can be thought of as the frozen (and portable) representation of the application component, which will be converted into an active component via scheduling and orchestration.

With this greater diversity and complexity of components, standardization is once again the weapon of choice that industry uses to manage and control their application stacks. A good example is Open Container Image (OCI) established in 2015 by Docker.

Images are becoming the industry preferred unit of packaging applications, including Java applications, even if the target platform is bare metal. The image is bundled with everything required to run the application, which includes the userspace components (such as a subset of operating system components) and the JVM.

Accordingly, OCI is responsible for defining the format of images, how images run as containers, and how images are distributed.

Let's explore some of the interesting aspects of building and running containers—and some of the potential issues to be aware of.

Building Images

One way to create an image as part of the software build process is to define the image instructions in a Dockerfile. Each line in the Dockerfile represents a new layer. A layer is an immutable change to the file system, which will be represented within the container and is stored in the build cache. Each existing layer in the build cache can be reused as a building block for new images.

> Docker is often confused between the use as a technology and the commercial entity and registry provider. In this chapter, we refer to Docker as the de facto standard format that is supported in open source and by excellent tooling.

In the following example, we can see the keyword FROM, which essentially uses another image layer as a basis for adding in our Java application animals-demo-1.0-SNAPSHOT.jar.

The USER, RUN, COPY, and WORKDIR commands set up the app folder and move the built jar to the /app folder, ready to be executed by the container entry point command CMD:

```
FROM registry.access.redhat.com/ubi8/openjdk-17:1.13-1
USER root
RUN mkdir /app
COPY target/animals-demo-1.0-SNAPSHOT.jar  /app
WORKDIR /app
CMD ["java", "-jar" , "animals-demo-1.0-SNAPSHOT.jar", \
    "io.opentelemetry.examples.animal.AnimalApplication"]
```

Other tools have been developed as alternatives to the Dockerfile approach, which have more information available to make build and layer optimization decisions.

Jib (*https://oreil.ly/hnAr-*) runs as part of a Java build system (e.g., Maven) to create the image and, therefore, has the advantage of having more information about the structure of your Java application and the dependencies. It organizes the image into distinct layers, including dependencies, resources, and classes. Jib only modifies the layers that have changed. The theory is that Java library dependencies and resources in the project change infrequently compared to the classes in your application code. By splitting layers out in this way, the immutable layers do not experience as much churn, decreasing the time of builds and startup during development.

Using Jib has the added benefit of keeping all dependencies fresh with each build of your application, for both Java-level libraries and lower image layers. Using the Dockerfile approach works too, but it is necessary to ensure that base images are updated as patches and newer versions are released. Jib has potential benefits for security patching and performance by assisting in keeping dependencies fresh.

It is also possible to run multistage builds in Docker by using it to both build the jar and then use the jar in a second stage to construct the image. The layers used as part of the first build stage are discarded, and only the target jar is copied across into the final image. The advantage of this is ensuring a standardized build environment by containerizing and simplifying the build process. The following example Dockerfile demonstrates this multistage approach.

The first part of the Dockerfile sets up base images with Maven and OpenJDK 17 to execute the build, creating a jar. The AS builder identifies the stage in subsequent stages of the build. The second part of the Dockerfile builds the target image and includes the jar using the --from=builder statement.

```
#This first stage acts as a builder using a maven base image to create the jar
FROM maven:3.9-openjdk-17 AS builder
COPY src /usr/src/app/src
COPY pom.xml /usr/src/app
RUN mvn -f /usr/src/app/pom.xml package

FROM registry.access.redhat.com/ubi8/openjdk-17:1.13-1
USER root
RUN mkdir /app
#Copy the jar created by the first stage
COPY --from=builder /usr/src/app/target/animals-demo-1.0-SNAPSHOT.jar /app
WORKDIR /app
CMD ["java", "-jar" , "animals-demo-1.0-SNAPSHOT.jar"]
```

A typical image stack for a Java application includes OS dependencies, the JVM and configuration, and a jar. A minimal base image is the Universal Base Image (UBI) Minimal (*https://oreil.ly/OFTvm*) from Red Hat, which is only 37.1 MB in compressed size. Layering OpenJDK on the AMD64 architecture results in a base image of 147.8 MB in compressed size. The final layer depends on the build size of your application. The images can get quite sizable; for example, a Windows AMD64 Eclipse Temurin image is 2.27 GB.

In "Challenges with Containers and Scheduling" on page 221, we will consider how the size of an image has the potential to impact scheduling.

Running Containers

Containers provide a mechanism for running applications in an isolated environment. They are controlled using two Linux kernel constructs: *namespaces* and *cgroups*. Namespaces control access and visibility to resources on the host machine, and cgroups enforce limits to machine resources—especially CPU utilization and memory.

One aim of container abstraction is to provide process isolation between different containers. This is somewhat similar to virtual machines—the major conceptual difference is that containers do not use a hypervisor like VMs. Instead, applications in containers execute directly on the host operating system and access the host's kernel without the additional indirection of a hypervisor.

This makes containers lightweight and quick to start on compute, forming the basis of the orchestration systems we will discuss in Chapter 9.

Let's now look at the importance of networking when running containers.

Networking

Containers and orchestration systems use *ephemeral compute*, so developers should expect workloads to not be reliably in the same "place" (i.e., physical or virtual host). Ephemeral compute has an advantage optimizing for cost, as it enables dynamic scale up and scale down.

Scaling up/down can be within a given footprint, or perhaps, dynamically adding to the footprint as needed (e.g., adding more nodes into a cluster). This can take advantage of spot computing, the ability to use unutilized plant resources at a reduced cost. Spot instances are not reserved or guaranteed; when demand for those resources occurs, the spot instances will be terminated without advance notice.

From a networking perspective, things won't be as stable as fixed on-premises data centers, and components won't always have a dedicated IP address or continuously available compute. As a result, when thinking about networking and application communication, it is often best to think about the abstraction of traffic. Traffic can be generalized into to categories, north → south and east → west.

North → south is traffic that is not part of your system and will originate from either somewhere else on cloud or perhaps from the internet. North → south traffic needs to have a fixed IP address and is often referred to as an ingress. We will cover this in more detail in "Connecting to Services on the Cluster" on page 220.

One option for ingress is to use a highly available load balancer, and many orchestration platforms utilize a load balancer supplied by the cloud provider. The individual applications would then set up the corresponding routing into the cluster. This allows for a fixed IP address for external calls but still provides the ability to scale up and add more workloads behind the scenes to respond to scale.

East → west often refers to service-to-service calls within the orchestration tier, and here you can use the internal service discovery provided by the orchestration platform to scale up and down. Within an orchestration system like Kubernetes, we can use a service to create a lightweight and local DNS entry, available to other services within the cluster. We will revisit this in "Services" on page 219 when we dive deeper into this topic.

To finish this chapter, let's introduce a fleshed-out example system as a way to illustrate the concepts of cloud native applications, and later, build and deployment, and then observability.

Introducing the Fighting Animals Example

In this book, we have tried to ensure that we provide complete and working examples that go beyond "Hello World" but are still simple enough to be understood and used as a starting point for real systems. This is for several reasons, but one of the most important is that newcomers to the cloud stack frequently find it difficult to progress beyond initial, often semi-trivial, sample projects.

When observability is layered onto the example, the situation gets more complex, as overly simple examples do not always generalize easily to an actual implementation that can form the basis of an actual production observability system.

There is also a certain amount of irreducible complexity involved in implementing an observability system, and this can be tricky to set up, as there are so many variables and options that may or may not apply to a specific observed system.

Therefore, we have made the decision to introduce the "Fighting Animals" example application here first. After this, in Chapters 10 and 11, you will discover the observability considerations in more detail.

Fighting Animals is a simple Java application with a microservice architecture, available on GitHub (*https://oreil.ly/NMV7j*). The main version is written as a Spring Boot application, but there is an alternative version (*https://oreil.ly/TSeKt*) based on Quarkus. In the book text we will stick to the Spring Boot version, though.

The application is run as a collection of Docker containers (e.g., via Docker Compose) and exposes a REST endpoint on port 8080. Hitting the endpoint returns a simple JSON representation of two animals from several different biological clades that will battle each other.[3]

Call GET /battle to get a battle that looks like this:

```
{
  "good": <animal1>,
  "evil": <animal1>
}
```

There are several branches that we will explore further (mostly in the upcoming chapters):

main
: No observability

micrometer_only
: Micrometer metrics only

micrometer_with_prom
: Micrometer metrics with Prometheus

manual_tracing
: OpenTelemetry tracing using manual spans

auto_otel
: Use of the OpenTelemetry Java agent to trace automatically

k8s-with-argo
: An example using Kubernetes and rolling out change using deployment strategies

logging_only
: SLF4J logging exported to OpenTelemetry

micrometer_with_otel
: Micrometer with OpenTelemetry metrics

otel_metrics_raw_api
: OpenTelemetry metrics using the raw API

distributed_systems
: Enhancing Fighting Animals with Kafka

---

3 The application started life as a "battle" application that used characters from a well-known entertainment giant. This had to be changed for the book for fairly obvious copyright reasons.

`with_infinispan`
    Enhancing Fighting Animals with Kafka and Infinispan

In Figure 8-3, we can see the simple structure and API invocations of the Fighting Animals system.

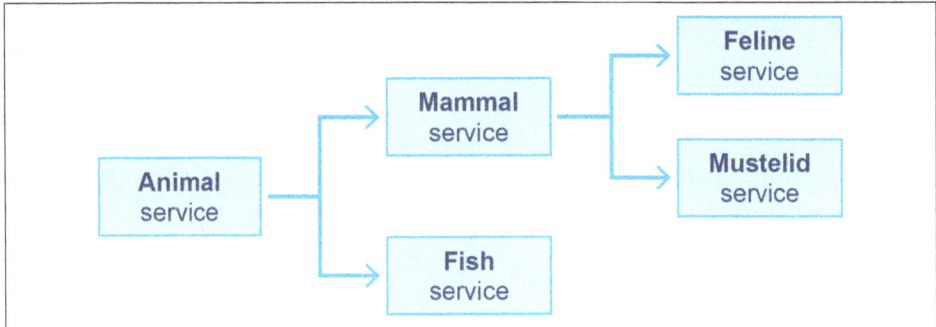

Figure 8-3. Fighting Animals microservices

The initial call results in further downstream calls to other microservices to fulfill the incoming request.

A Word About Version Numbers

In all the Fighting Animals examples, we are using *pinned versions* of our dependencies and containers. This is to ensure the examples are reproducible and do not change over time. In a system that uses *floating versions* (like `latest`), the versions will change over time. This can make it very difficult to understand what has changed and why—and this problem only gets worse as the system gets more complex. We do use `latest` for our own application containers, but that's because they are under our control and we can ensure that they are always up to date.

Summary

In this chapter, you have learned about how cloud platforms and components challenge our traditional model of optimization and performance.

MicroProfile is an excellent standard for building applications that are both cloud native and microservice-based architecture ready. Beyond considering Java standards in isolation, CNCF provides a guide for platform considerations and projects that should be considered for a cloud native architectural approach.

Virtualization is an important aspect of the cloud native stack and the principal building block for compute. Although there are low-level details in virtualization, the bigger benefits are gained from looking at the right VM configuration for the task. It is possible to mix bare metal and virtualization in a clustered deployment.

Images and containers are the de facto unit of deployment in a cloud native environment. There are different approaches to creating and layering images for Java and some common gotchas that need to be considered. Networking is an important aspect of the cloud native stack, and with that, the concerns of service discovery and traffic routing. We introduced the Fighting Animals project, which we will use throughout the upcoming chapters to describe more complexities in the cloud stack.

In the next chapter, we will look at running cloud native Java processes in more detail. We will start by looking at running containers locally and then how to schedule and deploy on cloud native infrastructure.

## CHAPTER 9

Deploying Java in the Cloud

In Chapter 8, we covered the foundational aspects of the cloud stack. In this chapter, we will take this topic further and look at the practical aspects of deploying Java processes on cloud native platforms.

We will begin by covering working locally with containers and understanding some of the basics of how containers interact when deployed. The interaction and details of how things are deployed will lead into looking at how container orchestration works and what you need to be aware of.

One enormously useful aspect of cloud native platforms is the access to ephemeral compute and the ability to scale—but this needs to be *coordinated* to be useful. With these basics in place, you will learn about options for release and deployment patterns. Deployment techniques are incredibly helpful when rolling out change to your JVM-based processes quickly, whilst still mitigating the risk of bugs.

If you are a developer, you might be wondering if deployment is really an important aspect for you to consider. Historically, you may have built software and handed it over to an operations team to run. However, one of the major changes with cloud native development is that the lines have blurred between operations and development, hence the term "DevOps."

For example, it is much simpler to create consistent environments for production and nonproduction systems. As a result, many teams are choosing to operate as "build and run" teams, finding a balance between building and supporting services. Building and operating as a single team can result in improved efficiency (or "velocity"). Efficiency gains arise from fewer miscommunications and frustrations or errors from the dev to ops handover. Build and run teams develop a deep expertise and a sense of responsibility for the stack as a whole. Working in a build and run team results in an engaged team with an increased job satisfaction.

Let's start by looking how you can work with containers locally.

Working Locally with Containers

In "Images and Containers" on page 202, we covered a primer for the basics of images and containers. One of the benefits of containers is creating a more representative environment at deployment time on your local machine. Containers eliminate all of the hassles that were associated with ironing out the differences between the operating system of the developer's machine and the runtime machine.

Running the following commands will build and launch mammal_demo from the Fighting Animals demo. However, running the curl statement won't actually work due to dependencies—i.e., the other services not being available:

```
git clone https://github.com/kittylyst/fighting-animals.git .
git checkout main

mvn clean package
docker build -t mammal_demo -f src/main/docker/mammal/Dockerfile .
docker run -p 8081:8081 -t mammal_demo
curl localhost:8081/getAnimal
  {"timestamp":"2024-04-29T17:18:00.170+00:00","status":500,
  "error":"Internal Server Error","path":"/getAnimal"}
```

Looking at the map of services in MammalController shown in the following code, there is a DNS dependency at the code level. Both the mustelid and feline services are referred to as mustelid-service and feline-service in the URL. Later in this chapter, we will demonstrate how DNS works in orchestration platforms; however, for now we need a way to recreate this locally:

```
private static final Map<String, String> SERVICES =
    Map.of(
        "mustelids", "http://mustelid-service:8084/getAnimal",
        "felines", "http://feline-service:8085/getAnimal");
```

One option is to run a Kubernetes cluster locally; another is to use Docker Compose, which is a simpler place to start.

Docker Compose

Docker Compose is a tool for defining and running multicontainer Docker applications locally during development. A docker-compose.yml is used to configure your application's services and define the dependencies between them. Then, with a single command, docker-compose up, you can create and start all the services based upon your configuration.

The following YAML is an example `docker-compose.yml`. The Fighting Animals example has a simple setup with five services, each of which is defined in a separate Dockerfile. The `depends_on` clauses define the service topology and the name of the services (e.g., `mustelid-service`) create a lightweight DNS entry that other containers can address:

```yaml
# Fish service
fish-service:
  image: fish_demo:latest
  ports:
    - "8083:8083"
# Mustelid service
mustelid-service:
  image: mustelid_demo:latest
  ports:
    - "8084:8084"
# Feline service
feline-service:
  image: feline_demo:latest
  ports:
    - "8085:8085"
# Mammal service
mammal-service:
  image: mammal_demo:latest
  ports:
    - "8081:8081"
  depends_on:
    - feline-service
    - mustelid-service
# Animal service
animal-service:
  image: animals_demo:latest
  ports:
    - "8080:8080"
  depends_on:
    - fish-service
    - mammal-service
```

Running `docker-compose` up launches five distinct microservices in this example, each of them listening on a different TCP port. Running `curl localhost:8081/get Animal` will provide a response from the mammal service. The feline and mustelid dependencies are set up on a named service and can be referenced from the other containers.

It is worth noting that the curl command had to be on localhost, as outside the containers the named services are not visible. The abstraction of the named service is useful for creating local service names; this is consistent with orchestration systems.

> One challenge for developers is that there is a lot of tooling in the development loop; in our example, there is Maven, Docker, and Docker Compose.

Without changing our build and local deployment tools, it would be helpful to make changes and see this reflect in our local running environment.

Tilt

Tilt (*https://tilt.dev*) is a toolkit that nicely coordinates other tools to create a local workflow with microservices. After installation (*https://oreil.ly/oUlW-*), a Tiltfile is created containing the recipe. The recipe contains multiple tasks required to compile, run, and deploy the example and will redeploy parts of your application as files identified by local_resource, as in the following Tiltfile example.

The monorepo-java-compile task rebuilds code after it is changed. Following this, docker_build runs across all the images and will be redeployed in the configuration set out by docker_compose:

```
local_resource(
  'monorepo-java-compile',
  'mvn clean package',
  deps=['src', 'pom.xml'])

docker_build(
  'animals_demo',
  '.',
  dockerfile='./src/main/docker/animal/Dockerfile')

// ... All other docker_build tasks elided

docker_compose("deploy/docker-compose.yml")
```

Figure 9-1 is an example of the Tilt UI, which provides visual feedback on the state of the build and running containers. It has some useful features in addition to seeing the current state of local deployments, such as quickly accessing the logs from a running container.

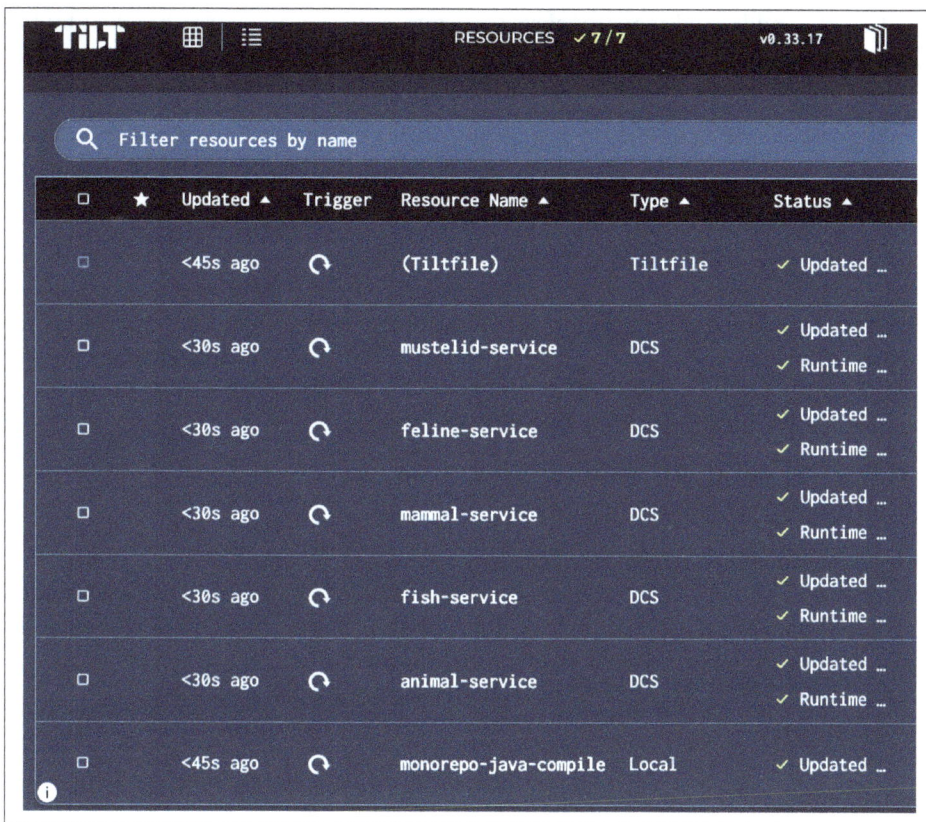

Figure 9-1. Tilt user interface

Container Orchestration

There are a variety of options for orchestrating containers; in this chapter, we will focus on Kubernetes, which is by far the most common choice.

> The name "Kubernetes" comes from Ancient Greek, and it means "helmsman" or "pilot." Various other tools in the space play on this theme with their naming.

Cloud native container orchestration is generally implemented with two high-level fundamental components, a control plane and data plane.

The control plane is where actions are taken to adjust the state of the data plane. The data plane is where the work happens and where the five Fighting Animals services will run. From a developer perspective, thinking about where the service is running and how it is addressed is nicely abstracted into a platform concern handled by the control plane.

> Control plane operations are eventually consistent, meaning operations applied will take time to apply to the data plane. Tradeoffs are made between consistency and availability; Kubernetes, by design, aims for availability. You will learn more about distributed patterns in Chapter 14.

There are a couple of approaches to running Kubernetes locally (*https://kubernetes.io/docs/setup*), which will construct a local cluster. For the rest of this chapter, we will assume that you have picked one of the possible configurations—all of the instructions should work regardless of the choice you've made.

Let's take the mammal service and look at the interactions with the Kubernetes control plane to get the service running.

The key command to perform Kubernetes operations is kubectl, which is short for "Kubernetes Control." In practice, many developers will create Kubernetes aliases for working with kubectl. For example, k is a common alias you'll see in documentation and examples on the internet.

Deployments

A Deployment describes what should happen to the workloads running in the data plane. In the example deployment, the mammal-service is defined along with the container specification. The deployment shown in the following example is defined in a deployment-mammal.yaml. Running kubectl apply -f deployment-mammal.yaml applies our deployment in the cluster:

```
apiVersion: apps/v1
kind: Deployment
metadata:
  name: mammal-service
spec:
  replicas: 1
  selector:
    matchLabels:
      app: mammal-service
  template:
    metadata:
      labels:
        app: mammal-service
    spec:
      containers:
        - name: mammaldemo
          image: mammal_demo
```

```
    ports:
      - containerPort: 8081
```

Once the `Deployment` is applied, the Kubernetes scheduler will create a Pod and orchestrate the deployment onto a node in the data plane. A Pod is one or more containers deployed together on a node in a Kubernetes cluster. In the deployment for mammal service, a single Pod will be created with a single container.

For example, in the following output, the Pod has a unique name and 1/1 containers running—meaning that the Pod has a single container running and expects to have a single container running; in other words, the Pod has reached a consistent state:

```
kubectl get Pods
NAME                               READY   STATUS    RESTARTS   AGE
mammal-service-79b4ccb9bb-4bqrj    1/1     Running   0          3m56s
```

Let's explore some of the reasons you might wish to run multiple containers within a Pod.

Sharing Within Pods

Developing with Pods creates powerful abstractions and is the heart of several common deployment architectures:

- Containers that run within a Pod have shared access to shared storage volumes and network.
- Containers deployed together in a Pod have a close coupling or a compositional dependency on each other.
- Containers deployed in a single Pod share `localhost`, making it possible for latency-sensitive services with out-of-process communication to be deployed together. This is possible because of the loopback adapter, which intercepts traffic as it travels down the network stack before it hits the physical network. This fact could be part of your design for application deployment, and it is also commonly used within infrastructure-level projects.

Egressing from one Pod to another will incur additional network latency and is something you will want to observe in the performance of your overall request flow. The impact of this will be higher if the connecting service is located on a different node in the cluster.

Service mesh is a group of CNCF projects that relies on Pods to be configured such that it can take control of network traffic and routing. A full coverage of service mesh can be found in *Mastering API Architecture* by James Gough et al.

Service mesh projects such as Istio (*https://istio.io*) deploy an Envoy proxy into the same Pod as a user's application container. It could be tempting to think this would require code to change to route through the proxy, which will be running on localhost. However, it is possible to manipulate the IP tables (i.e., routing and firewall rules) inside the Pod to alter the behavior of the local, Pod-level network. To set up the Pod in this way, an Istio-supplied init-container process executes setting any required state and configuration in the Pod's IP tables, and then exits.

Service mesh is used to provide additional features beyond what is provided out of the box by Kubernetes:

- The proxy can enforce that all traffic uses TLS or mTLS when traversing a cluster. This is transparent to the developer, and this is due to the intercept at the Pod level. The application connects to its local proxy, and the proxy takes on the responsibility of adding the encryption.

- As traffic is encrypted at the proxy, the proxy has access to the payload unencrypted. This enables a point of integration for telemetry collection at the network level.

- The proxy is capable of finer grain routing of traffic to target services. One example would be to prioritize traffic for human users versus traffic that is for batch or longer running processes.

Pods offer a consistent abstraction as a building block for more complex systems. With the ability to manipulate and configure shared resources consistently, Pods provide a highly flexible, consistent abstraction on top of the physical node.

Container and Pod Lifecycles

Additional nonfunctional requirements are necessary for applications running in distributed and scheduled environments.

One essential requirement is the need to provide *liveness* and *readiness* health checks. A liveness check assesses if the application is running at all, and a readiness check indicates whether the process is ready to serve requests. Accuracy of these health checks ensures that the orchestration or traffic flow systems deliver reliability and resiliency.

Note that defining readiness is down to the implementor or architect, and it should consider whether all the dependencies are in place to successfully serve a request. It is important to be able to observe both independent container health and the overall health of the system.

Pods have an execution cycle described by the current lifecycle phase, which directly taps in to the liveness and readiness checks at the container level. Pods have conditions PodScheduled, ContainersReady, Initialized, and Ready. For more information, consult the Kubernetes Documentation for Pod Lifecycle (*https://oreil.ly/iGoqq*).

Ensuring that liveness and readiness checks are accurate in our application means that a Pod will not be scheduled into rotation (attached to a service) until it is in the Ready state. The blog post "Kubernetes Probes: Startup, Liveness, Readiness" (*https://oreil.ly/RiZA9*) by Levent Ogut documents this in more detail.

Pods are ephemeral, so to consistently connect to containers running inside Pods, it is necessary to introduce a capability of routing to multiple Pods across the cluster—this is where services come in.

Services

A Service provides an abstraction over Pods deployed in the cluster and is the basis for advertising a lightweight DNS entry and routing across the cluster.

In the following example, we deploy a Service with the name mammal-service. We will create a DNS entry at the cluster level—similar to that used for docker-compose. The selector matches our deployment; however, it is possible to specify version matches and matches on other metadata:

```
apiVersion: v1
kind: Service
metadata:
  name: mammal-service
spec:
  selector:
    app: mammal-service
  ports:
    - protocol: TCP
      port: 8081
      targetPort: 8081
```

> In simple deployments, manually typing and retyping string metadata is OK, but this can get complicated quite quickly. Tools like Helm (*https://helm.sh*) and Kustomize (*https://kustomize.io*) help address this issue by introducing data types, templates, and variables.

Running kubectl get services will display the Services that are running on the cluster in the default namespace as demonstrated by the following output. A Service created in this way is designed for communication within the cluster:

```
kubectl get services
NAME             TYPE        CLUSTER-IP        EXTERNAL-IP   PORT(S)    AGE
kubernetes       ClusterIP   10.96.0.1         <none>        443/TCP    16d
mammal-service   ClusterIP   10.105.113.150    <none>        8081/TCP   57s
```

For clusters to accept external traffic, an external ingress point needs to be configured.

Connecting to Services on the Cluster

The Pods and Services created so far are visible only within the cluster. This is a valuable feature of cluster deployments, but in many applications it will be necessary to expose an entry point to the cluster. There are several options for this; however, a common approach is to create a LoadBalancer on an IP address accessible external to the cluster.

In the Fighting Animals example, only the *animal service* should be exposed outside the cluster. The other services are only referenced as internal services, which can use Service for internal cluster routing. In the following Service YAML, the animal-service is created with a LoadBalancer on the spec. This will indicate that an external load balancer with an IP address should be registered:

```
apiVersion: v1
kind: Service
metadata:
  name: animal-service
spec:
  type: LoadBalancer
  selector:
    app: animal-service
  ports:
    - protocol: TCP
      port: 8080
      targetPort: 8080
```

Creating this ingress point will expose an external IP address, which you can connect to from outside the cluster. Running kubectl get services in the following output displays the services with ClusterIP and the animal-service LoadBalancer type along with the external IP (20.108.87.2) and port (8080). You can now connect using the external IP address on http://20.108.87.2:8080:

```
NAME               TYPE           CLUSTER-IP       EXTERNAL-IP    PORT(S)
animal-service     LoadBalancer   10.106.223.136   20.108.87.2    8080:31762/TCP
feline-service     ClusterIP      10.101.233.232   <none>         8085/TCP
fish-service       ClusterIP      10.101.40.193    <none>         8083/TCP
kubernetes         ClusterIP      10.96.0.1        <none>         443/TCP
mammal-service     ClusterIP      10.111.138.65    <none>         8081/TCP
mustelid-service   ClusterIP      10.98.142.128    <none>         8084/TCP
```

LoadBalancer implementations vary depending on the variant of Kubernetes you are running. For example, when deploying to a cloud provider, this will be a load balancing solution offered by the provider's network.

Next, let's look at some of the common challenges with using Kubernetes as your production environment.

Challenges with Containers and Scheduling

As with many deployment environments, it is simple to get things up and running and to work locally with Kubernetes—however, operating environments at scale can pose various challenges. The full operation of a Kubernetes cluster is outside the scope of this book, but we will cover some aspects that may surprise developers.

As the cluster increases in complexity, both in terms of number of applications and number of nodes in the cluster, it can be difficult to discover the root cause of ongoing or retrospective problems. It is also tricky to view the path of a faulty request that has executed across multiple services. It is possible to look manually at logs, but with multiple running instances, this can be time-consuming and tricky to find which Pods and containers were involved in a failing request.

It is our opinion that three-pillar observability is mandatory for operating Kubernetes workloads at scale; we will cover this further in Chapter 10. Adopting three-pillar observability also provides monitoring of the overall cluster health, which can assist in capacity management.

Image loading is an important aspect of container scheduling. The size of the image is an important discussion for platforms, especially when considering the cost of a *cold start*, a term that describes the situation when you request a container that is not in the local container registry.

The larger the image size, the longer it will take to download and be available for the process to start. This will also place more load on your networking infrastructure, and in some cases, you will pay for this bandwidth. For longer running processes, the impact is not as significant, as the startup cost is amortized over a long-running application. However, for an application that runs for only a few seconds, the cost is extremely high.

Image size is only part of the issue because start-up times for Java can be slow under certain frameworks. This has created a myth around Java not being suitable for deployment on cloud native platforms. As we saw in "Ahead-of-Time (AOT) Compilation" on page 163, there are AOT compilation techniques that make Java applications launch in ~0.029 seconds and also take up significantly less image space.

To help mitigate the impact of cold starts, Kubernetes maintains a local container registry at the node level, storing cached images. In the `Deployment` object, there is an `imagePullPolicy` that is set to determine how Kubernetes should treat the relationship between the local and remote container registries. `imagePullPolicy` can have the following values:

- `IfNotPresent` will pull an image that doesn't exist on a node. The idea is that the cost of pulling the image is paid only once. This is the default when the `:latest` tag is not used for the image.

- Always will always pull a newer image from the remote container registry. Using Always may seem inefficient; however, a check is performed to only pull new layers as required. Always may be required if registry tags are not immutable and the registry permits updating an existing image tag.

- Never will never look in the remote container registry; however, this assumes that you have configured a mechanism for loading into the container registry.

One thing to avoid is using the tag :latest when specifying the image in a production cluster, for two reasons: first, because it essentially sets the policy to Always and can cause unnecessary network traffic. Second, and more important, not using a versioned image in production can potentially result in uncontrolled changes hitting your production environment.

In the worst case, this can even mean breaking changes—but more insidious is the possibility of your deployment changing underneath you without your knowledge or explicit intent. This could happen when your application is auto-scaled, introducing a partial old and new version mixture. This is a major red flag (and may even subject you to criminal liability in regulated or audited industries)—you should always know exactly what is running in production and be able to reconstruct the system state if necessary.

This might not be obvious if you are used to having Java ecosystems working from a static class path and library-based binary dependencies. Using a meaningful/versioned tag ensures that you will get a pinned version, and IfNotPresent reduces the risk of pulling new images unexpectedly.

> Tags are not immutable, so investigating how your image dependencies work is an important consideration when operating your cluster.

For resiliency production, clusters should always contain multiple nodes. Node placement is an important consideration, and nodes should be positioned in different data centers or public cloud availability zones. Losing a node in Kubernetes should not be a big deal, but it requires accurate placement and enough capacity to ensure that the remaining nodes can handle the placement of containers in a partial failure.

Kubernetes will generally perform a smooth distribution of containers across the various nodes in the cluster. However, operators can also control the placement/anti-placement of containers with respect to nodes using node affinity. If you are using specialized nodes for certain workloads, performance testing will ensure that you make the most out of the resources available.

Securing the Kubernetes cluster is an important challenge that needs to be considered carefully. The Kubernetes control plane is a key target for hackers—essentially because manipulating the control plane can compromise the entire cluster. The OWASP Security Cheat Sheet (*https://oreil.ly/IalaA*) is a good place to start in ensuring the security of your control plane and cluster. Ingress points must be secured at the outset, as these will often be broadly available. One of the authors ran a demo of an insecure application as part of a workshop, and after being deployed for 15 minutes, it was under active attack.

Using `namespaces` is a large topic that is mostly out of the scope of this book, but as groups of applications grow, namespaces are a key mechanism to reduce operational risk. Namespaces are essentially a grouping of resources on a cluster, which also provides isolation and configuration that applies only within a namespace. Access to control namespaces from the control plane can be locked down, so only operators from one team can deploy resources in a team's namespace.

Kubernetes Best Practices by Brendan Burns et al. (O'Reilly, 2023) is a great resource covering these topics.

Working with Remote Containers Using "Remocal" Development

In "Working Locally with Containers" on page 212, we presented options for working locally with containers. Another option is to make your local container appear as though it is part of a remote cluster. This is where *remocal development* provides the advantage of working locally with your IDE and container to use debugging and profiling tools. In complicated architectures, it has the benefit of not needing to run all services locally to fully test your application.

Telepresence (*https://www.telepresence.io*) is a tool that provides this capability by creating a proxy between the local machine and the cluster. You can configure which services resolve locally and which should resolve to the remote cluster.

Deployment Techniques

When working in cloud native environments, understanding the difference between *deployment* and *release* helps unlock new techniques for rolling out software change. Deployment refers to changing application components (code and/or config) or infrastructure. Release is used only when a feature or change is made available to end users. There are two main consequences of considering deployment and release as separate operations:

- Deployments can change production systems without releasing features, so deploys can be more frequent.
- Releases change user-visible behavior, but deploys may or may not.

For example, with the Fighting Animals demo, you can deploy a new version of the fish_demo into the production environment. From this point, we have options about how we release the new fish_demo into our running ecosystem. Although deployed, the new feature is not active or executed by interactions with the production system.

Several useful deployment techniques can help diagnose many of the problems we'll discuss in this section (and many others besides):

- Blue/green deployments
- Canary deployments
- Feature flags and how they can contribute to an evolutionary architecture

Blue/Green Deployments

Blue/green is one of the easier techniques to understand and provides a good starting point when looking at release separation for the first time. In most cases, it can also serve as a deployment pattern without using a fully cloud native platform. To implement it, you need a *decision point* to switch between the blue and green environments in your architecture.

A decision point is a component, for example, a load balancer, that is configured for traffic to flow to different targets. The decision to configure the load balancer for blue or green is a point-in-time decision accompanying the release step. Behind the decision point, an entire copy of your software stack is running—referred to as your *blue* environment. A second copy behind the decision point is also stood up—but this one is referred to as your *green* environment and conceptually represents the next version of your platform.

There are multiple options for how blue/green can be modeled in Kubernetes. One approach is to create new services, e.g., fighting-animals-blue and fighting-animals-green.

An Ingress is a Kubernetes resource, which provides an entry point but also provides a richer set of configuration options than exposing a service directly on a load balancer. You can push a configuration change to the Ingress to flip between blue and green services. Figure 9-2 highlights how this option would work with Fighting Animals.

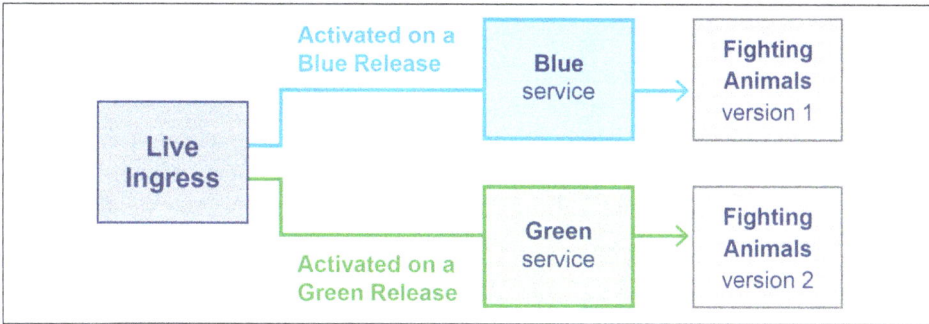

Figure 9-2. Example of a blue/green setup with Fighting Animals

During deployment of the green environment, the new changes and any regression testing can be performed in production. At the point of releasing the new change, live traffic is flipped over from blue to green. If a problem is spotted, it is a quick rollback to the previous version by updating the feature flag or which environment the gateway or ingress points to.

Moving between blue and green environments can be done as a big bang approach, and this might be a first step for developing a rollout strategy. Once all traffic is fully transferred from blue to green, the blue processes can move to standby (e.g., in case of a need to roll back). The next release will be back to the blue environment, with any new deployments created and configured against this environment. Managing ingress and services to manually move between blue and green can be a bit fiddly.

> Accessing either blue or green directly, for the purposes of regression testing, is required to verify the environment. This is necessarily different from how end users, who are oblivious to whether blue/green is active, access the environment. This can produce subtle bugs, for example, if the access is controlled by a path in the URL, and there is a bug in the path evaluation logic that doesn't manifest during regression but would manifest during go live.

In the next section on *canaries*, we will introduce Argo CD, which can also be used for blue/green deployments.

One potential downside with blue/green deployment is that you need to have all services duplicated, which can be costly. So, let's look at how *canary deployments* can provide more flexibility when replacing services without needing full replication of a blue/green environment.

Canary Deployments

Canary deployments replace running services independently and flow a small percentage of production traffic to the canary as part of a staged release sequence. The term canary originates from mining, where a canary was sent in ahead of the miners to test for any toxic gasses that might be present in the environment. The unfortunate death of the canary would prevent the onward progress of the miners (analogous to the full release).

Tools like Argo CD (*https://oreil.ly/gm3A0*) provide a rich set of tools for automating canary releases within Kubernetes clusters. In this section, we'll demonstrate a rollout where we set up five replicas of the `mammal_demo` image at the latest version. We will create a strategy that requires a manual intervention after the verification of the first 20% of the rollout. Following this, the rollout will introduce 20% more traffic on the new version at ten-second intervals.

To try the example yourself, you will need to install Argo CD on your cluster. You can do this by running the following commands or following the installation guide (*https://oreil.ly/GRYr2*):

```
git checkout k8s-with-argo

kubectl create namespace argo-rollouts
kubectl apply -n argo-rollouts -f \
https://github.com/argoproj/argo-rollouts/releases/latest/download/install.yaml
```

To create the strategy, you need to apply a rollout definition to the Kubernetes cluster `kubectl apply -f operations/k8s-canary-rollout-demo.yaml`. The rollout definition is picked up by ArgoCD, which you installed to the cluster.

The following YAML displays the contents of `operations/k8s-canary-rollout-demo.yaml`; you can find this example in the Fighting Animals `k8s-with-argo` branch in `operations/k8s-canary-rollout-demo.yaml`. The rollout defines the requirement for five replicas that will initially be set to the `mammal_demo` image. The strategy is defined as canary and states that 20% should release first, and `pause: {}` instructs the rollout to wait for user input. The `pause: {duration: 10}` will not wait for user input and proceed with the next weighting after waiting for ten seconds. The starting point is five replicas running at the original version, awaiting a command to promote to a new version:

```
apiVersion: argoproj.io/v1alpha1
kind: Rollout
metadata:
  name: rollouts-demo
spec:
  replicas: 5
  strategy:
    canary:
```

```
      steps:
        - setWeight: 20
        - pause: {}
        - setWeight: 40
        - pause: {duration: 10}
        - setWeight: 60
        - pause: {duration: 10}
        - setWeight: 80
        - pause: {duration: 10}
    revisionHistoryLimit: 2
    selector:
      matchLabels:
        app: mammal-service
    template:
      metadata:
        labels:
          app: mammal-service
      spec:
        containers:
          - name: mammal-service
            image: mammal_demo
            ports:
              - name: http
                containerPort: 8081
                protocol: TCP
            resources:
              requests:
                memory: 32Mi
                cpu: 5m
```

Let's say that we want to release a v2 container into production. We would execute the following command:

```
kubectl argo rollouts set image rollouts-demo mammal-service=mammal_demo:v2
```

This command executes the strategy defined in the previous rollout and instigates a 20% canary deployment where one container is set to mammal_demo:v2. Figure 9-3 shows the rollout underway using the Argo CD Dashboard; you can see this by running kubectl argo rollouts dashboard.

In Figure 9-3, the rollout is held at the first pause step and visually shows that one container of v2 is running. In this rollout, manually pressing Promote will trigger the next 20% of the rollout. If a problem is found, pressing the Rollback button will remove the new version from production and perform a full rollback to the previous version.

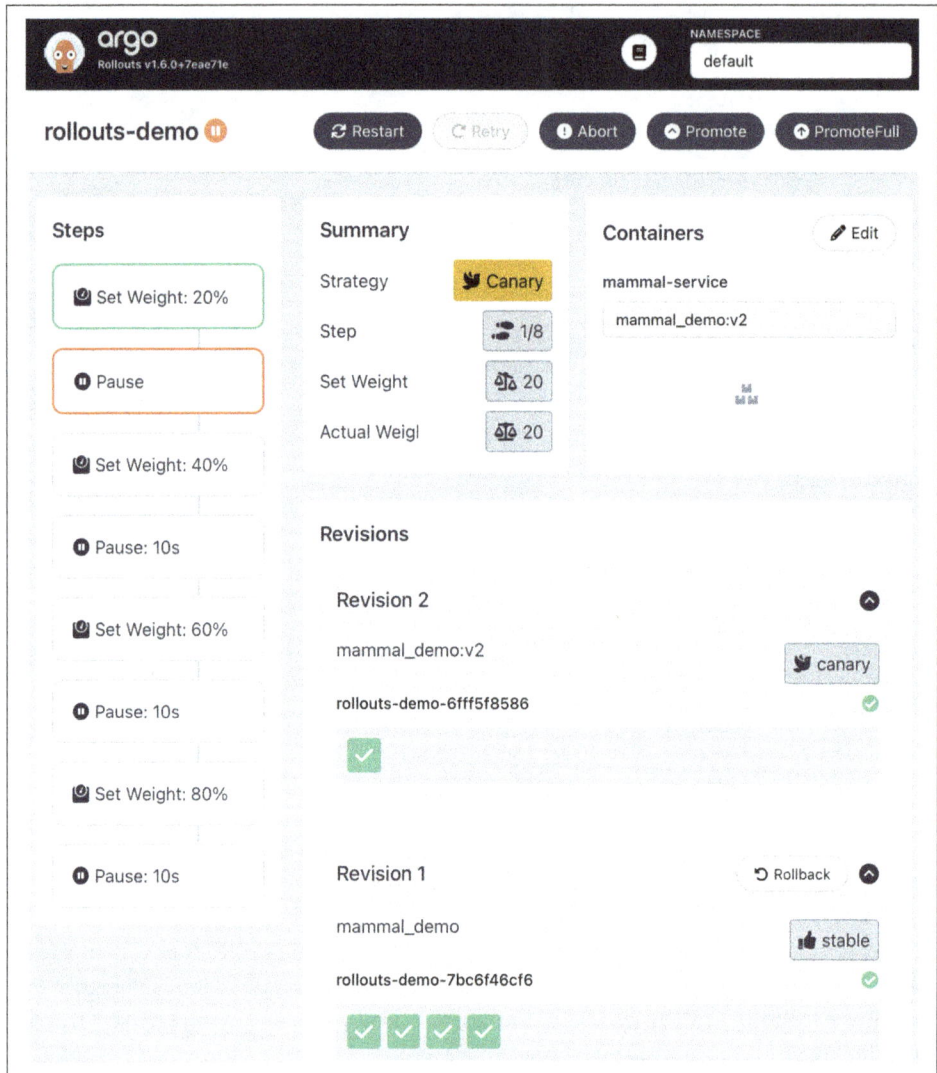

Figure 9-3. Execution of a canary release of the mammal service

In addition to manual user interaction to promote stages through the canary release, it is also possible to use signals to progress a release.

In Chapter 10, you will learn more about signals you could potentially use in monitoring for the success of a canary triggering the next stages of the release. The following is an example of an AnalysisTemplate that uses Prometheus metrics to look at the number of successful requests on a service.

The analysis stage would be applied as part of the rollout definition:

```yaml
apiVersion: argoproj.io/v1alpha1
kind: AnalysisTemplate
metadata:
  name: success-rate
spec:
  args:
  - name: service-name
  - name: prometheus-port
    value: 9090
  metrics:
  - name: success-rate
    successCondition: result[0] >= 0.95
    provider:
      prometheus:
        address: "http://prometheus.example.com:{{args.prometheus-port}}"
```

With many containers running at different versions and in different locations across the cloud native stack, understanding what is going on at any given moment can be quite a daunting problem. In Chapter 10, you will learn how to handle the new level of complexity introduced by a distributed platform.

Evolutionary Architecture and Feature Flagging

As architects, the authors are often asked about moving legacy code to participate in cloud native architectures. Blue/green and canaries are really good deployment mechanisms, but how do you migrate to use them? It is unlikely that we will change complex systems all at once because this approach introduces too much risk. Evolutionary architectures do not have the same problem.

Evolutionary architectures are designed with the expectation that the system will change over time and remain open to this. The idea behind an evolutionary architecture is an execution plan for moving toward a target state architecture. *Building Evolutionary Architectures* by Neal Ford et al. is a fantastic guide to the concept.

> Evolutionary architecture is a journey, and you will learn things along the way. It's likely that your target state will shift as you learn more about technologies.

In 2016, Amazon Web Services published a "six R's" approach to cloud migration (*https://oreil.ly/K1yIT*). If you are considering migrating your existing Java applications to the cloud, this represents a set of possible approaches of how you can migrate.

The six R's are:

- Retain or Revisit
- Rehost
- Replatform

- Repurchase
- Refactor/Re-architect
- Retire

It is important to know that, in some cases, it's OK to do nothing, and *Retain or Revisit* accepts that a system is too difficult to move, or perhaps adds significant value in current form.

Thinking that you need to move and change everything at once is an antipattern when adopting cloud native technologies. Only move things that are going to make a tangible difference to either your business case or improve the nonfunctional requirements in your architecture.

Rehosting takes the same platform model that you have today and moves it into the cloud architecturally unchanged in what is sometimes caled a *lift-and-shift* approach. This might seem like a pointless exercise, but there is an advantage to starting to consolidate and colocate your applications in the cloud.

This is often an initial step in an overall migration and can be seen as a useful decision point—i.e., whether to fully buy into cloud providers or understanding that a *hybrid architecture* between cloud and traditionally managed data centers makes more sense. Hybrid means that you'll use the best of cloud native platforms, but also accept that you will own or retain your own servers as well.

Replatform is somewhat similar to rehosting but involves a sliding scale of rework to adjust to the cloud environment. This might mean tweaking a few things to be able to take advantage of a slightly different solution, such as elastic managed database servers (e.g., RDS in AWS) instead of self-managed databases. At the upper end, replatforming can involve very significant changes to the application architecture and potentially overlaps with rearchitecting.

Repurchasing involves using an off-the-shelf SaaS product instead of something that you previously owned or operated.

Refactor/Re-architect is the most interesting from a technical perspective, as it provides the opportunity for adapting our software to make full use of platforms like Kubernetes.

Retiring is exactly as it sounds. Migrating might mean that some components are no longer required and can be decommissioned.

To support a migration to cloud, you will need different techniques to take advantage of new features in a controlled manner. In particular, a code-level construct is needed to provide migration at a granular level. *Feature flags* are a code-level check that use an external store of flags that can be configured to manipulate the flow of a running system, based on some condition.

This is a huge subject, and one that we will not be able to cover fully, but let's look at an example using pseudo-code from the popular Java feature-flagging tool LaunchDarkly (*https://launchdarkly.com*).

In the following code example, we are performing a user-based switch on features to decide whether the new mammal service is used or an internal library is providing the functionality. The feature flag "user.enabled.mammals" is checked and will default to false:

```
LDUser user = new LDUser("authors");
boolean mammalService =
    launchDarklyClient.boolVariation("user.enabled.mammals", user, false);
if (mammalService) {
  // Retrieves the mammal from the modern environment
}
else {
  // Retrieves the mammal from the existing monolithic codebase
}
```

With this type of flagging in place, there is full flexibility to introduce and turn on/off new features as needed, effectively separating deployment and release for any application. Using feature flags in combination with canary releases and blue/green is a good approach to application migration.

Feature flags have to be highly available in an architecture, but a sensible default is a fallback in the case of failure.

Feature flags are also commonly used as a primary mechanism for rolling out deployments. For example, in the Fighting Animals example, you could decide to use feature flags only for rolling out new changes to end users. Feature flags are at the heart of many systems that are too large to consider blue/green. For many applications that run 24-7, they are one of the few comprehensive ways of releasing change without requiring a time-consuming rollback. You must clean up feature flags and carefully consider the naming of feature flags. Feature flags should have a defined lifetime and should not exist indefinitely in the codebase.

Knight Capital (*https://oreil.ly/ClYpp*) is an extreme example where reusing feature flags and not tidying up led to half a billion dollars of electronic trading losses within a few hours. It is worth setting a policy for the naming and usage of feature flags in a system.

Finding a balance between the deployment options used for a particular stack of architecture is an important balance. Ensuring that things are not too complex, deployments are pushed quickly, and features are enabled as required in the target state.

Java-Specific Concerns

In this section, we will address some common concerns that are specific to Java deployments that applications delivered in other languages may not face. We have seen situations in production where using containers has gone wrong for a number of reasons. Let's explore some of these problems and what you should consider upfront to avoid this in your project.

Containers and GC

Both of the authors have seen situations where configurations have been set to force the JVM into a corner.

Research from Relic (*https://oreil.ly/7QqSdNew*) shows that 70%+ of Java applications are now deployed in containerized environments.[1]

By itself, this is not an issue—until we look at the distribution of CPUs commonly used in these containers. Roughly half of these containers are configured such that they appear to have only a single CPU. This is a problem because, as we discussed in "Java Implementations, Distributions, and Releases" on page 68, on startup the JVM dynamically sets some properties of the VM that control runtime behavior—including the GC configuration.

Recall that the default G1 collector is partially concurrent—but to run a concurrent collector, it needs multiple CPUs. On a single-CPU machine (which is what a single-core container presents as), the JVM ergonomics will detect that G1 cannot function effectively, so the Serial and SerialOld collectors will be selected instead.

For example, setting CPU: 1 constrains the runtime environment to have access to only one CPU. On the surface, this may seem like a reasonable idea; however, as we discussed in Chapter 5, modern garbage collectors are concurrent. The practical effect (*https://oreil.ly/PhDmJ*) of this constraint will mean that the JVM has to run GC as a serial operation, creating larger pause times, more application interruption, and lowered throughput.

As a performance engineer, you should be aware of this effect and ensure that you deploy into single-core containers only if you are absolutely sure that there is benefit

---

1 This is not a perfect view of the market as a whole but is based on data from tens of millions of production JVMs.

in doing so. Research by companies such as Red Hat and Microsoft indicates that for many workloads, large clusters of single-core containers are significantly less effective than smaller clusters with more CPUs per container.

In other words—it is very possible that deploying many single-core containers is wasteful, both in resources and money spent on cloud infrastructure. Therefore, the default assumption, in the absence of any other evidence, is that Java applications should be deployed in containers with two (or more) cores.

Memory challenges have caused significant issues with Java applications adopting containers—let's explore some of the effects for early adopters and developers not using the latest versions of the JVM.

Memory and OOMEs

The first issue is that older versions of the JVM historically did not observe the cgroups hints (as older versions of Java predate the development of the cgroups technology) and instead looked at the overall host machine details. What this means is that a JVM might try to use more memory than it actually has available, which would cause the operating system to kill the application. This is a major issue, because violating a cgroup limit means potential process termination, as the kernel does not fully enforce isolation using cgroups.

The cgroups functionality was backported to Java 8, but if you are using containers, you should use an up-to-date version of the JVM, as further optimizations have been added. For example, two major additions in Java 17 (*https://oreil.ly/NERCB*) are cgroups v2 support and container awareness in OperatingSystemMxBean.

> If you run an older JVM on a machine that only supports cgroups v2, you will find yourself in a situation where the JVM is looking at host-level details rather than the container constraints.

In general, it is always worth running with the latest LTS JVM where possible (ideally 17 or 21), especially in a containerized environment. Not only are there performance improvements with each LTS version of Java but running on anything less than Java 11 could also have unusual impacts on your application on certain hardware that may not be visible in local development.

The second issue is the configuration and settings between the container and the JVM. For example, if you allocate a quota of 1 GB to a container, the JVM maximum heapsize will auto-configure to 256 MB. You need to ensure that you leave space for container internals or other processes running, but this is likely going to result in an under-utilization.

Overriding the maximum heapsize -Xmx and running a performance test is a good practice to ensure maximum utilization. An alternative is setting the -XX:MaxRam option, which declares the physical RAM available to a process, enabling the JVM to decide how to size the heap. In addition to considering the heap sizing, it's important to consider the sizing of the stack and any direct memory or off-heap allocation in your application.

The reality is that you now have a series of options to configure, constrain, and tune. There are JVM configuration options and the runtime configuration options for the orchestration layer. The configuration options cannot always be considered or tested in isolation. It is possible to run with no constraints, and in a lift-and-shift,[2] this can be a good starting point. It is unlikely that you will want this to be the target state, as this likely will not address performance and resiliency objectives.

Summary

In this chapter, we have scratched the surface of a complicated shift toward a closer relationship between development and deployment of Java applications. You have learned about tools and approaches for working locally with containers and how to create lightweight DNS entries using Docker Compose.

We have reviewed a starting point for working with Kubernetes and some key concepts for the lifecycle of Pods and containers, including some common gotchas. We have explored by example how tools like Argo CD help with the automation of releases. Finally, we have looked at approaches for separating the concept of deployment and release using blue/green, canary, and feature flags for evolutionary architecture.

Using this tooling alone without a good way to manage services in production would be very challenging. In the next chapter, we will explore observability, which should be considered mandatory for the deployment options we have shared in this chapter.

---

2 Migrating an existing architecture to another platform with minimal changes.

## CHAPTER 10

Introduction to Observability

The topic of observability has come more and more to the forefront of software development in recent years.

> Observability is making the transition from being a niche concern to becoming a new frontier for user experience, systems, and service management in web companies and enterprises alike.
>
> —James Governor (*https://oreil.ly/Ybqvd*)

But why should Java developers care about observability? And what the hell is observability anyway?

In this chapter, we will explore the concepts and fundamentals of observability, and in Chapter 11, we will see how these techniques can be deployed in Java applications using open source libraries and technologies.

The What and the Why of Observability

Observability has a reputation, among some developers, of being vague and difficult to understand. This is, in our view, unwarranted—observability is conceptually simple and should be easy to explain. Observability tools are fundamentally a continuation, extension, and generalization of classic monitoring systems to provide capabilities that go beyond traditional monitoring techniques.

To help illustrate the concepts of observability, we will use the Fighting Animals example introduced in Chapter 8.

What Is Observability?

The steps involved in an observability solution are essentially:

1. Instrument production systems and applications to collect observability data.
2. Send this data to an external system that can store it.
3. Provide analysis tools that allow the extraction of insights into system behavior for DevOps, SREs, management, and so on.

It is essential that observability data is sent out of the production system and into an entirely separate observability system that is running on another cluster (which should be on physically separate hardware). This can be seen in Figure 10-1 for the Fighting Animals example.

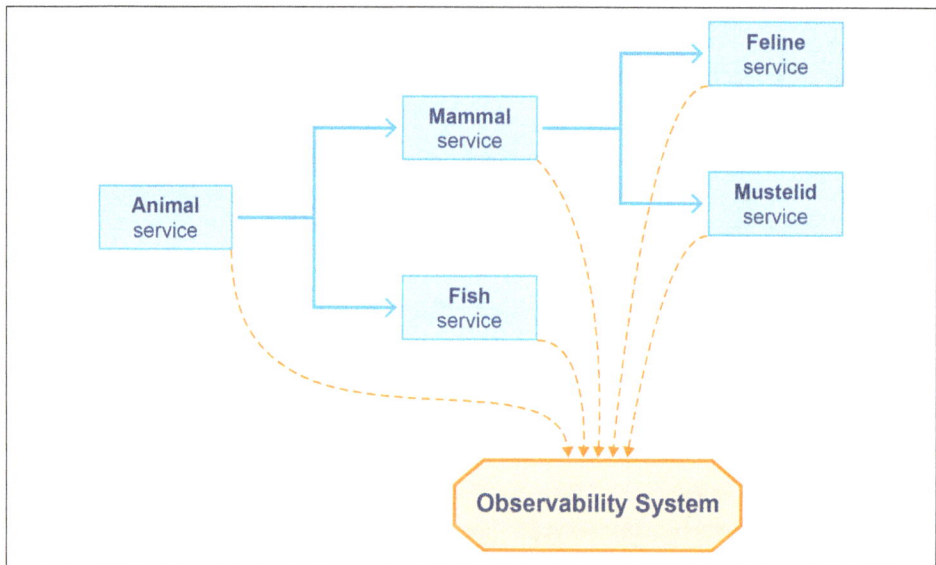

Figure 10-1. Sending observability data to a separate system

The reason for this is hopefully obvious, but to avoid doubt—observability data is used to solve runtime issues and outages. If the data needed to solve the outage is in the same system that is experiencing the outage, it may not be possible to use that data to resolve the outage.

Second, and for the same reason, the observability system must not be upgraded at the same time as the production system under observation.

Third, another extremely important aspect of observability solutions is the need for the analysis tools to be very flexible.

> Observability requires that you not have to predefine the questions you will need to ask, or optimize those questions in advance.
>
> —Charity Majors (*https://oreil.ly/stu61*)

An outage analysis based on observability data is exploratory and has aspects that resemble hypothesis testing in data or physical sciences. This means that some sort of graphical representation (including a graph plotter) and a query tool are common user interfaces for observability tools.

Finally, good observability data should provide actionable insights from the entire system, not just single aspects or facets, and this requires separate systems, services, and signal types to be correlated or linked in context. This is especially true for larger systems where the volume of observability data can be overwhelming.

Why Observability?

Three threads led to the practice of observability.

First and one of the most important is derived from system control theory, and specifically the question: "How well can the internal state of a system be inferred from outside?" This question naturally arises in incident resolution, but it also has wider utility.

> One way that observability differs from monitoring is that due to the complexity of modern apps, you can't really monitor the health of the application without knowledge of the application's internals. This means adopting some sort of DevOps approach and getting rid of the mentality that "monitoring is the ops team's responsibility and devs shouldn't need to care."

A second thread is the recognition that "cloud is different." Modern applications often use approaches such as immutable infrastructure as part of the deployment landscape. For example, a container containing the application is built by a continuous deployment system and pushed out to, say, a Kubernetes cluster.

The architectural differences in systems like Kubernetes, as compared to traditional systems, require a new operational approach. These deployments are not intended to be upgraded or to be particularly long-lived. Instead, if there are problems with it, it will be either reverted to a known-good version or rolled forward to a new candidate build.

This immutability of configuration does not work well with traditional system operation, such as SSH'ing into systems to perform interactive debugging and exploration. Observability is intended to deal with this change in emphasis (and scale) of operational practice.

A third and final thread that led to observability is application performance monitoring (APM). This area had originally been dominated by proprietary technology firms such as New Relic, Dynatrace, AppDynamics, etc.

In recent years, new entrants with a more open source approach have appeared, including Datadog and Honeycomb. The overall effect has been that the existing APM vendors have become more general observability-focused tools and have adopted more open source components as they do so.

The Three Pillars

The *three pillars* are a simple model to explain the primary data sources used in observability analysis. They are represented graphically in Figure 10-2.

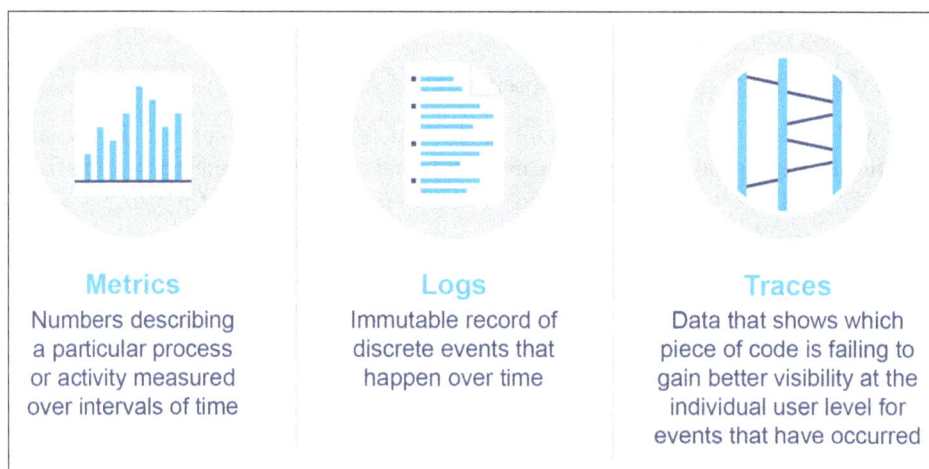

| **Metrics** | **Logs** | **Traces** |
| Numbers describing a particular process or activity measured over intervals of time | Immutable record of discrete events that happen over time | Data that shows which piece of code is failing to gain better visibility at the individual user level for events that have occurred |

Figure 10-2. The three pillars

The pillars refer to data sources that differ in fundamental aspects of shape and form:

- Metrics
- Logs
- Traces

Let's discuss the three pillars in that order.

Metrics

Many Java developers are already familiar with metrics, at least intuitively, but let's be specific about what we mean by a *metric*. Metrics are numbers that measure specific activity over a regular time interval. This means that metrics are often *counters* or *gauges*, and they represent aggregation of a set of data values into a time series.

In this aggregation, the precise detail of every distinct event is lost, but the resulting signal is much more compact, particularly for dashboards/alerts.

> Metrics can often be used as the starting point of an investigation. Logs and traces can then provide the detailed context that helps you piece together what happened.

There are typically four parts to a metric:

- Timestamp
- Name
- Value
- Dimensions (if any)

These should be fairly self-explanatory, except for possibly the last item—the *dimensions* of the metric.

Dimensions represent different values of some attribute (aka tag), which are recorded as a key/value pair. Crucially, to be suitable for use as a dimension, the metric values must allow for aggregation across dimensions.

As an example, the system and user percentages of CPU utilization can be sensibly aggregated—by adding them together to yield the total CPU utilization. We could represent the metric like this similarly to the common Prometheus format we'll meet later on:

```
cpu_memory_usage{type="system",} 0.12
cpu_memory_usage{type="user",} 0.66
```

This is a well-defined dimensional metric: it's named `cpu_memory_usage` and has a single dimension (`type`) with only two possible values—`system` and `user`—and the two values for the metric (`0.12` and `0.66`) can be sensibly aggregated into a total value.

On the other hand, the temperatures of separate rooms in your house, say kitchen and bedroom, do not have a particularly useful aggregate. Adding them together makes no sense, and the average is at best marginally useful. In this case, the temperatures are best represented using separate names, rather than dimensions.

Dimensions are also expected to be relatively *low cardinality*—which means there are only a small number of possible values for the dimension.

Additionally, in practice, metrics may well have multiple dimensions, and thus, the true max cardinality of the metric is the product of the sizes of the value set for each separate dimension. This can impact both query performance and storage volumes—

which, in turn, can raise the cost of implementing observability. It is also possible to experience problems visualizing and interpreting high-cardinality metrics. However, the actual observed cardinality may be less, since—in practice—some of the possible combinations may not occur.

> It's difficult to be precise about what constitutes too much cardinality for a dimension, but at one extreme, if your system has a million distinct users, then the user_id is not going to be a suitable choice for a dimension.

Once metrics are generated, they need to be exported to a storage and analytics system, just as for the other observability data types.

A simple but typical metrics observability installation can be seen in Figure 10-3.

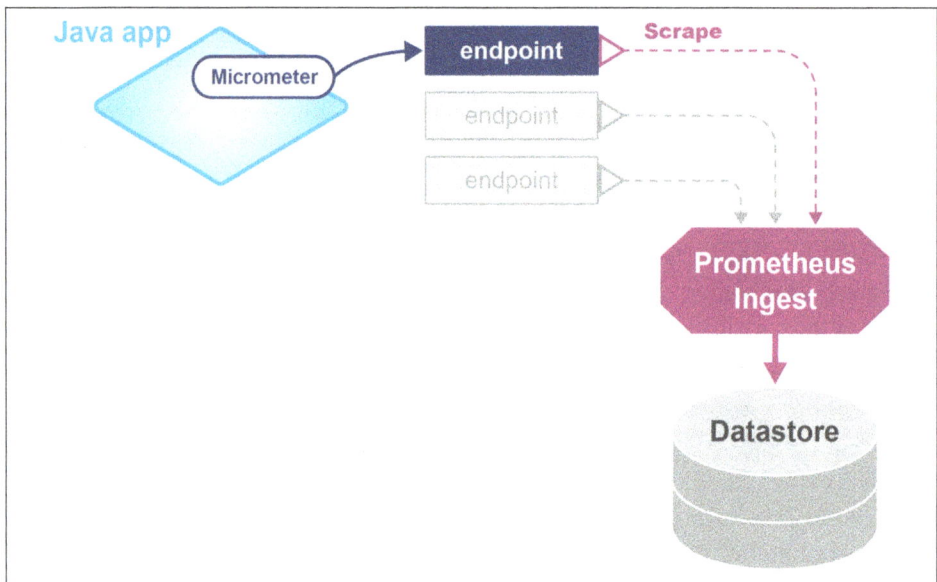

Figure 10-3. Example of metrics observability

As we discussed briefly in Chapter 8, Prometheus is one of the key technologies in the metrics space. In particular, it is probably the most common metrics storage system. We will have a bit more to say about it in the next chapter, but a full discussion of all of its aspects is outside the scope of this book—please consult the product documentation.

Finally, remember that metrics are time series data, i.e., they are reported at a fixed period. The JVM does produce data—for example, garbage collection—which is event-based and does *not* occur at a regular time cadence. These events are not amenable to standard time series analysis, as the technique normally assumes fixed-rate. Therefore, caution is required when using them as metrics—there are subtleties involved in the data handling.

For example, in the case of GC, to produce metrics, we must aggregate events over a fixed window. These metrics can be useful (especially when represented as histograms), but it's important to remember that information has already been lost compared to the underlying events.

Let's move on to look at the second pillar, logs, which is also likely to be familiar to Java developers.

Logs

Java development has had—and continues to have—a rich tradition of logs and log handling. Many, perhaps even most, Java teams are used to standard logging frameworks (SLF4J, Log4j, etc.).

The use of a logging facade pattern is very common, and to Java developers it's "just a logging API." In this model, the log configuration defines a suitable log exporter (which may be a file writer, a network logger, or something more elaborate, such as an exporter that sends to JDBC). The developer is agnostic to *how* the logs are handled, as the API is the same regardless of the plumbing, as this code example shows:

```
// SLF4J Code Example from logging_only branch
@RestController
public class AnimalController {
  private static Logger LOGGER = LoggerFactory.getLogger(AnimalController.class);

  // ...

  private String fetchRandomAnimal() throws IOException, InterruptedException {
    var pause = (int) (SERVICES.size() * Math.random());
    LOGGER.info("Pausing for: "+ pause);

    // ...
  }
}
```

But what actually is a log? Log entries are best thought of as records of discrete events that happen at a specific point in time. They are usually understood to be immutable after creation.

Examples include system and server logs (e.g., syslog), firewall or network system logs as well as the developer-focused platform and application logs. This type of log is unstructured text and usually has a severity associated with the log event.

The encoding of the log is often plain text, but there's no reason why it couldn't be binary—we consider this an implementation detail.

Logs have the characteristic that they are human-readable text. This brings useful abilities, such as being able to grep for keywords/phrases/regexes as well as graphing counts of specific messages over time.

In addition, log severity provides an easy verbosity control for how much data we want to look at. They can also be helpful as the data source for an audit tool or trail for forensic-style playback, although this depends upon proper design and architecting of the log system, as we will see later in this chapter.

> There is also the possibility of an *event*, which is a structured, immutable record of a discrete event that does not have a severity (but may have a name describing the class of the event). These are often represented in JSON format to provide a defined structure, and some practitioners refer to them as *structured logs*.

In a typical observability logging pattern, we aggregate logs from individual microservices to a single location over the network. This provides a single, unified dataset of logs that is searchable, filterable, and groupable. However, it is important to note that this is a *centralized* logging pattern—the logs are all in one place, even though they have come from different processes of a distributed system.

Note that aggregating logs from different sources requires us to have some consistency in how we log across those services.

By contrast, true *distributed logging* is much less common and much more technically complex. It is usually only seen when some aspect or constraint of the system prevents centralized logging from being possible—for example, contention with application processes for network or sheer excessive volume of logs that cannot be reduced. This is an edge case, and not one that most app developers will ever find themselves needing to address. Accordingly, we do not discuss distributed logging any further in this book.

When deploying a centralized logging solution as part of observability, there are a wide variety of open source and vendor tools to choose from. One commonly encountered term is the *ELK stack*. This is an acronym that describes a stack comprised of three popular projects:

Logstash
    Data processing pipeline for data ingestion (from multiple sources) and transform

Elasticsearch
    Data storage for search and analytics

Kibana
GUI component and KQL query language

When deployed, the ELK stack can look similar to the architecture shown in Figure 10-4.

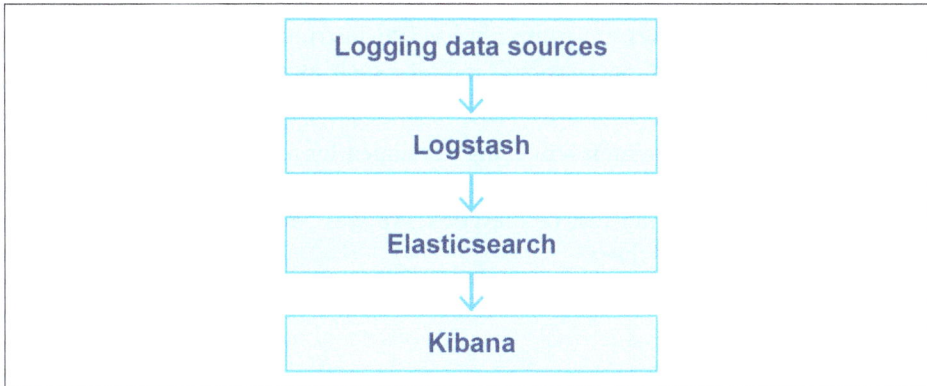

Figure 10-4. Example ELK stack

Running and maintaining an ELK stack can become expensive—not least due to the infrastructure costs involved in hosting it on one of the major cloud platforms. Various companies offer hosted versions of the ELK stack.

In general, DevOps staff are much more likely to be users of an ELK stack through a UI (whether self-hosted or from a vendor), rather than needing detailed knowledge of how to set it up and maintain it.

To complete the pillars, we also need to discuss traces—a subject that Java developers may not be as familiar with.

Traces

A *distributed trace* is a record of a single, top-level service invocation. In the normal case, this corresponds to a single request from an individual user, e.g., triggered by user activity. The trace includes the following metadata about each request:

- Which instance was called
- Which container each subrequest ran on
- Which method was invoked
- How the request performed
- Whether the request was successful or errored
- Optional additional custom metadata to enhance search and retrieval

In distributed architectures, which is the primary case we consider in this book, a single top-level service invocation typically triggers other actions that contribute to the overall trace. These actions are referred to as *spans* and can consist of, for example, a call to a method or a call to a remote service. Each span has the same type of associated metadata as the overall trace, so a trace forms a tree structure of spans.

Note that distributed traces are primarily used to instrument service calls that are request-response oriented, such as HTTP. Calls, such as asynchronous messaging, where there is no response, have additional difficulties associated with them.

In general, distributed tracing is still being developed for asynchronous messaging-- but it is actively being worked on by a number of interested parties. As the async story is still in flux, for the rest of the book, we will consider only synchronous, request-response-oriented flows.

An example span might look like this:

```
{
  "name": "/v1/app/foo",
  "context": {
    "trace_id": "kDMI7LTxLxTj220awNARJw==",
    "span_id": "9ir6veJ4Hdw="
  },
  "parent_id": "",
  "kind": 1,
  "start_time": "2021-10-22 16:04:01.209458162 +0000 UTC",
  "end_time": "2021-10-22 16:04:01.209514132 +0000 UTC",
  "status_code": "STATUS_CODE_OK",
  "status_message": "",
  "attributes": {
    "key": "attr",
    "string.value": "value2"
    // ... HTTP and transport details ommitted
  },
  "events": [
    {
      "name": "",
      "message": "OK",
      "timestamp": "2021-10-22 16:04:01.209512872 +0000 UTC"
    }
  ]
}
```

Note the trace_id, span_id, and parent_id—these three fields will be used to connect the different spans and reconstruct the distributed trace, as you will see. In our example, this is a root span, because there is no parent_id.

The span perspective corresponds to what is known as the *extrinsic view* of service calls in traditional monitoring. The parts of a single user call (the spans, in other words) are collected into a trace, which can be visualized as a *traceview*. This is a representation of how the tree of spans was generated.

You can see an example in Figure 10-5, which uses the Fighting Animals example again, and is visualized in the Jaeger UI.

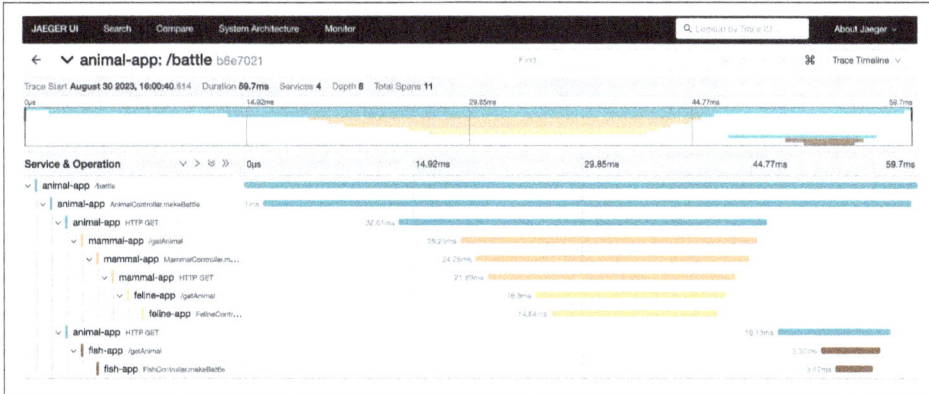

Figure 10-5. Example traceview

To implement distributed tracing, a team needs to consider several aspects of their architecture. The most important are:

- Instrumentation of application, middleware, and other components
- Propagation of trace context between services
- Trace data ingest and storage
- Search and retrieval of traces of interest
- Trace visualization

This can be done using either vendor tools (such as Datadog, New Relic, Dynatrace, Honeycomb, etc.) or by deploying a combination of open source tools. Some of the most common tools and projects used in open source tracing are OpenTelemetry, Jaeger, and Grafana Tempo. The tools provide different roles and are often combined to produce an overall solution.

For example, in Figure 10-6, you can see OpenTelemetry being used for instrumentation, trace context propagation, and data transport (aka *export* or *exfiltration*) to the observability system. Data storage is provided by Tempo and visualization by Jaeger.

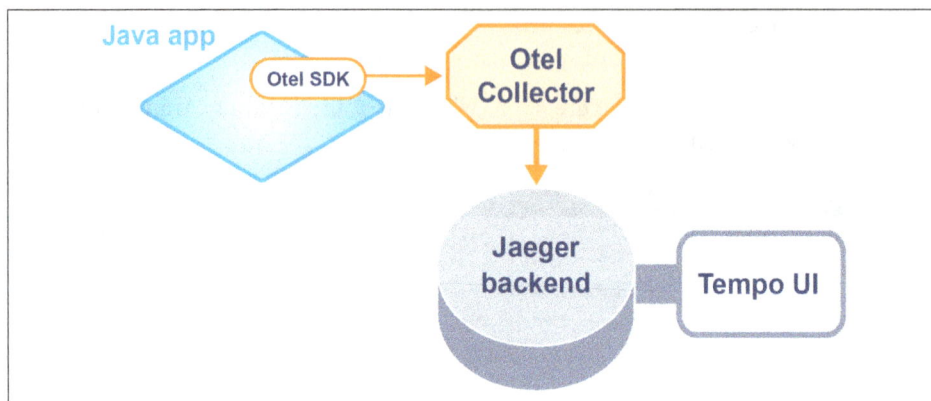

Figure 10-6. Example of distributed tracing observability

The context propagation part is handled by the three fields: `trace_id`, `span_id`, and `parent_id`. These values must be passed from microservice to microservice, and at first glance, it is difficult to see how this can be achieved, given that the services may be in different JVMs or physically separate hosts.

In practice, the values for these fields are carried in additional HTTP headers, as per the W3C Trace Context format (*https://oreil.ly/wDEUp*), which is a W3C Recommendation as of March 2024. These headers can either be handled manually by application code or via automatic instrumentation and injection. We will see examples of both (for the case of OpenTelemetry traces) in the next chapter.

In fact, visualization of traces is usually the hard part—the traceview is the usual form (e.g., Jaeger). However, this is often too low level and difficult to correlate with a larger overall picture of the system. At time of writing (August 2024), it very much seems as though some new forms of trace visualization are badly needed—especially as systems become more complex over time.

Finally, what about data sampling? Distributed tracing can produce very large volumes of data. Different sampling policies can be used to rationalize the data volumes arising from traces.

In practice, the overwhelming majority of traces will be for requests that return a success code (if not, then you have other problems), and it is not really necessary to handle the entirety of the dataset arising from successes.

> The W3C specification also defines the `trace-flags` field, which controls tracing flags such as sampling, trace level, etc. as recommendations from the caller to downstream services.

The intent of sampling is to preserve the statistical properties of the dataset. This is important because, for example, any changes in the distribution of response times due to a code change need to be observable.

As an example, the default sampler policy in OpenTelemetry is the "ParentBased Always On" sampler. This policy is: if there is no parent span, sample this span. If there is a parent, sample according to whether the parent was sampled. This essentially delegates the sampling decision to the origin point of the trace.

This has the benefit of simplicity, but has the problem that when the sampling decision is made, the sampler can't know whether the trace will succeed or have errors.

> Traces containing failure codes—whether client or server side, i.e., 4XX or 5YY in terms of HTTP—are typically more interesting than successes and ideally should always be collected unsampled, but this requires *tail-based sampling*, which remains challenging.

The sampling approach also explains why both `trace_id` and `parent_span_id` are propagated.

The Pillars as Data Sources

The three pillars approach essentially requires us to treat the signals from each pillar as separate data sources when they're generated. This is largely because the data sent from each pillar is structured very differently:

- Metrics are four fixed fields (with the dimensional field being a set of key-value pairs) that represent events aggregated over a regularly cadenced time period.
- Logs are unstructured text with a severity (and events are structured data with no severity) that occurred at a specific point in time (i.e., a Java `Instant`).
- Traces are made up of spans, which are defined, structured metadata that occurred over a duration (which can vary from trace to trace).

The data volumes produced also differ wildly from each other:

- Metric volumes don't grow with request traffic, as they are produced at fixed time intervals regardless of how many requests have been received.[1]

---

1 There are some subtleties here around exactly what happens when the mix of incoming requests includes many different dimension values.

- Log volumes do not have a simple relationship to request rates. In a system with poor logging discipline (whether in normal operation or when experiencing a lot of errors), the growth can be super-linear.

- Trace volumes are linearly related to request traffic. This remains more or less true when sampling traces.

These differences have caused open source projects that process observability data to tend to focus on only a single pillar. This siloing of projects has consequences for organizations that want to deploy integrated OSS observability.[2]

The real power of observability is bringing all this data together—the ideal is to be able to correlate across the different data types, not just collect and analyze each individually. Providing correlation between the signals is an active area of development in the open source tools, but at the time of writing (August 2024) this is not yet a solved problem.

Finally, it is worth noting that not every observability practitioner agrees with the three pillars as a basic model. In this book, we have chosen it as our primary approach for two reasons:

- Newcomers are likely to be familiar with the basic data types and the concepts that follow from them.

- The data types as discussed are, as we have seen, fundamentally different from each other.

Other approaches do exist, and you may well encounter them as you progress on their observability journey. As ever, our intent is to offer a starting point and encourage you to explore beyond.

Profiling—A Fourth Pillar?

In addition to the three standard pillars, there is a growing interest in seeing application profiling as a fourth data type and pillar. There are significant differences between profiling data and the other observability data types, though.

Implementing general, large-scale profiling also involves technical challenges. This is largely because profiling (whether of CPU or memory) can have significant overhead. For this reason, two separate approaches have evolved:

On-demand profiling
    Activated only when necessary, provides richer dataset

---

2 One of the selling points of vendor solutions is this type of correlation.

Continuous profiling
Always on, so overhead is reduced as much as possible

There are tradeoffs to both approaches. For example, continuous profiling will usually have lower overhead (because it has to), but it will also have lower data resolution—so it may be harder to spot problems in the collected data.

On the other hand, for on-demand profiling, something (either a human operator or a monitoring agent) needs to be able to turn profiling on and off again. This not only implies a control plane, but it also requires someone/something to notice that there is a problem in the first place.

It also means that it's hard (or impossible) to use for predictive problem analysis—i.e., being able to see an outage coming.

Profiling is the subject of Chapter 12, and we will have more to say about it there.

Observability Architecture Patterns and Antipatterns

We have already discussed the logging facade as a key pattern within observability. In this section, we will discuss some other patterns, especially in the area of metrics. We will finish by looking at a couple of antipatterns that teams should aim to avoid.

Architectural Patterns for Metrics

Metrics is a well-established aspect of observability for Java applications, and as a result, a number of different architectural styles have emerged to support it.

We have already met the concept of dimensionality, but not all metrics systems support dimensions. The key question we need to ask is: "Does the consumer support key/value annotation of the measurement?"

If yes, then the metric library being used is dimensional. If not, the alternative is to combine the information that is carried in the dimension into the metric name as suffixes to a base metric name.

For example, there are two primary conventions for metric naming:

Dotted
Used by OpenTelemetry Metrics and many vendor tools and libraries

Snake-cased names
Used primarily by Prometheus (but Prometheus also has dimensions, which it refers to as *metric labels*)

A dotted convention would look like this: `jvm.memory.used{area=heap,id=G1 Eden Space}` whereas the same metric in a nondimensional suffixed naming convention could look like this: `jvm_memory_used_heap_G1_Eden_Space`.

A second aspect of the architecture of metrics systems is *aggregation discipline*. This term refers to where the computation to aggregate metrics is performed:

Client-side
Discrete samples processed (e.g., converted to a rate) before being published out of the application

Server-side
Aggregation occurs at the observability server

In this respect, Prometheus also differs from the alternatives—it prefers to aggregate server-side, whereas most other metrics technologies use client-side aggregation.

This issue once again represents a tradeoff: sending every measurement over the network can be expensive, but so can the additional resources required for client-side temporary storage and math.

Finally, let's consider the question of how metrics should be delivered to the observability system. Two fundamentally different approaches are:

Server poll
The observability system collects metrics from the application.

Client push
The application being observed actively sends metrics to the observability system.

Of these, Prometheus uses server poll, which it refers to as *scraping*. This means that every service you wish to monitor using Prometheus must provide a Prometheus metrics endpoint available over HTTP. Prometheus also relies on services being known or discoverable, which presents challenges for short-lived jobs and for systems that can't (or don't want to) expose a metrics endpoint for security reasons.

To handle this, and also to integrate better with technologies like OpenTelemetry, Prometheus also ships a *remote-write* option, but it is not always deployed by teams.

We will discuss this in more detail in Chapter 11.

Manual Versus Automatic Instrumentation

Manual instrumentation involves making changes to application code to add in explicit calls to a telemetry library.

In the case of tracing, this provides full control over when traces and spans are created and finalized. However, it has two major downsides:

- It enforces direct coupling to observability libraries (at least an API).
- There is significant potential for human error—it assumes that the developer already knows what needs to be traced.

The second point is much more significant than many developers realize.

One of the key aspects of observability is that it must enable you to "find answers to questions you didn't know you had at the start." If you don't know what the questions are going to be, then how can you be sure that you have manually instrumented the subset of call paths that will allow you to ask those questions?

In other words, manual instrumentation of traces runs a very real risk of introducing observability blind spots into your application. This can be hugely harmful, as they can and will give a false impression of where the problems are.

Logging (e.g., SLF4J or Log4j) is almost always done manually, by explicitly including calls to a logging facade. This can lead to cases where necessary log events are missing or are being generated at the wrong severity level. However, compared to missing trace information, this is a minor annoyance, and teams are used to adding additional logging or changing severities in response to an incident.

Therefore, due to the inherent complexity, many teams prefer *automatic instrumentation* for tracing. This is provided either by using a Java agent or the built-in support provided by the framework your application is written in.

In the case of agents, the technique depends upon bytecode weaving. As noted in "Summary" on page 74, installing a Java agent allows the tooling component to modify the bytecode of any class loaded during the application's run. This allows the agent to automate the insertion of what can otherwise be rather tedious boilerplate code.

An OpenTelemetry example can be seen in "Manual Tracing" on page 292, if you want to read ahead.

Just as we discussed for garbage collection, a correct automatic system is not subject to human fallibility. However, the agent approach may still require some config (i.e., so it doesn't instrument absolutely everything). In addition, there may be possible startup time impact and runtime performance penalties—at least under some circumstances.

Some of the leading Java frameworks also ship with automatic tracing support—for example, Quarkus can switch on OpenTelemetry just by adding the Maven dependency:

```
<dependency>
    <groupId>io.quarkus</groupId>
    <artifactId>quarkus-opentelemetry</artifactId>
</dependency>
```

There are no mandatory configuration parameters for the extension to work—by default, it will try to send traces to port 4317 on `localhost` using OTLP over GRPC.[3]

To complete the picture, metrics typically combine aspects of both manual and automatic instrumentation. Developers can set up their own metrics for the items of interest that are specific to the application, and these are coded manually. These metrics can then be augmented with automatically generated metrics that are produced by libraries (or by the JVM itself). We will have more to say about this hybrid approach in Chapter 11, when we discuss Micrometer.

Antipattern: Shoehorn Data into Metrics

Recall that metrics are counters, gauges, or histograms—they represent data collected and/or aggregated over a fixed time period. Data that does not fit into this conceptual view is not a suitable candidate for a metric.

This also applies to dimensions—if the values of a dimension can't be aggregated, then it's not a dimension, and the values must be treated as separate metrics.

Remember that a metric, by nature, is a compression of a distribution of events into a time series. Information about the shape of the distribution is inevitably, irretrievably lost whenever we do this.

For example, let's suppose we are interested in the number of 500 error codes from one of our services. They obviously arrive at different times, but if we bundle them into a metric `errors.per.hour`, then the scenarios where one request per minute fails, and 60 requests failed in the last 0.1 s of the hour look identical according to this metric.

> As a statistic, averages (including the arithmetic mean) have many practical uses. Properly understanding a distribution isn't one of them.
>
> —Brendan Gregg (*https://oreil.ly/Pct9Q*)

In particular, don't aggregate percentiles—it doesn't work. The reason is very simple—to compute a percentile, you need the original data (population).

Without this, you do not have the ability to determine when your averaged percentiles are lying to you. For example, when you have lots of outliers, they could make unhealthy systems appear healthy, and vice versa.

---

3 The default changed in upstream OpenTelemetry in early 2024 to be port 4318 using HTTPS/protobuf.

These faulty aggregations can result in incorrect analysis and poor technical/business decisions. It's not only that the aggregations lie—it's worse than that. They are lies clothed as truth. The humans will look at the pretty charts and take them as the true state of the system—when, in fact, they can be completely misleading.

Another critical point is not to try to collect absolutely everything—not everything matters. This antipattern is sometimes seen when a development team is collecting, for example:

- Very detailed runtime-specific numbers
- Metrics that are too coarse-grained (e.g., five-minute CPU average)

The first case can occur when the team is interested in a number that appears to be pertinent to some problem they are solving, and they forget that it is not interesting in the general case. This can happen when a dev team is trying to make a metrics system provide data that should be coming from another source—such as a tracing system or a profiler. For certain types of triage, metrics just aren't the answer, and adding them unnecessarily may detract from the overall usability and health of the observability platform.

The second case is information that may not be actionable—by the time you notice that the five-minute CPU average is much too high, your system is already in trouble, and Kubernetes may have already started killing Pods.

A good rule of thumb is, when considering adding a metric, always ask: "What issue can this metric help us debug?" If you can't answer that question, then you probably don't need the metric. It's also worth checking whether the proposed new metric can be directly derivable from existing metrics—if so, then perhaps it should be synthesized by the metrics observability backend instead.

Antipattern: Abusing Correlated Logs

This is an attempt to somehow avoid deploying a real distributed tracing solution by pushing request metadata into logs instead. It is often characterized as:

"If we have an ID that flows through logs, we can follow requests."

This seems to be true at first glance, but it only holds true provided that:

- All logging components are set up correctly (e.g., log level).
- The IDs are always created the same way.
- The IDs do not contain PII/other sensitive data.
- The logging system can keep up with 100% of log flow.

In particular, the ID field must not be just a base-64 encoded form of some PII data (an appalling state of affairs that one of the authors has actually seen).

Not only that, but to make the homebrew log-correlator work, you also have to be prepared to:

- Pay for 100% of log storage for as long as you need it.
- Pay for enough compute to crunch 100% of log flow.
- Create and maintain custom code and integrations for every component in the solution.

Antipatterns are, of course, frequently encountered bad solutions to common problems. However, sometimes things just go wrong, even if we built and operated our systems perfectly. Let's move on to look at that—an introduction to what happens when systems just break, and how to use observability to spot the problems.

Diagnosing Application Problems Using Observability

It is very important to understand the most common ways in which an application can break so you can see how you might be able to detect—and fix—these failures using observability tools. So, in this section, we will discuss some of the most common errors that your applications may encounter.

> It is much easier after the event to sort the relevant from the irrelevant signals. After the event, of course, a signal is always crystal clear. We can now see what disaster it was signaling since the disaster has occurred, but before the event it is obscure and pregnant with conflicting meanings.[4]
>
> —Roberta Wohlstetter

Throughout the section, we'll also document some of the failure modes of distributed systems. There are many others, so this section is intended to serve only as a primer.

Performance Regressions

One of the simplest issues that observability can help detect is a performance regression. Sometimes, a code (or config) change can have unexpected impacts on some aspect of performance. This can be low-level aspects such as CPU utilization, memory usage, or allocation rate, or higher-level numbers such as overall transaction latency.

An observability tool, with a query interface and a graphing component, makes it possible to see the impact of a change by looking at a suitable observable before and

---

4 Roberta Wohlstetter, *Pearl Harbor: Warning and Decision* (Stanford University Press, 1962).

after the change. This can be done either by comparing performance before and after, or by using one of the deployment techniques we met in Chapter 9.

An example of the second type can be seen in Figure 10-7, where we are using a canary deploy.

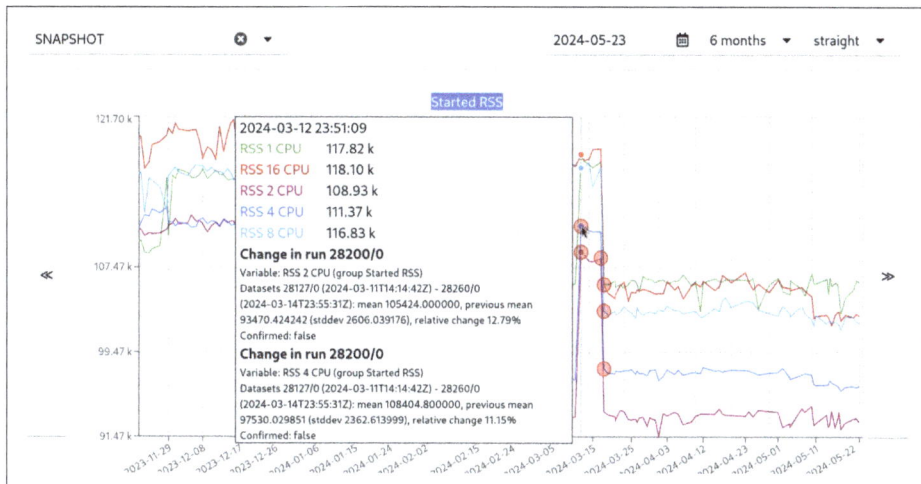

Figure 10-7. Seeing an outlier

Regressions are clear to see with these deployment techniques, because if the modified processes display a substantial divergence from the established baseline in performance behavior, then it should be visible in the relevant observable.

Faced with a straightforward regression like this, the team can decide to either accept the regression (if it's small enough) or to back out the change and do further analysis to modify the change to reduce the impact.

Ideally, the further analysis will take place in a development or testing sandbox. However, certain types of regression do not manifest cleanly outside of the production environment, and in this case, a fix-and-redeploy approach is necessary—which is a natural fit for a technique like canary deploys.

Setting service level objectives (SLOs) with an associated metric is a great way to validate throughout release and day-to-day operations that your system is performing as expected. Alerting or build failures can be set up in the situation where an SLO is no longer met, providing an opportunity to react and resolve the issue. Because performance is not an exact science, error budgets should be applied to set up a tolerance for a given metric. Considering using metrics as SLOs and applying error budgets fits into the SRE discipline and is extremely helpful in maintaining the desired performance of a system.

Unstable Components

Another common problem is a change introducing an instability to an application component. The easy cases of this, for example, when the entire component is destabilized, are often immediately apparent and can be backed out at once. However, it is quite common that the instability manifests only on certain code paths or for certain types of request. In this case, the change may be completely deployed to production before the component encounters code paths or requests that trigger the instability.

This type of issue is one example of the sort of problem that distributed traces can help solve. The detection methodology could involve comparing error rates of traces before and after a change, and looking at the error traces to see if there is a pattern, such as a particular URL or a particular service that is affected.

In this context, the service can be either one of our own services or some external dependency. It is helpful to have metrics for the error rate of these components, and this also demonstrates the exploratory nature of observability work. Digging into the problem can lead to investigating aspects of the system that were not obviously affected.

A compounding issue is that of *seasonality*. Many systems have code paths that are rarely exercised under normal circumstances, but that become over-represented at specific times (particular days of the week or quarter, or one-off special events). In this case, an instability can lie dormant—as the change that introduced it occurred at a time when the vulnerable code paths were not being called sufficiently often for the problem to manifest.

This means that when analyzing these types of problems, an observability engineer must ensure that they do not fall prey to *recency bias*—automatically assuming that the change that was just made is the cause, merely due to temporal proximity.

Repartitioning and "Split-Brain"

One classic problem in distributed systems is known as "split-brain": what happens when a cluster suffers a communication failure, such that certain members cannot reach all of the others?

In the worst case, the cluster can fracture into two or more pieces—with each fragment maintaining connectivity within itself but being disconnected from the others. As we will discuss in Chapter 14, when multiple nodes believe they are the Leader, this can lead to *network partition*—an example can be seen in Figure 10-8.

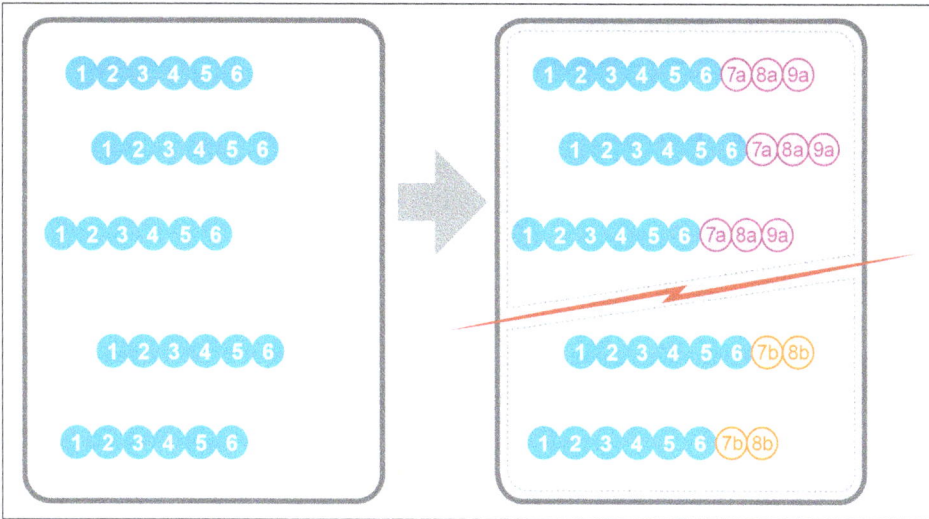

Figure 10-8. Split-brain

This is a significant problem for the observability engineer, as conflicting signals from the fragments can lead to incorrect inference. Even worse is the case where the fragments remain, broadly, in agreement in terms of the system observables.

Can we really tell the difference between a cohesive whole and two fragments that simply happen to be on similar trajectories for now? For this reason, we should ensure that cluster nodes report which node they consider their Leader, and alert if there is ever more than one Leader for a cluster.

> Network partitioning has been extensively studied, and various techniques for recovering from it, and ensuring data reconciliation, are known. We'll see some more details in "Basic Distributed Data Structures" on page 378.

Another related and important question is: if a cluster relies on partitioning techniques, then what happens if a node is lost?

Any system that does not keep multiple copies of the data partitions will lose data in the event of a hard failure (e.g., JVM crash or kernel panic). Therefore, realistic clustering solutions provide recovery and failover capabilities to prevent data loss. In the worst case, there should always be at least one backup of every piece of data, so the loss of a single member will never cause data loss.

However, even in this case, the partitions containing the data will need to be reassigned and balanced between the surviving nodes, as some partitions will now only have a single copy, and this must be corrected. This is referred to as a *repartitioning event*.

In many systems (e.g., Kafka), when a component is in repartitioning state, then no thread can read or process data. This effectively triggers a distributed stop-the-world event while the repartitioning event completes. These STW events are another signal that an observability engineer can, and should, look for and alert upon.

Thundering Herd

A *thundering herd* is a condition caused when some event triggers a large number of clients to make a request on a contented server resource. Typically only one (or a few) of these requests can be serviced (due to contention), which causes the majority of the requests to stall and possibly even time out.

This can often be caused by component restarts in the system—and it may be in a very different part of the system. Consider the restart of a database or database-like system; this results in closing all active connections. At the point of restart, a thundering herd of reconnects to the database results in increased response times, or worse, saturation that knocks over the resource.

Another way of thinking about thundering herds is by analogy with a highly contended Java synchronization lock—when all the threads are awoken, then only one can win the race to acquire the lock, and all others must block once again. The resource consumption caused by a thundering herd can be much more significant than just some unnecessary thread wakeups, however.

A common variation of this problem involves a cache—several readers attempt to read from the cache, fail, and therefore try to load it from the backing database. This causes huge, unnecessary database load, as each reading simultaneously executes the same (potentially expensive) query against the database.

Thundering herd events often show up as a sudden, unexpected burst of database or backend cache load, which is uncorrelated with incoming user requests, and this can be a useful signal to start from when diagnosing.

To help detect thundering herds, we can use metrics such as active connections. In particular, the derivative (rate of change) of that metric is a good way to detect the sudden ramp-up that corresponds to thundering herd.

In addition, a related popular mitigation strategy is to use a request queue to buffer incoming requests before sending them to the contended backend resource. If the request queue is some sort of `BoundedQueue`, then this technique forces senders to block, effectively throttling the number of requests, and applying *backpressure*.

Cascading Failure

In its simplest form, a *cascading failure* is when a single failing component of an application causes other subsystems to start to fail as a result of positive feedback.

For example, a single copy of a service can start to fail due to higher-than-usual load. This increases the number of in-flight requests, which increases load on the other copies in the cluster. In turn, this increases their failure probability, which can cause a *domino effect* that eventually takes down the entire service cluster, as can be seen in Figure 10-9.

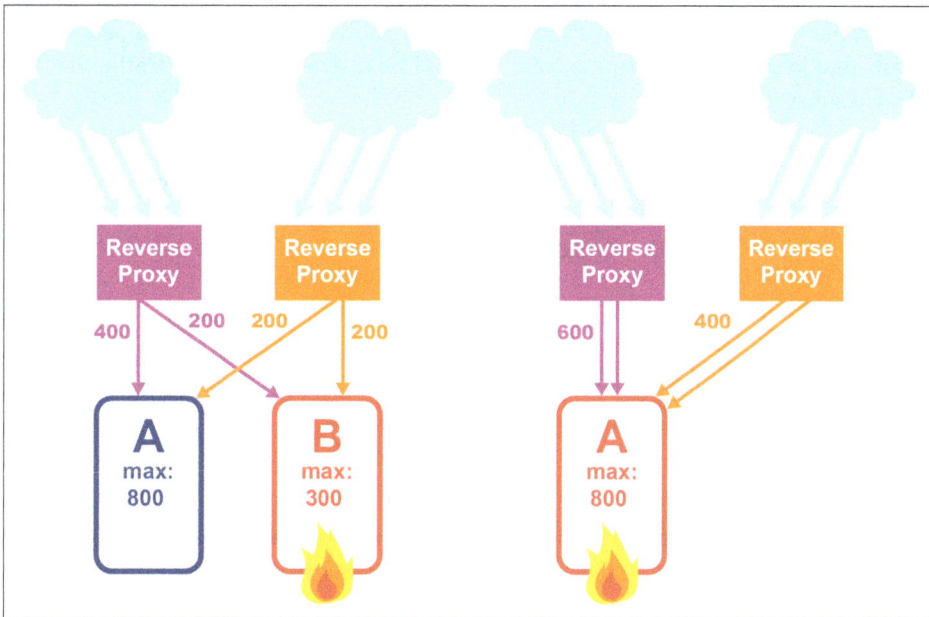

Figure 10-9. Cascading failure

The breakdown and reduction of useful work being done can spread beyond the initially impacted cluster and can potentially spread throughout the system.

For example, the system load balancer may respond to a crashed cluster by routing requests to other clusters. However, if the system is already close to its capacity limits, this can overload the servers in the new cluster, causing further contagion of the breakdown and ultimately leading to a service-wide failure.

The software version of this problem is named after a similar effect in cases such as high-voltage power systems. In that case, a single failure on a fully loaded system results in a sudden spike across all remaining nodes as the electricity is redistributed. This causes other nodes to go into overload and possibly also begin to fail, which makes the problem worse.

However, it is important to realize the limits of the metaphor and similar naming. In particular, physical power systems display two negative aspects that software does not have to deal with when handling a cascade.

Firstly, electrical systems can suffer permanent and irreversible damage if pushed to overload. Software may require some cooldown time, but that's about it—code does not permanently stop working if overloaded once.

Secondly, in electrical systems, the control signals—which would be needed to isolate or shut down other parts of the network to avoid damage—propagate at the same speed as the damaging load, so cannot outrun the cascade. In our case, a well-defined control plane will continue to function even if the data plane is swamped, which means that load balancers, routers, etc. can still be instructed to shed traffic to allow affected subsystems to recover.

This example illustrates just how essential it is that the control and observability infrastructure is distinct from the data plane. If observability fails, it becomes much more difficult (or outright impossible) to know what action to take in the control plane to limit and repair the cascading failure.

Compound Failures

In real outages, some of the failure modes just described can combine with each other to form new and interesting ways for an application to break.

For example, a component can become unstable due to increased downstream latency, which causes the upstream component's requests to sporadically time out.

This failure can be difficult to spot because it can manifest when nothing has changed in the upstream component. An even worse variant is when the only recent changes to upstream were cosmetic or unrelated and the important regression was introduced by a change to downstream (possibly made by a different team) but not immediately seen due to seasonality in the upstream component.

This is a good example of a problem that can be diagnosed with tracing (and that may be more difficult to spot with just metrics and logs), as the increased downstream latency can be correlated with the timeouts of the upstream component.

To take a second example, let's consider increased utilization causing extended processing time, causing request congestion leading to a long GC pause, which, in turn, causes healthchecks to begin to fail, so K8s recycles the Pod, which causes a Kafka repartition, which causes a cascading failure.

This sort of "perfect storm" failure can be difficult to work out, even with proper observability in place. In practice, an organization's observability practices will evolve over time—what to observe, what to alert on, and how to react to signals are as much a process as a fixed procedure.

Successful DevOps organizations will conduct retrospectives after these sorts of failures, during which the data collected and actions taken should be reviewed and critiqued. These should, of course, be seen as opportunities to improve observability and should be as blameless as possible.

Vendor or OSS Solution?

There are multiple different possible architectural approaches to deploying observability. Each has its own set of implications for both applications and observability components.

Broadly, the most common choices divide into an initial choice between build or buy—whether to maintain the capability in-house by deploying open source (or possibly on-premises proprietary) components or to pay money to a vendor, effectively outsourcing the observability function.

Organizations that choose to go the route of building their own capability (probably by combining existing open source components) will need to confront the simple fact that the three pillars represent very different data types with different shapes and behaviors. These differences make it very difficult to have a single software tool capable of processing and storing all of these data types—and in fact, there is, as yet, no credible single OSS project that covers all observability needs.

> The OpenTelemetry project, which we will discuss in Chapter 11, is the project that is closest to covering all aspects of observability, but its scope is limited to application instrumentation and signal exfiltration.

This means that organizations that want to use an open source stack that they will maintain in-house will need to make choices about the technologies they want to deploy (and support).

Broadly speaking, open source solutions fall into one of two options:

- Roll your own SaaS pipeline.
- Keep everything on cluster.

The first of these, building your own pipeline based on OSS components, is illustrated in Figure 10-10.

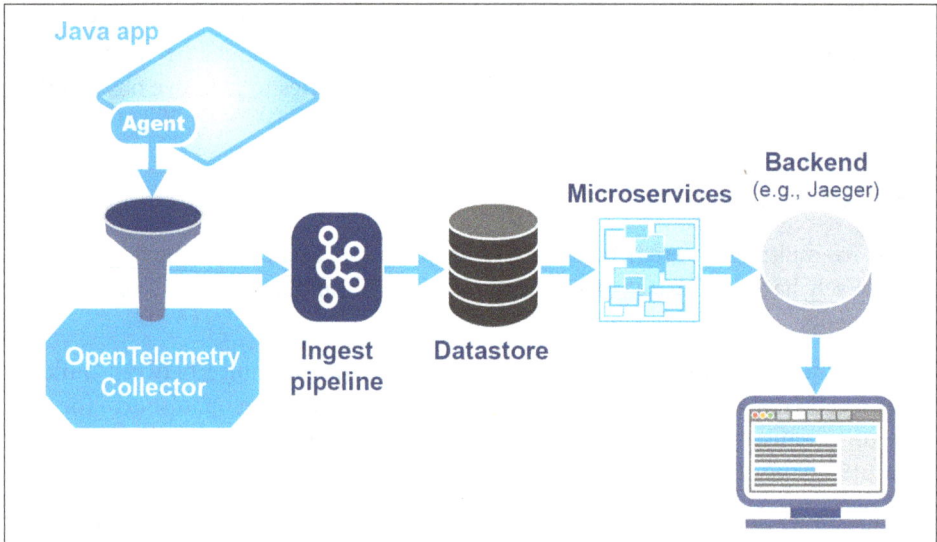

Figure 10-10. Example of an open source pipeline

The second alternative, keeping everything on a single cluster, is closely tied to orchestration techniques—predominantly K8s—and there are a number of different options, including solutions based on eBPF. They all share the drawback that they are single-cluster solutions and can make it harder to spot problems that span clusters.

Turning to the vendor solutions, commercial proprietary products may provide a more integrated experience, including components for which there is currently no viable OSS offering. Examples of vendor-specific components include:

- Alerting
- Serverless monitoring
- Synthetic monitoring
- Real user monitoring
- Outlier/anomaly detection
- Event correlation

Of these, the last is probably the one that most urgently needs to be addressed in the OSS approach, as it is used to tie signals from the three pillars together.

Different vendors offer different products, but two very common architectures for vendor solutions are:

- Aggregate observability data on app host and send aggregates to vendor SaaS
- Send all data to SaaS

The first option is the usual case, due to bandwidth and charging constraints (typically, vendors today use consumption-based pricing). However, some vendors also offer the second option, but this is often feasible only within a cloud region due to the costs of egress bandwidth charged by the hyperscaler cloud providers. Observability tools can produce a lot of data, so crossing region boundaries can result in large bandwidth bills.

Ultimately, each organization will have to make its own architectural decisions— especially the choice between OSS versus vendor. In larger companies or organizations, there might not be a single outcome. Different business units, different types of applications, different roles (debugging versus prod monitoring) may choose different solutions.

Although vendor solutions represent a direct monetary cost to run, the true cost of implementing and running an observability system (which will naturally be a critical system itself), including the staffing costs, should not be underestimated.

Summary

Observability is emerging as an absolutely essential discipline for cloud native applications.

In this chapter, we introduced you to the basic concepts behind observability. We talked about the three pillars model, which describes the main types of data sources used in observability analysis. We also discussed architecture and met some common observability patterns and antipatterns, including the important question of the choice between in-house and vendor solutions.

One of our key motivations in this chapter was to explain *what* observability can help you diagnose—the actionable insights that should be at the heart of the discipline.

In our next chapter, we will build on these foundations and explain in more detail how to implement an observability solution for a production Java application.

## CHAPTER 11

Implementing Observability in Java

In this chapter, you will see how to apply the principles and ideas of the last chapter to real, production Java/JVM systems. This will include the three pillars of metrics, traces, and logs.

We will use three primary technologies for our examples—Micrometer, Prometheus, and OpenTelemetry. However, it should be clearly understood that these technologies have different domains of applicability, and in practice, many real systems will use some or all of them together to provide a complete observability implementation.

There are also many other technologies in use in the field, with varying levels of maturity—in fact, one of the difficult problems in observability is managing the complexity of possible deployments.

A second, and related problem: observability is, by design, intended to be used to understand complex software systems and varied architectures. This means that, while there is an emerging set of patterns, there is no single "right" way to implement observability—the best solution for a particular software system depends on the details.

In this chapter, we'll be using Fighting Animals, from Chapter 8, as our example application.

> The architectural choices we make for observing Fighting Animals are not necessarily the best choices for other applications—a lot depends upon the details of the application architecture and the environment in which it is deployed.

Let's start looking at the Micrometer library to see how it can be applied to our example application.

Introducing Micrometer

At the time of writing (August 2024), one of the most common—and also most effective—of the current Java metrics libraries is Micrometer (*https://micrometer.io*), formerly developed as part of the Spring project but now standalone. It is a Java/JVM project, so teams that want to have the same library used across a heterogeneous architecture will need to consider alternatives.

The project is probably best described as a vendor-neutral application metrics facade, although it has other subprojects that also handle other observability data types, such as tracing.

Micrometer integrates with a large number of metrics data sources and backends, including: Azure Monitor, CloudWatch, Datadog, Dynatrace, Elastic, JMX, New Relic, OpenTelemetry Protocol (OTLP), Prometheus, SignalFx, and StatsD.

It is a library intended for use by the application developer, and as such, it expects the developer to consciously create and record the metrics they want to collect.

Meters and Registries

Micrometer provides a core library as a service provider interface (SPI) and uses pluggable *metric consumers*, which are service implementations that export to various vendor and OSS solutions. This is similar to how a logging framework operates (i.e., both are examples of the facade pattern). This structure enables the framework to handle any differences between metrics systems by delegating any required conversions to the consumers that export the data.

We met some of these differences in "Architectural Patterns for Metrics" on page 249, and Micrometer's interface is designed to be general enough to accommodate them. For example, not all metrics systems support dimensional annotation of the measurement, and instead, use hierarchical naming.

There is also the issue of *aggregation discipline* that determines how the metrics are created from individual samples. There are two general approaches, and different metrics systems make different decisions about which one to implement:

Client-side
> Discrete samples are converted to a fixed rate (aggregated) before they are sent to the server.

Server-side
> All samples are sent over the network, and aggregation occurs at the server.

Metrics systems also differ in how the data is actually transmitted (or published) to the server. There are two main options for this as well:

Client push

The application exporter connects to the server and sends updates to it.

Server poll

The metrics backend connects to a standard port (usually HTTP) and *scrapes* data from the application.

These aspects are properties of the exporters and are abstracted away by Micrometer. As a result, the developer who wants to work from a Java programming perspective can focus on the Micrometer API and not worry about the details of the metrics backend when implementing metrics in their code.

Within this API, the `Meter` is the key interface for collecting metrics. The different types of meter (the *instrument types*) are represented by instances of classes that implement various subinterfaces of `Meter`. Meters are named using all-lowercase with dot separators, and this is translated, if necessary, into the native naming scheme when exporting metrics.

Each meter lives in a specific *registry*, such as these examples:

`SimpleMeterRegistry`

In-memory only, used for development and unit testing

`LoggingMeterRegistry`

Also development and testing, but logs meters periodically

`CompositeMeterRegistry`

Holds multiple registries (multipub)

`Metrics.globalRegistry`

Static global registry

Micrometer autowires a test registry (`SimpleMeterRegistry`) when used in Spring apps. Non-Spring applications can simply instantiate an instance of it (and the same is true of `LoggingMeterRegistry`):

```java
// for testing non-Spring applications
MeterRegistry myRegistry = new SimpleMeterRegistry();

// produces some output
MeterRegistry withOutput = new LoggingMeterRegistry();
```

In our Fighting Animals example (from the `micrometer_only` branch), we want to use a `LoggingMeterRegistry` initially. We wire this up by providing a Spring bean in the application class, like this:

```java
@SpringBootApplication
public class AnimalApplication {
```

```java
@Bean
public MeterRegistry basicRegistry() {
  return new LoggingMeterRegistry();
}

public static void main(String[] args) {
  SpringApplication.run(AnimalApplication.class, args);
}
}
```

This will create a new `LoggingMeterRegistry` and make it available for autowiring in the controller. This will log the metrics to the console, which is a reasonable way to get started with Micrometer. Later, you'll see how to build something more sophisticated and similar to what we'd actually use in production.

Note that this plumbing has to be done for each of the `*Application` classes, as the different microservices run in different containers.

Micrometer supports a wide range of instrument types that cover most of the common use cases:

Counter
    Count of all events

Gauge
    Single metric value

Timer
    Count and total time of all timed events

DistributionSummary
    Tracks the distribution of nontimed events (histograms)

Less common instruments include `LongTaskTimer`, `TimeGauge`, `FunctionCounter`, and `FunctionTimer`.

In Micrometer, dimensions are represented as `Tag` objects. Tags are also named using a dotted lowercase convention and must have non-null values.

Counters

Let's look at a simple Micrometer code example that uses a counter:

```java
@RestController
public class AnimalController {
  // ...

  private final Counter battlesTotal;

  private final MeterRegistry registry;
```

```
  // ...

  public AnimalController(MeterRegistry registry) {
    this.registry = registry;
    this.battlesTotal = this.registry.counter("battles.total");
  }

  @GetMapping("/battle")
  public String makeBattle() throws IOException, InterruptedException {
    battlesTotal.increment();

    // ...
  }
}
```

A Micrometer `Counter` represents a *monotonic value*—one that can only increase over time. This makes it a good fit for a metric that represents the number of battles that have been fought.

They can be created using the `counter()` method on the registry or by using a fluent builder and `register()`:

```
this.battlesTotal = Counter
        .builder("battles.total")
        .description("Total number of battles fought")
        .register(this.registry);
```

The final step in the creation of a counter is to register it with the registry. There are also some optional methods—such as setting the units and any tags.

Gauges

Let's look at another example, this time using a `Gauge`. The gauge is a little more complex than the counter, as it needs to be able to change state both up and down rather than just increasing monotonically.

In this case, we want to track the percentage of feline animals that have been seen over time. For this, we need a class that acts as a carrier of a mutable double value. There isn't really anything suitable in the JDK, so we create our own class, `FelinePercent`, which extends `java.lang.Number`.

> The Java concurrency libraries do not provide an `AtomicDouble` class—which would otherwise have been an obvious choice (for the mutability rather than the concurrency aspect).

The resulting code for the controller looks a bit like this (details abridged to make the observability code clearer):

```
@RestController
public class MammalController {
  // ...
  private final FelinePercent felinePercent;
  private int felineCount = 0;
  private int mustelidCount = 0;

  private final MeterRegistry registry;

  public MammalController(MeterRegistry registry) {
    this.registry = registry;
    felinePercent = this.registry.gauge("battles.felinePercent",
      new FelinePercent(0.5));
  }

  @GetMapping("/getAnimal")
  public String getAnimal() throws IOException, InterruptedException {
    // ...

    var id = (int) (SERVICES.size() * Math.random());
    if (id == 0) {
      mustelidCount += 1;
    } else {
      felineCount += 1;
    }
    felinePercent.setValue((double) felineCount / (double) (felineCount
      + mustelidCount));

    // ...
  }
}
```

In this example, the key call is to `registry.gauge()`, which creates a new `Gauge` instance and registers it with the registry. In the Micrometer `MeterRegistry` class, the simplest form of the `gauge()` method is this:

```
@Nullable
public <T extends Number> T gauge(String name, T number) {
    return this.gauge((String)name, (Iterable)Collections.emptyList(),
      (Number)number);
}
```

Note that the generics require that the gauge class extends `Number`, so we use this simple class definition:

```
public final class FelinePercent extends Number {
  private volatile double value;

  public FelinePercent(double v) {
    if (v < 0.0 || v > 1.0) {
```

```
      throw new IllegalArgumentException("Require 0 < felinePercent < 1");
    }
    value = v;
  }

  public void setValue(double v) {
    if (v < 0.0 || v > 1.0) {
      throw new IllegalArgumentException("Require 0 < felinePercent < 1");
    }
    value = v;
  }

  @Override
  public int intValue() {
    return (int) value;
  }

  @Override
  public long longValue() {
    return (long) value;
  }

  @Override
  public float floatValue() {
    return (float) value;
  }

  @Override
  public double doubleValue() {
    return value;
  }
}
```

When an instance of `FelinePercent` is passed to the `gauge()` method, it effectively creates a watcher for the state—the percentage of feline animals that have been seen.

The programmer needs to update only the gauge value, and the rest of the metrics system is abstracted away. The watcher updates the gauge value whenever required—but note that this is on demand, so not every state change is necessarily observed, only the current value at the time the update is needed.

Meter Filters

Micrometer also implements *meter filters*—these provide greater control over:

- How and when meters are registered
- What kinds of statistics they emit

As a first example, filters can be used to adapt metrics to a new (or old) set of conventions without having to make widespread code changes.

Meter filters provide three basic functions:

- Deny/accept meters being registered
- Transform meters (change metric name, tags, units, etc.)
- Configure distribution statistics

Note that the last function can only be configured for appropriate meter types—meaning timers and distribution summaries. We will explain this final function in more detail later in this section when we meet the instrument types that it applies to.

Filters are represented as implementations of the `MeterFilter` interface. They can be added programmatically, often by using a factory method, like this:

```
// This next line prevents the internal metrics from being published
this.registry.config()
    .meterFilter(MeterFilter.denyNameStartsWith("internal"));
```

We don't actually have any internal metrics in our example, but this is a good demonstration of how to use a filter, and preventing internal metrics from being published is a common use case.

> `MeterFilter` is an interface, but not a functional interface, as it has three nonstatic methods, all of which are default methods (it does not have any mandatory methods at all).

We can also explicitly construct filter objects. For example, the filter from the previous example is equivalent to this code:

```
new MeterFilter() {
  @Override
  public MeterFilterReply accept(Meter.Id id) {
    if (id.getName().startsWith("internal")) {
      return MeterFilterReply.DENY;
    }
    return MeterFilterReply.NEUTRAL;
  }
};
```

The enum `MeterFilterReply` has three possible values: DENY, NEUTRAL, and ACCEPT. The DENY value prevents the meter from being registered, while ACCEPT immediately registers it, without looking at any further filters. NEUTRAL means that the filter has no opinion on the meter, and the next application filter for this metric (if any) should be consulted.

The implementation of `meterFilter()` is strictly additive, so the developer should consider the order in which filters are added to the chain.

Filters can also be used for more advanced use cases, such as using them as customizers for a `CompositeMeterRegistry`. This enables such patterns as sending a subset of metrics to an auxiliary backend. This can be very useful in production deployments, but a full discussion of this is outside the scope of this book.

Timers

Timers are a more complex data type that store at least three values internally:

- The sum of all recorded values
- A count of the values that have been recorded
- The maximum value seen within a time window, as a gauge

Timers can be configured to emit additional statistics, such as histogram data, precomputed percentiles, or even service level objective (SLO) boundaries.

Let's look at an example and focus on the timer code on the `micrometer_only` branch. Here's the code for the timer usage in the `AnimalController`:

```java
@RestController
public class AnimalController {
  // ...

  private final Timer responseTimer;

  private final MeterRegistry registry;

  // ...

  public AnimalController(MeterRegistry registry) {
    this.registry = registry;

    // ...

    this.responseTimer = Timer
            .builder("response.time")
            .description("Response time")
            .register(registry);
  }

  @GetMapping("/battle")
  public String makeBattle() throws Exception {
    Callable<String> callable = () -> {
```

```
      // Send the two requests and return the response body as the response
      var good = fetchRandomAnimal();
      var evil = fetchRandomAnimal();
      return  String.format("""
{ "good": "%s", "evil": "%s" }""", good, evil);
    };

    // ...

    return responseTimer.recordCallable(callable);
  }
}
```

In this code, we set up a block of code as a `Callable` and then pass it to the `recordCallable()` method of the timer. This will execute the code block and record the time taken to complete it.

Timers can also handle code represented as `Runnable` and `Supplier`. The appropriate `Timer` method is called `record()` in these cases—this is due to the signature collision between `Callable` and `Supplier`.

To conclude our discussion of Micrometer timers, we should point out that in general, timers are not the preferred approach for measuring the performance of methods in a distributed system. Distributed tracing, such as that implemented by OpenTelemetry, is usually a much better approach for this. We will discuss this approach later in this chapter.

So next, let's discuss the final instrument type we want to look at—the `Distribution Summary`.

Distribution Summaries

We've just met timers, and they provide statistics on the distribution of the timings that they've seen. In fact, they are a special case of the more general case of distribution summaries.

A *distribution summary* is, as the name suggests, an instrument used to summarize an entire set (or distribution) of values. They require more memory than a simple counter, as they need to store more data, but they still represent a lossy representation of an overall distribution.

> Distribution summaries should be used for things that are not timed. If the measurement quantity is a duration, then a timer should be used instead.

Let's look at an example and introduce a `DistributionSummary` into our `Animal Controller`:

```java
@RestController
public class AnimalController {
    // ...

    private static final Random random = new Random();

    private final DistributionSummary winSummary;

    private final MeterRegistry registry;

    public AnimalController(MeterRegistry registry) {
        this.registry = registry;

        // Summarizes the size of the attacker's strength when it wins
        this.winSummary = registry.summary("attacker.win.size");

        // ...
    }
}
```

To drive this demonstration of a summary, we'll also introduce some code for a `resolveFight()` method in the `AnimalController`. The aim is to simulate a fight between two animals and return the winner. We normalize the defender's strength to 0.5 and then use a random number for the attacker's strength to determine the winner:

```java
@GetMapping("/fight/{a}/{d}")
public String resolveFight(
        @PathVariable("a") String attacker, @PathVariable("d") String defender) {
    final String winner;
    // Defender's strength is taken to be 0.5
    var attackerStrength = random.nextDouble();
    if (attackerStrength > 0.5) {
        winner = attacker;
        // Add to the distribution summary
        winSummary.record(attackerStrength);
    } else {
        winner = defender;
    }
    return  String.format("""
{ "winner": "%s"}""", winner);
}
```

If the attacker wins, their "strength" is recorded in the distribution summary. This should produce a uniform distribution of values between 0.5 and 1.0, which the `DistributionSummary` will then summarize.

We'll use the `LoggingMeterRegistry` for this example, and the resulting output looks like this:

```
animal-service_1    | 2024-01-14T08:27:31.748Z  INFO 1 --- [trics-publisher] ↵
i.m.c.i.logging.LoggingMeterRegistry     : attacker.win.size{} ↵
throughput=0.183333/s mean=0.699785 max=0.98829
```

The default setup for distribution summaries is good enough for many purposes, but it is possible to use metric filters to set up more advanced configurations. The key to this is the third of the nonstatic methods in the `MeterFilter` interface, `configure()`, which is defined like this:

```java
@Nullable
default DistributionStatisticConfig configure(Meter.Id id,
        DistributionStatisticConfig config) {
    return config;
}
```

The default implementation represents an identity transformation of the configuration, but in general, a custom implementation will merge the supplied configuration with the input configuration.

By defining a custom filter that overrides this method, it is possible to configure optional distribution statistics (in addition to the basics of count, total, and max). These additional statistics can include precomputed percentiles, SLOs, and histograms.

For example, to configure precomputed "long-tail" percentiles (which we met in Chapter 2) for all JVM metrics, we could use a filter like this:

```java
new MeterFilter() {
    @Override
    public DistributionStatisticConfig configure(Meter.Id id,
            DistributionStatisticConfig config) {
        if (id.getName().startsWith("jvm")) {
            return DistributionStatisticConfig.builder()
                    .publishPercentiles(0.9, 0.99, 0.999, 0.9999)
                    .build()
                    .merge(config);
        }
        return config;
    }
};
```

This will add the 90th, 99th, 99.9th, and 99.99th percentiles to all JVM metrics—which can be very useful to observe the non-normal distribution of many of the JVM metrics.

It is important at this point to note that count, sum, and some other data associated with distribution summaries can be reaggregated across dimensions (or even across instances). However, precomputed percentile values cannot be reaggregated—to attempt to do so is a serious and all-too-common error.

The reason is that the way percentiles are created makes them unique to each dataset. Accurate percentiles across the entire dataset can only be computed by combining the original datasets and *then* calculating the percentiles. Once percentiles have been calculated, data has already been lost, and reaggregating the percentiles will not produce the correct result except in pathological special cases.

To conclude this discussion of Micrometer, let's take a quick look at the JVM metrics support that the library provides out of the box.

Runtime Metrics

In addition to programmer-defined metrics, Micrometer also provides the capability to collect and export a set of metrics associated with the JVM and other parts of the application runtime. There are a number of different sets of this type of metric that can be collected.

The key interface for this is `MeterBinder`, which is defined like this:

```
public interface MeterBinder {
    void bindTo(@NonNull MeterRegistry var1);
}
```

Two of the most important implementations of this are the JVM memory metrics and the processor metrics, as shown in this example:

```
@RestController
public class AnimalController {
  // ...

  private final MeterRegistry registry;

  // ...

  public AnimalController(MeterRegistry registry) {
    this.registry = registry;

    new ProcessorMetrics().bindTo(this.registry);
    new JvmMemoryMetrics().bindTo(this.registry);
  }

  // ...
}
```

The key to this is the `bindTo()` method, which makes the registry aware of the JVM-level metrics. It is not strictly necessary for Spring Boot applications, as the framework auto-installs them, but for other applications, they must be explicitly enabled. Other sets of metrics can be collected as well, but these are some of the most common ones.

To give some specific examples, the `JvmMemoryMetrics` class provides metrics such as `jvm.memory.used` and `jvm.memory.max`, while `ProcessorMetrics` provides metrics like `system.cpu.usage` and `system.load.average.1m`. One other important case is that of metrics from an `ExecutorService`, which can be enabled like this: `new Exec utorServiceMetrics(executor, executorServiceName, tags).bindTo(registry)` and enables easy monitoring of thread pools.

Having met the basic instruments and functionality provided by Micrometer, let's move on to meet Prometheus properly and see how we can integrate it with Micrometer.

Introducing Prometheus for Java Developers

We introduced Prometheus very briefly in Chapter 8 and made several references to it in the last chapter, but we didn't do a thorough treatment of the technology. In this section, we will discuss it in more detail, in particular, how it can be used by Java developers and projects.

Prometheus Architecture Overview

To recap, Prometheus is a CNCF project (originally created at SoundCloud) that provides a metrics backend, collection mechanism, and various integrations. It is designed to handle purely numeric, regular time series data and is not intended to be used for things like logs or traces.

Of the metrics architectural options discussed before, Prometheus uses server poll, which it refers to as scraping. This means that every service you wish to monitor using Prometheus must provide an HTTP endpoint from which the Prometheus scraper will collect metrics. In turn, this means that Prometheus also relies on services being known or discoverable, which potentially presents issues for short-lived jobs.

To handle these challenges, and also to integrate better with technologies like Open-Telemetry that use push-based architectures, Prometheus also ships a remote write capability. This is also more in accordance with the security model of systems like Kubernetes.

The overall architecture of a (relatively complex) Prometheus deployment can be seen in Figure 11-1.

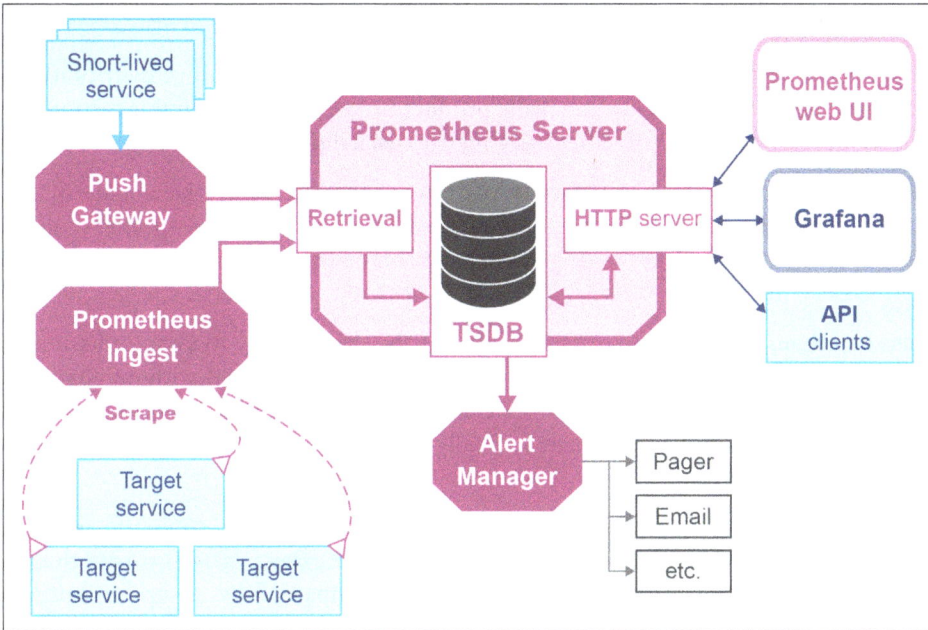

Figure 11-1. Prometheus architecture (source: Prometheus documentation (https://oreil.ly/hBFrH))

As the diagram makes clear, there are a large number of components, and the exact combination will depend upon the architectural choices made. Thus it is important to ask for clarification when people state that they are "using Prometheus."

Prometheus provides a query language known as PromQL, which is used to write queries against the collected data. Despite the name, PromQL is not SQL, and is instead a domain-specific language (DSL) designed to be used for querying time series data rather than traditional relational data. The queried data can then be visualized in a number of different ways.

Prometheus ships with a rudimentary UI, but this is frequently insufficient for production use. Instead, it is more common for other tools to layer on top of Prometheus—the open source Grafana graphing tools are a popular choice.

In general, developers and DevOps folk typically interact with Prometheus in two ways—either via the UI or by calling the metrics collection code from within their app code. However, a general awareness of the overall architecture of Prometheus (including its data storage capabilities) is useful for understanding how it fits into the overall observability picture—even if you're not directly responsible for maintaining the deployment.

Using Prometheus with Micrometer

In our initial examples, we used the `LoggingMeterRegistry` to output metrics to the console. This is, of course, not a realistic production configuration. In this section, we will see how we can use Prometheus as a metrics backend for Micrometer.

Recall that we want to use a facade pattern to abstract away the details of the metrics backend. The idea is that there should be no Prometheus-specific code in our application. This makes testing easier, as it can be run with a dummy or mocked metrics dependency.

It is sometimes said that use of facades means that it's possible to swap out components, such as replacing Prometheus for another metrics backend without changing our application code. This ability—to change the observability plumbing without requiring application changes—can be really important, and it is one of the major drivers for standardization.

Having said this, there are often details that make this not as straightforward in practice—vendor lock-in can be more subtle than we expect. It is also true that in many cases a major change of components is accompanied by an opportunity to revisit the overall architecture and make other changes as well.

Nevertheless, the facade nature of Micrometer's architecture makes the use of Prometheus as a metrics backend relatively straightforward. To implement Prometheus in our applications, we can use the SPI nature of the Micrometer library. All we need to do is to add another dependency to our project:

```
<dependency>
  <groupId>io.micrometer</groupId>
  <artifactId>micrometer-registry-prometheus</artifactId>
  <scope>runtime</scope>
</dependency>
```

This provides an additional exporter that can be used to send metrics to Prometheus.

To see this in `fighting-animals`, we need to make a few changes. To make this clearer, this is done on a separate branch (`micrometer_with_prom`).

We need to add this line to `application.properties`:

```
management.endpoints.web.exposure.include=health,info,prometheus
```

We are using Micrometer to directly expose the metrics from the application as a scrapeable endpoint that Prometheus can connect to.

You can also remove the logging registry to cut down on the amount of detail in the logs:

```
// Remove this bean to reduce log noise
@Bean
```

```
public MeterRegistry basicRegistry() {
  return new LoggingMeterRegistry();
}
```

The resulting architecture here is still fairly simple, as seen in Figure 11-2.

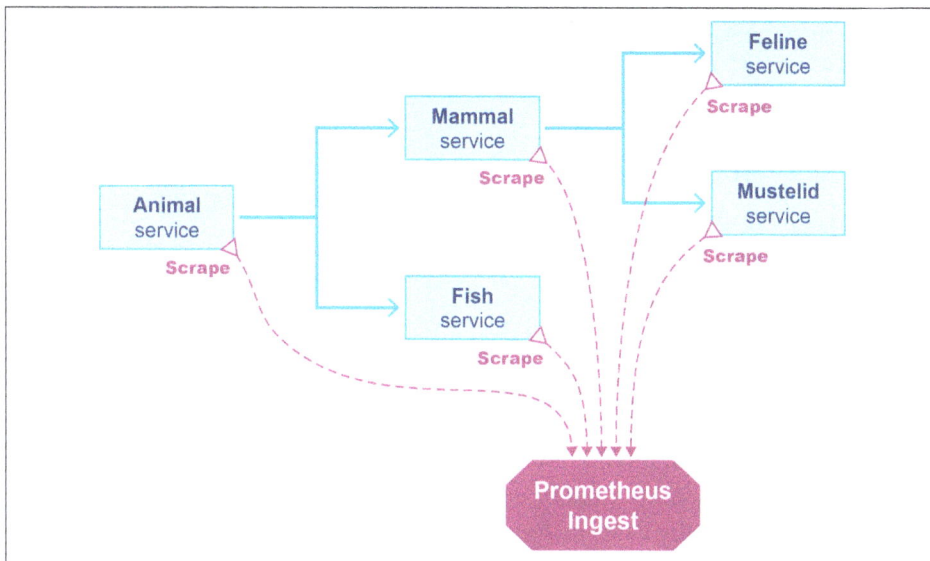

Figure 11-2. Fighting Animals with Prometheus

To configure Prometheus for this architectural configuration, we need to add a new service to our docker-compose.yml file:

```
# Prometheus
prom:
  container_name: prometheus
  image: prom/prometheus
  command:
    - "--config.file=/config/prometheus.yml"
  ports:
    - "9090:9090"
  user: root
  volumes:
    - './config:/config'
    - './target/data/prometheus:/prometheus'
```

This refers to a new configuration file, prometheus.yml, the bare bones of which look like this:

```
global:
  # Set the scrape interval to every 15 seconds. Default is every 1 minute.
  scrape_interval:     15s
  # Evaluate rules every 15 seconds. The default is every 1 minute.
  evaluation_interval: 15s
```

```
# scrape_timeout is set to the global default (10s).

# ...

scrape_configs:

- job_name: prometheus
  metrics_path: /metrics
  scheme: http
  static_configs:
  - targets:
    - localhost:9090

- job_name: animal
  metrics_path: /actuator/prometheus
  scrape_interval: 5s
  static_configs:
    - targets:
      - animal-service:8080

# Other services similarly configured
```

This is a simple configuration, but it has been tested to work across a real network rather than with everything running on localhost. This is quite deliberate, as many examples available on the internet do not work in a real network environment—only on localhost.

With our config, each service will expose its metrics on the same URI (/actuator/prometheus) on a different port, and Prometheus will scrape them all. Typical Prometheus output looks like this (from the animal service, deployed at a URL like http://<Target IP>:8080/actuator/prometheus):

```
# HELP system_load_average_1m The sum of the number of runnable entities queued ↵
to available processors and the number of runnable entities running on the ↵
available processors averaged over a period of time
# TYPE system_load_average_1m gauge
system_load_average_1m 0.2
# HELP process_files_open_files The open file descriptor count
# TYPE process_files_open_files gauge
process_files_open_files 34.0
# HELP jvm_classes_loaded_classes The number of classes that are currently ↵
loaded in the Java virtual machine
# TYPE jvm_classes_loaded_classes gauge
jvm_classes_loaded_classes 8934.0
# HELP tomcat_sessions_active_current_sessions
# TYPE tomcat_sessions_active_current_sessions gauge
tomcat_sessions_active_current_sessions 0.0
# HELP jvm_memory_committed_bytes The amount of memory in bytes that is ↵
committed for the Java virtual machine to use
# TYPE jvm_memory_committed_bytes gauge
jvm_memory_committed_bytes{area="nonheap",id="CodeHeap 'profiled nmethods'",}
```

```
    9109504.0
jvm_memory_committed_bytes{area="heap",id="G1 Survivor Space",} 4194304.0
# ... Other JVM metrics ommitted for brevity ...
jvm_memory_committed_bytes{area="nonheap",id="CodeHeap 'non-profiled nmethods'",}
    3145728.0
```

Note that many of these metrics are JVM metrics rather than application metrics. If we look further down the output, we can see some of our custom metrics:

```
# HELP battles_total
# TYPE battles_total counter
battles_total 5.0
```

Prometheus monitors itself using the same mechanism, so we can see the Prometheus metrics as well: http://<Target IP>:9090/metrics:

```
# HELP go_gc_duration_seconds A summary of the pause duration of garbage ↵
collection cycles.
# TYPE go_gc_duration_seconds summary
go_gc_duration_seconds{quantile="0"} 3.5e-05
go_gc_duration_seconds{quantile="0.25"} 7.8507e-05
go_gc_duration_seconds{quantile="0.5"} 9.9929e-05
go_gc_duration_seconds{quantile="0.75"} 0.000132907
go_gc_duration_seconds{quantile="1"} 0.000325268
go_gc_duration_seconds_sum 0.018079852
go_gc_duration_seconds_count 164
# HELP go_goroutines Number of goroutines that currently exist.
# TYPE go_goroutines gauge
go_goroutines 47
# HELP go_threads Number of OS threads created.
# TYPE go_threads gauge
go_threads 18
# HELP go_info Information about the Go environment.
# TYPE go_info gauge
go_info{version="go1.17.5"} 1
# ....
# HELP net_conntrack_dialer_conn_attempted_total Total number of connections ↵
attempted by the given dialer a given name.
# TYPE net_conntrack_dialer_conn_attempted_total counter
net_conntrack_dialer_conn_attempted_total{dialer_name="alertmanager"} 0
net_conntrack_dialer_conn_attempted_total{dialer_name="animal"} 42
net_conntrack_dialer_conn_attempted_total{dialer_name="default"} 0
net_conntrack_dialer_conn_attempted_total{dialer_name="feline"} 41
net_conntrack_dialer_conn_attempted_total{dialer_name="fish"} 41
net_conntrack_dialer_conn_attempted_total{dialer_name="mammal"} 42
net_conntrack_dialer_conn_attempted_total{dialer_name="mustelid"} 42
net_conntrack_dialer_conn_attempted_total{dialer_name="prometheus"} 2
```

The first group of metrics are the Go runtime metrics, including GC metrics and goroutine counts. As you can see, Prometheus is written in Go, and the Go language supports *goroutines*—lightweight threads that are managed by the Go runtime. These are very similar to the Java concept of virtual threads, which we will discuss in Chapter 14.

This provides an example of an important architectural principle that Prometheus exemplifies—the systems that support and convey observability signals should themselves be observable and well-architected from an observability perspective.

The basic Prometheus UI can be found at: `http://<Target IP>:9090/graph` and is shown in Figure 11-3.

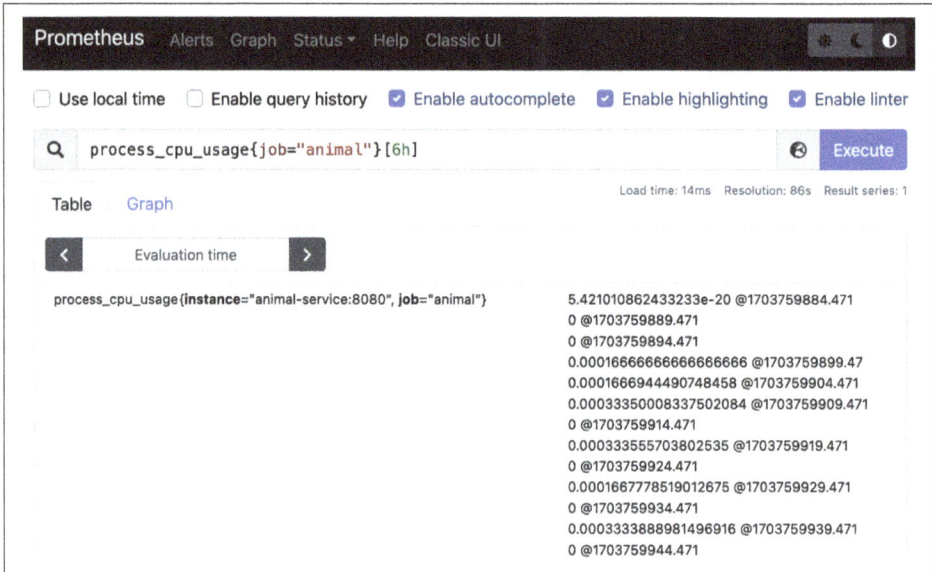

Figure 11-3. Prometheus query UI

Our query string here is `process_cpu_usage{job="animal"}[6h]`, which is a PromQL query that asks for all the data points representing the CPU usage of the `animal` job over the last six hours. This is known as a *range vector*, as it returns a vector of time series over a range of time.

Note that this is displayed here in the Table view, in the form: `<value> @ <time stamp>`. If we switch to the graphing view, then we need to change the query, as graphing requires an expression that is an *instant vector*.

The time series for the query `process_cpu_usage{job=~"m.*"}` is depicted graphically in Figure 11-4. This query returns the CPU metric for jobs that start with the letter `m`—in our case `mammal` and `mustelid`. This uses the Prometheus regular expression support, `=~`, which is very useful for selecting metrics.

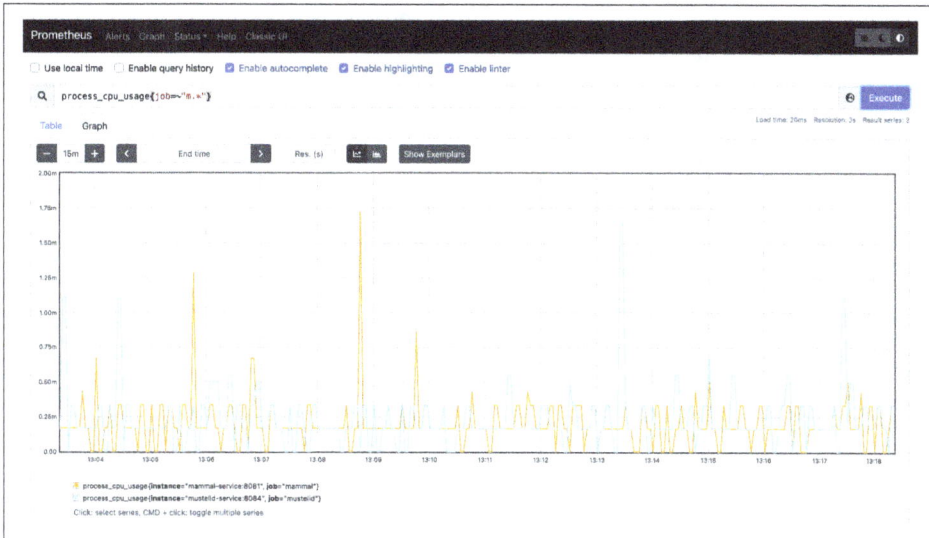

Figure 11-4. Prometheus graphs

A full discussion of PromQL is outside the scope of this book—the Prometheus documentation should be consulted for any serious work, as well as that for auxiliary components such as Grafana.

Instead, let's move on to discuss the third, and arguably most important, of our observability technologies—OpenTelemetry.

Introducing OpenTelemetry

In this section, we'll properly introduce OpenTelemetry (aka OTel), a new open standard from the CNCF for observability data, which we mentioned in Chapter 8. The project was formed by a merger of the OpenTracing (tracing) and OpenCensus (metrics) projects and is now an open standard that is rapidly gaining traction, showing rapid growth in adoption.

> OpenTracing and OpenCensus are now deprecated, and all new development should be done using OpenTelemetry.

This growth is even more impressive when you consider that the project is only a few years old and only reached its 1.0 release during 2023. The project is now stable and ready for production use and has been enthusiastically adopted by many companies and teams already—and that trend looks set to continue.

OTel can be used in a wide range of circumstances, but it is perhaps most at home in cloud-deployed, microservice-based applications, and it is generally suitable for heterogeneous (aka polyglot), distributed systems.[1]

What Is OpenTelemetry?

One of the key strengths of OTel is that it does not try to provide a solution for every problem but focuses on its core domain. OTel is *not* a data ingest or observability backend, and thus, is only one component of a complete observability system.

As we mentioned briefly in Chapter 10, OTel is focused on instrumentation of applications and the transport of data to a separate, external observability system.

The major project areas of OpenTelemetry are shown in Figure 11-5.

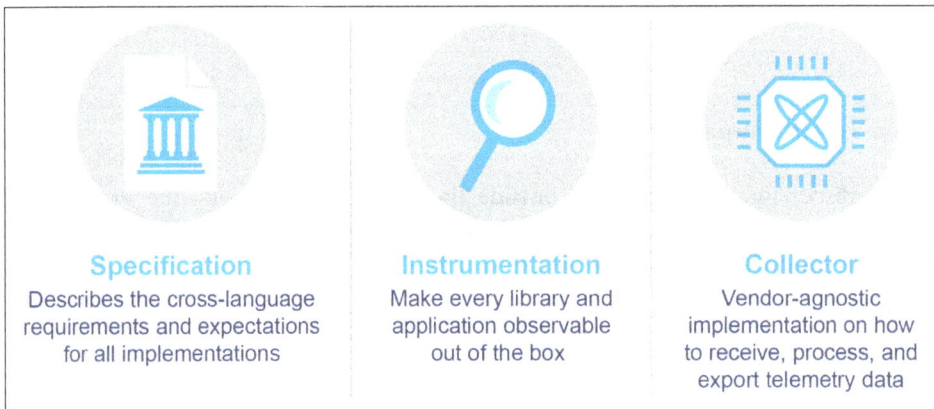

Specification	Instrumentation	Collector
Describes the cross-language requirements and expectations for all implementations	Make every library and application observable out of the box	Vendor-agnostic implementation on how to receive, process, and export telemetry data

Figure 11-5. Concerns of OpenTelemetry project

The specification defines formats and conventions for metrics, logs, and traces in a language-independent way and a protocol for transporting the data to the observability backend.

The various language implementations provide a set of APIs and SDKs that can be used to instrument applications written in virtually any mainstream language, and integrations to a wide range of frameworks. The Java implementation also provides a Java agent to instrument applications without needing to change code.

Finally, the OpenTelemetry Collector is a useful tool that can collect data from applications and send it to a variety of different backends, after having potentially

---

1 Status of the OTel components for various major languages can be found in OTel's documentation (*https://oreil.ly/pzorm*).

performed data processing and enrichment. You can think of it as a router or "switching station" that can also act as a protocol translator for observability data.

These design choices allow OTel to support various observability data architecture options—it is intended to be widely applicable and not prescriptive.

At a software level, the components provided for instrumentation can be seen in Figure 11-6.

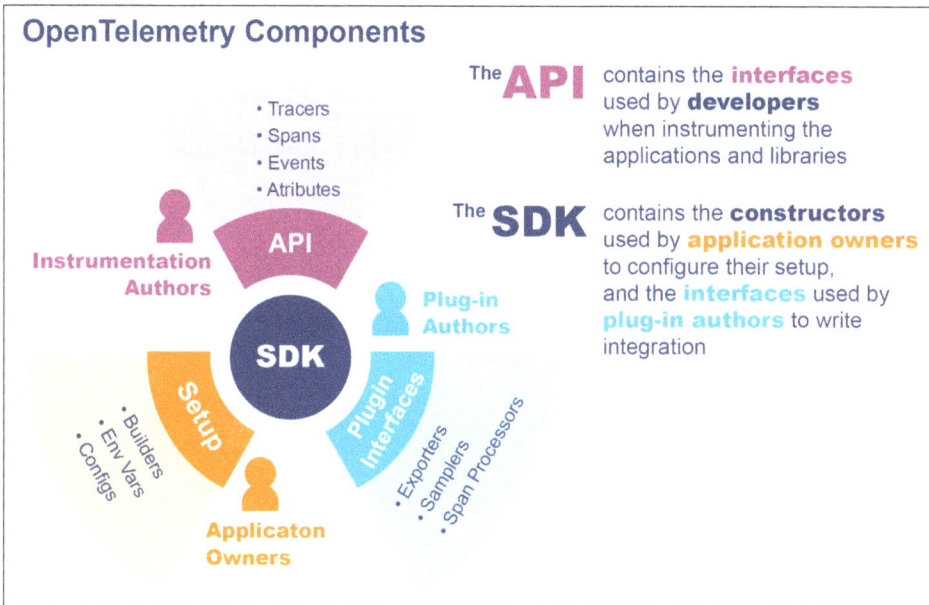

Figure 11-6. OpenTelemetry APIs and SDKs

The SDK is the primary aspect of OpenTelemetry that end users will interact with. It contains two main components:

- Constructors used by application owners to configure their deployment
- Interfaces used by plug-in authors to write integrations

This is the piece that teams deploying OpenTelemetry out of the box will use.

The API contains interfaces used by developers to write bespoke instrumentation for their apps and libraries.

> If an engineer wants to contribute code to the OpenTelemetry project, then the appropriate starting point for their contributions is usually providing some new instrumentation for an open source library or framework that does not currently have specific OTel support.

OTel places great emphasis on stability and backward compatability. The code follows *semantic versioning (https://semver.org)* conventions and provides, at minimum, long-term support for the stable versions of the API and SDK:[2]

API
Three-year support guarantee

Plug-in interfaces
One-year support guarantee

Constructors
One-year support guarantee

For Java, there are four main projects under the GitHub open-telemetry org:

opentelemetry-java
Core components including the API and SDK

opentelemetry-java-instrumentation
Library instrumentation and auto instrumentation agent

opentelemetry-java-contrib
Helpful and standalone libraries

opentelemetry-java-examples
Manual instrumentation examples[3]

The Java implementation initially focused on traces and metrics, with logs reaching 1.0 in late 2023.

Why Choose OTel?

The application performance monitoring (APM) market was originally dominated by proprietary vendors. As with many other market segments, demand for open source alternatives emerged—to reduce vendor lock-in, cut costs, and provide greater flexibility.

We have already met some of these open source projects, such as Jaeger for traces, Prometheus in the metrics space, and the ELK stack for logging.

A second market trend is more subtle, but no less important—the increasing complexity of software systems. As software continues to become more complex, and

---

2 These promises might be weaker than reality, specifically for opentelemetry-java (*https://oreil.ly/9Vq6V*). Supporting and providing backward compatibility on stable components is a major goal for the community, and publishing a major version would be an indication that breaking changes were being made.

3 See also the semantic conventions (*https://oreil.ly/Rcesz*).

as more languages and frameworks become popular, more and more resources are required to provide a credible instrumentation.

For proprietary observability products, this trend creates duplication and inefficiency, as each separate company must maintain its own suite of instrumentation libraries. This duplicated effort ultimately causes it to make more sense for observability vendors to collaborate on a single set of open source libraries rather than each maintaining its own. The value that an observability vendor provides is then in the user experience, backend capabilities, and cost rather than the instrumentation per se.

This represents a switch from proprietary to open source—at least, within the domain of the code that runs in the context of a customer's application. In recent years, we have indeed seen a number of proprietary vendors switch to an open source model.

This can be seen as an attempt by APM vendors to redefine themselves as observability providers. This has also been accompanied by an increasing number of observability startups that have always been more closely aligned with the open source model.

The protocol and instrumentation stack that vendors are converging on is, of course, OpenTelemetry.

The standard has been criticized for being slow moving, but the benefit of having stable, common naming conventions and associated semantic conventions is huge. In that light, it is perhaps no surprise that more and more companies and teams are adopting OpenTelemetry.

OTLP

A key part of the OpenTelemetry project is the OpenTelemetry Protocol (OTLP). OTLP does not try to define the entire protocol space, and instead focuses on its key concerns:

- Encoding
- Transport
- Delivery

Performance is a key consideration for OTLP, and it is typically implemented using HTTP/2 or gRPC (*https://grpc.io*)—which is essentially a *remote procedure call* (RPC) framework that uses the binary *Protocol Buffers* (protobuf) format over HTTP/2.[4] The core Java implementation can use either encoding and defaults to HTTPS/protobuf.

---

4 Other encodings are possible but not often seen in practice.

Before we start looking at the Java libraries that provide the SDK and APIs for OTel, we need to introduce a very important component—the OpenTelemetry Collector.

The Collector

The OTel Collector is a network service that works with streams of observability data and can receive, process, and export any or all of the three main types of observability data.

The simple architecture of the Collector is designed to be extensible and is vendor neutral. It is written in Go and is maintained by an open source team drawn from a variety of different companies. Despite the name, it also works with a wide variety of data formats, not just OTLP.

The Collector is configured using YAML and deploys to `http://localhost:4317` by default. The main configuration sections for the Collector are:

`receivers`
 Data sources that the Collector will listen to data from

`processors`
 Data transformations that the Collector will apply

`connectors`
 Optional components that transform one type of telemetry to another

`exporters`
 Where to send the data after transformation

`extensions`
 Any optional components (e.g., health-checking)

There is also a `service` section that is used to configure the pipelines of the Collector—it has separate sections for each observability signal that we want to handle. For example, this `service` section shows a simple trace pipeline:

```
service:
  pipelines:
    traces:
      receivers: [otlp]
      processors: [batch]
      exporters: [otlphttp]
```

Data will be accepted from the `otlp` receiver, processed by the `batch` processor, and then sent to the `otlphttp` exporter—and the data will be processed into batches before being sent. Note that, just like Prometheus, the Collector generates telemetry about itself in the (somewhat confusingly named) `telemetry` section beneath `service`.

The core architectural principles of the Collector are:

Usability
    Reasonable default config and should work out of the box

Performance
    Performant under varying loads and configurations

Observability
    Good example of an observable service

Extensibility
    Customizable without touching the core code

Unified
    Single codebase supports traces, metrics, and logs

In Figure 11-7 we show a sample architecture that uses OpenTelemetry to handle both metrics and traces. We can see that in this view, the Collector can be thought of as a shim between application processes (including short-lived) and data storage for metrics and traces.

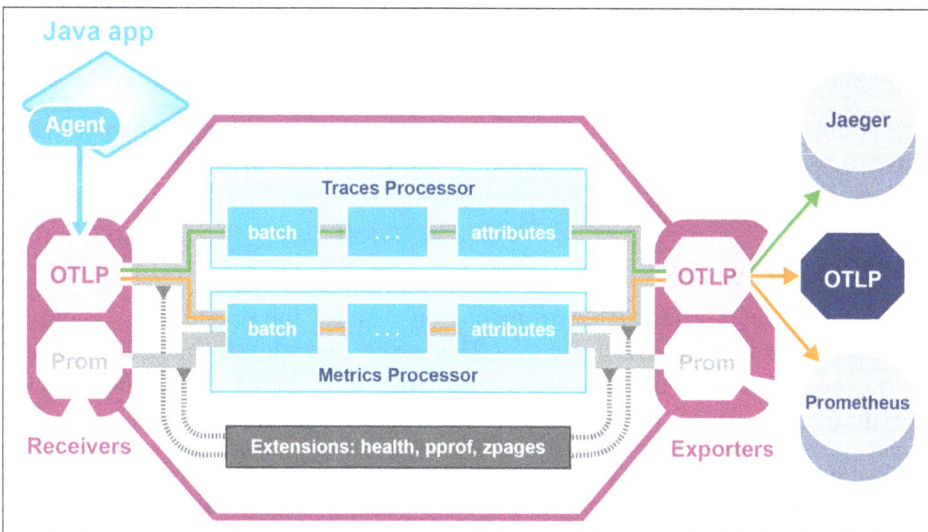

Figure 11-7. OpenTelemetry example architecture

In this example, the Collector instance receives data from multiple processes and exposes a single endpoint. For the case of metrics, this maintains flexibility of architectural choice—Prometheus either knows where the collectors are located, or the collectors can be configured to remote-write.

The Collector is actually a fairly simple, but very flexible, component in terms of configuration and operation, and we will return to it once we've introduced the Java libraries that will be sending data to it.

OpenTelemetry Tracing in Java

As we discussed earlier—OTel focuses on its core domain, which is instrumentation and data exfiltration. These are low-level concerns, so while OpenTelemetry does provide user-facing APIs, there are a number of approaches to adopting OpenTelemetry, some of which avoid explicit coupling to those APIs.

In addition, OTel does not attempt to provide a single unified API for all the different types of observability data in Java. Instead, where possible, it seeks to integrate with Java components that already exist and are widely used in the ecosystem.

As we'll see later, for logs, good patterns (and high-level APIs) exist, and OTel best practice is to use them. For traces, however, there is no existing candidate of suitable quality, so OpenTelemetry provides two different solutions—manual or automatic tracing.

Before we look at these two approaches, a quick word about OpenTelemetry architecture. It is designed to be used in a production deployment, so a certain amount of configuration is required, and a certain amount of extra complexity is unavoidable.

The following subsection, on manual tracing, is, therefore, longer than it really warrants. This is because it has to introduce infrastructure components (such as the Collector) and changes to the POM to bring in the required OTel dependencies.

Manual Tracing

As the name implies, manual instrumentation requires the developer to manually insert explicit calls to the tracing library. This means that while it is possible to use it for tracing, in practice, anything but a trivial example quickly becomes too complex to manage.

This is best shown with an example—so let's look at how we'd use manual tracing in Fighting Animals. In this section, we'll be looking at code taken from the `man ual_tracing` branch.

First of all, we need to depend upon the OpenTelemetry libraries directly in our project. The necessary changes to the POM are quite extensive—the key part is the addition of the `<dependencyManagement>` section and the use of a BOM, essentially to manage the dependencies as a group:

```
<dependencyManagement>
  <dependencies>
    <dependency>
```

```
    <groupId>io.opentelemetry</groupId>
    <artifactId>opentelemetry-bom</artifactId>
    <version>1.40.0</version>
    <type>pom</type>
    <scope>import</scope>
  </dependency>
  </dependencies>
</dependencyManagement>
```

We can then pull in additional OTel dependencies as required—we need the `opentelemetry-api`, `opentelemetry-sdk`, `opentelemetry-sdk-extension-autoconfigure`, and `opentelemetry-exporter-otlp` dependencies for this example.

We've also introduced an auto-configured `OpenTelemetry` bean in `AnimalApplication`, like this:

```
@Bean
public OpenTelemetry openTelemetry() {
  return AutoConfiguredOpenTelemetrySdk.initialize().getOpenTelemetrySdk();
}
```

This `OpenTelemetry` object is now available for use in our code, via constructor injection into the service controllers.

Now, let's look at the code changes required to add tracing to the main HTTP route from the `AnimalController` class:

```
@GetMapping("/battle")
public String makeBattle() throws IOException, InterruptedException {
  // Extract the propagated context from the request. In this case,
  // no context will be extracted from the request - this is the root span
  var extractedContext = extractContext(httpServletRequest,EXTRACTOR);

  try (var scope = extractedContext.makeCurrent()) {
    // Start a span
    var span = serverSpan("/battle", HttpMethod.GET.name(),
        AnimalController.class.getName(), "animal-service:8080");

    // Send the two requests and return the response body as the response
    // and end the root span.
    try {
      var good = fetchRandomAnimal(span);
      var evil = fetchRandomAnimal(span);
      return  String.format("""
{ "good": "%s", "evil": "%s" }""", good, evil);
    } finally {
      span.end();
    }
  }
  // ...
}
```

This is only one service, of course. Very similar tracing code must be added to every service if we are to avoid gaps in the tracing coverage of our code. For example, we need to modify `MammalController` like this:

```
@GetMapping("/getAnimal")
public String makeBattle() throws IOException, InterruptedException {
    // Context will be extracted from that propagated from the Animal Service.
    var extractedContext = extractContext(httpServletRequest,EXTRACTOR);

    try (var scope = extractedContext.makeCurrent()) {
        var span = serverSpan("/getAnimal", HttpMethod.GET.name(),
                MammalController.class.getName(), "mammal-service:8081");

        // Send the sub-request, return the response and end the span
        try {
            return fetchRandomAnimal(span);
        } finally {
            span.end();
        }
    }
}
```

Both of these controllers use the `serverSpan()` method, which is defined in the `Misc` helper class in our application:

```
public static Span serverSpan(Tracer tracer, String path, String method,
  String serviceName) {
   return tracer
       .spanBuilder(path)
       .setSpanKind(SpanKind.SERVER)
       .setAttribute(SemanticAttributes.HTTP_METHOD, method)
       .setAttribute(SemanticAttributes.HTTP_SCHEME, "http")
       .setAttribute(SemanticAttributes.HTTP_HOST, serviceName)
       .setAttribute(SemanticAttributes.HTTP_TARGET, path)
       .startSpan();
}
```

The `Tracer` object is akin to a logger, so it's best to initialize it once, in the constructor code. Having created spans, we need somewhere to send them, so in our *docker-compose.yml*, we have a Collector instance configured to receive them and then forward them on to Jaeger:

```
# Jaeger
# Local GRPC port (4317) needs to be remapped to appear as 14317
# to avoid a clash with the OTel collector's GRPC port
jaeger-all-in-one:
  image: jaegertracing/all-in-one:1.52.0
  ports:
    - "16686:16686"
    - "14317:4317"    # OTLP gRPC receiver
    - "4318:4318"     # OTLP HTTP receiver
```

```yaml
# Collector
otel-collector:
  image: otel/opentelemetry-collector:0.91.0
  command: ["--config=/etc/otel-collector-config.yaml"]
  volumes:
    - ./otel-collector-config.yaml:/etc/otel-collector-config.yaml
  ports:
    - "13133:13133" # Health_check extension
    - "4317:4317"   # OTLP gRPC receiver
    - "55681:55681" # OTLP HTTP receiver alternative port
  depends_on:
    - jaeger-all-in-one
```

As per "A Word About Version Numbers" on page 208, we use explicit version numbers to ensure that the example will work as is. For actual production usage, you should upgrade to a more recent version of these components before deployment, as older images may harbor security vulnerabilities or other bugs.

We also need to configure the Collector to send the spans to Jaeger, which we do in `otel-collector-config.yaml`:

```yaml
receivers:
  otlp:
    protocols:
      grpc:
      http:

exporters:
  otlphttp:
    endpoint: http://jaeger-all-in-one:4318

processors:
  batch:

extensions:
  health_check:

service:
  extensions: [health_check]
  pipelines:
    traces:
      receivers: [otlp]
      processors: [batch]
      exporters: [otlphttp]
```

These components are essentially infrastructure—they are not part of the application code, but are instead part of the observability infrastructure. This also provides a useful indirection point. The operations folks can make changes to the configuration of the Collector without needing to change the application.

We also need to tell the microservices where to find the Collector, as it's now running in its own container—in our example, we do this using a Java command-line parameter to set a system property: `-Dotel.exporter.otlp.endpoint=http://otel-collector:4317/`, which we include in the Dockerfile. This configuration can also be set using environment variables, such as `OTEL_EXPORTER_OTLP_ENDPOINT`. These could also be configured in the Dockerfile.

Just from the two controller classes we met in this section, we can see that the amount of code required to add tracing to our application is quite substantial. This provides a good example of what we mentioned in "Manual Versus Automatic Instrumentation" on page 250: the complexity of manual tracing quickly outstrips the ability of the programmer to manage it.

The solution to this sort of tedious, meticulous complexity is the same as it always is—we make the computer do it instead.

Automatic Tracing

This leads us to automatic instrumentation, which, in the case of OpenTelemetry, usually means deploying with an agent that can work with any Java 8+ application. Dynamic attachment of the agent is also possible and may be preferred in some circumstances. Finally, some frameworks, such as Quarkus, have built-in support and do not require—and should not use—the agent.

> As we discussed briefly in Chapter 3, a Java agent is a special jar file that contains code to be run before the main method is called. Building such things is an advanced topic, and the interested reader is advised to consult specialist material.

The agent adds extra bytecode to provide the timings of methods and other information that is needed to build a trace. In particular, this includes the trace ID and the span IDs, which will be used to link the spans together into a trace. The spans will be stored in memory temporarily, and then the OpenTelemetry exporters will send them to the backend.

> In addition to the instrumentation of core code and exporting by the agent, the `opentelemetry-java-instrumentation` project has modules that support over 100 of the most popular libraries and frameworks out of the box.

The branch `auto_tracing_only` of Fighting Animals contains an example of automatic tracing in action. It has a prebuilt agent jar available as part of the repo, and the location of this jar file must be passed to the JVM as a command-line argument, which you can see in the Dockerfile.

One major advantage of automatic tracing is that it is much easier to use than manual tracing, and it also keeps the project codebase free of explicit compile-time dependencies on OTel. You can see that by looking at this branch—there are no explicit dependencies on OTel in the POM, and no explicit code to create spans.

By default, the agent uses an OTLP exporter and points at `http://localhost:4317`, where it expects a local OpenTelemetry Collector to be running.

However, on this branch, the Collector setup is exactly the same as for manual tracing, so we won't repeat it here. So, just as we did for manual tracing, we need to add a command-line parameter to tell the application where to find the collector: `-Dotel.exporter.otlp.endpoint=http://otel-collector:4317/`.

The use of automatic tracing is a good example of the principle of *separation of concerns*—the application code is not concerned with the details (or even existence) of tracing, and the tracing capability is provided by the Java agent and some infrastructure configuration.

Before we move on from the subject of distributed tracing, there's one practical aspect that we still need to discuss—sampling.

Sampling Traces

In "Interpretation of Statistics" on page 37, we met the "hat/elephant" problem, a whimsical name for a very real problem: not all response categories have the same information content. For example, unless there are obvious degradations in response time, successful responses are not very interesting.

The same is true of traces—the vast majority of traces are successful, so are not very interesting. On the other hand, traces that are slow or fail are much more interesting, so we want to be able to see them.

> All happy families are alike; each unhappy family is unhappy in its own way.
> —Leo Tolstoy, *Anna Karenina* (*https://oreil.ly/1CuvU*)

One solution that the community has adopted is to vary the rate of sampling of traces, depending on the response code, and the number of transactions a service sees. In general, we always want to capture 100% of all errors (whether 4xx or 5xx errors) and then sample a percentage of the successful traces. For relatively high-volume services, this can be as low as 1% of successful traces.

This works because, if we have a high-volume service, then we will still get a statistically significant sample of successful traces, so any performance regressions will still be visible in the sampled data.

OpenTelemetry Metrics in Java

Let's turn our attention to OTel metrics. There is a manual API provided for handling metrics using the low-level OTel constructs. We'll see how this compares to Micrometer presently, but for the sake of completeness, let's look at a quick example from the `otel_metrics_raw_api` branch of Fighting Animals.

This branch has explicit dependencies on OTel libraries, just as for manual tracing. So, the POM changes are similar, and we also need the `opentelemetry-sdk-metrics` to be available.

Note that we have also removed the `spring-boot-starter-actuator` dependency. This is necessary to avoid conflicts with Spring Boot's bundled Micrometer, and we removed the bean providing a `MeterRegistry` bean. Instead, we're relying on the `OpenTelemetry` bean, just as we did for manual tracing.

In the code, we're using the instruments from the OTel metrics API in the package `io.opentelemetry.api.metrics` to handle our metrics. Let's look at an example in the `AnimalController`, which uses a `LongCounter` and an `ObservableDoubleGauge`.

First, let's declare our fields—a copy of the `OpenTelemetry` bean and the metrics we want to use:

```java
public class AnimalController {
  // ...

  private final OpenTelemetry sdk;

  private final Meter appMeter;
  private final Meter memoryMeter;
  private final LongCounter battlesTotal;
  private final ObservableDoubleGauge cpuTotal;
```

Next, in the constructor, we stash the `OpenTelemetry` bean in a field, and then use it to create the metrics we want to use:

```java
public AnimalController(OpenTelemetry sdk) {
  this.sdk = sdk;

  Meter appMeter = sdk.getMeter(INSTRUMENTATION_SCOPE + ".app");
  this.appMeter = appMeter;
  this.battlesTotal = createCounter(appMeter);

  Meter memoryMeter = sdk.getMeter(INSTRUMENTATION_SCOPE + ".memory");
  this.memoryMeter = memoryMeter;
  this.cpuTotal = createGauge(memoryMeter);
}
```

The creation of these two metrics is handled by static methods:

```
static LongCounter createCounter(Meter meter) {
  return meter
      .counterBuilder("battles.total")
      .setDescription("Counts total battles fought.")
      .build();
}

static ObservableDoubleGauge createGauge(Meter meter) {
  return meter
      .gaugeBuilder("jvm.memory.total")
      .setDescription("Reports JVM memory usage.")
      .setUnit("By")
      .buildWithCallback(
          result -> result.record(Runtime.getRuntime().totalMemory(),
            Attributes.empty()));
}
```

The counter is very similar to the Micrometer counter we saw earlier—and when a new battle is fought, we simply increment it, like this: `battlesTotal.add(1)`.

However, the gauge is a little different.

As we can see, the method that actually creates the gauge—`buildWithCallback()`—takes a callback function, which is used to record the value of the gauge. This will be called only when the gauge is observed—and the order of execution of callbacks between multiple gauges is not specified.

With this branch, the metrics are sent to the OTel Collector but only from the `animal_service`, as this makes things less noisy in the logs, and makes for a better illustrative example.

Only the `debug` exporter is configured for the collector's metrics pipeline, to avoid the need to configure a metrics backend.

OTel metrics also supports JVM-level metrics, and these can be gathered from JMX. There is also support for JFR integration.

It is possible to use the OTel metrics API directly, but many teams prefer the convenience and flexibility of a facading approach (such as Micrometer)—and that's our next topic.

On the branch `micrometer_with_otel`, we show an example of using Micrometer with an OTel exporter. This branch has a dependency on the `micrometer-registry-otlp` library, which provides an OTel exporter for Micrometer:

```
<dependency>
  <groupId>io.micrometer</groupId>
  <artifactId>micrometer-registry-otlp</artifactId>
  <scope>runtime</scope>
</dependency>
```

However, this is provided by the Micrometer libraries, so we do not require the OTel BOM, and there is no direct coupling to OTel in the POM. In fact, the code for `AnimalController` on this branch is identical to the code on the `micrometer_only` branch.

Note that the Micrometer registry is configured in `application.properties`:

```
management.otlp.metrics.export.url=http://otel-collector:4318/v1/metrics
management.otlp.metrics.export.step=10s
```

At the time of writing, this registry supports only compressed HTTP, not gRPC, so we must ensure the Collector is configured to accept OTLP over HTTP by adding the following to the ports section of `docker-compose.yml`:

```
- "4318:4318"   # OTLP http receiver
```

This exposes the HTTP port as well as the gRPC port, which matches the setting provided in `application.properties`. The configuration presented so far is somewhat bare-bones, but it does provide a starting point for good solutions for metrics and traces. However, we haven't said anything about how to get logs from the application into OTel, so let's discuss that next.

OpenTelemetry Logs in Java

The development of logs support in OpenTelemetry has proceeded with an eye on the architectural point that logs are expecting to follow the facading patterns already familiar to Java developers.

Therefore, our treatment of logs is going to be somewhat different from that of traces and metrics (where we displayed the low-level "raw" OTel API before discussing alternative approaches).

To be clear, OpenTelemetry does provide a "Logs Bridge" API, which allows logs to be emitted into the OTel pipeline. However, most teams should not use this approach, as it requires too much change to existing practice and codebases. Instead, one of the following alternatives is much more likely to be a better fit for your use case:

- Write logs from your service to a file, using a file-based appender, and arrange for this file to be scraped by the OpenTelemetry Collector, which then forwards to your logging backend via OTLP.

- Use an OTel instrumentation library to export logs from your logging framework of choice to the collector (usually alongside traces and metrics).[5]

---

5 Technically, if you use this option, you are using the Logs Bridge, just not directly.

There are pros and cons to both approaches—the first seems to serve architectural neutrality, but in practice, proves to be inflexible, whereas the second requires more upfront effort but seems to require less effort to maintain in the medium term.

In what follows, we will focus on the second option—the OTel logging docs (*https://oreil.ly/U4hWh*) should be consulted if you want to explore the first architectural option.

Unlike in the case of agent-based tracing or Micrometer-based metrics, there is no SPI or facading API for logs that does not involve an explicit dependency on OTel.

We have no choice but to directly couple to the OTel libraries in our POM. Just as for metrics, we will need to make an `OpenTelemetry` bean available for autowiring. We will also need to configure the Collector to receive logs, but this is a minor detail.

The boilerplate looks like this:

```
@ConditionalOnClass(LoggerContext.class)
@ConditionalOnProperty(name="otel.instrumentation.logback.enabled",
                       matchIfMissing=true)
@Configuration
static class LogbackAppenderConfig {
  @Bean
  ApplicationListener<ApplicationReadyEvent> logbackOtelAppenderInitializer(
      OpenTelemetry openTelemetry) {
    return event -> OpenTelemetryAppender.install(openTelemetry);
  }
}
```

We require a very similar collector config to previously; details can be found on the `logging_only` branch.

We're using the Logback appender, which needs to be included in the POM:

```
<dependency>
  <groupId>io.opentelemetry.instrumentation</groupId>
  <artifactId>opentelemetry-logback-appender-1.0</artifactId>
  <version>2.0.0-alpha</version>
</dependency>
```

and we configure it in `logback.xml` like this:

```
<appender name="OpenTelemetry"
          class="io.opentelemetry.instrumentation.logback.appender.v1_0. ←
OpenTelemetryAppender">
    <captureExperimentalAttributes>true</captureExperimentalAttributes>
    <captureKeyValuePairAttributes>true</captureKeyValuePairAttributes>
</appender>
```

and include an entry in `application.properties`:

```
otel.instrumentation.logback.enabled=true
```

to activate the conditional beans in the `AnimalApplication` class.

With this setup, developers can just continue to use SLF4J and Logback as normal, and the logs will be sent to the OTel Collector, which will forward them to the logging backend.

Bringing together the different approaches for traces, metrics, and logs, we can see that the recommended stack for Java that our applications could use might look something like:

- OTel agent for traces and JVM metrics
- Micrometer with OTLP registry for application metrics
- SLF4J with Logback OTLP logging appender for logs

The flows for each of these signals could be something like:

- Traces: Java agent → OTLP Exporter → OTel Collector → Jaeger
- Metrics: Micrometer → OTLP Exporter → OTel Collector → Prometheus
- Logs: SLF4J/Logback → OTLP Exporter → OTel Collector → Loki

The use of a local OTel Collector--generally one per cluster—provides a useful indirection point. This makes changing the architecture and handling cases like multipublication much easier, and it also isolates developers from many of the details of exactly how observability is architected.

Of course, this is not the only architectural approach—there are a large number of possible combinations of components that can be used to build an observability system. For example, OTel tracing can be either manual or automatic; Prometheus can be configured to either scrape from the OTel Collector or receive remote write from it.

Ultimately, it is a matter of understanding the overall architecture of the system as a whole—both in its current state and how it might evolve in the future. From this starting point, the team can then make architectural and deployment choices that work well in their particular circumstances.

Summary

In this chapter, we have taken a deep dive into the practicalities of implementing observability in Java cloud applications.

We have introduced some of the most important technologies in this space (Micrometer, Prometheus, and OpenTelemetry) and shown how they can be used together to build a complete open source observability system. We have also discussed some of the architectural principles that inform decisions about implementing observability systems for Java applications.

Where possible, we have tried to showcase approaches that do not impact the existing working practices of the development team. For example, use of the OpenTelemetry agent to provide automatic tracing, and use of the Micrometer registry for OTel to provide metrics.

This chapter also included a look at components such as the OpenTelemetry Collector and the use of the OTLP protocol for observability data transport.

One notable omission from this chapter is the subject of application profiling. This is a very important topic, but it is also a very large one, and it does not fit neatly into the framework for observability we have just introduced. In fact, it warrants a separate chapter of its own, and that is where we will turn our attention next.

CHAPTER 12
Profiling

The term *profiling* has a somewhat loose usage among programmers. There are, in fact, several different approaches to profiling that are possible, the two most common of which are:

- Execution
- Allocation

In this chapter, we will cover both of these topics. Our initial focus will be on execution profiling, and we will use this subject to introduce the tools that are available to profile applications. Later in the chapter, we will introduce memory profiling and see how the various tools provide this capability.

One of the key themes we will explore is just how important it is for Java developers and performance engineers to understand how profilers operate in general. Profilers are very capable of misrepresenting application behavior and exhibiting noticeable biases.

Execution profiling is one of the areas of performance analysis where these biases come to the fore. The cautious performance engineer will be aware of this possibility and will compensate for it in various ways, including profiling with multiple tools to understand what's really going on.

It is equally important for engineers to address their own cognitive biases, and to not go looking for the performance behavior that they expect. The antipatterns and cognitive traps that we met in Chapter 2 (and see also Appendix B) are a good place to start when training ourselves to avoid these problems.

Introduction to Profiling

In general, JVM profiling and monitoring tools operate by using some low-level instrumentation and either streaming data to an external tool (sometimes a GUI graphical console or a SaaS) or saving it in a log for later analysis. The low-level instrumentation often takes the form of either an agent loaded at application start or a component that dynamically attaches to a running JVM.

> Agents were introduced in "Monitoring and Tooling for the JVM" on page 62; they are a very general technique with wide applicability in the Java tooling space.

In broad terms, we need to distinguish between *monitoring tools* (whose primary goal is observing the system and its current state), *alerting systems* (for detecting abnormal or anomalous behavior), and *profilers* (which provide deep-dive information about running applications). These tools have different, although often related, objectives and a well-run production application can use all of them.

The focus of this chapter, however, is profiling, the aim of which is to identify user-written code that is a target for refactoring and performance optimization.

As discussed in "A Simple System Model" on page 184, the first step in diagnosing and correcting a performance problem is to identify which resource is causing the issue. An incorrect identification at this step can prove very costly.

> The scary thing about benchmarks is that they always produce a number, even if that number is meaningless. They measure something; we're just not sure what.
>
> —Brian Goetz, "Anatomy of a flawed microbenchmark" (*https://oreil.ly/SWxZW*)

In other words, profiling tools will always produce a number—it's just not clear that the number has any relevance to the problem being addressed. For this reason we introduced some of the main types of bias in Chapter 2 and delayed discussion of profiling techniques until now.

> A good programmer...will be wise to look carefully at the critical code; but only *after* that code has been identified.[1]
>
> —Donald Knuth

---

[1] "Structured Programming with go to Statements," *Computing Surveys*, vol. 6, no. 4 (December 1974): 268.

This means that before undertaking a profiling exercise, performance engineers should have already identified a performance problem. This identification can come from a number of sources, including:

- Performance regression tests in dev or CI pipelines
- UAT or dedicated performance testing environments
- Changes in production—for example, by observing the behavior of a canary
- Originally acceptable performance that has now become a problem—for example, by running out of capacity or data growth, exposing insufficient indexing

Note that performance regression tests can be difficult to write well, and most applications should structure them in the form of integration tests rather than microbenchmarks.

Once a performance problem has been identified (by whatever route), then the next step is to figure out what has caused it. It might be the case that application code is to blame, but it could also be something such as a library dependency upgrade that has brought in a performance regression. If you have performance regression tests as part of CI/CD, then you will want the deployment to fail and prevent that from going to Production.

In general, if the application is consuming close to 100% of CPU in user mode (which we can detect via metrics or alerts), then this is strong evidence for a performance problem that should be tackled with execution profiling. However, we must also remember that—even if the CPU is fully maxed out in user mode (not kernel time)—there is another possible cause that must be ruled out before profiling: garbage collection.

All applications that are serious about performance should be logging GC events, so this check is a simple one: consult the GC log and application logs for the machine and ensure that the GC log is quiet and the application log shows activity. If the GC log is the active one, then GC tuning should be the next step—not execution profiling.

Maxed-out CPU is not the only situation where an execution profiling can be useful, however. For example, if the application is not meeting latency SLAs in Production, you might choose to see what the profiler can tell you. If it's got high lock contention (which a profiler will tell you), then that will prevent it from using all the available cores.

As a second example, an application that's blocking on database I/O because a code change has put in a new, and expensive, SELECT query would also show up in an execution profiling run.[2] Some problems will only show up in profiling data from Production, however. This can occur when Staging does not have enough data in it for the missing index or expensive SELECT to hurt badly enough, but Production definitely does.

GUI Profiling Tools

In this section, we will discuss two different profiling tools with graphical UIs. There are quite a few tools available in the market, so we focus on two of the most common OSS tools rather than attempting an exhaustive survey. Our focus will be on execution profiling here, but the tools do offer a variety of other capabilities as well.

VisualVM

As a first example of a profiling tool, let's consider the VisualVM (*https://visualvm.git hub.io*), which we met in "Monitoring and Tooling for the JVM" on page 62. It includes both an execution and a memory profiler and is a very straightforward free profiling tool.

It is quite limited—it is rarely usable as a production profiler, but it can be helpful to performance engineers who want to understand the behavior of their applications in dev and QA environments.

We have already met some of the common screens in VisualVM—but let's consider the Monitor tab again. This shows basic telemetry information, as we can see in Figure 12-1, and is often the starting point for a profiling investigation.

---

2 This could include a full table scan or an ORM lazy-load issue, aka N + 1 problem.

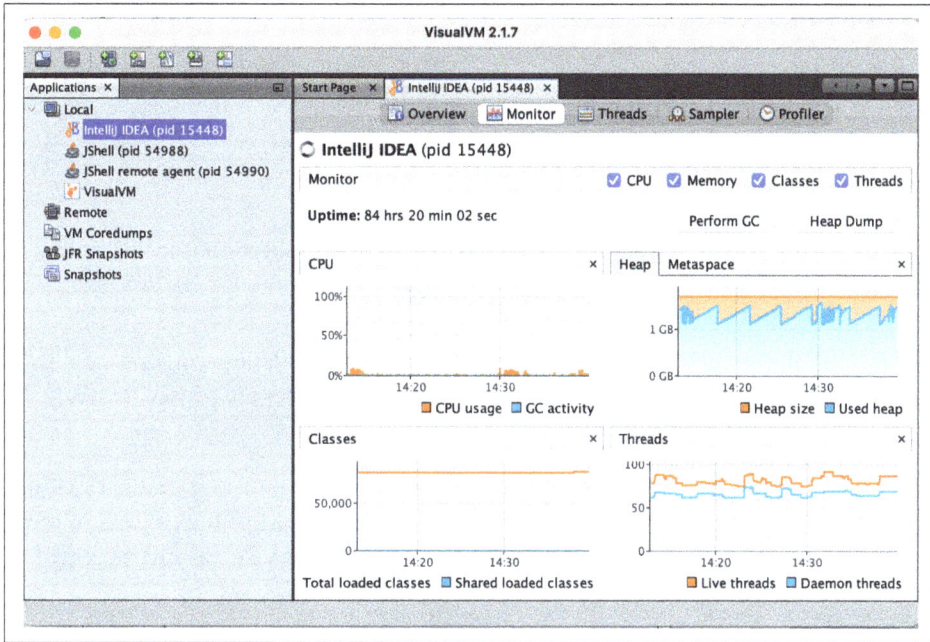

Figure 12-1. VisualVM monitor view

In Figure 12-2 we can see the execution profiling view of VisualVM from the Profiler tab.

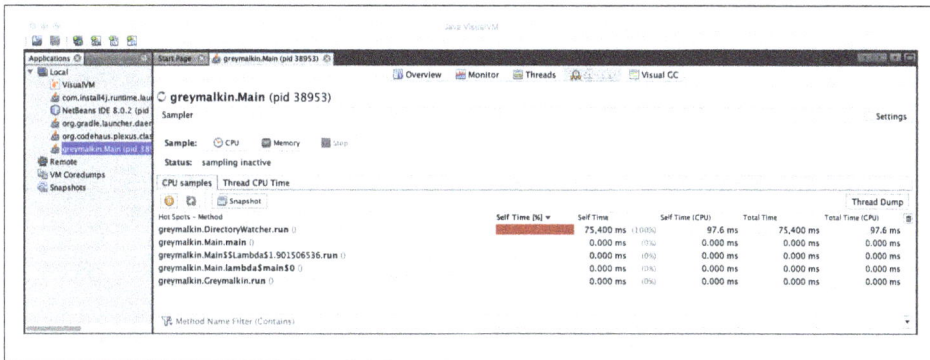

Figure 12-2. VisualVM execution profiler

This shows a simple view of executing methods and their relative CPU consumption. It can be a useful first tool for performance engineers who are new to the art of—and tradeoffs involved in—profiling. However, the amount of profiling drill-down that is possible within VisualVM's UI is really quite limited, and most performance engineers quickly outgrow it and turn to one of the more complete tools on the market.

JDK Mission Control

The JDK Flight Recorder and JDK Mission Control tools (*https://oreil.ly/IHLs8*) (known as JFR/JMC) are profiling and monitoring technologies that Oracle obtained as part of its acquisition of BEA Systems.

The two technologies are separate but related:

- JFR is a low-level, event-based, performance data collection capability that is embedded into the HotSpot JVM, and it provides events for the OS, the JVM, and JDK libraries.[3]
- JMC is the graphical component, and its initial installation consists of a JMX Console and a handler for JFR data, although more plug-ins can easily be installed from within Mission Control.

These tools were originally part of the tooling offering for BEA's JRockit JVM and were moved to the commercial version of Oracle JDK as part of the process of retiring JRockit. To support the port from JRockit, the HotSpot VM was instrumented to introduce a large basket of additional performance counters.

When Java 11 was released, JFR was donated to OpenJDK, and JMC was moved to a standalone project. Subsequently, JFR was backported to OpenJDK 8 as part of Update 272 (*https://oreil.ly/TMCtd*)—this means that recent releases of OpenJDK 8 have JFR available.

> The JMC desktop application can be built from source or downloaded from several places, including the Eclipse Adoptium project (*https://oreil.ly/xzTOU*).

JMC is started up by running the jmc binary. The startup screen for Mission Control can be seen in Figure 12-3.

---

3 Teams can also implement custom JFR events to add to their applications.

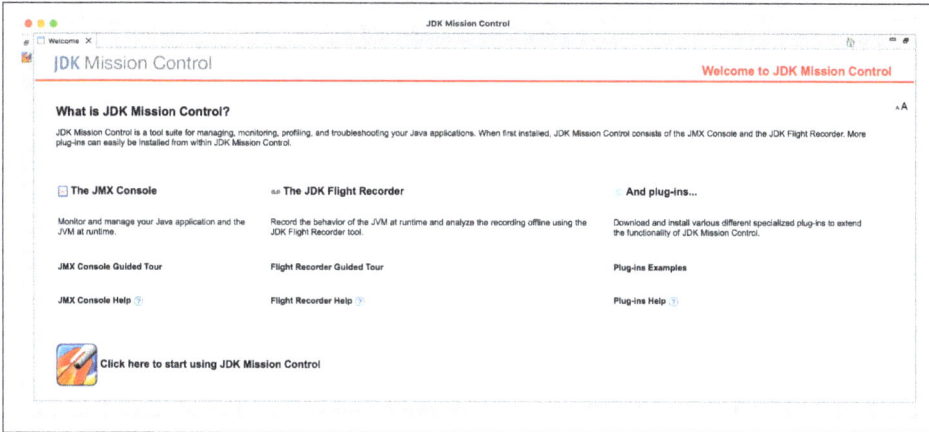

Figure 12-3. JMC startup screen

To profile, Flight Recorder must be enabled on the target application. You can achieve this in one of three ways: by starting the application with the JFR flags enabled or by dynamically attaching after the application has already started, or by starting the application and then using the jcmd command to start a JFR recording in a JVM on the local machine.[4]

Once it is attached, enter the configuration for the recording session and the profiling events, as shown in Figure 12-4.

---

4 It can be difficult to attach to a live production environment via JMX directly, so exfiltrating a JFR dump file is often an easier approach.

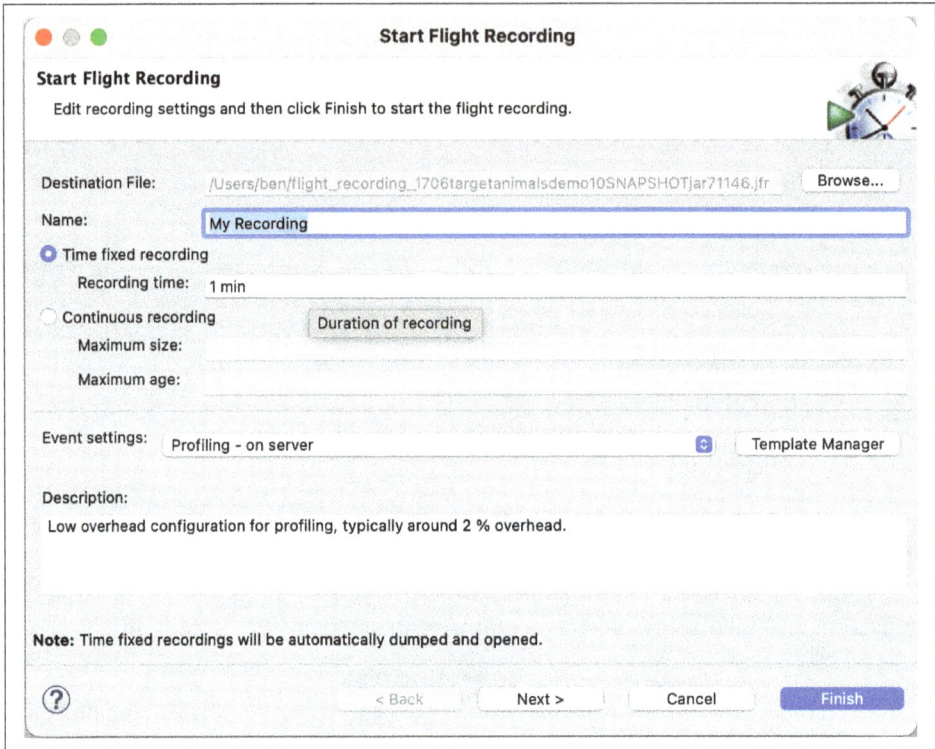

Figure 12-4. JMC recording setup

As discussed earlier in the chapter, execution profiling is very much not a silver bullet, and engineers must proceed carefully to avoid confusion and misconceptions. There are inevitable performance tradeoffs in the configuration of the tool, as well as a need for an awareness of the overhead of profiling.

> These screenshots depict the case of an application that is idle— i.e., not performing much (if any) work, so the images are for demonstration purposes only.

When the recording completes, an automated analysis is displayed in the main window, with the lefthand side showing a wide variety of available events. It looks like the view shown in Figure 12-5.

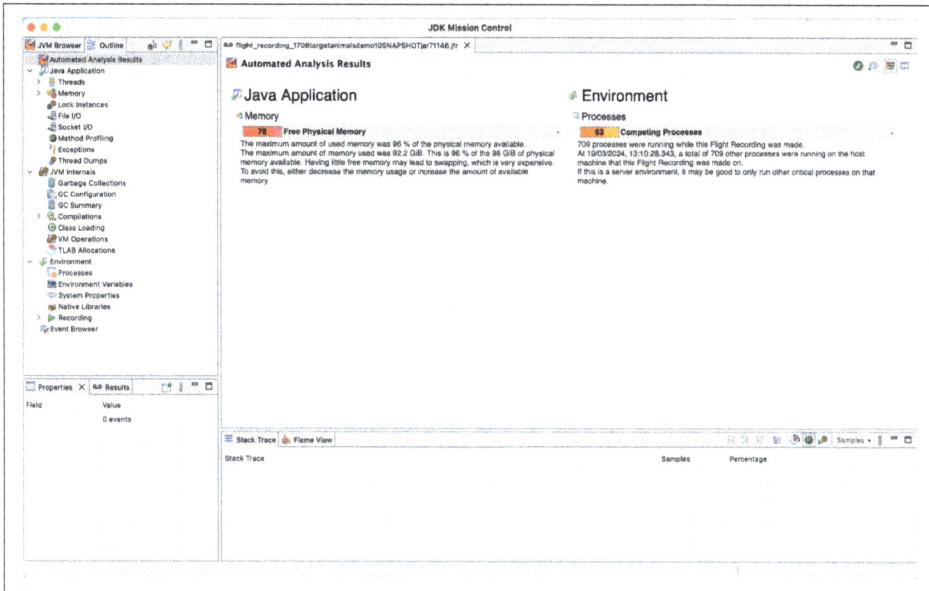

Figure 12-5. JMC automated analysis

Let's start by selecting the Method Profiling entry from the lefthand navigation. This results in a screen like Figure 12-6.

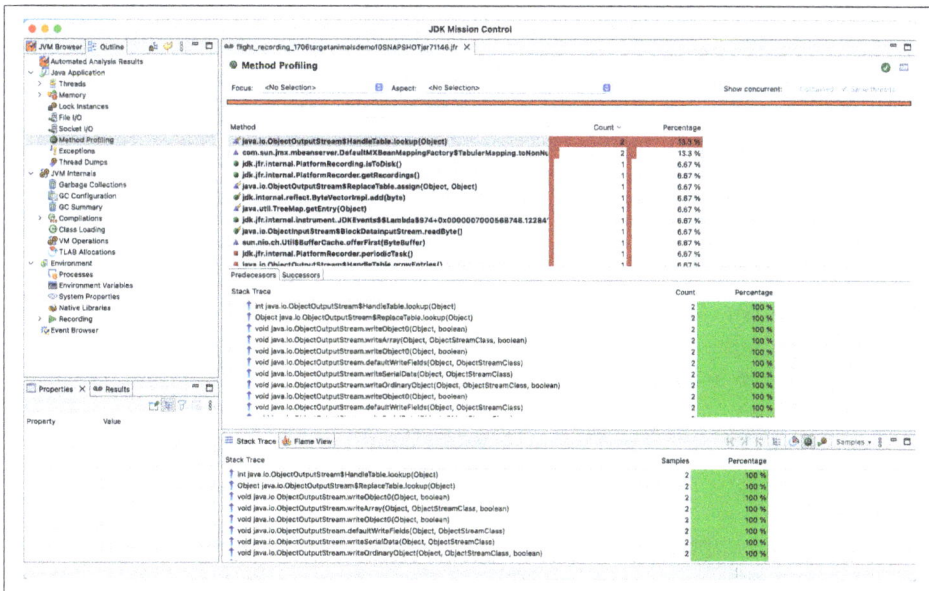

Figure 12-6. JMC Method Profiling

From here, we can start to look at which of the hot methods are occupying the majority of the application runtime and can also use techniques such as flame graphs (which we will discuss in more detail later)—provided that our profiling setup supports them.

Overall, JMC is a solid GUI-based profiling tool—but there are limits to this type of tooling. In particular, it can be difficult to see how to apply desktop-based profiling to the sorts of observability techniques we met in Chapters 10 and 11.

We will see how to bridge this gap presently, but first we need to discuss some details of how execution profilers actually operate.

Sampling and Safepointing Bias

Traditionally, execution profiling uses periodic sampling of stack traces to obtain a view of what code is running on each thread. This is because it is not cost-free to take measurements, so tracking all method entries and exits would represent an excessive data collection cost. So, instead, a sampled snapshot is taken—but this can only be done at a relatively low frequency without unacceptable overhead.

For example, the thread profiler in the New Relic Java agent will sample every 100 ms—and this is often considered a rule of thumb, or best guess, of a limit on how often samples can be taken without incurring unacceptably high overhead.

In other words, the sampling interval represents a tradeoff for the performance engineer. Sample too frequently, and the overhead becomes unacceptable, especially for an application that cares about performance. On the other hand, sample too infrequently, and the chance of missing important behavior becomes too large, as the sampling may not reflect the real performance of the application.

> By the time you're using a profiler it should be filling in detail—it shouldn't be surprising you.
>
> —Kirk Pepperdine (personal correspondence)

Not only does sampling offer opportunities for problems to hide in the data, but in many profilers, sampling has only been performed at JVM safepoints. This is known as *safepointing bias* and has two primary consequences:

- All threads must reach a safepoint before a sample can be taken.
- The sample can only be of an application state that is at a safepoint.

The first of these imposes additional overhead on producing a profiling sample from a running process. The second consequence skews the distribution of sample points by sampling only the state when it is already known to be at a safepoint.

Knowing that a profile is only showing running code because of the way it samples is crucial, because blocking and waiting are as large a headache as inefficient algorithms.

Sampling execution profilers use the `GetCallTrace()` function from HotSpot's C++ API to collect stack samples for each application thread. The usual design is to collect the samples within an agent, and then log the data or perform other downstream processing.

However, in its original implementation, `GetCallTrace()` had a quite severe overhead: if there are N active application threads, then collecting a stack sample caused the JVM to safepoint N times. This overhead is one of the root causes that set an upper limit on the frequency with which samples can be taken, at least for Java 8 and before.

This limitation was, to some extent, addressed by JEP 312, "Thread-Local Handshakes" (*https://oreil.ly/9MpFi*), which was also necessary groundwork for the Shenandoah and ZGC collectors that we discussed in Chapter 5. More recent versions, from Java 11 onward, have a significantly reduced overhead for thread profiling as a result of this change.

In general, the careful performance engineer will, therefore, keep an eye on how much safepointing time is being used by the application. If too much time is spent in safepointing, then the application performance will suffer, and any tuning exercise may be acting on inaccurate data. A JVM flag that can be very useful for tracking down cases of high safepointing time is:

```
-XX:+PrintGCApplicationStoppedTime
```

This will write extra information about safepointing time into the GC log. Some tools can automatically detect problems from the data produced by this flag and differentiate between safepointing time and pause time imposed by the OS kernel.

One example of the problems caused by safepointing bias can be illustrated by a *counted loop*. This is a simple loop, of a similar form to this snippet:

```
for (int i = 0; i < LIMIT; i += 1) {
    // only "simple" operations in the loop body
}
```

We have deliberately not defined the meaning of a "simple" operation in this example, as the behavior depends on the exact optimizations that the JIT compiler can perform. Further relevant details can be found in "Diagnosing Application Problems Using Observability" on page 254.

Examples of simple operations include arithmetic operations on primitives and method calls that have been fully inlined (so that no methods are actually within the body of the loop).

If LIMIT is large, then the JIT compiler will translate this Java code directly into an equivalent compiled form, including a back branch to return to the top of the loop. As discussed in "JVM Safepoints" on page 108, the JIT compiler inserts safepoint checks at loop-back edges. This means that for a large loop, there will be an opportunity to safepoint once per loop iteration.

However, for a small enough LIMIT this will not occur, and instead the JIT compiler will unroll this loop (*https://oreil.ly/J4z8P*). This means that the thread executing the small-enough counted loop will not safepoint until after the loop has completed.

Only sampling at safepoints has, thus, led directly to a biasing behavior that is sensitively dependent on the size of the loops and the nature of operations that we perform in them.

This is obviously not ideal for rigorous and reliable performance results. Nor is this a theoretical concern—loop unrolling can generate significant amounts of code, leading to long chunks of code where no samples will ever be collected.

However, there is an alternative to sampling profilers, and it's the subject of our next section.

Modern Profilers

In this section, we will discuss three modern open source tools that can provide better insight and more accurate performance numbers than traditional sampling profilers. These tools are:

- perf
- Async Profiler
- Honest Profiler

We'll discuss each in turn—let's start with the perf tool (*https://oreil.ly/JJap5*).

perf

perf is a useful lightweight profiling solution for applications that run on Linux. It is not specific to Java/JVM applications but instead reads hardware performance counters and is included in the Linux kernel, under tools/perf.

Performance counters are physical registers that count hardware events of interest to performance analysts. These include instructions executed, cache misses, and branch mispredictions. This forms a basis for profiling applications.

Java presents some additional challenges for perf, due to the dynamic nature of the Java runtime environment. To use perf with JVM applications, we also need a bridge to handle mapping the dynamic parts of VM execution.

This bridge is perf-map-agent (*https://oreil.ly/eUBUV*), an agent that will generate dynamic symbols for perf from unknown memory regions (including JIT-compiled methods). Due to HotSpot's dynamically created interpreter and jump tables for virtual dispatch, these must also have entries generated. perf-map-agent consists of an agent written in C and a small Java bootstrap that attaches the agent to a running Java process if needed.

In Java 8u60, a new flag was added to enable better interaction with perf:

```
-XX:+PreserveFramePointer
```

Unfortunately, this flag defaults to `false`, so when using perf to profile Java applications, it is strongly advised that you explicitly switch it on.

> Activating this flag disables a JIT compiler optimization, so it can decrease performance slightly.

One striking visualization of the numbers perf produces is the flame graph (*https://oreil.ly/tJREW*). This shows a highly detailed breakdown of exactly where execution time is being spent. An example can be seen in Figure 12-7.

The flame graph technique has evolved over time, so there are some important details about reading a flame graph that you should be aware of:

- The *x*-axis shows the stack profile population, sorted alphabetically.
- The *y*-axis shows stack depth, counting from the bottom.
- Each rectangle represents a stack frame, and the wider a frame is, the more often it was present in the stacks.
- The top rectangle shows what is on a specific CPU, and beneath it is its ancestry.
- Originally, flame graphs used random colors to help visually differentiate adjacent frames.

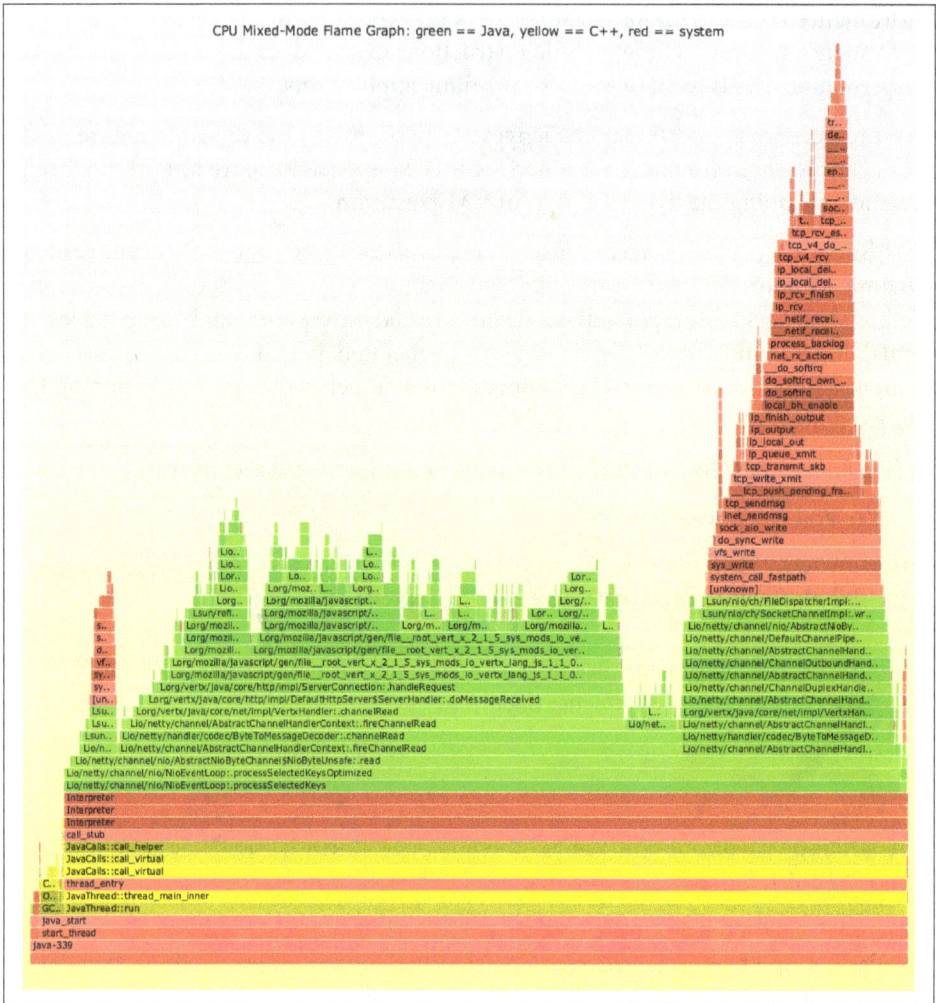

Figure 12-7. Java flame graph

Of these points, understanding that the *x*-axis is not the passage of time is perhaps the most important. Flame graphs organize the samples alphabetically and merge frames wherever possible—this gives a better overview of the big picture of the profile.

There have been several enhancements and variations on Gregg's original concept of flame graphs. For example, some implementations have begun using a consistent coloring scheme, in which the color of a rectangle has some semantic meaning (e.g., if it's a Java or a native frame), rather than just using the colors to make the graphs easy to read.

One important variation is *flame charts*, which were originally developed for Google Chrome's WebKit Web Inspector. Flame charts have time on the *x*-axis instead of the alphabetical sorting. This has the advantage that time-based patterns can be displayed but comes at the expense of only being able to sensibly display the pattern for a single thread. This is often fine for JavaScript applications, which are typically single-threaded, but is much less useful for Java applications.

The Netflix Technology Blog has some detailed coverage (*https://oreil.ly/KpAv9*) of how the team has implemented flame graphs on its JVMs.

You should also be aware of some issues with running perf in containers--remember that perf is based on hardware performance counters. The events that perf relies upon for CPU profiling may not be available in containers (or in seccomp environments).

Let's move on to look at Async Profiler, which uses perf as a building block for JVM profiling.

Async Profiler

The key goals of Async Profiler (*https://oreil.ly/Sn2pk*) are to:

- Remove the safepointing bias that most other profilers have.
- Operate with significantly lower overhead than traditional profilers.

To achieve this, Async Profiler uses a private API call: `AsyncGetCallTrace` (or AGCT) within HotSpot. This means, of course, that Async Profiler will not work on a non-OpenJDK JVM. It will work with OpenJDK-based JVMs (including builds from Adoptium, Amazon, Microsoft, Oracle, Red Hat, and Zulu from Azul) as well as HotSpot JVMs that have been built from scratch.

> In general, tools like Async Profiler are more commonly run in headless mode as data collection tools. In this approach, visualization is provided by other tooling or custom scripts.

Its reliance on perf means that Async Profiler also works only on the operating systems where perf works (primarily Linux). The implementation of Async Profiler uses the Unix OS signal `SIGPROF` to interrupt a running thread. The call stack can then be collected via the private `AsyncGetCallTrace()` method.

This only interrupts threads individually, so there is never any kind of global synchronization event. This avoids the contention and overhead typically seen in traditional sampling profilers. Within the asynchronous callback, the call trace is written into a lock-free ring buffer. A dedicated separate thread then writes out the details to a log without pausing the application.

There are some additional details about the operation of nonsampling profilers that you need to be aware of. First of all, let's consider this question:

When a CPU receives an "externally triggered" interrupt (e.g., a cache miss), at what point in the instruction stream is the CPU interrupted?

This question is especially important for modern out-of-order (OOO) CPUs, which is essentially everything a modern serverside application is likely to be running on.

If the output of a low-level profiler (such as perf) is examined, then it is possible to see an instruction tagged with, say, an L1 cache miss event that was not caused by this instruction. This is known as *skid* and is defined as the distance between the instruction that actually caused the event and the instruction where the event is tagged.

A related problem (specific to the JVM) is that there is also a hidden form of safepoint bias. Even though nonsampling profilers using AGCT or a similar technique are not safepoint biased for collecting stacktraces, the resolution of the last frame is still biased toward the recorded debug information, and unfortunately, by default, these are at safepoints.

To counteract this, nonsampling profilers try to activate the flag `-XX:+DebugNonSafe points` as soon as possible to have more precise resolution.

Async Profiler also tries to solve the `perf_events` issue that affects containers--by adding a new CPU sampling engine based on `timer_create` instead. This combines benefits of the older sampling engines, with the small tradeoff that it cannot collect kernel stacks.

This means that recent versions of Async Profiler work in containers by default, have reduced timing biases, and also do not consume file descriptors.[5]

> To use Async Profiler standalone, a certain amount of ceremony and scripting specific to your application is required. Rather than delve into those complexities, external resources, such as the Async Profiler GitHub page (*https://oreil.ly/nVNDr*) should be consulted.

Finally, an alternative choice to Async Profiler that was popular a few years ago is Honest Profiler (*https://oreil.ly/Cem59*). It uses the same internal API as Async Profiler, and is also an open source tool that runs only on HotSpot JVMs. However, it

---

5 This approach, based on `timer_create`, has also been adopted by the Go profiler as of 1.18.

does not seem to be actively maintained any longer, so it should not be used for new projects (and any existing installations of it should be migrated away from).

In the next section, we'll examine JFR—a built-in profiler that is, in many ways, similar to Async Profiler.

JDK Flight Recorder (JFR)

We met JFR in "GUI Profiling Tools" on page 308—it is a low-overhead tool shipped as part of OpenJDK for gathering diagnostics and profiling data. The intent is that it should be used by an in-flight Java application running on the HotSpot JVM in production.

For a production profiler, the overhead needs to be small enough to be tolerated both during normal and high-usage scenarios. JFR achieves this with the use of *profiles*— remember that JFR is event-based, so the different profiles correspond to different sets of events being enabled for JFR to respond to.

Out of the box, JFR ships with two profiles: "Continuous" (sometimes called "Default") and "Profiling." The XML config files corresponding to these profiles are present in the JDK installation as `default.jfc` and `profile.jfc`.

Of these two stock profiles, Continuous is designed for always-on profiling but may lack important detail, especially for allocation profiling. The "Profiling" profile (a truly classic example of why engineers shouldn't be allowed to name things) has much more detail but also a higher runtime overhead.

> Advanced users of JFR can choose to create a custom profile, containing a different set of events, which better reflects the performance interests of the group maintaining the application.

On the subject of overhead—according to Oracle presentations and demos—JFR profiling has about ~1% impact to steady state application performance for the Continuous profile. The authors are in broad agreement—having generally observed impact in the ~3% range for a profile that includes allocation profiling.

Alternatively, a more systematic study (but one conducted on microbenchmarks rather than full systems) can be found in "Don't Trust Your Profiler: An Empirical Study on the Precision and Accuracy of Java Profilers" (*https://oreil.ly/Sb4y2*).[6]

---

6 Humphrey Burchell, Octave Larose, Sophie Kaleba, and Stefan Marr, "Don't Trust Your Profiler: An Empirical Study on the Precision and Accuracy of Java Profilers," *MPLR 2023: Proceedings of the 20th ACM SIGPLAN*

This paper broadly follows the methodology of Georges et al. (2007), which we briefly discussed in Chapter 2, and compares JFR and several other profilers (including Async Profiler and Honest Profiler, which we have already met).

This consensus is that, in general, JFR induces an overhead that lies within the acceptable range for profilers, and that it is possible to use it to perform always-on profiling (although some applications may have resource requirements that make the overhead unaffordable).

Due to this, JFR has been used as a foundation to build many other observability and monitoring tools. For example, both Datadog and New Relic ship execution profilers that use JFR data as input data.

The key to understanding what's possible with JFR is the events, and what data can be found in them. So, let's take a closer look.

JFR events are typed data, and each event type has a name and a structure. For example, the event `jdk.CPULoad` represents a metric time series of CPU data, with several fields such as `jvmUser`, `jvmSystem`, and `machineTotal` as well as a timestamp represented by the event start time.

Other events have different structures—such as the GC events, which are fine-grained and may correspond to just a single phase of a collection cycle. Or the lock events, such as `jdk.JavaMonitorEnter`, which have a threshold value, enabling JFR to record only those instances where a Java monitor was held for longer than a specified time (e.g., 10 ms).

The JDK ships with a simple command-line tool that you can use to analyze a JFR dump file. These dump files can be created in one of three ways—using the JMC GUI, or via the command-line `jcmd` to control a running Java process, or by adding a suitable command-line switch to your Java startup.

For the `jcmd` route, we need to execute three separate commands to generate a file, one to start, one to dump, and then one to shut down the recording operation once we've collected enough data:

```
jcmd <pid> JFR.start name=MyRecording settings=default
jcmd <pid> JFR.dump filename=my-recording.jfr
jcmd <pid> JFR.stop
```

To begin a JFR recording at startup, we need to add this command-line switch and provide suitable options:

```
-XX:StartFlightRecording:<options>
```

International Conference on Managed Programming Languages and Runtimes (2023): 100–113, Association for Computing Machinery.

These recordings can be of a fixed duration or use a ring-buffer mode (as we will discuss later in the chapter). Once we've obtained a dump file, we can use the `jfr` tool that the JDK also provides to look at the events in it.

> The `jfr` tool has many subcommands—use `jfr --help` to see them all.

For example, we can see the `CPULoad` and `JavaMonitorEnter` events with a single `jfr print` command like this:

```
jfr print --events CPULoad,JavaMonitorEnter recording.jfr
```

which can produce output similar to this:

```
...

jdk.CPULoad {
  startTime = 11:51:57.745
  jvmUser = 8.75%
  jvmSystem = 0.57%
  machineTotal = 13.50%
}

jdk.JavaMonitorEnter {
  startTime = 11:51:58.065
  duration = 12.1 ms
  monitorClass = jdk.jfr.internal.PlatformRecorder (classLoader = bootstrap)
  previousOwner = "RMI TCP Connection(idle)" (javaThreadId = 32)
  address = 0x12CE66508
  eventThread = "JFR Periodic Tasks" (javaThreadId = 26)
}

...
```

By experimenting with a few `jfr print` commands, you can see the different shapes of the different event types. The `jfr` tool can also produce output in XML and JSON formats.

> An event browser for JFR events (*https://oreil.ly/OpLA6*) is maintained by the team at SAP and covers LTS and recent feature releases of OpenJDK.

It is also relatively simple to handle JFR dump files programmatically, as it's a simple matter of looping through a `RecordingFile` object:

```
String fileName = // ... some JFR file
var recording = new RecordingFile(Paths.get(fileName));
while (recording.hasMoreEvents()) {
    var event = recording.readEvent();
    if (event != null) {
        var details = decodeEvent(event);
        if (details == null) {
            System.err.println("Failed to recognize details");
        } else {
            // We'd process details here, for now just log
            System.out.println(details);
        }
    }
}
```

Of course, the events of interest still need to be decoded in the decodeEvent()
method. One way to do this is to use a static collection of mappers, which are applied
like this:

```
public Map<String, String> decodeEvent(final RecordedEvent e) {
    for (var ent : mappers.entrySet()) {
        if (ent.getKey().test(e)) {
            return ent.getValue().apply(e);
        }
    }
    return null;
}

private static Predicate<RecordedEvent> makePredicate(String s) {
    return e -> e.getEventType().getName().startsWith(s);
}

private static final Map<Predicate<RecordedEvent>,
        Function<RecordedEvent, Map<String, String>>> mappers =
    Map.of(makePredicate("jdk.CPULoad"),
        ev -> Map.of("timestamp", ""+ ev.getStartTime(),
                    "user", ""+ ev.getDouble("jvmUser"),
                    "system", ""+ ev.getDouble("jvmSystem"),
                    "total", ""+ ev.getDouble("machineTotal")
            ));
```

In this simple example, the makePredicate() method produces a Predicate object
to test whether an incoming event is of interest, and then transforms it to a map of
strings for output.

There are also lots of OSS tools available for handling JFR data. An interesting one
is JFR Analytics (*https://oreil.ly/W2Sje*) by Gunnar Morling. It presents a SQL-like
interface to querying JFR recording files and can be used with regular JDBC code.

Now that we understand the alternatives to sampling profilers and have seen JFR in context, it's time to return to the subject of how we use profiling within operational practice.

Operational Aspects of Profiling

Profilers are developer tools used to diagnose problems or understand the runtime behavior of applications at a low level. At the other end of the tooling spectrum are observability or operational monitoring tools. The latter exist to help a team visualize the current state of the system and determine whether the system is operating normally or is anomalous.

The space that these tools delineate is huge, and a single book simply cannot completely cover every tool in the space. Instead, we'll pick a few highlights to focus on.

These examples can serve as a starting point for you to begin to investigate the options and evaluate which is suitable for your applications. In observability and performance analysis, there is no easy path—you must engage fully and find the techniques that work for your specific domain of interest.

Using JFR As an Operational Tool

JFR has a long history, which is something of a double-edged sword. On the one hand, it has years of being battle-tested in production and is a best-in-class tool due to the deep integration with HotSpot.

However, it also comes from a much earlier time, when state of the art production profiling created a dump file (containing a lot of binary data and not human-readable) and then copied it back to a developer machine for offline analysis.

In our new world of cloud native applications, however, this may not be easy to achieve or very convenient. Simply put, we need new patterns and new methodology if JFR is to be a useful tool in the cloud native world.

One common operational pattern for using JFR is to start it in *ring buffer* configuration. This is usually done by starting the application with preconfigured JFR recording options that are passed to the -XX:StartFlightRecording switch, like this:

```
-XX:StartFlightRecording:disk=true,filename=/sandbox/service.jfr,maxage=4h, ↵
settings=profile
```

This tells JFR that we want to keep events matching the "Profiling" profile that are up to four hours old in memory (and discarding events older than that as new events come in), and when we request a recording, to dump the current state of the buffer into /sandbox/service.jfr.

This allows an operator to dump a file when required and "go back in time" to after an incident has already started, provided the ring buffer is large enough. This can be an extremely useful technique during outage recovery.

It is, of course, necessary to allow for the additional memory that will be used to buffer events in the container, and this has a somewhat-subtle consequence that you should be aware of.

Note that in our example, we are using the `maxage` parameter to indicate how long we want events to be kept for. Thus, because JFR is event-based, the amount of data it generates pends on the JVM's activity (e.g., number of garbage collections) and does not necessarily have a hard cap.

In turn, this means it is possible, if an application is close to the container memory limits, that a burst of unexpected activity can cause the size of the JFR event buffer to overrun that limit, resulting in the container runtime or OOM-killer enforcing the limit and killing the application process.

For this reason, some teams prefer to specify the `maxsize` parameter instead, which provides a guarantee that JFR will not cause the container to be killed. However, this comes at the expense of not being 100% sure how much "look-back" time window is provided by the JFR ring buffer.

In addition, JFR will spool to a file on the filesystem, so care must also be taken to have sufficient free disk space (on bare metal and VMs) and also not to get evicted by a container runtime (Docker or K8s) for excessive I/O in what's supposed to be a stateless container.

More recent versions of Java, including both 17 and 21, also have a JFR Event Streaming capability. This is an API that lets programs receive callbacks for JFR events so the application (or an observability thread, perhaps in a Java agent) can respond to them as they occur. The key class here is the `RecordingStream`, which allows the developer to register an interest in particular event types and indicate a callback object to handle it.

This is much more suitable as the foundation for building an observability tool, but it suffers from the problem that Java 17+ has only a ~35% market share as of April 2024 (*https://oreil.ly/ekd0_*). Instead, other tooling capabilities have been developed.

Red Hat Cryostat

Cryostat (*https://cryostat.io*) is a JFR tool for containerized Java/JVM applications. It was originally developed by Red Hat and is natively supported on the OpenShift hybrid cloud platform but is available as an upstream OSS project that will work on any Kubernetes distribution.

Cryostat seeks to reduce the complexity of working with JFR recording files within a Kubernetes cluster. It provides the capability for users to remotely start, stop, retrieve, and analyze JFR event data.

Cryostat requires cert-manager, Operator Lifecycle Manager (OLM), and Operator Hub to deploy successfully. It offers features such as:

- Application topology view
- Grafana view (for metrics)
- Automated rules
- Notifications
- Smart triggers

In Figure 12-8, we can see the topology view that the general Kubernetes version of Cryostat provides.

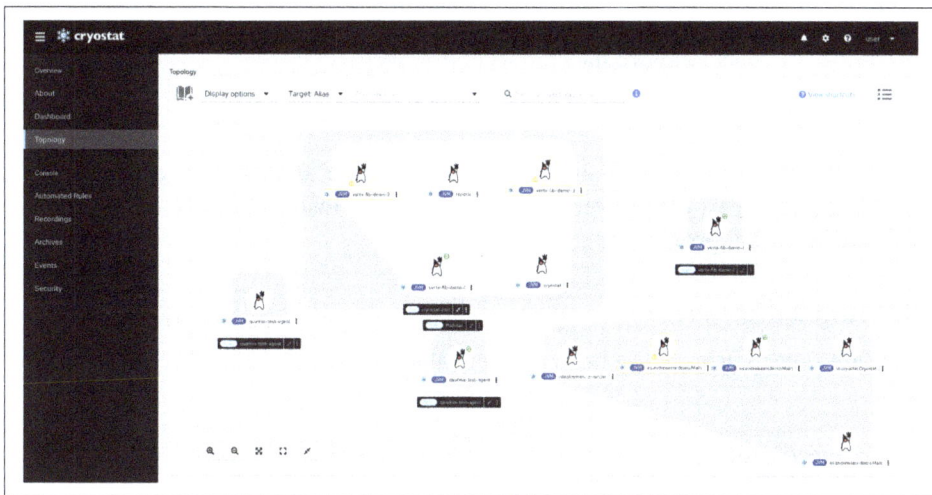

Figure 12-8. Cryostat topology view

The image shows a Kubernetes deployment of several pods, including both sample applications and the Cryostat pods themselves (another example of how observability services should themselves be observable).

Cryostat is an extremely useful tool for working with JFR, but a full discussion is outside the scope of this book. For completeness, in the proprietary tools space, both Datadog and New Relic (and possibly others) provide execution profilers that are based on JFR.

JFR and OTel Profiling

In "The Three Pillars" on page 238, we met the three pillars of observability and discussed the possibility of profiling as a fourth pillar. This enhancement is being actively discussed within the OpenTelemetry working groups. For Java, multiple different profilers would potentially be usable as data sources for a future OTel profiling signal type.

JFR could be one of the data sources that provides the profiling signal, but there are some complications. For example, a practical OTel implementation of profiling would need to be based upon JFR Event Streaming due to OTel's time window restrictions, and so it would only work for Java 17+.

There is also the problem that a the time of writing (August 2024), there is no simple way to associate a trace ID with a JFR profiling sample. Work in this space is ongoing, not just in Java but in the other languages that are in scope for OpenTelemetry.

> The `opentelemetry-java-instrumentation` project ships an implementation of OpenTelemetry JVM metrics based on JFR, which defines a standard set of JVM metrics.

Overall, JFR should be seen as an important contributor and data source for the OTel ecosystem and as part of the overall shift toward open instrumentation, but it is not a complete execution profiling solution by itself.

Choosing a Profiler

There are several aspects to choosing a profiler that you need to take into account, such as:

- Do I need a tool for working interactively in a GUI?
- Is this tool for production profiling or more for dev/CI usage?
- How much time and sophistication can I afford to invest in setting up my profiler?
- Do I have any constraints on the overhead I can tolerate for my profiling solution?

In general, you can characterize the open source profilers like this:

- VisualVM is a GUI tool that is easy to deploy but requires direct JMX connection or a snapshot to work from.
- JMC is another, more sophisticated GUI tool, which can also use JFR (but only via dump files—streaming events are not supported).

- JFR is a low-overhead headless profiling engine built into the JVM—which can integrate with a variety of other tools (both for offline and more operational use cases).

- perf is very low level and concerned with hardware events on Linux—it is not Java specific and needs some additional bridging tools.

- Async Profiler builds on top of `perf_events` and provides a low-overhead solution that does not suffer from safepoint bias, but it probably has fewer available integrations than JFR.

Finally, there are proprietary commercial profilers available, such as JProfiler (*https://oreil.ly/Id7Rd*) and YourKit (*https://www.yourkit.com*). These were once clearly superior to the freely available tools, but that gap has arguably closed in recent years, although some teams still find value in these tools. We do not discuss them in this book, however, as our tooling focus is on open source products.

To conclude this chapter, let's move on from execution profiling and look at the other major form of profiling—memory.

Memory Profiling

Execution profiling is an important aspect of profiling, but it is not the only one! Many applications will also require some level of memory analysis, and here we will consider two primary types—allocation profiling and heap dump analysis.

Allocation Profiling

As we discussed in Chapter 4, one of the most important aspects of performance analysis is to consider the allocation behavior of the application. This leads to the discipline of *allocation profiling*, and several possible approaches could be applicable.

For example, we could use the Visitor pattern that tools like `jmap` rely upon.[7] In Figure 12-9, we can see the memory profiling view of VisualVM, which uses this approach to produce a histogram of memory used by each type.

---

7 The Visitor pattern is a classic design pattern that extracts an operation (in this case, memory analysis) into a separate class that can traverse the subcomponents of a composite object.

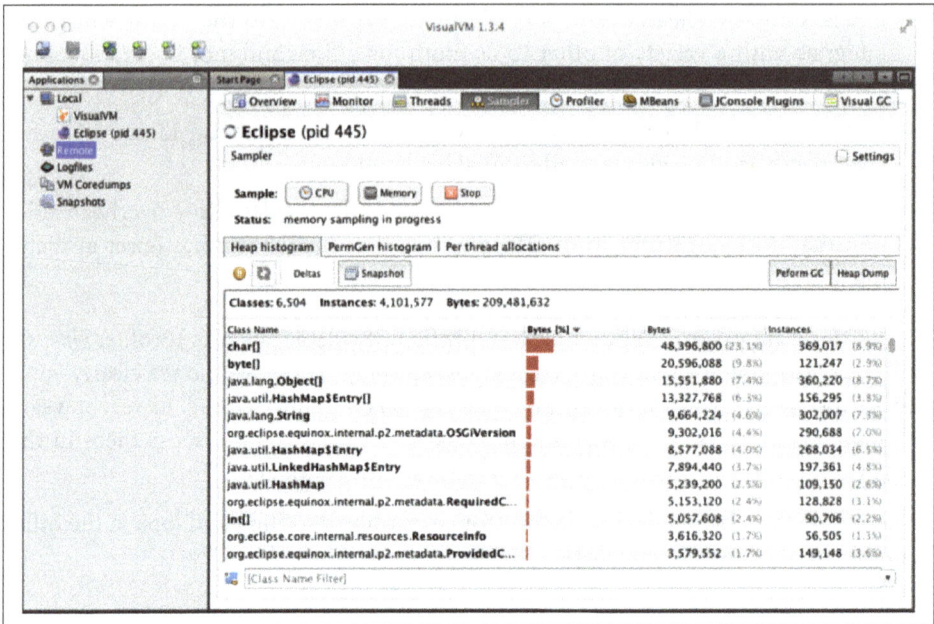

Figure 12-9. VisualVM memory profiler

This is a relatively simple view of memory, but there are a couple of things to point out here. First of all is that when producing this histogram, there are two options:

- A snapshot that's quick to produce but contains both live objects and garbage.

- An accurate snapshot, but one that needs an STW GC before being produced.

These two options correspond to the two command-line invocations: `jmap -histo` and `jmap -histo:live`.

Second, even a simple histogram can tell us a certain amount about an application's memory usage.

In most applications, strings are by far the most common data type. Inside a string is a reference to a `byte[]` (or a `char[]` in Java 8—the implementation changed with JEP 254 (*https://oreil.ly/Hzx8k*)), so we will expect to see at least as many `byte[]` objects as strings.

We also typically see other common objects, such as `HashMap` entries and `Object[]`. Business applications will also often see their domain objects appear in the list of most common objects—and this can provide a quick check by asking the question: "Is the observed amount of domain objects in the right ballpark for my application?"

Moving on from VisualVM, and slightly shifting focus from heap utilization to profiling GC, we can use the JMC tool to collect statistics that contain some values not available in the traditional Serviceability Agent (although the majority of counters presented are duplicates of the SA counters).

The advantage is that the cost for JFR to collect these values so that they can be displayed in JMC is much lower than it is with the SA. The JMC displays also provide greater flexibility to the performance engineer in terms of how the details are displayed.

Another approach to allocation profiling is to look at the TLABs, which you met in Chapter 4. In particular, JFR uses events to receive notifications when an object is allocated:

- In a TLAB (the `jdk.ObjectAllocationInNewTLAB` event)
- Outside of a TLAB (the "slow path," `jdk.ObjectAllocationOutsideTLAB` event)

This allows JFR to calculate how quickly memory is being allocated.

The Allocations view of JMC/JFR is capable of displaying the TLAB allocation view. Figure 12-10 shows a sample image of JMC's view of allocations.

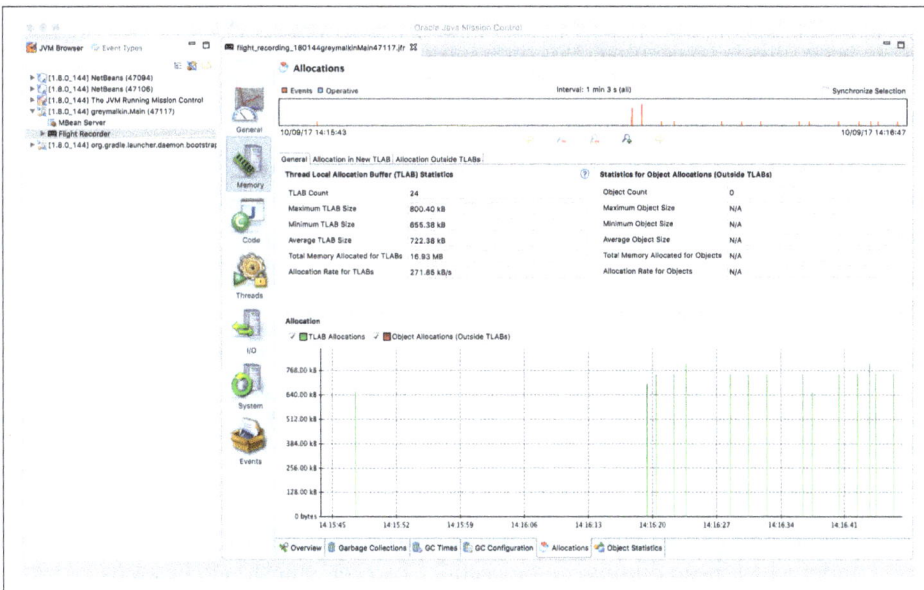

Figure 12-10. JMC Allocations profiling view

JFR also comes with events that can act as a form of memory leak profiler. It samples object allocations to track their lifetimes, using the `jdk.OldObjectSample` event, and over time, can provide suggestions for a starting point to investigate as a potential memory leak.

Heap Dumps

Another memory profiling technique is *heap dump analysis*. Unlike allocation profiling, this is an offline process, in which a snapshot of an entire heap is created and dumped to a file.

This can be achieved by the `jmap` command, for example, like this:

```
jmap -dump:live,format=b,file=heap.bin <pid>
```

This dump file can then be examined and analyzed by a separate tool to determine salient facts, such as the live set and numbers and types of objects, as well as the shape and structure of the object graph. These tools can either be batch mode or interactive.

With a heap dump loaded in an interactive tool, performance engineers can then traverse and analyze the snapshot of the heap at the time the heap dump was created. They will be able to see live objects and any objects that have died but not yet been collected.

One major drawback of heap dumps is their sheer size. A heap dump can frequently be 300%–400% the size of the memory being dumped, and for a production multigigabyte heap, this is substantial. Not only must the heap be written to disk, but for a real production use case, it must be retrieved over the network as well (which may not be easy for a containerized application).

Once retrieved, it must then be loaded on a workstation with sufficient resources (especially memory) to handle the dump without introducing excessive delays to the workflow. Working with large heap dumps on a machine that can't load the whole dump at once can be very painful, as the workstation pages parts of the dump file on and off disk.

Production of a heap file also requires the same tradeoff as we saw for the heap histogram—either garbage shows up alongside the live objects, or the process stops-the-world while the heap is traversed and the dump written out. In a modern cloud-based system, such an STW pause could cause the JVM process to appear down while a large heap was traversed, and this could result in the pod being killed.

Despite these difficulties, there are circumstances (such as difficult-to-isolate memory leaks) under which heap dumps can be useful. However, you should be aware of some of the limitations surrounding them, and avoid degrading or killing your production pods accidentally. Let's move on to discuss how to create and work with heap dumps.

As we saw in Figure 12-9, VisualVM can produce a heap dump. You can also use the tool to browse the contents of a heap dump file, but in practice, production heap dumps are somewhat unwieldy and difficult to work with in VisualVM.

An alternative is the Eclipse Memory Analyzer (*https://eclipse.dev/mat*) (aka MAT), which is a standalone tool that can be used to analyze heap dumps.

A lot of the power of MAT comes from its ability to traverse the object graph and generate reports based on the structure of the heap. For example, MAT can be used to find potential memory leaks, analyze the top consumers and dominators of memory, and perform other memory-related tasks.

Figure 12-11 shows an example of MAT with several standard reports visible in tabs.

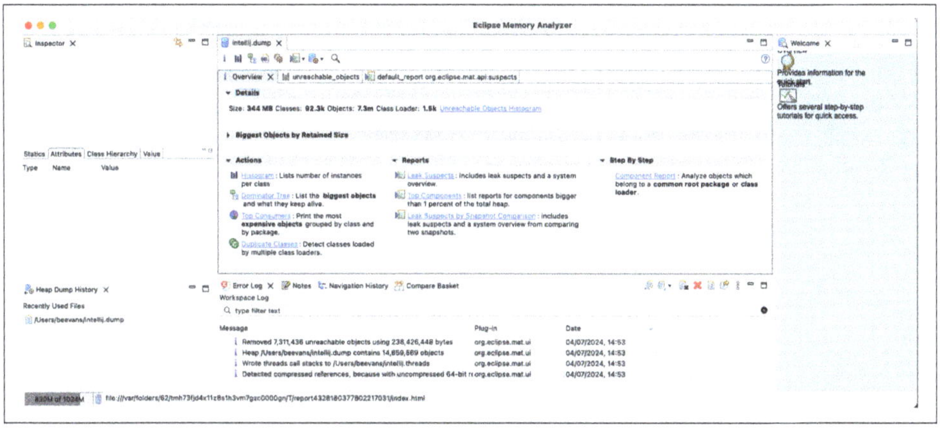

Figure 12-11. Example MAT view

In general, MAT is an advanced tool, and while the basic out-of-the-box reports are useful, the real power of MAT comes from spending some time learning how to use it effectively.

Allocation and heap profiling are of interest for the majority of applications that need to be profiled, and performance engineers are encouraged not to over-focus on execution profiling at the expense of memory.

As a final note, older texts may refer to the hprof heap profiling native agent. This was intended as a reference implementation for the JVMTI technology rather than as a production-grade profiler, and the documentation frequently points this out.

Despite this, quite a large number of developers started to consider hprof a suitable tool for actual use. For this reason, the hprof tool was removed in Java 9, although the ability to create heap dumps in the hprof format was retained in tools such as jmap. If your current toolchain uses hprof, then you should migrate to a supported tool such as MAT.

Summary

The subject of profiling is one that is often misunderstood by developers. Both execution and memory profiling are necessary techniques. However, it is very important that performance engineers understand what they are doing—and *why*. Simply using the tools blindly can produce completely inaccurate or irrelevant results and waste a lot of analysis time.

Profiling modern applications requires the use of tooling, and there are a wealth of options to choose from, including both commercial and open source options.

In the next chapter, we will move on from profiling and talk specifically about concurrency and how to use it efficiently in your Java apps. This will include key techniques that generalize to the distributed systems case, so they will be relevant to the cloud native case.

## CHAPTER 13

Concurrent Performance Techniques

In the history of computing to date, software developers have typically written code in a sequential format. Programming languages and hardware generally only supported the ability to process one instruction at a time. In many situations a so-called "free lunch" was enjoyed, where application performance would improve with the purchase of the latest hardware. The increase in transistors available on a chip led to better and more capable processors.

Many readers will have experienced the situation where moving the software to a bigger or a newer box was the solution to capacity problems, rather than paying the cost of investigating the underlying issues or considering a different programming paradigm.

Moore's law originally predicted the number of transistors on a chip would approximately double each year. Later the estimate was refined to every 18 months. Moore's law held fast for around 50 years, but it has started to falter. The momentum we have enjoyed for over 50 years is increasingly difficult to maintain.

The impact of the technology running out of steam can be seen in Figure 13-1, a central pillar of "The Free Lunch Is Over," a 2005 article written by Herb Sutter that aptly describes the arrival of the modern era of performance analysis.[1]

We now live in a world where multicore processors are the norm. Well-written modern applications must take advantage of distributing application processing over multiple cores. Application execution platforms such as the JVM are at a distinct advantage.

---

1 Herb Sutter, "The Free Lunch Is Over: A Fundamental Turn Toward Concurrency in Software," *Dr. Dobb's Journal* 30 (2005): 202–210.

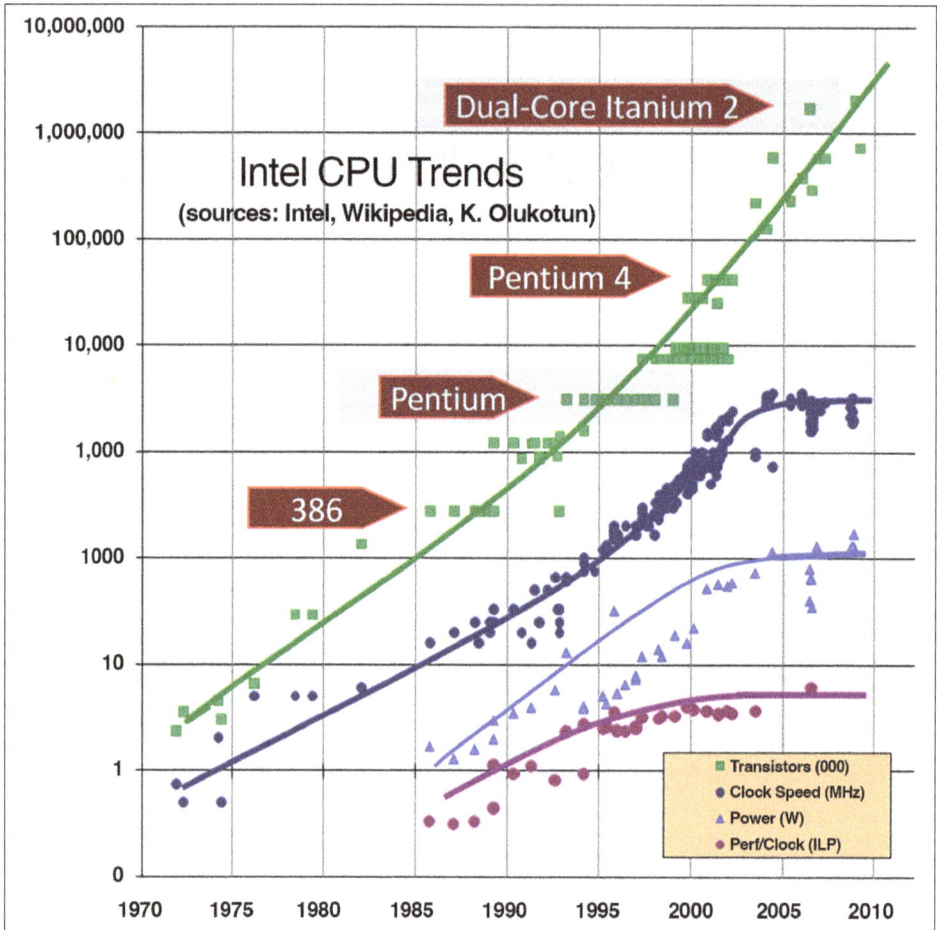

Figure 13-1. The Free Lunch Is Over (Sutter, 2005)

This is because there are always VM threads that can take advantage of multiple processor cores for operations such as JIT compilation and garbage collection. This means even JVM applications that have only a single application thread benefit from multicore hardware.

To make full use of current hardware, the modern Java professional must have at least a basic grounding in concurrency and its implications for application performance. This chapter is a basic overview but is not intended to provide complete coverage of Java concurrency. Instead, a guide such as *Java Concurrency in Practice* by Brian Goetz et al. (Addison-Wesley Professional) should be consulted in addition to this discussion.

Introduction to Parallelism

For almost 50 years, single-core speed increased, and then around 2005 it began to plateau at about 3 GHz clock speed as a result of physical constraints on hardware. Software engineers have been forced to focus more on performance techniques, as only limited improvements to hardware performance can be expected.

In this section, we will discuss some fundamental theoretical underpinnings of parallelism and concurrency.

One of the most important basic concepts is the distinction between *data parallelism* and *task parallelism*.

Data parallelism is about subdividing a single, large task that operates on a large pool of data. This involves distributing chunks of data over different processors, for example, an application that needs to process payroll and can allocate each CPU core a block of employees to process.

Task parallelism, on the other hand, involves distributing execution of different operations over processors, as seen in Figure 13-2. In Java, this will be achieved using threads and Executor objects—for example, the pattern whereby each thread services a user in Java REST app.

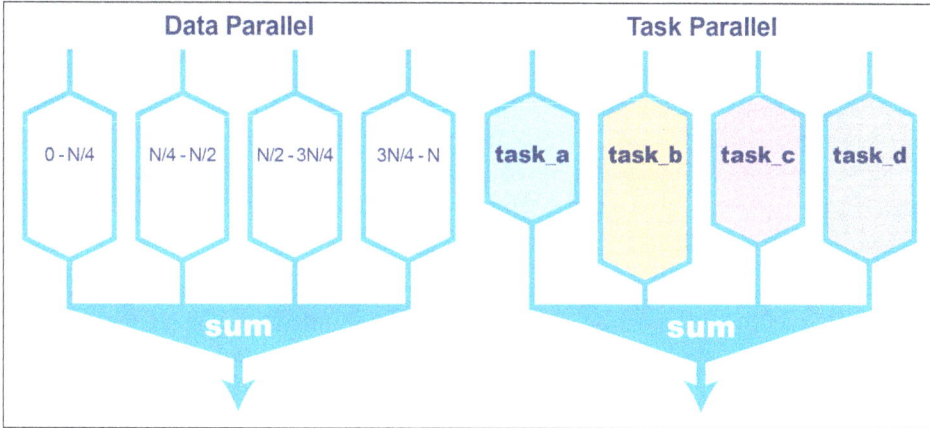

Figure 13-2. Data and task parallel concurrency

It is important to understand when to use each approach, and in this chapter, we will discuss patterns and relevant theory that apply to both cases.

Let's start by meeting a famous law of computation.

Amdahl's Law

In today's multicore world, *Amdahl's law* has emerged as a major consideration for improving the execution speed of a computation task—usually one that is obviously data-parallel.

We introduced Amdahl's law in Chapter 1, but we now need a more formal description. Consider a data-parallel computing task that can be divided into two parts—one part that can be executed in parallel, and one that has to run serially (e.g., for collating results or dispatching units of work for parallel execution).

Let's refer to the serial part as S and the total time needed for the task as T. We can use as many processors as we like for the task, so we denote the number of processors as N. This means we should write T as a function of the number of processors, $T(N)$. The concurrent part of the work is $T - S$, and if this can be shared equally among N processors, the overall time taken for the task is:

```
T(N) = S + (1 / N) * (T - S)
```

This means that no matter how many processors are used, the total time taken can never be less than the serial time. So, if the serial overhead is, say, 5% of the total, then no matter how many cores are used, the effective speedup will never be more than 20x. This insight and formula make up the underlying theory behind the introductory discussion of Amdahl's law in Chapter 1. The impact can be seen in another way in Figure 13-3.

Only improvements in single-threaded performance, such as faster cores, can reduce the value of S. Unfortunately, trends in modern hardware mean that CPU clock speeds are no longer improving by any meaningful amount. As a consequence of single-core processors no longer getting faster, Amdahl's law is often the practical limit of software scaling.

One corollary of Amdahl's law is that if no communication between parallel tasks or other sequential processing is necessary, then unlimited speedup is theoretically possible. This class of workloads is known as *embarrassingly parallel*, and in this case, concurrent processing is fairly straightforward to achieve.

The usual approach is to subdivide the workload between multiple worker threads without any shared data. Once shared state or data is introduced between threads, the workload increases in complexity and inevitably reintroduces some serial processing and communication overhead.

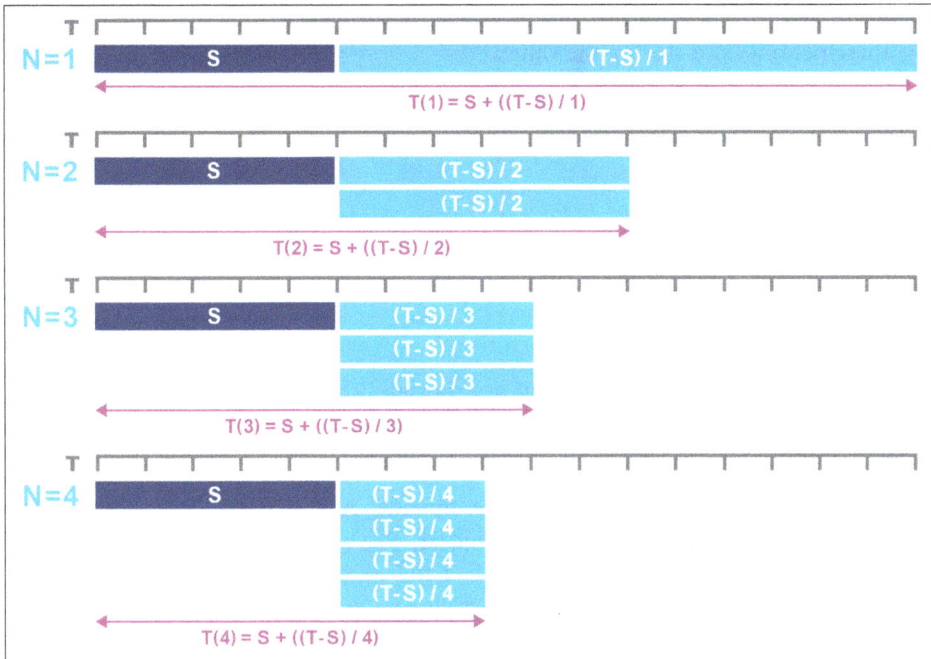

Figure 13-3. Amdahl's law revisited

> Writing correct programs is hard; writing correct concurrent programs is harder. There are simply more things that can go wrong in a concurrent program than in a sequential one.
>
> —*Java Concurrency in Practice*, Brian Goetz et al. (Addison-Wesley Professional)

In turn, this means that any workload with shared state requires correct protection and control. For workloads that run on the JVM, the platform provides a set of memory guarantees called the Java Memory Model (JMM). Let's look at some simple examples that explain the problems of Java concurrency before introducing the model in some depth.

Fundamental Java Concurrency

One of the first lessons learned about the counterintuitive nature of concurrency is the realization that incrementing a counter is not a single operation. Let's take a look:

```java
public class Counter {
    private int i = 0;
    public int increment() {
        return i = i + 1;
    }
}
```

Analyzing the bytecode for this produces a series of instructions that result in loading, incrementing, and storing the value:

```
public int increment();
   Code:
    0: aload_0
    1: aload_0
    2: getfield      #2  // Field i:I
    5: iconst_1
    6: iadd
    7: dup_x1
    8: putfield      #2  // Field i:I
   11: ireturn
```

If the counter is not protected by an appropriate lock and is accessed by another thread, it is possible a load could happen before another thread stores the value. This problem results in lost updates.

To see this in more detail, consider two threads, A and B, that are both calling the increment() method on the same object. For simplicity's sake, suppose they are running on a machine with a single CPU and that the bytecode accurately represents low-level execution (so, no reordering, cache effects, or other details of real processors).

As the operating system scheduler causes context switching of the threads at nondeterministic times, many different sequences of bytecodes are possible with even just two threads.

Suppose the single CPU executes the bytecodes as shown (note that there is a well-defined order of execution for the instructions, which would not be the case on an actual multiprocessor system):

```
A0: aload_0
A1: aload_0
A2: getfield #2 // Field i:I
A5: iconst_1
A6: iadd
A7: dup_x1
B0: aload_0
B1: aload_0
B2: getfield #2 // Field i:I
B5: iconst_1
B6: iadd
B7: dup_x1
A8: putfield #2 // Field i:I
A11: ireturn
B8: putfield #2 // Field i:I
B11: ireturn
```

Each thread will have a private evaluation stack from its individual entry into the method, so only the operations on fields can interfere with each other (because the object fields are located in the heap, which is shared).

The resulting behavior is that, if the initial state of i is 7 before either A or B starts executing, then if the execution order is precisely as just shown, both calls will return 8 and the field state will be updated to 8, despite the fact that increment() was called twice.

> This issue is caused by nothing other than OS scheduling—no hardware trickery was required to surface this problem, and it would be an issue even on a very old CPU without modern features.

A further misconception is that adding the keyword volatile will make the increment operation safe. By forcing the value to always be reread by the cache, volatile guarantees that any updates will be seen by another thread. However, it does not prevent the lost update problem just shown, as it is due to the composite nature of the increment operator.

The following example shows two threads sharing a reference to the same counter:

```java
public class CounterExample implements Runnable {

    private final Counter counter;

    public CounterExample(Counter counter) {
        this.counter = counter;

    }

    @Override
    public void run() {
        for (int i = 0; i < 100; i++) {
            System.out.println(Thread.currentThread().getName()
                    + " Value: " + counter.increment());
        }
    }
}
```

The counter is unprotected by synchronized or an appropriate lock. Each time a program runs, the execution of the two threads can potentially interleave in different ways.

On some occasions the code will run as expected and the counter will increment fine. This is down to the programmer's dumb luck! On other occasions the interleaving may show repeated values in the counter due to lost updates, as seen here:

```
Thread-1 Value: 1
Thread-1 Value: 2
Thread-1 Value: 3
Thread-0 Value: 1
Thread-1 Value: 4
Thread-1 Value: 6
Thread-0 Value: 5
```

In other words, a concurrent program that runs successfully most of the time is not the same thing as a correct concurrent program. Proving it fails is not the same thing as proving it is correct—it is sufficient to find one example of failure to demonstrate it is not correct.

To make matters worse, reproducing bugs in concurrent code can be extremely difficult. Dijkstra's famous maxim that "testing shows the presence, not the absence of bugs" applies to concurrent code even more strongly than to single-threaded applications.

We could use synchronized to control the updating of a simple value such as an int.[2]

The problem with using synchronization is that it requires some careful design and upfront thought. Without this, just adding synchronization to permit concurrency can slow down the program.

This is counter to the whole aim of adding concurrency: to increase throughput. Accordingly, any exercise to parallelize a code base must be supported by performance tests that fully prove the benefit of the additional complexity.

> Adding synchronization blocks, especially if they are uncontended, is a lot cheaper than it was in older versions of the JVM (but it sill should not be done if not necessary).

To do better than just a shotgun approach to synchronization, we need an understanding of the JVM's low-level memory model and how it applies to practical techniques for concurrent applications.

Understanding the JMM

Java has had a formal model of memory, the JMM, since version 1.0. This model was heavily revised, and some problems were fixed in JSR 133,[3] which was delivered as part of Java 5.

---

2 And before Java 5, synchronized was the only choice.

In the Java specifications, the JMM appears as a mathematical description of memory. It has a somewhat formidable reputation, and many developers regard it as the most impenetrable part of the Java specification (except, perhaps, for generics).

The JMM seeks to provide answers to questions such as:

- What happens when two cores access the same data?
- When are they guaranteed to see the same value?
- How do memory caches affect these answers?

Anywhere shared state is accessed, the platform will ensure that the promises made in the JMM are honored. These promises fall into two main groups: guarantees related to ordering and those concerned with visibility of updates across threads.

As hardware has moved from single-core to multicore to many-core systems, the nature of the memory model has become increasingly important. Ordering and thread visibility are no longer theoretical issues but are now practical problems that directly impact the code of working programmers.

At a high level, there are two possible approaches that a memory model like the JMM might take:

Strong memory model
    All cores always see the same values.

Weak memory model
    Cores may see different values, and there are special cache rules that control when this occurs.

From the programming point of view, a strong memory model seems very appealing—not least because it doesn't require programmers to take any extra care when writing application code.

In Figure 13-4, we can see a (greatly) simplified view of a modern multi-CPU system. We saw this view in Chapter 5 and again in Chapter 7, where it was discussed in the context of NUMA architectures.

---

3 The Java platform evolves through Java Specification Requests (JSRs) that track enhancements to the platform standards.

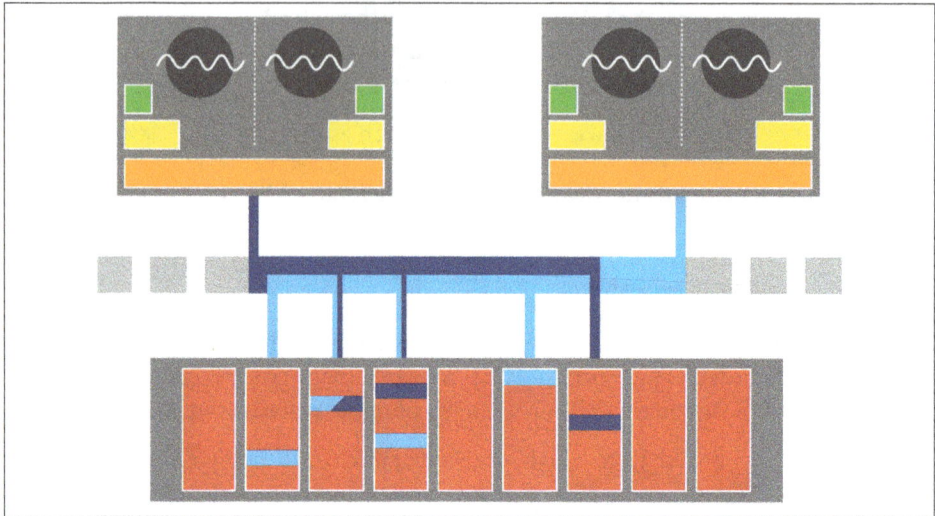

Figure 13-4. Modern multi-CPU system

If a strong memory model were to be implemented on top of this hardware, this would be equivalent to a writeback approach to memory. Notification of cache invalidation would swamp the memory bus, and effective transfer rates to/from main memory would nosedive. This problem would only get worse as the number of cores increases, which makes this approach fundamentally unsuitable for the many-core world.

It is also worth remembering that Java is designed to be an architecture-independent environment. This means that if the JVM were to specify a strong memory model, it would require additional implementation work to be done in software running on top of hardware that does not support a strong memory model natively. In turn, this would greatly increase the porting work required to implement a JVM on top of weak hardware.

In reality, the JMM has a very weak memory model. This fits better with trends in real CPU architecture, including MESI (described in "Memory Caches" on page 172). It also makes porting easier, as the JMM makes few guarantees.

It is very important to realize that the JMM is a minimum requirement only. Real JVM implementations and CPUs may do more than the JMM requires, as discussed in "Hardware Memory Models" on page 178.

This can lead to application developers being lulled into a false sense of security. If an application is developed on a hardware platform with a stronger memory model than the JMM, then undiscovered concurrency bugs can survive—because they do not manifest in practice due to hardware guarantees. When the same application is deployed onto weaker hardware, the concurrency bugs can become a problem as the application is no longer being protected by the hardware.

The guarantees provided by the JMM are based upon a set of basic concepts:

Happens-before
One event definitely happens before another.

Synchronizes-with
The event will cause its view of an object to be synchronized with main memory.

As-if-serial
Instructions appear to execute in order outside of the executing thread.

Release-before-acquire
Locks will be released by one thread before being acquired by another.

One of the most important techniques for handling shared mutable state is locking via synchronization. It is a fundamental part of the Java view of concurrency, and we will need to discuss it in some depth to work adequately with the JMM.

For developers who are interested in performance, a passing acquaintance with the `Thread` class and the language-level basic primitives of Java's concurrency mechanism is not enough.

In this view, threads have their own description of an object's state, and any changes made by the thread have to be flushed to main memory and then reread by any other threads that are accessing the same data. This fits well with the write-behind view of hardware as discussed in the context of MESI, but in the JVM, there is a considerable amount of implementation code that wraps the low-level memory access.

From this standpoint, it is immediately clear what the Java keyword `synchronized` refers to: it means that the local view of the thread holding the monitor has been synchronized-with main memory.

Synchronized methods and blocks define touchpoints where threads must perform syncing. They also define blocks of code that must fully complete before other synchronized blocks or methods can start.

The JMM does not have anything to say about unsynchronized access. There are no guarantees about when, if ever, changes made on one thread will become visible to other threads. If such guarantees are required, then the write access must be protected by a synchronized block, triggering a writeback of the cached values to main memory. Similarly, the read access must also be contained within a synchronized section of code to force a reread from memory.

Prior to the arrival of modern Java concurrency, using the Java keyword `synchron ized` was the only mechanism of guaranteeing ordering and visibility of data across multiple threads.

The JMM enforces this behavior and offers various guarantees that can be assumed about Java and memory safety. However, the traditional Java `synchronized` lock has several limitations, which have become increasingly severe:

- All `synchronized` operations on the locked object are treated equally. There is not an opportunity to specify priority strategies or differentiate between read and write access.

- Lock acquiring and releasing must be done on a method level or within a `synchronized` block within a method.

- Either the lock is acquired or the thread is blocked; there is no way to attempt to acquire the lock and carry on processing if the lock cannot be obtained.

A very common mistake is to forget that both read and write operations on locked data must be treated equitably. If an application uses `synchronized` only on write operations, this can lead to lost updates.

For example, it might seem as though a read does not need to lock, but it must use `synchronized` to guarantee visibility of updates coming from other threads.

> Java synchronization between threads is a cooperative mechanism, and it does not work correctly if even one participating thread does not follow the rules.

One resource for newcomers to the JMM is the JSR-133 Cookbook for Compiler Writers (*https://oreil.ly/F2tLe*). This contains a simplified explanation of JMM concepts without overwhelming the reader with detail.

For example, as part of the treatment of the memory model, a number of abstract barriers are introduced and discussed. These are intended to allow JVM implementors and library authors to think about the rules of Java concurrency in a relatively CPU-independent way.

The rules that the JVM implementations must follow are detailed in the Java specifications. In practice, the actual instructions that implement each abstract barrier may well be different on different CPUs. For example, the Intel CPU model automatically prevents certain reorderings in hardware, so some of the barriers described in the cookbook are actually no-ops.

One final consideration: the performance landscape is a moving target. Neither the evolution of hardware nor the frontiers of concurrency have stood still since the JMM was created. As a result, the JMM's description is an inadequate representation of modern hardware and memory.

In Java 9, the JMM has been extended in an attempt to catch up (at least partially) to the reality of modern systems. One key aspect of this is compatibility with other programming environments, especially C++11, which adapted ideas from the JMM and then extended them. This means that the C++11 model provides definitions of concepts outside the scope of the Java 5 JMM (JSR 133). Java 9 updates the JMM to bring some of those concepts to the Java platform and to allow low-level, hardware-conscious Java code to interoperate consistently with C++11.

To delve deeper into the JMM, see Aleksey Shipilëv's blog post "Close Encounters of the Java Memory Model Kind" (*https://oreil.ly/fU3vW*), which is a great source of commentary and very detailed technical information.

Building Concurrency Libraries

Despite being very successful, the JMM is hard to understand and even harder to translate into practical usage. Related to this is the lack of flexibility that intrinsic locking provides.

As a result, since Java 5, there has been an increasing trend toward standardizing high-quality concurrency libraries and tools as part of the Java class library and moving away from the built-in language-level support. In the vast majority of use cases, even those that are performance-sensitive, these libraries are more appropriate than creating new abstractions from scratch.

The libraries in `java.util.concurrent` have been designed to make writing multi-threaded applications in Java a lot easier. It is the job of a Java developer to select the level of abstraction that best suits their requirements, and it is a fortunate confluence that selecting the well-abstracted libraries of `java.util.concurrent` will also yield better "thread hot" performance. We use the term "thread hot" to refer to concurrent profiles where threads spend the majority of their time executing and not contending with other threads performing tasks on the same structures.

The core building blocks provided fall into a few general categories:

- Locks and semaphores
- Latches
- Atomics
- Executors
- Blocking queues

In Figure 13-5, we can see a representation of a typical modern concurrent Java application that is built up from concurrency primitives and business logic.

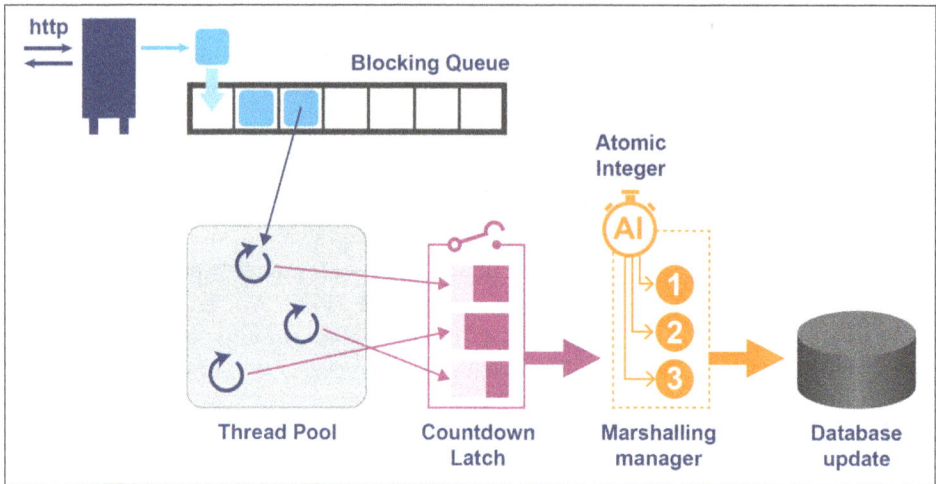

Figure 13-5. Example concurrent application

Some of these building blocks are discussed in the next section, but before we review them, let's look at some of the main implementation techniques used in the libraries. An understanding of how the concurrent libraries are implemented will allow performance-conscious developers to best use them. For developers operating at the extreme edge, knowing how the libraries work will give teams who have outgrown the standard library a starting point for choosing (or developing) ultra-high-performance replacements.

In general, the libraries try to move away from relying upon the operating system and instead work more in user space where possible. This has a number of advantages, not least that the behavior of the library is then hopefully more globally consistent, rather than being at the mercy of small but important variations between Unix-like operating systems.

Method and Var Handles

In Chapter 6, we met `invokedynamic`. This major development in the platform brings much greater flexibility in determining which method is to be executed at a call site. The key point is that an `invokedynamic` call site does not determine which method is to be called until runtime.

Instead, when the call site is reached by the interpreter, a special auxiliary method (known as a *bootstrap method*, or BSM) is called. The BSM returns an object (a *method handle*, provided by the Method Handles API) that represents the actual method that should be called at the call site. This is known as the *call target* and is said to be *laced into* the call site.

In the simplest case, the lookup of the call target is done only once —the first time the call site is encountered—but there are more complex cases whereby the call site can be invalidated and the lookup rerun (possibly with a different call target resulting).

At its core, the Method Handles API provides the ability to decide upon, obtain, and call a method at runtime, without any foreknowledge required at compile time. It is similar, in many ways, to the better-known (but much older) Reflection API-- however, the API is generally better, less cumbersome, and with several significant design flaws corrected.

It's not too much of a stretch to think of method handles as a more modern version of reflection and, as of Java 21, the reflection capability is actually implemented on top of method handles.

A `MethodHandle` object from the package `java.lang.invoke` in `java.base` represents a *directly executable* reference to a method. These method handle objects have a group of several related methods that allow execution of the underlying method. Of these, `invoke()` is the most common, but there are additional helpers and slight variations of the primary invoker method.

Just as for reflective calls, a method handle's underlying method can have any signature. Therefore, the invoker methods present on method handles need to have a very permissive signature to have full flexibility. However, method handles also have a new and novel feature that goes beyond the reflective case.

To understand this new feature, and why it's important, let's first consider some simple code that invokes a method reflectively:

```
Method m = ...
Object receiver = ...
Object o = m.invoke(receiver, new Object(), new Object());
```

This produces the following rather unsurprising piece of bytecode:

```
17: iconst_0
18: new           #2  // class java/lang/Object
21: dup
22: invokespecial #1  // Method java/lang/Object."<init>":()V
25: aastore
26: dup
27: iconst_1
28: new           #2  // class java/lang/Object
31: dup
32: invokespecial #1  // Method java/lang/Object."<init>":()V
35: aastore
```

```
36: invokevirtual #3   // Method java/lang/reflect/Method.invoke
                       // :(Ljava/lang/Object;[Ljava/lang/Object;)
                       // Ljava/lang/Object;
```

The `iconst` and `aastore` opcodes are used to store the zeroth and first elements of the variadic arguments into an array to be passed to `invoke()`. Then, the overall signature of the call in the bytecode is clearly `invoke:(Ljava/lang/Object;[Ljava/lang/Object;)Ljava/lang/Object;`, as the method takes a single object argument (the receiver) followed by a variadic number of parameters that will be passed to the reflective call. It ultimately returns an `Object`, all of which indicates that nothing is known about this method call at compile time—we are punting on every aspect of it until runtime.

As a result, this is a very general call, and it may well fail at runtime if the receiver and `Method` object don't match or if the parameter list is incorrect.

In contrast, let's look at a similar simple example carried out with method handles:

```
MethodType mt = MethodType.methodType(int.class);
MethodHandles.Lookup l = MethodHandles.lookup();
MethodHandle mh = l.findVirtual(String.class, "hashCode", mt);

String receiver = "b";
int ret = (int) mh.invoke(receiver);
System.out.println(ret);
```

There are two parts to the call: first the lookup of the method handle, and then the invocation of it. In real systems, these two parts can be widely separated in time or code location; method handles are immutable stable objects and can easily be cached and held for later use.

The lookup mechanism seems like additional boilerplate, but it is used to correct an issue that has been a problem with reflection since its inception—access control.

When a class is initially loaded, the bytecode is extensively checked. This includes checks to ensure that the class does not maliciously attempt to call any methods that it does not have access to. Any attempt to call inaccessible methods will result in the classloading process failing.

For performance reasons, once the class has been loaded, no further checks are carried out. This opens a window that reflective code could attempt to exploit, and the original design choices made by the reflection subsystem (way back in Java 1.1) are not wholly satisfactory, for several reasons.

The Method Handles API takes a different approach: the lookup context. To use this, we create a context object by calling `MethodHandles.lookup()`. The returned immutable object has state that records which methods and fields were accessible at the point where the context object was *created*.

This means that the context object can either be used immediately, or stored. This flexibility allows for patterns whereby a class can allow selective access to its private methods (by caching a lookup object and filtering access to it). By contrast, reflection only has the blunt instrument of the `setAccessible()` hack, which completely subverts the safety features of Java's access control.

Let's look at the bytecode for the lookup section of the method handles example:

```
 0: getstatic     #2 // Field java/lang/Integer.TYPE:Ljava/lang/Class;
 3: invokestatic  #3 // Method java/lang/invoke/MethodType.methodType:
                     // (Ljava/lang/Class;)Ljava/lang/invoke/MethodType;
 6: astore_1
 7: invokestatic  #4 // Method java/lang/invoke/MethodHandles.lookup:
                     // ()Ljava/lang/invoke/MethodHandles$Lookup;
10: astore_2
11: aload_2
12: ldc           #5 // class java/lang/String
14: ldc           #6 // String hashCode
16: aload_1
17: invokevirtual #7 // Method java/lang/invoke/MethodHandles$Lookup.findVirtual:
                     // (Ljava/lang/Class;Ljava/lang/String;Ljava/lang/invoke/
                     // MethodType;)Ljava/lang/invoke/MethodHandle;
20: astore_3
```

This code has generated a context object that can see every method that is accessible at the point where the `lookup()` static call takes place. From this, we can use `findVirtual()` (and related methods) to get a handle on any method visible at that point. If we attempt to access a method that is not visible through the lookup context, then an `IllegalAccessException` will be thrown. Unlike with reflection, there is no way for the programmer to subvert or switch off this access check.

In our example, we are simply looking up the public `hashCode()` method on `String`, which requires no special access. However, we must still use the lookup mechanism, and the platform will still check whether the context object has access to the requested method. Next, let's look at the bytecode generated by invoking the method handle:

```
21: ldc           #8  // String b
23: astore        4
25: aload_3
26: aload         4
28: invokevirtual #9  // Method java/lang/invoke/MethodHandle.invoke
                      // :(Ljava/lang/String;)I
31: istore        5
33: getstatic     #10 // Field java/lang/System.out:Ljava/io/PrintStream;
36: iload         5
38: invokevirtual #11 // Method java/io/PrintStream.println:(I)V
```

This is substantially different from the reflective case because the call to `invoke()` is not simply a one-size-fits-all invocation that accepts any arguments, but instead describes the expected signature of the method that should be called at runtime.

The bytecode for the method handle invocation contains better static type information about the call site than we would see in the corresponding reflective case.

In our case, the call signature is `invoke:(Ljava/lang/String;)I`, and nothing in the JavaDoc for `MethodHandle` indicates that the class has such a method.

Instead, the `javac` source code compiler has deduced an appropriate type signature for this call and emitted a corresponding call, even though no such method exists on `MethodHandle`. The bytecode emitted by `javac` has also set up the stack such that this call will be dispatched in the usual way (assuming it can be linked) without any boxing of varargs to an array.

Any JVM runtime that loads this bytecode is required to link this method call as is, with the expectation that the method handle will, at runtime, represent a call of the correct signature and that the `invoke()` call will be essentially replaced with a delegated call to the underlying method.

This slightly strange feature of the Java language is known as *signature polymorphism* and applies only to method handles.

This is, of course, a very un-Java-like language feature, and the use case is deliberately skewed toward language and framework implementors.

For many developers, one simple way to think of method handles is that they provide a capability similar to reflection but done in a modern way with maximum possible static type safety. Unsurprisingly, they are a very useful toolkit for implementing concurrency and other high-performance libraries.

Historically the only option for implementing low-level concerns has been performed using `Unsafe`. It was the only way to directly access CPU and other hardware features, manage off-heap memory, and generally bypass Java's well-placed constraints. Despite the intention of `Unsafe` to reside within the use of the JDK, it became ubiquitous in almost all Java frameworks. Methods and var handles are important, as they represent the path forward and underpinnings for concurrency libraries, including atomics and CAS.

Atomics and CAS

Java's atomic integer class (`java.util.concurrent.AtomicInteger`) has composite operations to add, increment, and decrement, which combine with a `get()` to return the affected result. This means that an operation to increment on two separate threads will return `currentValue + 1` and `currentValue + 2`. The semantics of atomic variables are an extension of `volatile`, but they are more flexible. Thread-based operations are performed without the need to synchronize to guarantee visibility of other interactions.

Note that atomics do not inherit from the base type they wrap, and they do not allow direct replacement. For example, `AtomicInteger` does not extend `Integer`—for one thing, `java.lang.Integer` is (rightly) a final class and, for another, `Integer` represents an immutable value, whereas an `AtomicInteger` is explicitly a thread-safe mutable value.

Atomics, along with some of the other concurrency libraries (notably the locks in `java.util.concurrent`) rely on low-level processor instructions and operating system specifics to implement a technique known as *compare and swap* (CAS).

This technique takes a pair of values, the "expected current value" and the "wanted new value," and a memory location (a pointer). As an atomic unit, two operations occur:

1. The expected current value is compared with the contents of the memory location.
2. If they match, the current value is swapped with the wanted new value.

CAS is a basic building block for several crucial higher-level concurrency features, so this is a classic example of how the performance and hardware landscape has not stood still since the JMM was produced.

Despite the fact that the CAS feature is implemented in hardware on most modern processors, it does not form part of the JMM or the Java platform specification. Historically, it was, therefore, handled as an implementation-specific extension, and access to CAS hardware was provided via the `sun.misc.Unsafe` class.

However, in recent versions of Java, increasing efforts have been made to remove `Unsafe` and replace it with method and var handles.[4]

---

[4] A full treatement of `Unsafe` is outside the scope of this book—especially as it is an API that the OpenJDK team is actively trying to remove. Further details can be found in this article in Oracle's Java magazine (*https://oreil.ly/ZR9WH*).

It is vital for effective use of atomics that developers use the facilities provided and do not roll their own implementations of, say, an atomic integer. Rest assured that the standard library already takes advantage of method handles (and Unsafe, where permitted).

Let's look at a quick example that shows how we might approach replacing Unsafe:

```java
public class AtomicIntegerWithVarHandles extends Number {

    private volatile int value = 0;
    private static final VarHandle V;

    static {
        try {
            MethodHandles.Lookup l = MethodHandles.lookup();
            V = l.findVarHandle(AtomicIntegerWithVarHandles.class, "value",
                int.class);
        } catch (ReflectiveOperationException e) {
            throw new Error(e);
        }
    }

    public final int getAndSet(int newValue) {
        int v;
        do {
            v = (int)V.getVolatile(this);
        } while (!V.compareAndSet(this, v, newValue));

        return v;
    }
    // ....
```

The sample demonstrates the usage of a loop to repeatedly retry a CAS operation. This is to deal with the situation where the comparison fails so the update is not performed. Usually this occurs when another thread just performed an update between the read and the write (as seen by this thread).

This retry loop produces a linear degradation of performance if multiple retries are required to update the variable. When considering performance, it is important to monitor the contention level to ensure throughput levels remain high.

With this caveat, we can see that atomics are lock-free and therefore cannot deadlock.

Locks and Spinlocks

The intrinsic locks that form the basis of synchronized in Java operate by invoking the operating system from user code. The OS is used to put a thread into an indefinite wait until signaled. This can be a huge overhead if the contended resource is only in use for a very short time.

Lock-free techniques start from the premise that blocking is bad for throughput and can degrade performance. Instead, it may be much more efficient to have the blocked thread stay active on a CPU, accomplish no useful work, and "burn CPU" retrying the lock until it becomes available.

This technique is known as a *spinlock* and is intended to be more lightweight than a full mutual-exclusion lock. In modern systems, spinlocks are usually implemented with CAS, assuming the hardware supports it. Let's look at a simple example in low-level x86 assembly:

```
locked:
        dd      0

spin_lock:
        mov     eax, 1
        xchg    eax, [locked]
        test    eax, eax
        jnz     spin_lock
        ret

spin_unlock:
        mov     eax, 0
        xchg    eax, [locked]
        ret
```

The exact implementation of a spinlock varies between CPUs, but the core concept is the same on all systems:

- The "test and set" operation—implemented here by xchg—must be atomic.
- If there is contention for the spinlock, processors that are waiting execute a tight loop.

CAS essentially allows the safe updating of a value in one instruction if the expected value is correct. This helps us to form the building blocks for a lock.

Of course, these techniques also come at a cost. Occupying a CPU core is expensive in terms of utilization and power consumption: the machine is going to be non-idle, but this spinning also implies hotter, which means more power will be required to cool the core that's processing nothing.

Summary of Concurrent Libraries

Concurrency in Java was originally designed for an environment where long-running blocking tasks could be interleaved to allow other threads to execute—for example, I/O and other similar slow operations—but where the underlying hardware often had only one execution core. Nowadays, almost every machine is a multicore system (even mobile phones), so making efficient use of the available CPU resources is very sensible.

However, when the notion of concurrency was built into Java, it was not something the industry had a great deal of experience with. In fact, Java was the first industry-standard environment to build in threading support at language level—with the Thread API. As a result, many of the painful lessons developers have learned about concurrency were first encountered in Java. In Java, the approach has generally been not to deprecate features (especially core features), so the Thread API is still a part of Java and always will be.

This has led to a situation where, in modern application development, threads are quite low level in comparison to the abstraction level at which Java programmers are accustomed to writing code. For example, in Java we do not deal with manual memory management, so why do Java programmers have to deal with low-level threading creation and other lifecycle events?

Fortunately, modern Java offers an environment that enables significant performance to be gained from abstractions built into the language and standard library. This allows developers to have the advantages of concurrent programming with fewer low-level frustrations and less boilerplate.

We've seen an introduction to the low-level implementation techniques used to enable atomic classes and simple locks. Now, let's look at how the standard library uses these capabilities to create fully featured production libraries for general-purpose use.

Locks in java.util.concurrent

Java 5 reimagined locks and added a more general interface for a lock in `java.util.concurrent.locks.Lock`. This interface offers more possibilities than the behavior of intrinsic locks:

`lock()`
Traditionally acquires the lock and will block until the lock is available.

`newCondition()`
Creates conditions around the lock, which allows the lock to be used more flexibly. Allows a separation of concerns within the lock (e.g., a read and a write).

`tryLock()`
Tries to acquire the lock (with an optional timeout), allowing for a thread to continue the process in the situation where the lock does not become available.

`unlock()`
Releases the lock. This is the corresponding call following a `lock()`.

In addition to allowing different types of locks to be created, locks can now also span multiple methods, as it is possible to lock in one method and unlock in another. If a thread wants to acquire a lock in a nonblocking manner, it is able to do so using the tryLock() method and back out if the lock is not available.

The ReentrantLock is the main implementation of Lock and basically uses a compare AndSwap() with an int. This means that the acquisition of the lock is lock-free in the uncontended case. This can dramatically increase the performance of a system where there is less lock contention while also providing the additional flexibility of different locking policies.

> The idea of a thread being able to reacquire the same lock is known as *re-entrant locking*, and this prevents a thread from blocking itself. Most modern application-level locking schemes are re-entrant.

The actual calls to compareAndSwap() and the usage of Unsafe can be found in the static subclass Sync, an extension to AbstractQueuedSynchronizer. AbstractQueued Synchronizer also uses the LockSupport class, which has methods that allow threads to be parked and resumed. The LockSupport class works by issuing permits to threads, and if there isn't a permit available, a thread must wait.

The idea of permits is similar to the concept of issuing permits in semaphores, but here there is only a single permit (a binary semaphore). If a permit is not available, a thread will be parked, and once a valid permit is available, the thread will be unparked. The methods of this class replace the long-deprecated methods of Thread.suspend() and Thread.resume().

There are three forms of park() that influence the following basic pseudocode:

```
while (!canProceed()) { ... LockSupport.park(this); }}
```

They are:

park(Object blocker)
  Blocks until another thread calls unpark(), the thread is interrupted, or a spurious wakeup occurs.

parkNanos(Object blocker, long nanos)
  Behaves the same as park() but will also return once the specified nano time elapses.

parkUntil(Object blocker, long deadline)
  Is similar to parkNanos() but instead uses an absolute point in time (deadline) specified in milliseconds from the Epoch.

Read/Write Locks

Many components in applications will have an imbalance between the number of read operations and write operations. Reads don't change the state, whereas write operations will. Using the traditional synchronized or ReentrantLock (without conditions) will follow a single lock strategy. In situations like caching, where there may be many readers and a single writer, the data structure may spend a lot of time unnecessarily blocking the readers due to another read.

The ReentrantReadWriteLock class exposes a ReadLock and a WriteLock that can be used within code. The advantage is that multiple threads reading do not cause other reading threads to block. The only operation that will block is a write. Using this locking pattern where the number of readers is high can significantly improve thread throughput and reduce locking. It is also possible to set the lock into "fair mode," which degrades performance but ensures threads are dealt with in order.

The following implementation for AgeCache would be a significant improvement over a version that uses a single lock:

```java
public class AgeCache {
    private final ReentrantReadWriteLock rwl = new ReentrantReadWriteLock();
    private final Lock readLock = rwl.readLock();
    private final Lock writeLock = rwl.writeLock();
    private Map<String, Integer> ageCache = new HashMap<>();

    public Integer getAge(String name) {
        readLock.lock();
        try {
                return ageCache.get(name);
        } finally {
                    readLock.unlock();
            }
    }

    public void updateAge(String name, int newAge) {
        writeLock.lock();
        try {
                ageCache.put(name, newAge);
        } finally {
                writeLock.unlock();
        }
    }
}
```

However, we could make it even more optimal by considering the underlying data structure. In this example, a concurrent collection would be a more sensible abstraction and yield greater thread hot benefits.

Semaphores

Semaphores offer a unique technique for allowing access to a number of available resources—for instance, threads in a pool or database connection objects. A semaphore works on the premise that "at most, X objects are allowed access" and functions by having a set number of permits to control access:

```
// Semaphore with 2 permits and a fair model
private Semaphore poolPermits = new Semaphore(2, true);
```

`Semaphore::acquire()` reduces the number of available permits by one, and if there are no permits available, will block. `Semaphore::release()` returns a permit and will release a waiting acquirer if there is one. Because semaphores are often used where resources are potentially blocked or queued, it is most likely that a semaphore will be initialized as fair to avoid thread starvation.

A one-permit semaphore (binary semaphore) is equivalent to a mutex, but with one distinct difference. A mutex can only be released by a thread that the mutex is locked on, whereas a semaphore can be released by a non-owning thread. A scenario where this might be necessary would be forcing the resolution of a deadlock. Semaphores also have the advantage of being able to ask for and release multiple permits. If multiple permits are being used, it is essential to use fair mode; otherwise, there is a chance of thread starvation.

Concurrent Collections

Since Java 5, implementations of the collections interfaces have been specifically designed for concurrent uses. These concurrent collections have been modified and improved over time to give the best possible thread hot performance.

For example, the map implementation (`ConcurrentHashMap`) uses a split into buckets or segments, and we can take advantage of this structure to achieve real gains in performance.

Each segment can have its own locking policy—that is, its own locks. Having both a read and a write lock enables many readers to be reading across the `ConcurrentHash Map`, and, if a write is required, the lock only needs to be held on that single segment. Readers generally do not lock and can overlap safely with `put()`- and `remove()`-style operations. Readers will still observe the happens-before ordering for a completed update operation.

It is important to note that iterators (and the spliterators used for parallel streams) are acquired as a sort of snapshot, meaning that they will not throw a `ConcurrentModifi cationException`. The table will be dynamically expanded when there are too many collisions, which can be a costly operation. It is worthwhile (as with the `HashMap`) to provide an approximate sizing if you know it at the time of writing the code, either as a constant or as a variable.

Java 5 also introduced the `CopyOnWriteArrayList` and `CopyOnWriteArraySet`, which in certain usage patterns can improve multithreaded performance. With these, any mutation operation against the data structure causes a fresh copy of the backing array to be created. Any existing iterators can continue to traverse the old array, and once all references are lost, the old copy of the array is eligible for garbage collection. Again, this snapshot style of iteration ensures that no `ConcurrentModificationExcep tion` is raised.

This tradeoff works well in systems where the copy-on-write data structure is accessed for reading many more times than mutating. If you are considering using this approach, make the change with a good set of tests to measure the performance improvement. Given the broad usage of collections, using tools such as JMH and microbenchmarks should be considered and is discussed in Appendix A.

Latches and Barriers

Latches and barriers are useful techniques for controlling the execution of a set of threads. For example, a system may be written where worker threads:

1. Retrieve data from an API and parse it.
2. Write the results to a database.
3. Finally, compute results based on a SQL query.

If the system simply started all the threads running, there would be no guarantee on the ordering of events. The desired effect would be to allow all threads to complete task #1 and then task #2 before starting on task #3. One possibility would be to use a *latch*. Assuming we have five threads running, we could write code like this:

```java
public class LatchExample implements Runnable {

    private final CountDownLatch latch;

    public LatchExample(CountDownLatch latch) {
        this.latch = latch;
    }

    @Override
    public void run() {
        // Call an API
        System.out.println(Thread.currentThread().getName() + " Done API Call");
        try {
            latch.countDown();
            latch.await();
        } catch (InterruptedException e) {
```

```
            e.printStackTrace();
        }
        System.out.println(Thread.currentThread().getName()
            + " Continue processing");
    }

    public static void main(String[] args) throws InterruptedException {
        CountDownLatch apiLatch = new CountDownLatch(5);

        ExecutorService pool = Executors.newFixedThreadPool(5);
        for (int i = 0; i < 5; i++) {
            pool.submit(new LatchExample(apiLatch));
        }
        System.out.println(Thread.currentThread().getName()
            +" about to await on main..");
        apiLatch.await();
        System.out.println(Thread.currentThread().getName()
            + " done awaiting on main..");
        pool.shutdown();
        try {
            pool.awaitTermination(5, TimeUnit.SECONDS);
        } catch (InterruptedException e) {
            e.printStackTrace();
        }
        System.out.println("API Processing Complete");
    }
}
```

In this example, the latch is set to have a count of 5, with each thread making a call to countdown() reducing the number by one. Once the count reaches 0, the latch will open, and any threads held on the await() function will be released to continue their processing.

It is important to realize that this type of latch is single-use only. Once the result is 0, the latch cannot be reused; there is no reset.

> Latches are extremely useful in examples such as cache population during startup and multithreaded testing.

In our example, we could have used two different latches: one for the API results to be finished and another for the database results to complete. Another option is to use a CyclicBarrier, which can be reset. However, figuring out which thread should control the reset is quite a difficult challenge and involves another type of synchronization. One common best practice is to use one barrier/latch for each stage in the pipeline.

Executors and Task Abstraction

In practice, most Java programmers should not have to deal with low-level threading concerns (except perhaps for the fire-and-forget use cases of virtual threads). Instead, we should be looking to use some of the `java.util.concurrent` features that support concurrent programming at a suitable level of abstraction. For example, keeping threads busy using some of the `java.util.concurrent` libraries will enable better thread hot performance (i.e., keeping a thread running rather than blocked and in a waiting state).

The level of abstraction that offers few threading concerns can be described as a *concurrent task*—that is, a unit of code or work that we require to run concurrently within the current execution context. Considering units of work as tasks simplifies writing a concurrent program, as the developer does not have to consider the thread lifecycle for the actual threads executing the tasks. This approach also helps with controlled shutdown (i.e., ensuring that threads complete tasks cleanly), as we will see a bit later.

Introducing Asynchronous Execution

One way of fulfilling the task abstraction in Java is by using the `Callable` interface to represent a task that returns a value. The `Callable<V>` interface is a generic interface defining one function, `call()`, that returns a value of type `V` and throws an exception in the case that a result cannot be calculated. On the surface, `Callable` looks very similar to `Runnable`; however, `Runnable` does not return a result and does not throw an exception.

> If `Runnable` throws an uncaught unchecked exception, it propagates up the stack and, by default, the executing thread stops running.

Dealing with exceptions in the lifetime of a thread is a difficult programming problem. It should also be noted that threads are be treated as OS-style processes, meaning they can be expensive to create on some operating systems. Getting hold of any result from `Runnable` can also add extra complexity, particularly in terms of coordinating the execution return against another thread, for instance.

The `Callable<V>` type provides us with a way to deal with the task abstraction nicely, but how are these tasks actually executed?

An `ExecutorService` is an interface that defines a mechanism for executing tasks on a pool of managed threads. The actual implementation of the `ExecutorService` defines how the threads in the pool should be managed and how many there should be. An ExecutorService can take either Runnable or Callable via the submit() method and its overloads.

The helper class Executors has a series of new* factory methods that construct the service and backing thread pool according to the selected behavior. These factory methods are the usual way to create new executor objects, some of the most common are:

newFixedThreadPool(int nThreads)
> Constructs an ExecutorService with a fixed-size thread pool, in which the threads will be reused to run multiple tasks. This avoids having to pay the cost of thread creation multiple times for each task. When all the threads are in use, new tasks are stored in a queue.

newCachedThreadPool()
> Constructs an ExecutorService that will create new threads as required and reuse threads where possible. Created threads are kept for 60 seconds, after which they will be removed from the cache. Using this thread pool can give better performance with small asynchronous tasks.

newSingleThreadExecutor()
> Constructs an ExecutorService backed by a single thread. Any newly submitted tasks are queued until the thread is available. This type of executor can be useful to control the number of tasks concurrently executed.

newScheduledThreadPool(int corePoolSize)
> Has an additional series of methods that allow a task to be executed at a point in the future that take Callable and a delay.

Once a task is submitted, it will be processed asynchronously, and the submitting code can choose to block or poll for the result. The submit() call to the ExecutorSer vice returns a Future<V> that allows a blocking get() or a get() with a timeout, or a nonblocking call using isDone().

Selecting an ExecutorService

Selecting the right ExecutorService allows good control of asynchronous processing and can yield significant performance benefits if you choose the right number of threads in the pool.

It is also possible to write a custom ExecutorService, but this is not often necessary. One way in which the library helps is by providing a customization option: the ability to supply a ThreadFactory. The ThreadFactory allows the author to write a custom thread creator that can set properties on threads such as name, daemon status, and thread priority.

The ExecutorService will sometimes need to be tuned empirically in the settings of the entire application. Having a good idea of the hardware that the service will run on and other competing resources is a valuable part of the tuning picture.

One metric typically used is the number of cores versus the number of threads in the pool. Selecting a number of threads to run concurrently that is higher than the number of processors available can be problematic and cause contention. The operating system will be required to schedule the threads to run, and this causes a context switch to occur.

When contention hits a certain threshold, it can negate the performance benefits of moving to a concurrent way of processing. This is why a good performance model and being able to measure improvements (or losses) is imperative. Chapter 2 discusses performance testing techniques and antipatterns to avoid when undertaking this type of testing.

Fork/Join and Parallel Streams

Java offers several different approaches to concurrency that do not require developers to control and manage their own threads. This includes the Fork/Join framework, which provides a new API intended to work efficiently with multiple processors. It is based on a new implementation of ExecutorService, called ForkJoinPool.

This class provides a pool of managed threads, which has two special features:

- It can be used to efficiently process a subdivided task.
- It implements a *work-stealing* algorithm.

The subdivided task support is introduced by the ForkJoinTask class. This is a thread-like entity that is more lightweight than a standard Java thread. The intended use case is that potentially large numbers of tasks and subtasks can be hosted by a small number of actual threads in a ForkJoinPool executor.

The key aspect of a ForkJoinTask is that it can subdivide itself into "smaller" tasks until the task size is small enough to compute directly. For this reason, the framework is suitable only for certain types of tasks, such as computation of pure functions or other *embarrassingly parallel* tasks. Even then, it may be necessary to rewrite algorithms or code to take full advantage of this part of Fork/Join.

Despite this, the work-stealing algorithm part of the Fork/Join framework can be used independently of the task subdivision.[5] For example, if one thread has completed all the work allocated to it and another thread has a backlog, it will steal work from the queue of the busy thread. This rebalancing of jobs across multiple threads is a simple but clever idea, yielding considerable benefit.

In Figure 13-6, we can see a representation of work stealing.

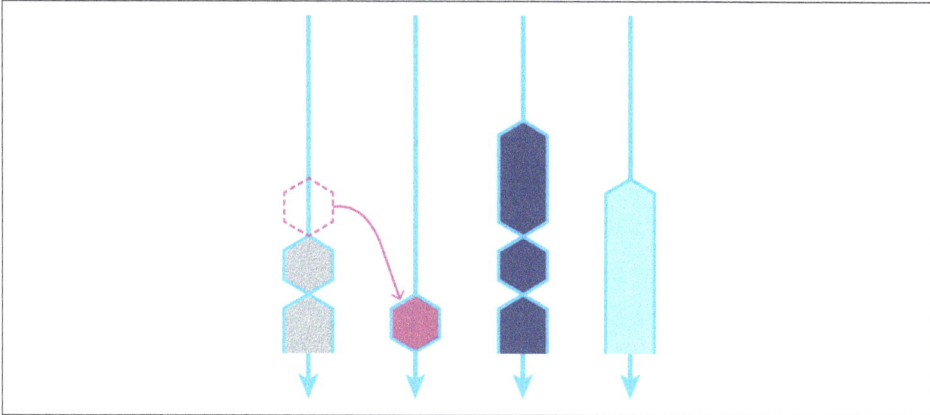

Figure 13-6. The work-stealing algorithm

ForkJoinPool has a static method, commonPool(), that returns a reference to the system-wide pool. This prevents developers from having to create their own pool and provides the opportunity for sharing. The common pool is lazily initialized so will be created only if required.

The sizing of the pool is defined by Runtime.getRuntime().availableProces sors()–1. However, this method does not always return the expected result.

Writing on the Java Specialists mailing list (*https://oreil.ly/Rniob*), Heinz Kabutz found a case where a 16-4-2 machine (16 sockets, each with 4 cores and 2 hyper-threads per core) returned the value 16. This seems very low; the naive intuition gained by testing on our laptops may have led us to expect the value to be $16 \times 4 \times 2 = 128$.

However, if we were to run Java 8 on this machine, it would configure the common Fork/Join pool to have a parallelism of only 15.

---

5 Arguably, it is the more useful of the two capabilities that Fork/Join provides.

> The VM doesn't really have an opinion about what a processor is; it just asks the OS for a number. Similarly, the OS usually doesn't care either, it asks the hardware. The hardware responds with a number, usually the number of "hardware threads." The OS believes the hardware. The VM believes the OS.
>
> —Brian Goetz

Thankfully, there is a flag that allows the developer to programmatically set the desired parallelism:

```
-Djava.util.concurrent.ForkJoinPool.common.parallelism=128
```

As discussed in Chapter 2, though, be careful with magic flags. And as we will discuss with selecting the `parallelStream()` option, nothing comes for free!

The work-stealing aspect of Fork/Join is becoming more utilized by library and framework developers, even without task subdivision.

By far the biggest change in Java 8 (arguably the biggest change ever) was the introduction of lambdas and streams. Used together, lambdas and streams provide a sort of "magic switch" to allow Java developers to access some of the benefits of a functional style of programming.

Leaving aside the rather complex question of just how functional Java 8 actually is as a language, we can say that Java now has a new paradigm of programming. This more functional style involves focusing on data rather than the imperative object-oriented approach that it has always had.

A stream in Java is an immutable sequence of data items that conveys elements from a data source. A stream can be from any source (collection, I/O) of typed data. We operate on streams using manipulating operations, such as `map()`, that accept lambda expressions or function objects to manipulate data. This change from external iteration (traditional `for` loops) to internal iteration (streams) provides us with some nice opportunities to parallelize data and to lazily evaluate complicated expressions.

All collections now provide the `stream()` method from the `Collection` interface. This is a default method that provides an implementation to create a stream from any collection, and behind the scenes a `ReferencePipeline` is created.

A second method, `parallelStream()`, can be used to work on the data items in parallel and recombine the results. Using `parallelStream()` involves separating the work using a `Spliterator` and executing the computation on the common Fork/Join pool. This is a convenient technique to work on *embarrassingly parallel* problems, because stream items are intended to be immutable, so they allow us to avoid the problem of mutating state when working in parallel.

The introduction of streams has yielded a more syntactically friendly way of working with Fork/Join than recoding using `RecursiveAction`. Expressing problems in terms of the data is similar to task abstraction in that it helps the developer avoid having to consider low-level threading mechanics and data mutability concerns.

It can be tempting to always use `parallelStream()`, but there is a cost to using this approach. As with any parallel computation, work has to be done to split up the task across multiple threads and then to recombine the results—a direct example of Amdahl's law.

On smaller collections, serial computation can actually be much quicker. You should always use caution and performance-test when using `parallelStream()`. In terms of using parallel streams to gain performance, the benefit needs to be direct and measurable, so don't just blindly convert a sequential stream to parallel.

The arrival of Java 8 also raised the usage level of Fork/Join significantly, as behind the scenes `parallelStream()` uses the common Fork/Join pool.

Actor-Based Techniques

In recent years, several different approaches to representing tasks that are naturally *smaller* than a thread have emerged. We have already met this idea in the `ForkJoin Task` class, and we will meet it again in the section on virtual threads. Another popular approach is the *actor paradigm*.

Actors are small, self-contained processing units that contain their own state, have their own behavior, and include a mailbox system to communicate with other actors. Actors manage the problem of state by not sharing any mutable state and communicating with each other only via immutable messages. The communication between actors is asynchronous, and actors react to the receipt of a message to perform their specified task.

By forming a network in which they each have specific tasks within a parallel system, actors take the view of abstracting away from the underlying concurrency model completely.

Actors can live within the same process, but they are not required to. This opens up a nice advantage that actor systems can be multiprocess and even potentially span multiple machines. Multiple machines and clustering enables actor-based systems to perform effectively when a degree of fault tolerance is required. To ensure that actors work successfully in a collaborative environment, they typically have a fail-fast strategy.

For JVM-based languages, Apache Pekko is a popular framework for developing actor-based systems.[6] It is written in Scala but also has a Java API, making it usable for Java and other JVM languages as well.

The motivation for an actor-based system is based on several problems that make concurrent programming difficult. The Pekko documentation (*https://oreil.ly/O-YLZ*) highlights three core motivations for considering the use of Pekko over traditional locking schemes:

- Encapsulating mutable state within the domain model can be tricky, especially if a reference to the object's internals is allowed to escape without control.
- Protecting state with locks can cause significant reduction in throughput.
- Locks can lead to deadlock and other types of liveness problems.

Additional problems highlighted include the difficulty of getting shared memory usage correct and the performance problems this can introduce by forcing cache lines to be shared across multiple CPUs.

The final motivation discussed is related to failures in traditional threading models and call stacks. In the low-level threading API, there is no standard way to handle thread failure or recovery. Pekko standardizes this and provides a well-defined recovery scheme for the developer.

Overall, the actor model can be a useful addition to the concurrent developer's toolbox. However, it is not a general-purpose replacement for all other techniques. If the use case fits within the actor style (asynchronous passing of immutable messages, no shared mutable state, and time-bounded execution of every message processor), then it can be an excellent quick win.

If, however, the system design includes request-response synchronous processing, shared mutable state, or unbounded execution, then careful developers may choose to use another abstraction for building their systems.

Let's move on and meet one of the most talked-about new features of Java 21.

Virtual Threads

One of the great strengths of Java is that it is very adaptable—it will take ideas for new features from anywhere. It does so carefully and deliberately, however—the aim is to have the best and most "Javaish" version of a feature, even if it takes more time to arrive.

---

6 Pekko was forked from an earlier project (Akka) when the original project adopted a non-open source license.

One of the most important innovations in Java concurrent programming in many years—*virtual threads* (vthreads)—arrived with Java 21 (but the groundwork for them had been laid much earlier). These can be seen as Java's take on *goroutines*, from the Go programming language (or *cooperative processes* in Erlang).

Let's take a first look at them.

Introduction to Virtual Threads

In the very earliest Java versions, the JVM's threads were multiplexed onto OS (aka *platform*) threads in what were referred to as *green threads*.

However, this practice died around the Java 1.2/1.3 era, and modern versions (before Java 21) running on mainstream operating systems basically implement the rule that "one Java thread is exactly one platform thread."

Calling `Thread.start()` invokes the thread creation system call (e.g., `clone()` on Linux) and actually creates a new OS thread (until then, the `Thread` object consists of metadata for a thread that doesn't actually exist yet).

This mechanism—whereby the OS creates, manages, and destroys threads (and processes) has some significant consequences. To see this, recall that the memory space of a process has a standard layout—this goes back to the earliest days of Unix.

Java programs (and the platform threads within them) obey this standard layout and add some specializations within that layout, as can be seen in Figure 13-7.

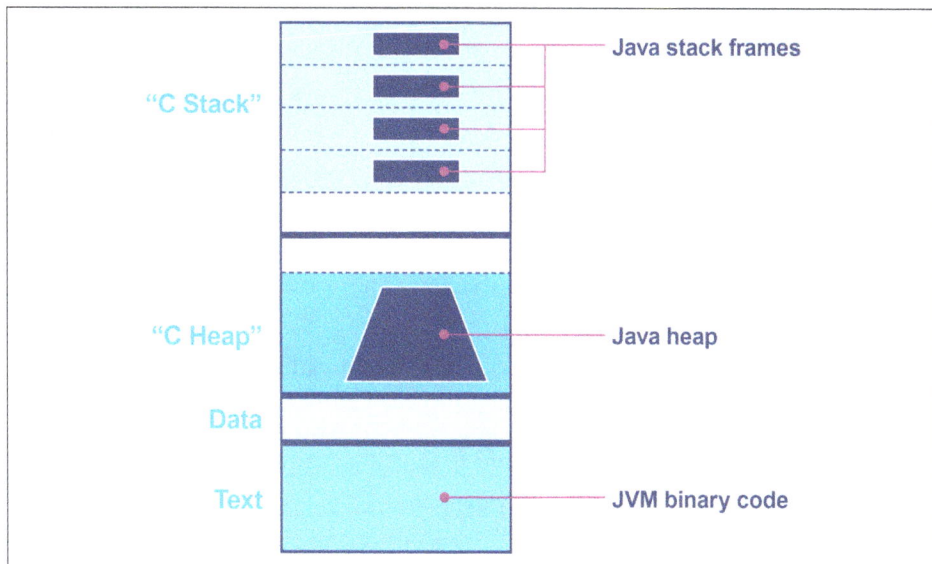

Figure 13-7. Simplified memory layout of a Java process

One aspect of this layout is that OS processes have a *stack segment*. This is a fixed amount of memory that is reserved, per-thread, within the process virtual address space (only one thread's stack segment is shown in the diagram). It is reserved when each thread is created and is not reclaimed until the thread exits.

On Linux x64, the default user space stack size is 1 MB. This means that 1 MB is reserved by the OS each time we launch a new thread.

The math is pretty simple—even for "only" 20,000 threads we need 20 GB of memory. This is an issue—referred to as the *thread bottleneck* problem—especially for thread-per-request and similar architectures.

Virtual threads (which were developed under the codename "Project Loom") are a response to that problem and attempt to find a solution to it.

That solution can be explained as a question: what if there was a new kind of thread that had these properties:

- Created and managed by the JVM, *not* the OS
- Doesn't have a dedicated platform thread—must share a pool of *carrier threads*
- Replaces static allocation of thread segments with a more flexible model
- Designed for tasks that do (at least some) I/O

Virtual threads are "just" runnable Java objects—they require a platform thread to run upon, but these platform threads are shared as carrier threads. This removes the 1:1 relationship between Java threads and OS threads, and instead establishes a temporary association of a virtual thread to a carrier thread—but this lasts only while the virtual thread is executing.

It also means that when a carrier thread switches between different virtual threads, the context switch may be even cheaper, as there is now no involvement by the operating system. Instead, the switch happens entirely in user space.

Secondly, virtual threads use Java objects within the garbage-collected heap to represent stack frames. This is much more dynamic and removes the static bottleneck caused by stack segment reservation.

To see how we can achieve this, let us consider the thread lifecycle again (as shown in Figure 7-6). It is certainly possible that threads can run to completion purely in user mode, perhaps doing some calculations, for AI/ML or similar tasks. This means that they would use up their entire CPU timeslice and be swapped out by the OS scheduler. In practice, though, this rarely happens.

Instead, threads often hit a blocking call (e.g., I/O) and switch into kernel space, so the operating system can perform some task on their behalf. Virtual threads use these execution points as a key part of the implementing mechanism.

It's important at this point to be precise about our terminology—Java does not have *bare* syscalls, as it is a fully managed environment. All "system calls" (such as I/O) are actually JDK library calls. Within the implementations of those library calls, the JVM makes syscalls on behalf of the user thread.

Next, remember that Java provides both blocking and nonblocking variants of I/O. As of Java 17, the Java Socket API has been reimplemented in terms of nonblocking I/O (NIO)—previously, it had been based on blocking I/O. This did not change the API (only the internals), but it provides an important building block for vthreads.

Essentially, every time a vthread makes a "blocking" I/O call, it actually performs a nonblocking call instead and yields up its carrier thread. The actual I/O proceeds while the vthread is paused, but another vthread can now use the carrier thread instead.

There's nothing particularly special about carrier threads—they're just a standard Java thread pool (`ExecutorService`), and they show up as standard platform threads to the OS.

> It is possible to explicitly give up the carrier thread by calling `yield()` from the vthread, but this is generally discouraged. As noted in the JavaDoc for `Thread.yield()`, "It is rarely appropriate to use this method" for any type of thread.

It is important to know that code has to specifically create a vthread—there is never any "automatic virtualization" of threads. This is important for several reasons, but one of the most important is that the arrival of virtual threads should not change the meaning—or performance characteristics—of any existing code.

In terms of the Java class hierarchy, virtual threads have been added by introducing a new sealed subclass of thread, with a single, final subclass `VirtualThread`, as shown in Figure 13-8.

This accommodates existing code that subclasses `Thread` directly (and subclassing `Thread` always gives a platform thread), while ensuring that all virtual threads are created from a `Runnable`.

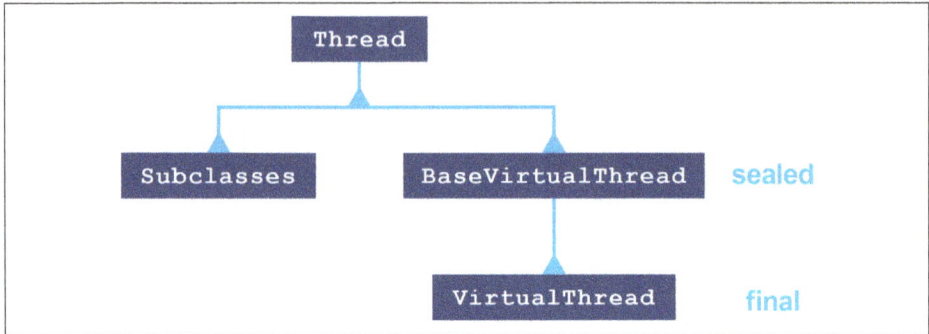

Figure 13-8. New Java thread inheritance hierarchy

To obtain a virtual thread, new static methods have been added to Thread, as well as a *Builder* pattern. It can be used like this:

```
Thread.Builder tb = Thread.ofVirtual();
tb.name("MyVirtualThread");
Thread t = tb.unstarted(() -> System.out.println("Hello World!"));
System.out.println(t);
t.start();
```

Note that new methods can be used to get a thread builder object: .ofPlatform() and .ofVirtual(). Thread builders can set a name and then be built into either a started or unstarted thread by supplying a Runnable task. There are also thread factories available from builders via the .factory() method for additional flexibility.

Care has been taken to isolate vthreads—for example, a vthread cannot directly observe its current carrier; Thread.currentThread() will return the vthread, and the stack frames from the carrier do not show up in stack trace of vthreads.

> The JVM language Kotlin has *coroutines*, which might seem super-ficially similar to vthreads, but they are, in fact, very different. The Kotlin source compiler transforms coroutines into a state machine that is visible in the compiled bytecode, whereas vthreads have support at the Java SDK (and VM) level.

Virtual threads do come with some limitations, including:

- A vthread will yield only if a blocking I/O call is made—there is no preemption.
- JNI calls and the synchronized keyword (but not the locks in java.util.concur rent) pin a vthread to its carrier and prevent unmounting. When a virtual thread is scheduled, it is mounted or assigned to a platform thread. Unmounting usually occurs at the point where a virtual thread is blocked waiting on I/O or code

execution to complete, freeing up the platform thread for other usage. Pinning vthreads in this way can lead to resource issues and unintending blockages.

- vthreads are always daemon threads with normal priority.
- vthreads do not interact well with the Object Pool pattern; vthreads are intended to be short lived, and underlying caching techniques will result in retaining unusable weak references to garbage objects that cannot be reused as intended.

From a tooling perspective, the potentially vast numbers of vthreads can complicate the use of tools such as JMC (and JFR), and new observability patterns will have to be developed to work effectively with them.

> The story for `ThreadLocal` is more complex for vthreads, and it may be better to use the `ScopedValue` approach (which we will meet in Chapter 15).

Let's conclude this introduction with a few dos and don'ts for vthreads:

- Do expect to learn some new intuitions for vthreads.
- Don't think of vthreads as a free lunch.
- Do learn what types of problems they'll help with—don't just apply them blindly.
- Don't use vthreads for compute-bound tasks—they need blocking calls to yield.

In fact, some of the best advice might be to go and talk to other developers—if you have friends who develop in Go, ask them how they use goroutines and what patterns might be transferable.

Virtual Thread Concurrency Patterns

In practice, one of the most immediately obvious benefits of virtual threads is that they should completely remove the need for developers to use the nonblocking form of the NIO APIs directly. Instead, programs can create a dedicated virtual thread that uses the blocking API, and let the runtime sort it out.

The intent is that this is essentially the same thing as using nonblocking I/O in terms of performance, while providing a simpler programming model. Avoiding more complex programming models that display *asynchronous contagion* (such as async-await or *colored functions*[7]) was a major design goal for Project Loom.

---

7 Named as such in the blogpost "What Color is Your Function?" (*https://oreil.ly/BuPbg*) although the author incorrectly assumes that Java is planning to support async-await.

At the same time, bringing explicit "reactive approaches" into the JDK was a definite non-goal. The end result was the form of virtual threads that we see in Java 21.

Building upon this language feature, we want to examine some relevant patterns, starting with one of the most obvious: just replacing some of a program's threads with vthreads.

Recall that carrier threads are threads from a `ForkJoinPool` executor and will yield on (most) blocking operations. This means that for threads that do at least some I/O, there is a potential performance benefit by switching them to virtual. Remember that Java 21 does not do any automatic virtualization—unless you explicitly construct a virtual thread, then you will always get a platform thread.

Of course, as the point of converting some threads to virtual is that we might be able to obtain a performance boost, then we have to test the change—in a real-world complete system—to ensure that we actually realize the expected benefit.

As well as manual creation of virtual threads, there is also a new executor type, which we can get from `Executors.newVirtualThreadPerTaskExecutor()`. As the name suggests, rather than relying upon a traditional threadpool that is reused for multiple tasks, this executor creates a new virtual thread for each task that is submitted.

To accommodate this new executor type, the `ExecutorService` interface is now `AutoCloseable`—so it can be used in try-with-resources blocks.

This is a great example of a new pattern designed specifically for virtual threads. Executors for platform threads are typically long-lived objects—because they create threads at startup, which is an expensive operation. Therefore, it doesn't make sense to create them as local objects within a method—they're much more likely to be seen as (possibly static) fields.

Virtual threads, on the other hand, are very cheap to create—they're just Java objects. The creation of an executor for virtual threads is similarly cheap, so creating a locally scoped executor doesn't incur the same performance penalty.

This leads to code like this example showing the bare bones of a web server, which uses the block-scoped virtual thread executor:

```
private volatile boolean isShutdown = false;

void handle(Socket socket) {
    // Handle incoming request
}

void serveVT(ServerSocket serverSocket) throws IOException,
    InterruptedException {
        try (var executor = Executors.newVirtualThreadPerTaskExecutor()) {
            try {
                while (!isShutdown) {
```

```
                    var socket = serverSocket.accept();
                    executor.submit(() -> handle(socket));
                }
            } finally {
                // If there's been an error, or we're interrupted,
                // we stop accepting
                executor.shutdown();
            }
        }
    }

    public shutdown() {
        isShutdown = true;
    }
}
```

The server socket is passed into the main `serveVT()` method and handles each incoming request by starting a new virtual thread.

Every request is isolated from every other request, so there is no need to share data or context, and the requests will all complete in bounded time (and require network I/O). We can call this type of operation *fire-and-forget*, and this pattern is very suitable for implementing a simple web server using vthreads.

It's also important to note that this code uses the *Volatile Shutdown* pattern, which uses the `volatile` field `isShutdown` to force a reread of the flag before accepting any new connection. This is an extremely standard pattern for handling graceful shutdown of Java server applications.

Summary

This chapter only scratches the surface of topics that you should consider before aiming to improve application performance using multithreading. When converting a single-threaded application to a concurrent design:

- Ensure that the performance of straight-line processing can be measured accurately.
- Apply a change and test that the performance is actually improved.
- Ensure that the performance tests are easy to rerun, especially if the size of data processed by the system is likely to change.

Avoid the temptation to:

- Use parallel streams everywhere.
- Create complicated data structures with manual locking.
- Reinvent structures already provided in `java.util.concurrent`.

Aim to:

- Improve thread hot performance using concurrent collections.
- Use access designs that take advantage of the underlying data structures.
- Reduce locking across the application.
- Provide appropriate task/asynchronous abstractions to prevent having to deal with threads manually.

Taking a step back, concurrency is key to the future of high-performance code. However:

- Shared mutable state is hard.
- Locks can be challenging to use correctly and expensive in terms of hardware resources.
- Both synchronized and asynchronous state sharing models are needed.
- The JMM is a low-level, flexible model.
- The thread abstraction is very low level.

The trend in modern concurrency is to move to a higher-level concurrency model and away from threads, which are increasingly looking like the "assembly language of concurrency." Recent versions of Java have increased the amount of higher-level classes and libraries available to the programmer. On the whole, the industry seems to be moving to a model of concurrency where far more of the responsibility for safe concurrent abstractions is managed by the runtime and libraries.

In the next chapter, we will see how some of the techniques and patterns we have met can be applied to the clustered and distributed case. We will also see what new complications arise when nontrivial network latency and cluster failure states enter the picture, and how we can overcome them.

## CHAPTER 14

Distributed Systems Techniques and Patterns

In this chapter, we will introduce some fundamental techniques of distributed systems. Some of these are generalizations of the concurrent patterns we have already met, but others are new abstractions caused by one or more of the *fallacies of distributed computing* enumerated by L. Peter Deutsch and James Gosling (*https://oreil.ly/6Cg3K*) in the mid-1990s.

The fallacies are:

- The network is reliable.
- Latency is zero.
- Bandwidth is infinite.
- The network is secure.
- Topology doesn't change.
- There is one administrator.
- Transport cost is zero.
- The network is homogeneous.

Some of these effects will impact us more than others—for example, the question of latency is of particular importance, as is the possibility of topology change within a cluster. In addition, architecture styles like service-oriented architecture (SOA) and microservice-based architectures can significantly increase the number of distributed connections, which, in turn, increases the potential impact of the fallacies.

That is, we may discover that although we distributed our app as a means of optimizing it and allowing it to scale, instead we did the exact opposite because we failed to take into account one or more of the fallacies. To counteract this possibility, we need some tools and techniques to help immunize us from the impact of the fallacies.

In this chapter, we will introduce several of these useful technologies and will point out which of the fallacies are relevant to each case. Our first section discusses a number of low-level, or basic, *distributed data structures*. After that, we discuss the concept of consensus, which is broadly the idea that cluster members will need to agree on some mutable data value for distributed computation to be viable.

In the second half of the chapter, we will discuss examples of libraries that can simplify the process of building distributed systems in Java. As we cover each topic, we will see how one or more of the fallacies is mitigated by each technology. Finally, we will bring the topics together and see how to enhance Fighting Animals with some of these technologies.

Basic Distributed Data Structures

To construct distributed data structures, we will start by introducing some basic building blocks. This is by no means an exhaustive list—many others are useful and relevant but these are a starting point (and many are reused in the higher-level libraries we discuss later).

Clocks, IDs, and Write-Ahead Logs

One of the simplest building blocks of distributed data structures is the generation clock (*https://oreil.ly/DjA0l*). This is a monotonically increasing value that is used to order events in a distributed system. It is attached to all messages sent in the system (and stored in replicated logs).

For example, it can be used in leader-follower clusters to handle the possibility of the leader being temporarily disconnected from the followers. If a new leadership election occurs, then the generation clock will advance, so the follower nodes know they should discard messages from the old leader if it reconnects to the cluster.

A technique that can be easily generalized from single-machine concurrent programming to distributed systems is the use of immutable objects. Provided that immutable objects can be serialized and deserialized, they can be sent over the network without fear. There is no possibility of lost updates—because the object state cannot be updated after it has been created.

One other basic need is for unique cluster-wide IDs. There are several techniques for generating unique IDs in a distributed system, but one of the simplest is to use a cluster-wide segment. The leader node is responsible for handing out segments to the follower nodes, which can then generate IDs from that segment and request a new segment when it is exhausted.

For example, each follower claims a segment of, for example, one million IDs to allocate. Behind the scenes, this could be done by the leader process using an `AtomicLong` and incrementing that atomic when a follower claims a segment.

After claiming the segment, the cluster member can increment a local counter each time a new ID is required. Once all IDs in the segment are used, the follower can claim a new segment.

The consequence of this approach is that network traffic is vastly reduced—almost all the ID generation can be done in memory and is extremely fast. Another consequence is that this approach scales a lot better than a raw `AtomicLong` because there is a lot less contention—it is much more efficient and faster to get segments of `1_000_000` `AtomicLong` IDs from the leader than requesting them one at a time.

There will not be any duplicate IDs, but there are some issues you need to be aware of:

- IDs generated by different followers will be out of order.
- If a member goes down without fully using its segment, there might be gaps. In most cases, for ID generation, this isn't relevant.
- If the cluster leader restarts, then (in the simplest case) the ID generator is reset and will start again from 0.

The last of these issues can be mitigated by using persistent storage (e.g., a database) to record the last segment handed out. There are also alternative solutions for creating cluster-wide unique IDs, such as `java.util.UUID` or other forms of UUID, but in many cases a simple numeric ID suffices.

To conclude this section, let's introduce the *write-ahead log* (WAL). This technique is widely deployed in database systems to provide atomicity and durability (two of the *ACID properties* for databases). The log is an ordered, append-only data structure that lives on persistent storage.

It is traditionally used to implement crash recovery—when a process restarts, it can check the log and see whether the changes had been completed, or if they need to be rolled back and the log entries discarded.

For our purposes, we can think of this technique as a log of changes that a node wants to make but has only made on a speculative basis. When a completion condition is reached, the log has reached a checkpoint, applies the changes, and clears the log.

Two-Phase Commit

The two-phase commit is a very common technique in distributed programming. For example, it often appears when a transaction needs to be persisted to a database and also propagated to a messaging system. Handling this as two separate transactions would be problematic because of the possibility that the database transaction completed, but then the messaging transaction failed.

The basic structure of the two-phase commit is to use separate *prepare* (aka *voting*) and *commit* phases. Let's walk through this in a leader-follower system.

In the prepare phase, the leader writes to a write-ahead log. The leader replicates the change over the network to the followers, which write it to their local WALs and reply with a promise—that they're ready to commit.

When sufficient followers have replied with a promise, the leader begins the commit phase. It marks the entry as final and sends out a completion message. Followers can apply their local WAL entry, and then complete their promise by sending back an acknowledgment (ACK).

Once sufficient ACKs are received, the commit is complete.

This technique has some useful advantages. First of all, it is simple and easy to understand. Secondly, it provides atomicity and consistency—the transaction either succeeds or fails, and there is no way for different nodes to end up with different results for the transaction. It also ensures liveness—eventually, we will reach a consensus, although this can take multiple iterations of the transaction.

However, two-phase commit has multiple downsides:

- It requires promises and acknowledgments from every node, and this scales linearly with the size of the cluster.

- A single error or conflict from any of the nodes causes the transaction to be aborted and retried from scratch.

- The leader waits for everybody in the group to reply, which means the overall latency is at least that of the slowest node.

The protocol also has possible blocking behavior. This is because, in the prepare phase, nodes must allocate resources needed to complete the transaction. This means that the entire cluster is waiting with an unacknowledged promise for the entry in the write-ahead log.

Until the transaction commits or rolls back, they can't accept new updates that apply to any of the affected resources.

Practical versions of two-phase commit will also need to deal with timeouts and aim to provide at least basic fault-tolerance—when one node is unavailable or slow or is temporarily unavailable (perhaps due to a GC pause). The interested reader could consult a text such as *Designing Data-Intensive Applications* by Martin Kleppmann for a deeper treatment of this subject.

Object Serialization

Serialization in Java has a long, and somewhat inglorious, history. Broadly, it is the conversion of the state of an object instance into a byte stream. This byte stream can then be written to disk or moved across a network, where it can be *deserialized* back into an object instance.

It has been a built-in feature of the platform since Java 1.1, but the language-level mechanism has multiple severe drawbacks and is now widely recognized as being deeply flawed in the general case.

> Serialization constitutes an invisible but public constructor, and an invisible but public set of accessors for your internal state.
>
> —Brian Goetz, "Towards Better Serialization" (*https://oreil.ly/nJEI7*)

Built-in serialization has also contributed to a large number of security issues over Java's long history. As a result, most application teams have opted for a library-level solution instead of relying on the built-in mechanism.

For example, JSON is one attractive choice for a serialization format, for several reasons:

- It is extremely simple.
- It is human-readable.
- Libraries exist for it in basically every programming language.

However, this is counter-balanced by some other factors—such as the size of the serialized objects, which can contribute to poor performance for larger messages. For high-performance applications, binary encodings are preferable—and there a great many to choose from, including Protocol Buffers (*https://protobuf.dev*) and Avro (*https://avro.apache.org*).

The tradeoff and architectural choices for data serialization relate to two of the fallacies we met at the start of the chapter: "Transport cost is zero" and "Bandwidth is infinite." Performance of serialization libraries has been an important aspect of the overall design of distributed systems for many years.

For example, more than twenty years ago, one of the authors was doing performance work on service architectures where the primary gating factors for performance were:

- The serialization and deserialization of Java objects to XML
- Finding the correct granularity of services (largely to reduce the amount of the above)

While the on-the-wire serialization format you work with is probably not XML anymore, the stated general principles remain as major concerns for modern systems.

Data Partitioning and Replication

We met partitioning briefly in Chapter 10, as a problem that can be detected by observability. In this section, we'll introduce it properly and place it in context as a key technique for distributed systems.

In its simplest form, data partitioning (aka *sharding*) is the dividing of a large dataset into smaller, more manageable subsets—the *partitions*. Each partition contains a subset of the overall data, and they are distributed across multiple nodes.

There are a couple of different ways that the data can be partitioned. For example, *horizontal partitioning*, dividing the data based on rows, and *vertical partitioning*, dividing the data based on columns.

In the case of horizontal partitioning, there are several well-known techniques for splitting the data into partitions. For example, the data can be partitioned by some key—an ID or a hash of important fields. As we will discuss later, this is the approach taken by systems such as Apache Kafka.

One very common approach is to use a combination of heartbeating network connections between hosts in the cluster, along with a *quorum* system for ensuring that a distributed transaction has sufficient "votes" to complete (more about this in the next section).

For fault tolerance, there may be multiple copies of each partition to mitigate the effects of a node becoming unavailable (this is the "The network is reliable" fallacy). The most obvious default is one synchronous copy, but other strategies are possible—such as two synchronous copies to permit a rolling update across the cluster while still protecting against unexpected failure of a node.

For example, we could choose to deploy multiple synchronous backups, but this would come at the cost of higher memory consumption across the cluster (as each backup consumes memory equivalent to the size of the original data structure).

However, it is important to realize that all synchronous backups require locking between the copies to prevent a distributed version of the *Lost Update* antipattern we met in Chapter 13. The more backup copies are held, the more costly this locking becomes.

In some applications, persisting an in-memory data store to a backing store can be advantageous. However, this durability comes with a potential performance problem—as for full reliability, each change to the in-memory data has to be "written through" to the physical store before the change can be fully confirmed. This is similar to the case of main memory versus cache, which we discussed in the previous chapter.

There are plenty of use cases where this behavior is overkill, and a short window of potential data loss can be tolerated by the application architecture. Under these circumstances, many systems can be configured to "write-behind," in which case the writes to backing store effectively become asynchronous.

Observability can also be beneficial when deploying replication and partitioning. In addition to ensuring that data continues to flow through the pipeline, observing repartitioning events—not only that they occur, but also their duration—can be early indicators that the application is nearing the capacity constraints of the messaging infrastructure.

Repartitioning is *at best* linear in the number of nodes (and is sometimes as bad as quadratic). Being able to observe repartitioning across the cluster is important, because the perspective of any given node may be insufficient to form a complete overall picture.

CAP Theorem

The CAP theorem (*https://oreil.ly/NtLPj*) is one of the most recognizable pieces of theory in distributed systems. The name comes from the three initials for behavioral aspects of a system—consistency, availability, and partition-tolerance.

The theorem indicates that only two of the three aspects are possible for any system. Different technologies may make different choices, for example, an AP system chooses availability and partition-tolerance.

The theorem relates to two of the fallacies of distributed computing: "The network is reliable" and "Topology doesn't change." In fact, a network partition is a classic example of a topology change, and hence, a lack of reliability.

One, somewhat loose, way to approach the theorem is to consider that if you have a network that may drop messages, then you cannot have both complete availability and perfect consistency in the event of a partition.

So, in the event of a network partition where nodes remain up and connected to different groups of clients, one strategy is to give up consistency and remain available while partitioned. This is the same concept that we met as the split-brain in "Repartitioning and "Split-Brain"" on page 256.

The effect for the user in the event of a partition would be that clients connected to one partition would see locally consistent results. However, clients connected to different partitions would not necessarily see the same result. For example, a supposedly atomic value could now potentially have different values in different partitions.

Another approach is to note that network partitions—indicated by total loss of messages—are very rare on modern LANs (or within data centers). As a result, many people consider the CAP theorem to apply only over wide-area (and possibly global) networks.

If the system's clients are always made aware of a list of cluster nodes they could connect to, in the event of loss of a datacenter (or region), clients would simply reconnect to unaffected nodes.

Consensus Protocols

In this section, we will briefly discuss two of the most commonly used *consensus protocols*. These protocols are used in distributed systems to ensure that coordinating cluster members agree on some mutable data value (the consensus) that is needed during computation.

> The use of consensus algorithms relate to the same two fallacies as we saw for the CAP theorem, i.e., "The network is reliable" and "Topology doesn't change."

Our treatment will build upon the discussion of the two-phase commit earlier in the chapter. There is also an excellent presentation from Devnexus 2023 (*https://oreil.ly/XMw2r*) that covers both algorithms in simple language.

This area also provides a case study of another component of successful observability: knowing what any cluster transition events look like.

Based on this, you should configure observability not to alert until there is an actual problem. This may not be at the first occurrence—these transition events are relatively rare, but they do occur naturally in normal operation. For example, when monitoring systems like ZooKeeper, there should never be two consecutive monitoring intervals (minutes, by default) during which multiple nodes report being a leader.

Paxos

Paxos (*https://oreil.ly/3HT-4*) is a popular voting-based consensus algorithm (or, more properly, a family of algorithms) used in many systems, such as Cassandra, DynamoDB, and Chubby (a distributed lock system from Google).[1] It was introduced

---

1 In addition, ZooKeeper uses the ZAB protocol, which can be thought of as a Paxos variant that is specifically tailored to ZooKeeper's use case.

by Leslie Lamport in the 1980s and uses some concepts that we have already met (such as the generation clock.

The protocol has two basic roles that cluster nodes can perform:

- Proposer
- Acceptor

In general, messages are identified with a *round number* N (which is the generation clock time), and they may also have a to-be-agreed-upon value.

Paxos has two phases, each with two subphases:

Phase 1a: Prepare
   Proposer creates a `Prepare` message and sends it to all known Acceptors.

Phase 1b: Promise
   When any Acceptor receives a `Prepare` message from any Proposer, it returns a `Promise` to that Proposer—essentially, that it agrees to honor a value to be provided by that Proposer.

Phase 2a: Accept
   Once a Proposer has received promises from a quorum of Acceptors, it needs to set a value V to its proposal. It does so by sending `Accept` messages, denoted by the pair (N, V), to all Acceptors that have promised to honor the proposal.

Phase 2b: Accepted
   If an Acceptor receives an `Accept` from a Proposer, it must accept it if and only if it has not already promised (in Phase 1b) to only consider proposals having a higher round number (i.e., a number greater than N).

Paxos is a quorum-based protocol, so a simple majority is enough to move forward—this is to ensure that forward progress can still be made even if some nodes are disconnected, slow, or overwhelmed. One critical part of the protocol is the acceptance criteria—this is designed to prevent conflicting values from disrupting convergence to a consensus.

Paxos has been very well studied and has many different possible extensions. One of the most obvious is to include a third role—the *Learner* (sometimes known by other names, such as *observer* in ZooKeeper).

Learners are passive observers of the cluster—they don't propose new values, and they don't vote in the ballot. Instead, they're just notified about the outcome when the value is agreed upon—and both Acceptors and Proposers can notify Learners once the value is fixed. This can be very useful for reducing read load on the nodes participating in the consensus algorithm.

In practice, many Paxos implementations merge the roles, so an Acceptor can also be a Learner.

We should also mention one of the most significant theoretical results about consensus algorithms at this point—known as the Fischer, Lynch, and Paterson (FLP) Impossibility result.

Their 1985 paper (*https://oreil.ly/XNA84*) (which has a very readable simplified overview (*https://oreil.ly/AcboU*)) establishes that in an asynchronous system, consensus algorithms will provide only two of the three properties of safety, liveness, and fault tolerance.

This is a strong result, but a number of workarounds have been developed to minimize its restrictions. For example, introducing a short random delay between proposed values would reduce the chances of a liveness failure (essentially a distributed LiveLock similar to the one we met in Chapter 13), but the underlying theoretical possibility cannot be completely ruled out.

Let's move on to look at the other consensus algorithm—Raft.

Raft

When Raft (*https://raft.github.io*) was created, one of its major design goals was to provide a simple and easy-to-understand (*https://raft.github.io/raft.pdf*) consensus algorithm. It approaches this by decomposing the consensus problem into two distinct subproblems:

- Leader election
- Log replication

To further promote the idea of simplicity, Raft is based on the idea that every node has only two possible election states (Stable and Election), and three possible role states (Leader, Follower, and Candidate). It's a leader-follower based protocol, so only one of the nodes will be a Leader, and every other node is a Follower, at least while an election is not running.

Every update goes through the Leader, which writes to its log and asynchronously replicates the change to its Followers. Once the Leader has successfully replicated the data to a quorum, the commit index is advanced, the operation is applied to the state machine, and the update is deemed successful.

Followers in Raft are totally passive; they just accept the updates sent to them by the Leader. Leader nodes in Raft send out heartbeat messages to all Followers at regular intervals (e.g., 100 ms). If a Follower notices that the Leader is no longer sending heartbeats, then it can send out a message to its peers and call for an election, as we will see.

Like Paxos, Raft is based on the idea of generation clocks, which are also referred to as *terms*. Every node in the cluster knows which node is the Leader and what the current term number is. It also has a list of the Followers (which are peers of one another).

The two messages are AppendEntry to send an update from Leader to Followers (it also serves as the heartbeat message, by just sending a null update payload), and RequestVote, which is sent to all peers if a Follower has not received an AppendEntry within a timeout.

The AppendEntry message, and its response, can be represented in Java like this:

```
record AppendEntry (
    int term,
    int leaderId,
    List<Payload> payloads,
    int prevLogIndex,
    int prevLogTerm,
    int leaderCommit) { }

record AppendEntryResponse (
    int term,
    boolean accepted,
    int conflictIndex,
    int conflictTerm) { }
```

with the RequestVote and RequestVoteResponse looking like this:

```
record RequestVote (
    int term,
    int candidateId,
    int lastLogIndex,
    int lastLogTerm
) {}

record RequestVoteResponse(
    int term,
    boolean inFavor
) {}
```

The resulting state machine for Raft can be seen in Figure 14-1.

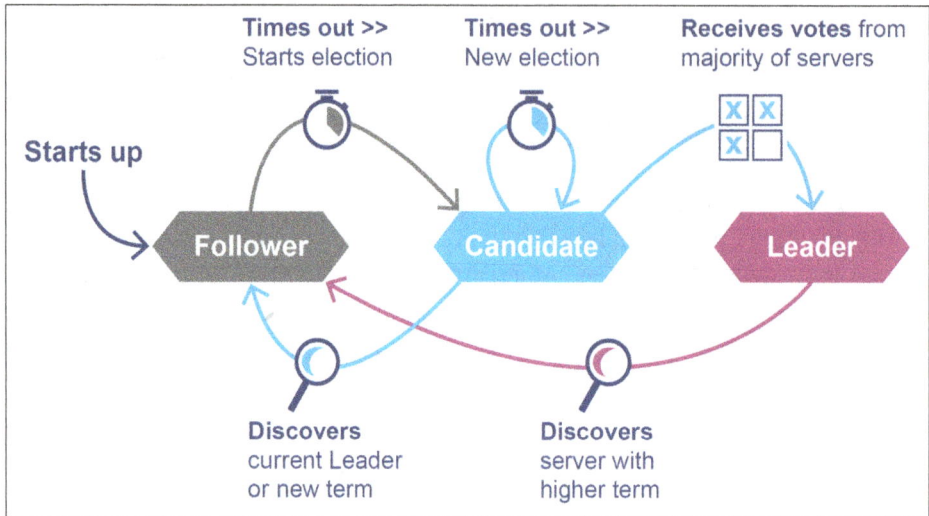

Figure 14-1. Raft state machine

Note that, when the cluster starts, there's no Leader node—so every node starts as a Follower. To handle this, nodes can self-promote to Candidate—to do so, they increment the term number and send every other node a `RequestVote`.

Raft has been extensively studied, and the algorithm has been shown to not fully guarantee liveness (*https://oreil.ly/6XbP6*) in the event of a network fault without additional modifications. This means that it's still possible an election can theoretically continue forever.

However, Raft minimizes this probability by introducing a random election timeout (and that a Candidate cannot win an election unless its log is up to date). In practice, this means that LiveLock does not occur, but just as for Paxos, we cannot prove it is impossible—another consequence of the FLP result.

Finally, we should note that just because an algorithm is correct does not mean the implementation code is also correct. For Raft, one of the possible Java implementations is the version provided by the jgroups-raft project (*https://oreil.ly/Qm2AA*)—which is used in products like Red Hat's Infinispan—and has been extensively tested for correctness bugs (*https://oreil.ly/BoKOO*).

Distributed Systems Examples

In this section, we will discuss some case studies of how these distributed techniques are used in practice by real systems. Our examples are basically infrastructural, in that they are designed to enable the programmer to separate the distributed systems' aspects from their business logic. Let's get started by discussing an example of a distributed database.

Distributed Database—Cassandra

Cassandra (*https://oreil.ly/CjNX9*) is one of the most popular open source NoSQL distributed databases. It is written in Java and is nonrelational and column-oriented. By default, Cassandra is an AP (available, partition-tolerant) database, but this consistency can be configured on a per-query level.

It is relatively common for NoSQL systems to display this type of *eventual consistency* behavior. Cassandra provides the concept of a *consistency level*, which specifies how many replicas nodes must acknowledge the write before the coordinator reports success to the client. Some common values of the consistency level are:

- ONE: Only a single acknowledgement from any replica is sufficient to confirm the write.
- LOCAL_QUORUM: Acknowledgement from a simple majority of nodes in the same datacenter is needed to confirm.
- QUORUM: Acknowledgement from a simple majority of cluster nodes globally is needed to confirm.
- ALL: Acknowledgement from all nodes is required.

These options are ordered from fastest to slowest. Cassandra is optimized for writing large amounts of data quickly, so the more stringent the consistency level, the slower the writes will become.

Note that typical deployments of Cassandra may be globally distributed, so QUORUM and ALL may well involve WAN traffic, which can have write-confirmation times in the tens or hundreds of milliseconds (due to speed-of-light limitations).

> The ALL setting is not recommended, as it is not only the slowest but also affects availability—a single failed node can cause writes to fail. This goes against the design of Cassandra as an AP database, and if you are tempted to use it, then this can be an "architecture smell" of something wrong somewhere else in the system design.

The primary interface into the Cassandra DB is Cassandra Query Language (CQL). This is a query language that is somewhat similar to SQL (despite Cassandra being a NoSQL database), in that both have the same basic concept of a table constructed of columns and rows. However, Cassandra is nonrelational, so it does not support joins or subqueries.

If we look at some basic examples of CQL, then it can be deceptively similar to SQL. For example, all of these examples are *both* valid SQL and valid CQL:

```
CREATE TABLE IF NOT EXISTS demoTable (id INT PRIMARY KEY);
ALTER TABLE demoTable ADD newField INT;
CREATE INDEX myIndex ON demoTable (newField);
INSERT INTO demoTable (id, newField) VALUES (1, 2);
SELECT * FROM demoTable WHERE newField = 2;
SELECT COUNT(*) FROM demoTable;
DELETE FROM demoTable WHERE newField = 2;
```

However, just as this statement:

```
var x = 15;
```

is both valid Java and JS but has substantial semantic difference in the two environments, it is important not to take too much from surface impressions and simple examples.

There is actually a substantial amount of difference between CQL and SQL, despite the identical syntax. For example, INSERT and DELETE both behave very differently in Cassandra than is typical in SQL databases.

It is also true that what we're referring to as a table is more properly called a *columnfamily* in CQL—the alias "table" is really there to make new arrivals with SQL experience more comfortable. Likewise, a Cassandra *keyspace* is a namespace that defines how data is replicated on nodes and is broadly analogous to a database schema for a SQL RDBMS.

Keyspaces are designed to control data replication for a set of tables. This replication is controlled on a per-keyspace basis, so data that has different replication requirements typically resides in different keyspaces. As a consequence of this, a cluster will typically have one keyspace per application that the cluster serves.

Note that there are cases where Cassandra's default of eventual consistency just doesn't work—i.e., sometimes you need to maintain a strict order of reads and writes.

For these cases, *linearizable consistency (https://oreil.ly/0qjCU)* is useful, and Cassandra has two sorts of CQL operations—regular (which we've already met) and *lightweight transactions*, which provide linearizable consistency for conditional updates.

The lightweight transaction syntax is different from that of regular operations, and it uses an implementation of Paxos to support this feature. In their simplest form, lightweight transactions are CAS operations that look something like INSERT ... IF NOT EXIST.

Normal operations should not be mixed with lightweight transactions—if your application is an appropriate use case for lightweight transactions, then they should be used throughout.

The SERIAL consistency level is used for lightweight transactions and ensures that conditional writes are isolated and applied atomically. Cassandra lightweight transactions are, therefore, only really lightweight when compared to transaction strategies in other DB types or to two-phase commit.

In-Memory Data Grid—Infinispan

Infinispan (*https://infinispan.org*) is a distributed cache and key-value NoSQL in-memory data store developed by Red Hat as the successor to JBoss Cache. As well as being in-memory, Infinispan can also persist data to a more permanent *cache store*. These are pluggable, and many different implementations exist to allow Infinispan data to be persisted in an existing system.

The technology can be used to add clustering and high availability to libraries and frameworks. By delegating state management to Infinispan, the internal distributed data structures that Infinispan provides can provide clustering capability.

The jgroups library is a useful toolkit that provides reliable, group network communication for Infinispan and many other projects. It provides many useful features, such as node discovery, both point-to-point and point-to-multipoint, failure detection, and data transfer.

The fault tolerance capability is based on the jgroups-raft component, which (as the name suggests) is an implementation of the Raft protocol. Infinispan provides a configurable replication factor, working as an AP system, similar to Cassandra.

Infinispan exposes a `Cache` interface, which extends `java.util.Map`—so, from an end-user perspective it can be seen, in its simplest terms, as a "big `HashMap` that can extend across machines"—Infinispan also supports non-JVM platforms as clients.

Transactional use cases--both JTA and XA—are also supported, and Infinispan can participate in distributed transactions brokered by a JTA transaction manager. Transactions in Infinispan are optional and can be disabled for higher performance, depending on your application.

For observability, Infinispan has good support for tracing, including OpenTelemetry traces—despite not being based on HTTP, the jgroups protocol has been extended to include OTel support.

Event Streaming—Kafka

Apache Kafka (*https://kafka.apache.org*) is a key piece of infrastructure technology that provides a stream of events in a publish-subscribe paradigm. The events are used both as triggers for actions and the means of distributing state to nodes. This is a common pattern for implementing microservice architectures.

Unlike other messaging systems (such as JMS and AMQP), Kafka was built with scale and throughput as the primary design goals. It is a client-broker system, so messages are sent from clients to clusters of Kafka broker processes.

In addition to authorization, Kafka provides the capability to authenticate at transport level, and this mitigates the fallacy "The network is secure."[2] Of course, to fully mitigate this issue, we would also need to include authentication on all of our microservices as well.

The heart of Kafka is an ordered, replicated log. This allows efficient implementation of both reads and writes, as shown in Figure 14-2.

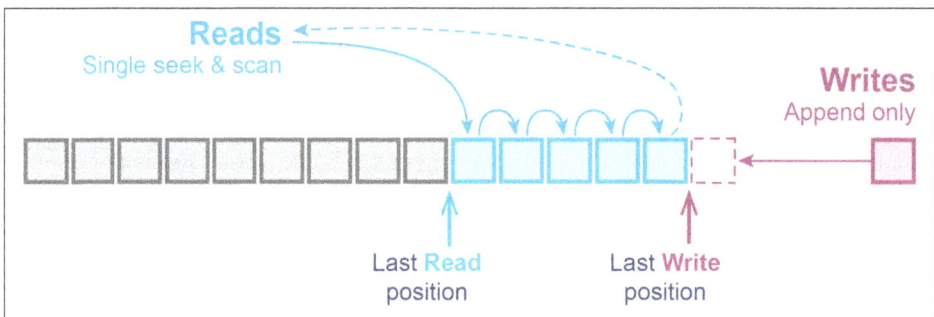

Figure 14-2. Kafka reads and writes

The bouncing arrow represents a seek-and-scan read, and note that there are no updates—Kafka is append-only. This means that reads and writes are sequential operations. In turn, this allows them to work with the linear nature of underlying media (e.g., memory and disk) to leverage things like prefetch and memory caches as well as providing an opportunity to batch operations together.

Kafka processors subscribe to *topics*, which are always divided into one or more partitions. Topics are a useful abstraction that is essentially a label and common configuration for a set of partitions. The partitions have two properties:

---

2 This capability enables some useful fine-grained patterns—such as granting consumers read-only access only to a specific topic (or topics), and granting the producer only write access, with no consumer allowed to see the contents of any topic not explicitly granted to it. This is very helpful in multitenant environments and for GDPR type work.

- Each partition is consumed by exactly one consumer.

- A single consumer can consume more than one partition.

Therefore, the number of active consumers must be less than or equal to the number of partitions.[3] These properties enable Kafka to provide both ordering guarantees and load balancing over a pool of consumers.

Kafka guarantees the order of events within the same partition. However, it does not (by default) guarantee a total order of events across all partitions.

The key class to examine is `ProducerRecord` in the package `org.apache.kafka.cli ents.producer`, which has these fields:

```
public class ProducerRecord<K, V> {
    private final String topic;
    private final Integer partition;
    private final Headers headers;
    private final K key;
    private final V value;
    private final Long timestamp;

    // ...
}
```

In most deployments the destination partition will be computed from a hash of the key. This allows Kafka to guarantee that messages having the same key always land in the same partition, and therefore, are always in order.

However, it is possible to change this behavior—either by explicitly providing the partition number or by just allowing Kafka to round-robin the messages. Note that in this final case, different messages with the same key may well be handled by different consumers, which can destroy the ordering properties.

Kafka used to use a standalone ZooKeeper service but has switched to its own implementation of Raft--known as KRaft. This somewhat simplifies adopting Kafka, as it reduces the number of components that need to be deployed, maintained, and observed.

Let's move on to discuss a concrete example—and think about how we might use some of these technologies to enhance Fighting Animals.

---

3 It is possible to have additional consumers that are idle and are present to provide hot standbys.

Enhancing Fighting Animals

First of all, let's introduce a `VeterinaryHospital` service for any animals that might have been injured in any of the battles. The hospital's purpose is to take care of any animal that has been fighting in too many battles.

We could use any of the technologies from the last section to implement the hospital service. For example:

- Existing services could write to a shared instance of Cassandra when one of their animals fights.
- Infinispan could store all currently available animals in a collection of maps, and each existing service could use that instead of holding a local map of animals.
- Existing services could communicate with the hospital via Kafka.

We could also consider ideas like using jgroups-raft to implement a cluster of our existing web services, but as they are effectively stateless, this is almost certainly overkill—instead, we should rely on K8s to provide our load balancing and related concerns.

Let's start with the third option, and implement an initial version of `VeterinaryHospital` that receives updates via Kafka. We can iterate on this initial design later in the chapter.

Introducing Kafka to Fighting Animals

We need three pieces to build out to introduce Kafka. Obviously, we will need some Kafka infrastructure in the form of a cluster of Kafka brokers. We also need the hospital service—note that it will still be a microservice, but it will differ from all of our existing services, because it does not communicate over HTTP but instead listens for messages on Kafka topics.

In addition, we have to modify each of the existing "leaf" microservices (those that return an animal, so Feline, Fish, and Mustelid) so that they will publish a Kafka message that says which animal was returned. Each microservice will have its own topic, so the hospital will need to listen to them all.

We can see the new layout of components in Figure 14-3.

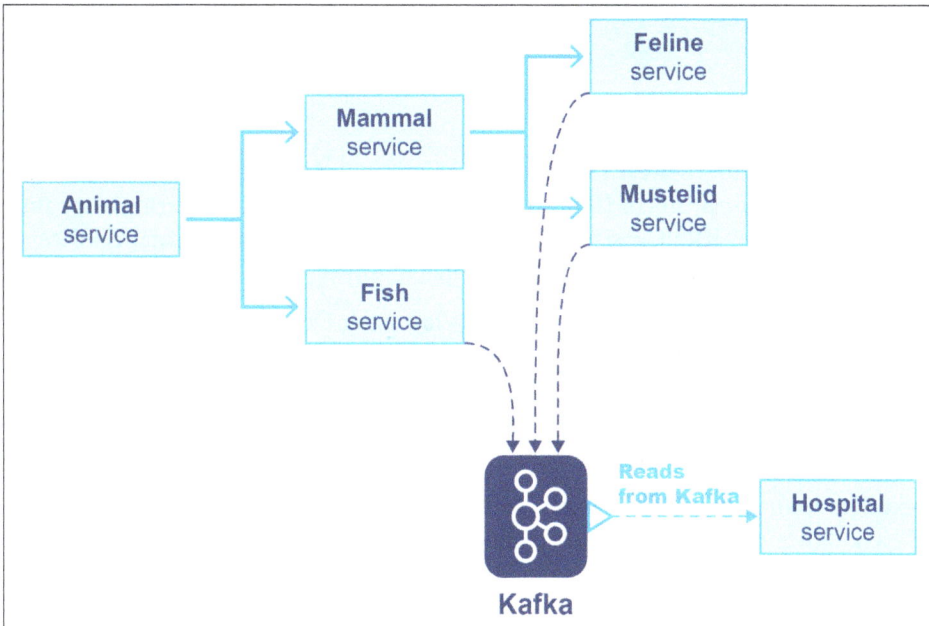

Figure 14-3. Fighting Animals with Kafka

To implement this, first of all, we'll need some Kafka infrastructure. The `dis tributed_systems` branch of the Fighting Animals repo has the code and config changes. We're using the Kafka Docker image (*https://oreil.ly/UdlQc*) from the Debezium project (*https://debezium.io*), and once again, we're using a pinned version rather than floating (like `latest`).

We have the new Kafka nodes set up like this in `docker-compose.yml` (and similarly for `kafka-2` and `kafka-3`):

```
# Kafka
kafka-1:
  image: debezium/kafka:2.7.0.Final
  ports:
    - "19092:9092"
    - "19093:9093"
  environment:
    - CLUSTER_ID=g4xWbaRgd-b-zQYgIS1rY5
    - NODE_ID=1
    - KAFKA_CONTROLLER_QUORUM_VOTERS=1@kafka-1:9093,2@kafka-2:9093,3@kafka-3:9093
```

and we also need to make the leaf node services depend upon Kafka, like this:

```
# Feline service
feline-service:
  image: feline_demo:latest
  ports:
```

```
      - "8085:8085"
    depends_on:
      - kafka-1
      - kafka-2
      - kafka-3
```

We're also using the newest (at the time of writing, August 2024) version, which supports the KRaft protocol (*https://oreil.ly/zTbb2*) rather than requiring a separate ZooKeeper cluster. KRaft is significantly more performant than external ZooKeeper and is intended to become the default for Kafka in time.

There is now a lot more noise in the startup log using Docker Compose, and startup (and shutdown) now takes significantly longer. We could have avoided some of this noise by using a single-node Kafka cluster, but we feel it's more informative to be able to see some of the details of clustering, leadership elections, and KRaft as the application starts up and runs.

Next, let's look at the code changes. Each of the leaf services needs to notify Kafka of each choice by producing and sending a message to a suitable topic. The Feline service has been modified like this (and the changes to Fish and Mustelid are similar):

```java
@RestController
public class FelineController {
  private final List<String> CATS = List.of("tabby", "jaguar", "leopard");

  private final KafkaProducer<String, String> producer;

  public FelineController() {
    Properties properties = new Properties();
    properties.put("bootstrap.servers", "kafka-1:9092"); // PLAINTEXT
    properties.put(ProducerConfig.KEY_SERIALIZER_CLASS_CONFIG,
      StringSerializer.class);
    properties.put(ProducerConfig.VALUE_SERIALIZER_CLASS_CONFIG,
      StringSerializer.class);
    producer = new KafkaProducer<>(properties);
  }

  @GetMapping("/getAnimal")
  public String makeBattle() throws InterruptedException {
    // Random pause
    Thread.sleep((int) (20 * Math.random()));

    // Return random cat (and also send to Kafka)
    var cat = CATS.get((int) (CATS.size() * Math.random()));
    var key = UUID.randomUUID().toString();
    var producerRecord = new ProducerRecord<>("FELINE", key, cat);
    producer.send(producerRecord);
    return cat;
  }
}
```

The changes to the constructor are just to set the Kafka producer to allow messages to be sent to the broker. We use the Kafka `ProducerRecord` class, as it allows us to specify the topic as well as the key and value for the message.

When we send the first requests to the Kafka-enabled animal service, we see lines like this in the log:

```
kafka-1-1          | 2024-07-14 09:13:19,275 - INFO  [data-plane-kafka-request- ↵
handler-7:Logging@66] - Sent auto-creation request for Set(MUSTELID) to the ↵
active controller.
kafka-1-1          | 2024-07-14 09:13:19,275 - INFO  [quorum-controller-1-event- ↵
handler:ReplicationControlManager@670] - [QuorumController id=1] CreateTopics ↵
result(s): CreatableTopic(name='MUSTELID', numPartitions=1, ↵
replicationFactor=1, assignments=[], configs=[]): SUCCESS
kafka-1-1          | 2024-07-14 09:13:19,276 - INFO  [quorum-controller-1- ↵
event-handler:ReplicationControlManager@457] - [QuorumController id=1] Replayed ↵
TopicRecord for topic MUSTELID with topic ID cnzLVYp8QOO7FIUd6mUkzg.
```

This shows the Kafka topics and partitions being auto-created and set up, so our modified services are connecting and sending, although we don't log the outgoing messages. Next, we need the Hospital service, so something is listening and responding to the message flow.

A Simple Hospital Service

The hospital has been implemented as a simple Kafka-based Quarkus service. This slightly complicates the setup, because it is usually easier to have Spring Boot and Quarkus components in separate Maven projects.[4]

Don't worry if you're not that familiar with Quarkus—one of the points of this example is to show how simple it can be. We won't use anything that requires any specific Quarkus knowledge—just Maven and Docker.

A skeleton for the service can be generated by installing the Quarkus CLI tool and then using the `create app` command, specifying the Kafka extension (*https://oreil.ly/ wWty8*). The project derived from this, which we'll use for these examples, is available on GitHub as the "Fighting Animals Hospital" (*https://oreil.ly/YLGb0*). For now, we'll be using the `listen_and_log` branch.

Our hospital is just one class:

```
@ApplicationScoped
public class VeterinaryHospital {

    public static final String FISH_CHANNEL = "fish";
```

---

4 It is entirely possible to have the two technologies coexist in the same Maven build, but it requires separate submodules, and Fighting Animals hasn't been set up that way, so the extra complexity is not worth it for our example.

```
public static final String FELINE_CHANNEL = "feline";
public static final String MUSTELID_CHANNEL = "mustelid";

@PostConstruct
public void init() {}

void onStart(@Observes StartupEvent ev) {
  Log.infof("Hospital starting up");
}

@Incoming(FISH_CHANNEL)
@Incoming(FELINE_CHANNEL)
@Incoming(MUSTELID_CHANNEL)
public CompletionStage<Void> processMainFlow(Message<String> message) {
  var payload = message.getPayload();
  var topic = message.getMetadata(IncomingKafkaRecordMetadata.class)
                     .get().getTopic();

  Log.infof("Processed: %s on topic %s, benching them for the next round",
    payload, topic);

  return message.ack();
}
}
```

Overall, the code should be easy to understand. We have a single `@Application Scoped` class, which is going to act as a controller and respond to Kafka messages. We have included a couple of callback hooks—`init()` and `onStart()`—which don't really do anything in this example except point out two useful points in the service lifecycle where a more complex service might want to take some action.

The code in our message handler `processMainFlow()` is deliberately a little more complex than a simple "Hello World" Kafka service would be. In particular, Quarkus offers several different ways to interact with Kafka, and in our example, we're using manual control of the Kafka ACK, via the final `message.ack()`.

This is more complex than the simplest case would be but also less "magical." The return type (`CompletionStage<Void>`) of our message handler method also gives us a clue that this is intended to fit into part of a larger flow.

> If a service uses manual Kafka ACKs, then you must ensure that every possible path through the method (including any exceptional paths) performs a `message.ack()` before exiting the method. Failing to do this can result in the Kafka consumer position not advancing, and so the consumer may end up re-consuming the message (including after a restart).

Also note the repeated @Incoming annotation—this arises because we want the same code to handle multiple incoming topics. We use the getMetadata() method on the message, so we can extract the topic the message was received on—a service that listened to multiple topics but didn't care which topic a message was received on wouldn't need to do this, of course.

We don't usually look at the import statements of our examples, but in this case, it's interesting to note how a few Quarkus-specific classes are being used:

```
import io.quarkus.logging.Log;
import io.quarkus.runtime.StartupEvent;
import io.smallrye.reactive.messaging.kafka.api.IncomingKafkaRecordMetadata;
import jakarta.annotation.PostConstruct;
import jakarta.enterprise.context.ApplicationScoped;
import jakarta.enterprise.event.Observes;
import org.eclipse.microprofile.reactive.messaging.Incoming;
import org.eclipse.microprofile.reactive.messaging.Message;

import java.util.concurrent.CompletionStage;
```

One aspect that should be briefly discussed is that this service does *not* use the standard Kafka consumer classes. Instead, it uses the Kafka support provided by Smallrye and Microprofile *reactive messaging*.

However, this is largely an implementation detail. The Quarkus framework deals with the reactive and nonblocking aspects and leaves the developer free to focus on just implementing a handler that processes Message objects as they arrive.

The hospital service also needs some config, which is in src/main/resources/appli cation.properties:

```
# Kafka bootstrap applies to all topics
kafka.bootstrap.servers=kafka-1:9092,kafka-2:9092,kafka-3:9092

# Kafka boilerplate
kafka.sasl.jaas.config = ""
kafka.sasl.mechanism = PLAIN
kafka.security.protocol = PLAINTEXT

# Input queue
mp.messaging.incoming.fish.connector=smallrye-kafka
mp.messaging.incoming.fish.topic=FISH
mp.messaging.incoming.feline.connector=smallrye-kafka
mp.messaging.incoming.feline.topic=FELINE
mp.messaging.incoming.mustelid.connector=smallrye-kafka
mp.messaging.incoming.mustelid.topic=MUSTELID

# Logging
quarkus.log.level=INFO
```

There is a small amount of additional complexity here, because we want the hospital to listen to multiple topics. To achieve this, we specify each one as a separate `mp.messaging.incoming` stanza in our config, and then use a corresponding repeated annotation in the code.

As the hospital service needs to be brought up as part of our cluster, we have to include it in the main `docker-compose.yml` file in the `fighting-animals` repo, like this:

```
# Hospital
hospital-service:
  image: hospital_demo:latest
  ports:
    - "8000:8000"
  depends_on:
    - kafka-1
    - kafka-2
    - kafka-3
```

This makes the deployment a little more complex, as we must build the jars and containers from both the main project and the hospital project before running `docker compose up`.

An Active Hospital

The next step is to make the hospital service actually do something. A hospital that can't do anything while the casualties continue to arrive is of extremely limited use.

Our next iteration is to add the capability for the hospital to tell the other services that an animal is injured and should not be included in the next fight.

We're going to do this by using Infinispan as a remote cache. The code is on the `with_infinispan` branch and can be seen in Figure 14-4.

We're also going to dial down the Kafka cluster to a single node—just to make it easier to see what's going on. We saw the extra complexity and startup latency that was induced by the multinode Kafka cluster in the last section, and now we want to focus on the changes the new Infinispan component brings in.

> If you have previously used a multinode Kafka cluster, then when you switch to the branch with a single node, you will need to purge the multinode config. You can do this by switching to a non-Kafka branch (e.g., `main`) and running `docker compose up --remove-orphans` to completely remove the old Kafka containers and then switching to the single-node branch.

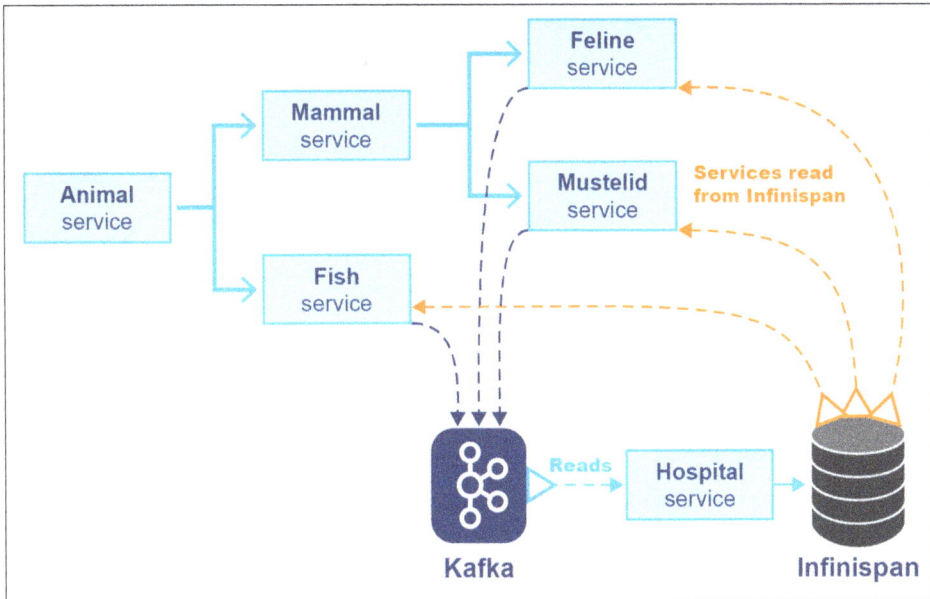

Figure 14-4. The full Fighting Animals system

To get started, we'll add this dependency to the hospital service:

```
<dependency>
  <groupId>io.quarkus</groupId>
  <artifactId>quarkus-infinispan-client</artifactId>
</dependency>
```

and we also need a code change to the `VeterinaryHospital` class:

```
@Inject
@Remote("animals")
RemoteCache<String, String> lastBattledAnimal;
```

This will store the last animal from each clade that was involved in a battle. We only need to include the single line:

```
lastBattledAnimal.put(topic, payload);
```

in the `processMainFlow()` method before calling `message.ack()`. We also need some cache configuration, which is stored partly in `application.properties`:

```
# Infinispan
quarkus.infinispan-client.cache.images.configuration-uri=animals.yaml
quarkus.infinispan-client.devservices.port=11222
quarkus.infinispan-client.hosts=infinispan-1:11222
quarkus.infinispan-client.username=xxxxxx
quarkus.infinispan-client.password=yyyyyy
```

and in the `animals.yaml` file (the name is chosen to coincide with the annotation and the application property):

```yaml
replicatedCache:
  mode: "SYNC"
  statistics: "true"
  encoding:
    key:
      mediaType: "application/x-protostream"
    value:
      mediaType: "application/x-protostream"
  locking:
    isolation: "REPEATABLE_READ"
  indexing:
    enabled: "true"
    storage: "local-heap"
    startupMode: "NONE"
```

We need to make changes to the main Fighting Animals project as well. To start with, we need to modify the controller classes for all the leaf services, like this example from `FelineController`:

```java
@GetMapping("/getAnimal")
public String makeBattle() throws InterruptedException {
  // Random pause
  Thread.sleep((int) (20 * Math.random()));

  // Look up last injured animal
  var injured = cacheManager.getCache(InfinispanConfiguration.CACHE_NAME)
                        .get("FELINE");
  String cat;
  do {
    Thread.sleep(1);
    cat = CATS.get((int) (CATS.size() * Math.random()));
    System.out.printf("Looking up uninjured cat - is %s OK?", cat);
  } while (injured == null || injured.equals(cat));

  // Return random uninjured cat (and also send to Kafka)
  var key = UUID.randomUUID().toString();
  var producerRecord = new ProducerRecord<>("FELINE", key, cat);
  producer.send(producerRecord);
  return cat;
}
```

The code uses a simple do loop to keep selecting a random cat until we choose one that is uninjured (i.e., is not in the cache maintained by the hospital service). This relies on a `RemoteCacheManager` that we inject into the controller classes:

```java
@Autowired private RemoteCacheManager cacheManager;
```

We also need a configuration class to set up the animals cache on this side:

```
@Configuration
public class InfinispanConfiguration {
  public static final String CACHE_NAME = "animals";

  @Bean
  @Order(Ordered.HIGHEST_PRECEDENCE)
  public InfinispanRemoteCacheCustomizer caches() {
    return b -> {
      URI cacheConfigUri;
      try {
        cacheConfigUri = this.getClass().getClassLoader()
                             .getResource("animals.xml").toURI();
      } catch (URISyntaxException e) {
        throw new RuntimeException(e);
      }

      b.remoteCache(CACHE_NAME).configurationURI(cacheConfigUri);
    };
  }
}
```

We also need some configuration in `application.properties`, like this:

```
infinispan.remote.server-list=infinispan-1:11222
infinispan.remote.auth-username=xxxxxx
infinispan.remote.auth-password=yyyyyy
infinispan.remote.marshaller=org.infinispan.commons.marshall.ProtoStream ↵
Marshaller
```

and a cache config (in our case, `animals.xml`):

```
<?xml version="1.0"?>
<distributed-cache name="animals" mode="SYNC" statistics="false">
    <encoding media-type="application/x-java-object"/>
    <indexing enabled="false" />
</distributed-cache>
```

With all these pieces in place, the full system should now start:

```
infinispan-1-1  | 2024-07-22 13:47:19,215 INFO  (main) [org.infinispan. ↵
CONTAINER] ISPN000104: Using EmbeddedTransactionManager
infinispan-1-1  | 2024-07-22 13:47:19,445 INFO  (ForkJoinPool.commonPool- ↵
worker-2) [org.infinispan.server.core.telemetry.TelemetryServiceFactory] ↵
ISPN000953: OpenTelemetry integration is disabled
infinispan-1-1  | 2024-07-22 13:47:19,475 INFO  (main) [org.infinispan.SERVER] ↵
ISPN080018: Started connector Resp (internal)
infinispan-1-1  | 2024-07-22 13:47:19,491 INFO  (ForkJoinPool.commonPool- ↵
worker-1) [org.infinispan.SERVER] ISPN080018: Started connector HotRod (internal)
infinispan-1-1  | 2024-07-22 13:47:19,544 INFO  (ForkJoinPool.commonPool- ↵
worker-2) [org.infinispan.SERVER] ISPN080018: Started connector REST (internal)
infinispan-1-1  | 2024-07-22 13:47:19,559 INFO  (main) [org.infinispan.SERVER] ↵
Using transport: Epoll
infinispan-1-1  | 2024-07-22 13:47:19,640 INFO  (main) [org.infinispan.SERVER] ↵
ISPN080004: Connector SinglePort (default) listening on 0.0.0.0:11222
```

```
infinispan-1-1  | 2024-07-22 13:47:19,641 INFO  (main) [org.infinispan.SERVER] ↵
ISPN080034: Server '8239b401a660-45518' listening on http://0.0.0.0:11222
infinispan-1-1  | 2024-07-22 13:47:19,676 INFO  (main) [org.infinispan.SERVER] ↵
ISPN080001: Infinispan Server 14.0.21.Final started in 10421ms
```

The architecture we have built is partially asynchronous—HTTP requests hit the microservices, and then data is handed off via Kafka to the hospital service, which updates the in-memory cache. This design forces us to consider the possibility of *partial availability*—what happens if the hospital is unavailable? Should the animal services continue, or does the failure of the hospital mandate the unavailability of others?

In this context, because the possibility exists of requests coming in so quickly that a hospitalized animal will still be selected, then arguably, the failure of the hospital should not cause a total outage. From this perspective, the same should also be true of the infrastructure components (i.e., Kafka and Infinispan).

Before we move on, it is important to once again highlight the role of observability— it is absolutely crucial that these distributed infrastructure components be observable. We need to be able to make sense of what's happening in all the components of our cloud app, including the infrastructure components.

For clarity, we disabled OpenTelemetry support in the Infinispan node, but in a real production system, this would be essential. The ability to observe, and also correlate, behaviors between our services and components is not only very powerful but also increasingly important.

Summary

In this chapter, we introduced some basic building blocks for building distributed systems—both distributed generalizations of single-machine concurrent data structures and genuinely new structures.

We outlined the two most common consensus protocols—Paxos and Raft. We have looked at some case studies of common cloud infrastructure components (all built in Java) that use the consensus algorithms and other low-level concepts to provide highly available solutions to common application and architectural problems. To bring it all together, we showed how to use two of these technologies to enhance our Fighting Animals example and discussed the tradeoffs that naturally arise when doing so.

In the next, and final, chapter we will look ahead and show you what new developments in the Java and JVM world will have the most impact on cloud-deployed applications in the coming years.

## CHAPTER 15

Modern Performance and The Future

In this chapter, we will look to the future of performance for Java and the JVM, especially as it relates to the reality of cloud native deployments. We will discuss several technologies that are not present (or present only as incubator or preview features) in Java 21. This reflects the principle that we only cover final features present in an LTS version in the main part of the book, and we reserve discussion of non-final features until this chapter.

New Concurrency Patterns

In this section, we're going to discuss some new patterns for concurrent systems that are enabled by virtual threads and some related new features that "follow on" from virtual threads—specifically *structured concurrency* (JEP 453) and *scoped values* (JEP 446).

Note that, as of JDK 21, both structured concurrency and scoped values are in preview state, so they cannot be used in production applications.

Structured Concurrency

The first of the two new APIs is known as *structured concurrency*. This is an API for thread handling, which provides an approach for cooperating tasks (usually virtual threads) to be considered and managed collectively as a collection of subtasks.

It might help to recall the discussion of Amdahl's law in Chapter 13, where we described the application of concurrent techniques to data-parallel problems.

In contrast, structured concurrency is designed for task-parallel problems and, because of its affinity to virtual threads, it is primarily useful for tasks that involve some amount of I/O (especially calls to remote services). However, the approach is much less useful for operations that act solely (or mostly) on in-memory data, as the virtual threads will contend with each other for CPU time.

The general flow for a structured concurrency task looks something like this:

1. Create a scope—the creating thread *owns* the scope. The scope enables the grouping of subtasks to coordinate the tasks in the group.

2. Fork concurrent subtasks in the scope (each is a virtual thread).

3. Scope owner joins the scope (all subtasks) as a unit.

4. Scope's `join()` method blocks until all subtasks have completed.

5. After joining, handle any errors in forks and process results.

6. Close the scope.

It's worth pointing out that the version of structured concurrency that shipped in Java 21 included some minor API changes over Java 20. The main one is that `fork()` now returns a `Subtask` (which implements `Supplier`) instead of a bare `Future` (as it was in Java 20).

> Java's release cadence and preview APIs are key in providing early access for real-world feedback.

The reason for this new interface, rather than just using `Future`, is that results are queried only after a `join()` because structured concurrency treats multiple subtasks as single unit of work. As a result, neither blocking calls to `get()` nor checked exceptions from subtasks are useful, so `Future` was something of an awkward interface; `Subtask` is a checked-exception-free interface.

Let's see structured concurrency in action in an example using the calculation of a stock tip, a record class that we'll define like this:

```
record StockTip(String symbol, double sentiment, double delta24) {}
```

We'll assume that the strength of the market's attitude to the stock (the *sentiment*) and the possible change in price over the next 24 hours (the *delta24*) are to be calculated by some external process. These elements may take some time to compute, and this is likely to involve network traffic.

We can therefore use structured subtasks to compute them, like this:

```
String symbol = "IBM";

try (var scope = new StructuredTaskScope.ShutdownOnFailure()) {
```

```
        Callable<Double> getSentiment = () -> getSentiment(symbol);
        Subtask<Double> fSentiment = scope.fork(getSentiment);

        Callable<Double> getDelta = () -> getDelta24(symbol);
        Subtask<Double> fDelta = scope.fork(getDelta);

        scope.join();
        scope.throwIfFailed();

        return new StockTip(symbol, fSentiment.get(), fDelta.get());
    } catch (ExecutionException | InterruptedException e) {
        throw new RuntimeException(e);
    }
}
```

This follows the general flow for structured concurrency that we established previously.

Closing the scope is handled implicitly via the try-with-resources block—this shuts down the scope and waits for any straggling subtasks to complete. Structured TaskScope has different Shutdown policies. In the previous example, we used ShutdownOnFailure(); in the next example, we will use ShutdownOnSuccess() in try-with-resources.

We should also mention a couple of other points.

First, joining the subtasks can also be canceled by calling a shutdown() method. Second, there is also a timed variant of join(), called joinUntil(), which accepts a deadline (as an Instant parameter).

There are two built-in shutdown policies for the scope (and custom shutdown policies are also supported):

- Cancel all subtasks if one of them fails (ShutdownOnFailure).
- Cancel all subtasks if one of them succeeds (ShutdownOnSuccess).

We met the first of these built-in options in our first example, so let's move on to meet the second option.

Consider a library method where multiple subtasks are launched (possibly multiple copies of the same subtask), and the first result (from any of the subtasks) will do. The tasks are racing each other to complete, and the rest of the virtual threads should be shut down as soon as the first success occurs, so we should use the ShutdownOn Success policy, like this:

```
<T> T race(List<Callable<T>> tasks, Instant deadline)
        throws InterruptedException, ExecutionException, TimeoutException {

    try (var scope = new StructuredTaskScope.ShutdownOnSuccess<T>()) {
        for (var task : tasks) {
```

```
            scope.fork(task);
    }
    return scope.joinUntil(deadline)
            .result();  // Throw if none of the subtasks
                        // completed successfully
}
}
```

This has an obvious dual operation: all tasks must run to completion, and a failure of any subtask should cancel the entire task. To achieve this, we'll use `ShutdownOn` `Failure` again:

```
<T> List<T> runAll(List<Callable<T>> tasks)
        throws InterruptedException, ExecutionException {

    try (var scope = new StructuredTaskScope.ShutdownOnFailure()) {
        List<? extends Subtask<T>> handles =
            tasks.stream().map(scope::fork).toList();

        scope.join()
            .throwIfFailed();  // Propagate exception if any subtask fails

        // Here, all tasks have succeeded, so compose their results
        return handles.stream().map(Subtask::get).toList();
    }
}
```

Note that this version of the code rematerializes the results into a `List`, but it's also possible to imagine a version that had a different terminal operation, which reduced the results and returned a single value.

We can build more complex structures as well—the subtasks we created using forks can themselves create scopes (subscopes). This naturally induces a tree structure of scopes and subtasks, which is useful when we want to condense a final value out of a tree of subtasks.

If, however, the main point of our code is to operate via side effects, then it is possible to use a `StructuredTaskScope<Void>`—i.e., use a task scope that returns `void`, such as in this example:

```
void serveScope(ServerSocket serverSocket) throws IOException,
    InterruptedException {
        try (var scope = new StructuredTaskScope<Void>()) {
            try {
                while (true) {
                    final var socket = serverSocket.accept();
                    Callable<Void> task = () -> {
                        handle(socket);
                        return null;
                    };
                    scope.fork(task);
                }
```

```
        } finally {
            // If there's been an error or we're interrupted,
            // we stop accepting
            scope.shutdown();  // Close all active connections
            scope.join();
        }
    }
}
```

However, this is arguably often better handled using a fire-and-forget pattern, such as `newVirtualThreadPerTaskExecutor()`. There are also some small wrinkles with the generics here—such as needing to explicitly return `null`.

One recurring theme in all the patterns that we have met so far is that using these techniques requires applying design thinking and knowledge of the domain and context of the problem being solved. There is no software tool that can tell with 100% accuracy whether a thread is a good candidate for being converted to a vthread—that is a task for a human software engineer.

Likewise, the restructuring of a task into subtasks and the definition of the relevant scopes requires the programmer to have a good understanding of the domain and any data dependencies between the subtasks.

Let's move on to look at the second of the new APIs that we want to discuss.

Scoped Values

As well as structured concurrency, the new *Scoped Values* API arrived in Java 21 as a preview. It is based on a new class, `ScopedValue<T>` in `java.lang`, and it represents a *binding* of a value to a variable within a specific scope. This value is written once and is then immutable on a per-scope basis.

The scope-specific bound value can be retrieved at any point down any call chain within the scope, but only within the scope in which it was set—this provides robustness and a form of encapsulation.

In particular, there is no need to explicitly pass the scoped value down the call chain. It can be thought of as *implicitly* available, but this is a much more controlled (and more Javaish) form than, say, Scala's implicit method parameters.

The Scoped Values API can also be thought of as a modern alternative to thread-local variables but with a number of enhancements, such as immutability. This means there is no `set()` method to let faraway code change a scoped value. This also enables possible future runtime optimizations, as the runtime can be certain that a scoped value cannot change.

Some goals of the API are:

- To share data within a thread and with child threads.

- Controlled and bounded lifetime of values.

- Lifetimes visible from the structure of code.

- Immutability allows sharing by lots of threads.

- Immutability and explicit lifetime is often a better fit.

It is not necessary for programmers to move away from `ThreadLocal`, but scoped values combine well with virtual thread patterns, such as fire-and-forget. It therefore seems quite likely that as scoped values are adopted, then `ThreadLocal` will be gradually replaced for almost all use cases.

Let's rewrite the virtual thread web server to use scoped values:

```
public class ServerSV {
    private final static ScopedValue<Socket> SOCKETSV =
        ScopedValue.newInstance();

    void serve(ServerSocket serverSocket) throws IOException,
        InterruptedException {
        while (true) {
            var socket = serverSocket.accept();
            ScopedValue.where(SOCKETSV, socket)
                        .run(() -> handle());
        }
    }

    private void handle() {
        var socket = SOCKETSV.get();
        // handle incoming traffic
    }
}
```

Note that the `handle()` method now no longer takes a parameter; instead, the socket is accessed via the scoped value—this is the implicit availability we discussed previously. This example is very simple, as all we're really doing is replacing the parameter passing with a scoped value—an almost trivial application. `ScopedValue.where` presents a scoped value and the object it is to be bound to. On the execution of `run`, the value is bound, which provides a copy specific to the current thread. Calling `.get()` reads the scoped value, and on completion of the method, the binding is destroyed.

The real power of scoped values is that the call chains and the scoping and subscoping can be arbitrarily complex, and the scoped value will still be available.

Overall, the intent of scoped values is to provide a *dynamic scope*, a concept that has not been seen in Java before. This approach to scopes is similar to that found in some other languages—such as shells, Lisp dialects, and Perl. It's also important to notice that the creation of the `private final static` field happens in object context (as the class is loaded), but the dynamic scope must be created within a method.

We can contrast it with the traditional Java form of scoping—usually called *lexical scoping*. This is where the scope of a variable is determined by the structure of the code, usually defined by a matching pair of curly braces.

Our dynamic scoping example shows a key pattern in action:

- Using a `static final` field as a holder for a scoped value
- Declaring the `ScopedValue` instance in class scope
- Creating the dynamic scope (e.g., `runWhere()`) within a method
- Using a lambda to define the scope body (where the call chains will live)

Scoped values are intended to be very useful for passing values like transaction contexts and other examples of *ambient context* data.

Scoped values interact well with structured concurrency, as they can be constructed for a scope and then *rebound* by subscopes. Any values that are not rebound will be inherited by the subscope. This technique allows for "privilege escalation" and similar patterns, such as in this example, where we will consider two security access levels:

```
enum SecurityLevel { USER, ADMIN }
```

We'll use a scoped value to hold the current security level and another to hold the current request number:

```
private static final ScopedValue<SecurityLevel> securitySV =
    ScopedValue.newInstance();
private static final ScopedValue<Integer> requestSV = ScopedValue.newInstance();

private final AtomicInteger req = new AtomicInteger();

public void run() {
    //Present the binding of the current security level
    ScopedValue.where(securitySV, level())
            //Present the binding the current request number
            .where(requestSV, req.getAndIncrement())
            //Bind the values
            .run(() -> process());
}
```

To demonstrate rebinding, let us assume that `ADMIN` privileges are not available, so any attempt to use them will result in a fallback to user privileges:

```
private void process() {
    if (!securitySV.isBound()) {
        throw new RuntimeException(
            "ScopedValue not bound - this should not happen");
```

```
    }

    var level = securitySV.get();
    if (level == SecurityLevel.USER) {
        System.out.println("User privileges granted for " +
            requestSV.get() +" on: "+ Thread.currentThread());
    } else {
        //ADMIN is not available in our implementation
        System.out.println("Admin privileges requested for " +
            requestSV.get() +" on: "+ Thread.currentThread());
        System.out.println(
            "System is in lockdown. Falling back to user privileges");
        //Present and bind the USER level and execute process
        //again with the new security level
        ScopedValue.where(securitySV, SecurityLevel.USER)
                .run(() -> process());
    }
}
```

To conclude this section, we should also point out that classes that represent continuations and other low-level building blocks for virtual threads and other components do exist in Java 21. However, they are in the package jdk.internal.vm, so they are not intended for direct use by Java programmers as of this release.

We can expect both of these APIs to continue to be developed, and hopefully arrive in a final form in some future version of Java. Let's move on to look at some of the major OpenJDK projects being developed over the last few years.

Panama

Project Panama is a major new OpenJDK project that gets its name from the *Panama Canal*, which connects the Atlantic and Pacific Oceans. In Project Panama's case, it connects the JVM and native code.

> ...[I]mproving and enriching the connections between the Java virtual machine and well-defined but "foreign" (non-Java) APIs, including many interfaces commonly used by C programmers.
>
> —Project Panama (*https://oreil.ly/IJbPH*)

It comprises JEPs in two main areas:

- Foreign Function and Memory API
- Vector API

The Foreign Function and Memory (FFM) API was originally proposed as a preview feature in Java 19 and subsequently refined in Java 20 and Java 21, before being finalized in Java 22.

However, because Java 22 is not an LTS release, we choose to cover Panama here rather than earlier, as there is no current LTS that contains the API as a final feature. As of Java 21, the API lives in the `jdk.incubator.foreign` package in the `jdk.incubator.foreign` module, and in the Java 22 final feature in the package `java.lang.foreign` in the `java.base` module.

Panama provides direct support in Java for:

- Foreign memory allocation
- Manipulation of structured foreign memory
- Lifecycle management of foreign resources
- Calling foreign functions

The implementation builds upon the MethodHandles and VarHandles APIs, and its overall design goals are:

Productivity
> Replace the brittle machinery of native methods and the Java Native Interface (JNI) with a concise, readable, and pure-Java API.

Performance
> Provide access to foreign functions and memory with overhead comparable to, if not better than, JNI and `sun.misc.Unsafe`.

Broad platform support
> Enable the discovery and invocation of native libraries on every platform where the JVM runs.

Uniformity
> Provide ways to operate on structured and unstructured data, of unlimited size, in multiple kinds of memory (e.g., native memory, persistent memory, and managed heap memory).

Soundness
> Guarantee no use-after-free bugs, even when memory is allocated and deallocated across multiple threads.

Integrity
> Allow programs to perform unsafe operations with native code and data but warn users about such operations by default.

Two of the most important concepts in Panama are the *arena* and the *memory segment*. A simple demonstration of them can be seen in this example:

```java
public class Main {
    private static final int INT_SIZE = 4;
```

```
    private static final long ARENA_SIZE = 4 * 1024 * 1024 * 1024L;

    public static void main(String[] args) {
        long l = 0;
        try (var arena = Arena.ofConfined()) {
            MemorySegment segment = arena.allocate(INT_SIZE * ARENA_SIZE);
            for (l = 0 ; l < ARENA_SIZE ; l += 1) {
                segment.setAtIndex(ValueLayout.JAVA_INT, l, (int)(l % 16));
            }
        }
        System.out.println("l = "+ l);
    }
}
```

There are several things to note:

- The `Arena` class is used to control the lifecycle of memory segments.
- Arenas use the familiar try-with-resources construct to guarantee deterministic deallocation (which may need to be coordinated across segments).
- Memory segments are allocated from the arena.
- The `allocate()` method takes a `long` argument, allowing larger chunks of memory to be allocated than allowed by the `ByteBuffer` class (or arrays).

In this example, we are using a *confined arena*—this is the simplest case, as it represents an arena that can only be used by the current thread. Panama also supports shared arenas, a global arena, and also an automatic arena (which is managed by the JVM's GC).

You may have noticed that we have discussed the Foreign Memory API but have not mentioned the Vector API. This is because the Vector API has made the decision to incubate until certain necessary features of Project Valhalla (see "Valhalla" on page 420) become available as preview features.

This places the Vector API farther out, and on a much more speculative basis, than some of the other features we are discussing in this chapter.

So, instead, let's take a look at a new OpenJDK project that is relevant to the discussion of evolving Java execution, but that may need to be coordinated, and is still in its very early stages at the time of writing (August 2024).

Leyden

Project Leyden is named for *Leyden jars*, which were an early form of electrical capacitor dating from the 18th century and invented in the city of Leyden in the Netherlands.

Another name for a capacitor is a *condenser*, which has some significance in terms of naming aspects of the project, as we will see later.

The overall aim of the project is:

> To improve the startup time, time to peak performance, and footprint of Java programs.
>
> —Project Leyden (*https://oreil.ly/YJMD6*)

Colloquially, the name is intended to invoke "capturing lightning in a bottle"—i.e., preserving the semantics of Java programs without requiring the overhead of the general-purpose dynamic capabilities that HotSpot provides.

This is rooted in the idea that the JVM balances both static and dynamic reasoning about runtime states and optimization, rather than the "choose one, lose one" approach taken by other languages.

For example, languages like C++ choose static reasoning and compilation, and give up dynamism, whereas languages like Python choose dynamic reasoning and then struggle to add back limited forms of static reasoning.

In contrast, HotSpot speculatively optimizes dynamic states at runtime, in effect converting them to static states. In Leyden, the goal is that such optimizations can be shifted and speculatively optimized before application startup.

Note that this is more general than just "provide AOT compilation." As we discussed in Chapter 6, there is a distinction between an outcome and a mechanism—and Leyden is focused on outcomes.

Leyden draws upon the practical experience that has already been gained by projects such as GraalVM and Quarkus, and it seeks to generalize this experience and bring it into the core of OpenJDK and the Java standards.

The two fundamental mechanisms being explored in Leyden currently are:

- Condensers
- Premain archives

Let's look at each in turn.

Images, Constraints, and Condensers

One of the most important ideas within the project is that of a *static run-time image*. This is understood to be a standalone program, derived from an application and a JDK, which runs solely on that specific application.

A related concept is that of the *closed world* constraint. An application that signs up to this constraint indicates that it is prepared to accept some strict limitations on classes that it can load: during the runtime phase, it cannot load classes from outside the image, nor can it create classes dynamically.

The closed-world constraint imposes very strict limits on Java's natural dynamism, particularly on the run-time reflection and class-loading features. However, so many of Java's existing libraries and frameworks depend upon these aspects, and as a result, not all applications are well suited to this constraint, and not all developers are willing to live with it.

Therefore, rather than adopt the closed-world constraint as a primary and singular goal, Leyden instead pursues a gradual and incremental approach—it seeks to explore what intermediate states exist. This is expressed in terms of constraints weaker than closed world that are still useful and appropriate for a meaningful number of Java workloads.

Noting that Java and the JVM—by design—have dynamic features that make static analysis difficult (or even impossible), Leyden's approach gives developers the control to trade functionality for performance—and to do so selectively.

One of the key concepts is *computation shifting*—moving certain types of computation out of the startup and warmup phases of an application into earlier (or in some cases later) phases.

We can shift two kinds of computation:

- Work expressed directly by a program (e.g., invoke a method)
- Work done on behalf of a program (e.g., compile a method to native code)

Java implementations already have some features that can shift computation automatically:

- Compile-time constant folding (shifts computation earlier)
- Pre-digested class-data archives (earlier)
- Lazy class loading and initialization (later)

Both Quarkus's build time computation and the AOT compilation capabilities of GraalVM can be seen as shifting compilation earlier (although these capabilities are tied to the framework and are not standardized).

From a certain point of view, even garbage collection can be seen as shifting computation to later phases.

Whenever shifting occurs, it must always preserve program meaning, per the Java specifications, this is necessary to ensure compatibility. Leyden will explore new ways to shift computation.

Some kinds of shifting will likely require no specification changes, but some of the possibilities being considered definitely will, and the intent is also to provide new features that allow developers to express their intent to shift computation directly.

A *condenser* is a transformation that is intended to shift computation from runtime to earlier phases by examining the entire program image—i.e., it is a *meaning-preserving whole-program transformation*.

Condensers will transform a program image into a new image that may contain:

- New code (AOT compiled methods)
- New data (serialized heap objects)
- New metadata (such as preloaded classes)
- New constraints

Note that condensers are intended to be composable—the image output by one condenser can be the input to another, and a particular condenser can be applied multiple times, if necessary.

> Experience with Quarkus Native Mode suggests that when unit testing or debugging, don't bother performing the program transformations—just run normally. Performing this type of test would be a net result in testing the framework and not provide value.

Shifting computation generally requires accepting constraints, with the overall idea that you can trade functionality for performance via the condensers that you choose.

Given sufficiently powerful condensers, if you shift enough computation earlier or later in time, you might even be able to produce a fully static native image, although this will likely require accepting many constraints.

This means that Leyden need not necessarily specify fully static native images directly. Instead, it will enable sufficient shifting of computation and constraining of dynamism, so that fully static native images can fall out as an emergent property.

At the time of writing (August 2024), a number of design efforts are underway, but not much work toward condensers has landed in mainline yet.

This aspect of the project is still early in its development and has commenced by looking at such ideas as resolving `invokedynamic` linkages at compile time, where possible (e.g., for lambdas), and the development of lazily computed static final fields.

Let's move on to look at the other major aspect of Leyden—the premain.

Leyden Premain

The aim of Leyden premain is to reduce warmup activity—which we define as optimization effort (by the JVM, not app) to reach peak performance. Peak performance may be defined as a statistical maximum (with some noise still present).

As the JVM is usually quite a noisy environment, with noise often in the 3%-5% range, then we can define a rule that peak is reached at 95% throughput or better. The warmup time is, therefore, defined to be the time it takes to reach 95% throughput.

To achieve this, the premain aspect of Leyden builds on the concept of *class-data sharing* (CDS).

This is not a new idea—CDS has been available in Java since version 8 and has been part of the default installation starting (for the LTS versions) with Java 17. The basic idea is that when the JVM starts, a shared archive is memory-mapped in to allow immediate availability of read-only JVM metadata for a selection of classes, thus shortening startup time.

In current versions of Java, by default, those classes come from the standard Java library. However, recent enhancements also allow for application class-data sharing (AppCDS), which are more flexible and under the control of the developer. They have been introduced to extend the CDS concept to include selected classes from the application class path.

This even includes the ability (as of Java 17) to produce *dynamic AppCDS archives*, whereby metadata can be recorded during an initial *training run* and then used in subsequent *deployment runs* by specifying the switch `-XX:SharedArchive File=<dynamic archive>`.

Leyden premain seeks to take this further, by using training runs to capture much more metadata and code for reuse in deployment runs.

In general, a training run is considered to be a representative execution of an application, with typical inputs and config, which runs startup through expected paths and states and warms up to a steady state.

This will work best on systems that handle a lot of similar, repetitive tasks, leading to stable peak performance. Not all systems are like this, of course.

During training, the JVM gathers initial states, profiles, and JIT code and produces a log (or CDS archive). Optionally, multiple training runs are executed, and resulting logs of data are merged. The application is then *distilled* (essentially by applying a condenser) into the optimized version.

One interesting long-term possibility is to auto-train and hide some or all of the training steps "under the hood"—but there's a lot of shorter-term work needed before this becomes possible.

Executing the optimized application is called a deployment run. The deployment run starts with initial states and benefits from archived profiles and code.

In general, the startup phase of an application resolves symbols, runs class init methods (`<clinit>`), and runs `invokedynamic` BSMs (e.g., for lambdas). This work can be performed in a training run and saved for replay in deployment, along with some initialization states and code.

The code can be reused from the various tiers of HotSpot's tiered compiler, including C1 (which is a "conservative" JIT that does not make speculative optimizations and, thus, never needs to de-optimize) and the optimized code from C2 (i.e., Tier 4). See Chapter 6 for more details on HotSpot's JIT compilers and tiering.

The C1-compiled code can be used in place of interpreted code, which improves startup by avoiding both online recompilation and the interpreter. This helps particularly in the case of non-hot code paths that may never be compiled or that are encountered at startup but not after that. Initial performance results indicate that these time savings are significant.

It is also the intent that JIT code can be regenerated during startup from persisted profiles, if necessary.

At a high level, training runs (which observe the app) can be seen as the dynamic flip side of static app analysis—or alternatively, a second-order form of profile-guided optimization.

The dynamic observations can be used as if they were statically deduced, provided we retain the possibility of de-optimization. Once captured, such data "looks static," but it was "born dynamic," and it can change, triggering re-optimization. This combination of speculative techniques with "escape hatches" allowing for unplanned future events is a core competency of HotSpot.

In fact, there are very practical reasons why this approach is superior to total AOT compilation (as found in e.g., GraalVM Native Image, etc.).

For example, it is relatively common for workloads to have "unusual days."

In the financial industry, examples could be the U.S. non-farm payroll (NFP) dates or the option maturity dates (once per quarter).

On these unusual dates, a fully AOT-compiled system is likely to perform much worse than one with a dynamic VM still in the loop. This is because the fully static

AOT version cannot back out the assumptions about code path execution that were derived from training runs, whereas Leyden could de-optimize and recompile.

At the time of writing (August 2024), the status of premain work is:

- Premain activities are derived automatically from training runs.
- Optimizable states generated for premain are dumped into the archive.

In the future, it is anticipated that user-defined activities could participate as well. However, this will require work on characterizing things such as which user code is trusted as pure (e.g., via such things as new purity annotations).

This is to be expected—Leyden is an evolving technology that is still relatively early-stage.

Let's move on to meet another long-term project within OpenJDK—Valhalla.

Valhalla

Project Valhalla is a long-running project that seeks to reorder the JVM at a very deep level.

In detail, the major goals of the project are:

- Aligning JVM memory layout behavior with the cost model of modern hardware.
- Extending generics to allow abstraction over all types, including primitives, values, and even void.
- Enabling existing libraries, especially the JDK, to compatibly evolve to fully take advantage of these features.

Buried within this description is a hint of one of the most complex efforts within the project: exploring the possibility of *value classes* within the JVM.

> Valhalla was launched in 2014, and over the last 10 years, the implementation design has changed significantly several times. Be very careful when reading about Valhalla that the information is up to date. For example, the description given in the first edition of this book is now completely wrong.

Recall that, up to and including version 21, Java has had only two types of values: primitive types and object references. To put this another way, the Java environment deliberately does not provide low-level control over memory layout.

To be a venue to explore and incubate advanced Java VM and language feature candidates.

—Project Valhalla (*https://oreil.ly/JU4dP*)

As a special case, this means that Java has no such thing as structs, and any composite data type can only be accessed by reference.

To understand the consequences of this, let's look at the memory layout of arrays. In Figure 15-1 we can see an array of primitive ints. As these values are not objects, they are laid out at adjacent memory locations.

Figure 15-1. Array of ints

By contrast, the boxed integer is an object and so is handled by reference. This means that an array of Integer objects will be an array of references. This is shown in Figure 15-2.

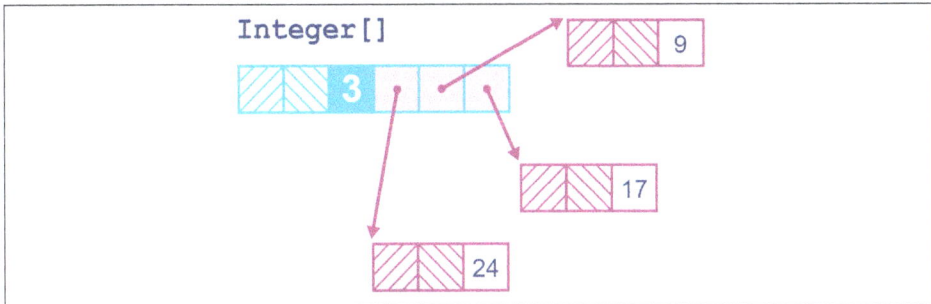

Figure 15-2. Array of integers

For over 25 years, this memory layout pattern has been the way that the Java platform has functioned. It has the advantage of simplicity but has a performance tradeoff— dealing with arrays of objects involves unavoidable indirections and attendant cache misses.

As a result, many performance-oriented programmers would like the ability to define types that can be laid out in memory more effectively. This would also include removing the overhead of needing a full object header for each item of composite data.

For example, a point in three-dimensional space, a `Point3D`, really only comprises the three spatial coordinates. As of Java 21, such a type can be represented as an object type with three fields:

```
public record Point3D(double x, double y, double z) {}
```

Therefore, an array of points will have the memory layout shown in Figure 15-3.

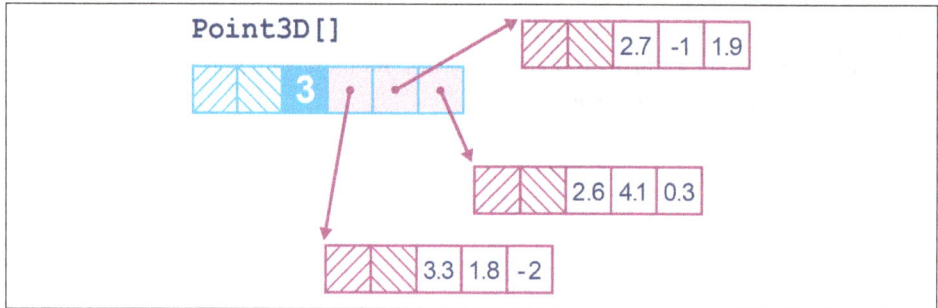

Figure 15-3. Array of Point3Ds

When this array is being processed, each entry must be accessed via an additional indirection to get the coordinates of each point. This has the potential to cause a cache miss for each point in the array, for no real benefit.

It is also the case that object identity is meaningless for the `Point3D` types. This means they are equal if and only if all their fields are equal. This is broadly what is meant by a *value class* in the Java ecosystem.

If this concept can be implemented in the JVM, then for simple types such as spatial points, a memory layout such as that shown in Figure 15-4 could be far more efficient.

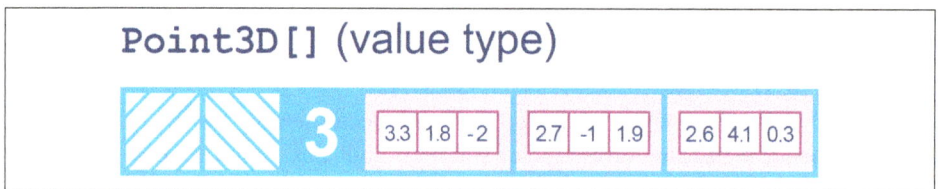

Figure 15-4. Array of "struct-like" Point3Ds

Iterating over an array of these nested points is now much more efficient because of memory and cache locality, as well as saving the cost of the headers of the individual objects. Not only this, but then other possibilities (such as user-defined types that behave in a similar way to built-in primitive types) also emerge.

With "struct-like" arrays, there is the potential to call foreign functions using Project Panama. One example would be to offload the struct to a GPU for a vector processing operation for faster and less power-intensive processing.

However, there are some key conceptual difficulties in this area. One important problem is related to the original design decisions made in the early days of Java. This is the fact that the Java type system lacks a *top type*, so there is no type that is the supertype of both `Object` and `int`. We can also say that the Java type system is not *single-rooted*.

As a consequence, when generics were added way back in Java 5, it was decided that type variables could range only over reference types (subtypes of `Object`). Thus, there is no obvious way to construct a consistent meaning for, say, `List<int>`. Instead, Java uses *type erasure* to implement backward-compatible generic types over reference types.

Sometimes people complain about type erasure, but this mechanism is not responsible for the lack of a top type and the resulting lack of primitive collections.

If the Java platform is to be extended to include value types, then the question naturally arises whether value types can be used as type parameter values. If not, then this would seem to greatly limit their usefulness. Therefore, the design of value types has always included the assumption that they will be valid as values of type parameters in an enhanced form of generics.

> Valhalla may be motivated by performance considerations, but a better way to view it is as enhancing abstraction, encapsulation, safety, expressiveness, and maintainability—without giving up performance.
>
> —Brian Goetz (*https://oreil.ly/lb94S*)

The current design of Valhalla strives to live up to the principle: "Codes like a class, works like an int." There is just a single new keyword (`value`) to indicate that a class is a value class—all current classes are now understood to be *identity classes* (a concept that has not been needed until now).

The JVM bytecode also has only minor changes and does not currently require any new bytecodes to be defined.

One of the most obvious changes is in the implementation of value comparison (i.e., the `if_acmpeq` bytecode). In current versions of Java, this is just a bitwise comparison—two primitives are equal if they have the same bits, and two object references are equal if they point to the same memory location.

However, comparison of value objects is more complex—two value objects are the same if and only if all their fields have the same value. This can cause problems, because value classes can have fields that are also value classes.

For example:

```
public value record VR0(VR1 vr1) {}
public value record VR1(VR2 vr2) {}
public value record VR2(VR3 vr3) {}
// ... and so on
public value record VRN(int i) {}
```

Now, consider comparing two objects of type VR0. They will be equal if and only if the embedded instances of VRN hold the same int value, as we can see for the case N=3:

```
var vr0a = new VR0(new VR1(new VR2(new VR3(42))));
var vr0b = new VR0(new VR1(new VR2(new VR3(73))));
var vr0c = new VR0(new VR1(new VR2(new VR3(42))));

System.out.println(vr0a == vr0b);
System.out.println(vr0a == vr0c);
System.out.println(vr0b == vr0c);
```

which will output:

```
false
true
false
```

However, to ascertain this, the VM must recurse through the definitions of equality for all the intermediate types.

This means there is now the possibility of arbitrary-depth recursive behavior in if_acmpeq, and this has important potentially negative performance consequences.

Note that these types of dependency chains must terminate sometime—value classes are not allowed to have fields that would cause cyclic dependencies, as it would be impossible to know how much space was required to lay out an object of that type.

In terms of JIT compilation, the major impact is in the required support in the C2 compiler, basically to avoid allocations as much as possible and implement "fancy boxing" for value objects. In terms of handling the new equality semantics, there are cases where the JIT compiler can infer behavior, but also cases where it can't.

Finally, these changes to the VM must be extremely carefully implemented. They must not, even in the worst possible case, cause performance regressions in existing code when Valhalla is not enabled.

At the time of writing (August 2024), it is unclear which release of Java will eventually introduce value types as a production feature.

Conclusions

In the new edition of this book, we have taken forward the material from the first edition that is still relevant to the modern Java developer. At the same time, we have introduced the techniques of cloud technology that are increasingly essential for applications that live in the cloud.

It is no longer enough for a performance-conscious Java engineer to have a journeyman's knowledge of the JVM's execution model and GC. New, cloud native techniques such as orchestration and observability are now part of the daily work of many—perhaps even most—Java developers and operations staff.

At the same time, the fundamentals of software performance engineering (in any environment) have not changed and still require the same knowledge and diligent application. Engineers now have more layers and more complex multivariate optimization problems to solve day to day. The body of knowledge also continues to grow, resulting in more specialization and coordination among engineers.

We hope that you will find the information and techniques we have presented in this book useful. It is intended as the starting point for your own unique performance journey rather than a complete guide. Good luck!

Microbenchmarking

In this appendix, we will consider the specifics of measuring low-level Java performance numbers directly. The dynamic nature of the JVM means that performance numbers are often harder to handle than many developers expect. As a result, there are a lot of inaccurate or misleading performance numbers floating around on the internet.

A primary goal of this appendix is to ensure that you are aware of these possible pitfalls and only produce performance numbers that you and others can rely upon. In particular, the measurement of small pieces of Java code (*microbenchmarking*) is notoriously subtle and difficult to do correctly, and this subject and its proper usage by performance engineers is a major theme throughout this appendix.

The Feynman quote we met way back in Chapter 2 is especially relevant when applied to microbenchmarks.

The second portion of this appendix describes how to use the gold standard of microbenchmarking tools: JMH. If, even after all the warnings and caveats, you really feel that your application and use cases warrant the use of microbenchmarks, then you will need to avoid numerous well-known pitfalls and "bear traps" by starting with the most reliable and advanced of the available tools.

Introduction to Measuring Low-Level Java Performance

In "Java Performance Overview" on page 4, we described performance analysis as a synthesis between different aspects of the craft that has resulted in a discipline that is fundamentally an experimental science.

That is, if we want to write a good benchmark (or microbenchmark), then it can be very helpful to consider it as though it were a science experiment.

This approach leads us to view the benchmark as an "opaque box"—it has inputs and outputs, and we want to collect data from which we can conjecture or infer results. However, we must be cautious: it is not enough to simply *collect* data. We need to ensure that we are not *deceived* by our data.

> Benchmark numbers don't matter on their own. It's important what models you derive from those numbers.
>
> —Aleksey Shipilëv

Our ideal goal is, therefore, to make our benchmark a fair test—meaning that, as far as possible, we only want to change a single aspect of the system and ensure any other external factors in our benchmark are controlled. In an ideal world, the other possibly changeable aspects of the system would be completely invariant between tests, but we are rarely so fortunate in practice.

> Even if the goal of a scientifically pure fair test is unachievable in practice, it is essential that our benchmarks are at least repeatable, as this is the basis of any empirical result.

One central problem with writing a benchmark for the Java platform is the sophistication of the Java runtime. A considerable portion of this book is devoted to illuminating the automatic optimizations that are applied to a developer's code by the JVM. When we think of our benchmark as a scientific test in the context of these optimizations, then our options become limited.

That is, to fully understand and account for the precise impact of these optimizations is all but impossible. Accurate models of the "real" performance of our application code are difficult to create and tend to be limited in their applicability.

Put another way, we cannot truly divorce the executing Java code from the JIT compiler, memory management, and other subsystems provided by the Java runtime. Neither can we ignore the effects of operating system, hardware, or runtime conditions (e.g., load) that are current when our tests are run.

> No man is an island, entire of itself.
>
> —John Donne

It is easier to smooth out these effects by dealing with a larger aggregate (a whole system or subsystem). Conversely, when we are dealing with small-scale or microbenchmarks, it is much more difficult to truly isolate application code from the background behavior of the runtime. This is the fundamental reason why microbenchmarking is so hard, as we will discuss.

Let's consider what appears to be a very simple example—a benchmark of code that sorts a list of 100,000 numbers. We want to examine it with the point of view of trying to create a truly fair test:

```java
public class ClassicSort {

    private static final int N = 1_000;
    private static final int I = 150_000;
    private static final List<Integer> testData = new ArrayList<>();

    public static void main(String[] args) {
        Random randomGenerator = new Random();
        for (int i = 0; i < N; i++) {
            testData.add(randomGenerator.nextInt(Integer.MAX_VALUE));
        }

        System.out.println("Testing Sort Algorithm");

        double startTime = System.nanoTime();

        for (int i = 0; i < I; i++) {
            List<Integer> copy = new ArrayList<Integer>(testData);
            Collections.sort(copy);
        }

        double endTime = System.nanoTime();
        double timePerOperation = ((endTime - startTime) / (1_000_000_000L * I));
        System.out.println("Result: " + (1 / timePerOperation) + " op/s");
    }
}
```

The benchmark creates an array of random integers and, once this is complete, logs the start time of the benchmark. The benchmark then loops around, copying the template array, and then runs a sort over the data. Once this has run for I times, the duration is converted to seconds and divided by the number of iterations to give us the time taken per operation.

The first concern with the benchmark is that it goes straight into testing the code, without any consideration for warming up the JVM. Consider the case where the sort is running in a server application in production. It is likely to have been running for hours, maybe even days. However, we know that the JVM includes a just-in-time compiler that will convert interpreted bytecode to highly optimized machine code. This compiler only kicks in after the method has been run a certain number of times.

The test we are conducting, therefore, is not representative of how it will behave in production. The JVM will spend time optimizing the call while we are trying to benchmark. We can see this effect by running the sort with a few JVM flags:

```
java -Xms2048m -Xmx2048m -XX:+PrintCompilation ClassicSort
```

The -Xms and -Xmx options control the size of the heap, in this case, pinning the heap size to 2 GB. The PrintCompilation flag outputs a log line whenever a method is compiled (or some other compilation event happens). Here's a fragment of the output:

```
Testing Sort Algorithm
  73   29   3    java.util.ArrayList::ensureExplicitCapacity (26 bytes)
  73   31   3    java.lang.Integer::valueOf (32 bytes)
  74   32   3    java.util.concurrent.atomic.AtomicLong::get (5 bytes)
  74   33   3    java.util.concurrent.atomic.AtomicLong::compareAndSet (13 bytes)
  74   35   3    java.util.Random::next (47 bytes)
  74   36   3    java.lang.Integer::compareTo (9 bytes)
  74   38   3    java.lang.Integer::compare (20 bytes)
  74   37   3    java.lang.Integer::compareTo (12 bytes)
  74   39   4    java.lang.Integer::compareTo (9 bytes)
  75   36   3    java.lang.Integer::compareTo (9 bytes) made not entrant
  76   40   3    java.util.ComparableTimSort::binarySort (223 bytes)
  77   41   3    java.util.ComparableTimSort::mergeLo (656 bytes)
  79   42   3    java.util.ComparableTimSort::countRunAndMakeAscending (123 bytes)
  79   45   3    java.util.ComparableTimSort::gallopRight (327 bytes)
  80   43   3    java.util.ComparableTimSort::pushRun (31 bytes)
```

The JIT compiler is working overtime to optimize parts of the call hierarchy to make our code more efficient. This means the performance of the benchmark changes over the duration of our timing capture, and we have inadvertently left a variable uncontrolled in our experiment. A warmup period is, therefore, desirable—it will allow the JVM to settle down before we capture our timings. Usually this involves running the code we are about to benchmark for a number of iterations without capturing the timing details.

Another external factor that we need to consider is garbage collection. Ideally, we want GC to be prevented from running during our time capturing, and also to be normalized after setup. Due to the nondeterministic nature of garbage collection, this is incredibly difficult to control.

One improvement we could definitely make is to ensure that we are not capturing timings while GC is likely to be running. We could potentially ask the system for a GC to be run and wait a short time, but the system could decide to ignore this call. As it stands, the timing in this benchmark is far too broad, so we need more detail about the garbage collection events that could be occurring.

Not only that, but as well as selecting our timing points we also want to select a reasonable number of iterations, which can be tricky to figure out through trial and improvement. The effects of garbage collection can be seen with another VM flag:

```
java -Xms2048m -Xmx2048m -verbose:gc ClassicSort
```

This will produce GC log entries similar to the following:

```
Testing Sort Algorithm
[GC (Allocation Failure)  524800K->632K(2010112K), 0.0009038 secs]
[GC (Allocation Failure)  525432K->672K(2010112K), 0.0008671 secs]
Result: 9838.556465303362 op/s
```

Another common mistake made in benchmarks is to not actually use the result generated from the code we are testing. In the benchmark, copy is effectively dead code, and it is, therefore, possible for the JIT compiler to identify it as a dead code path and optimize away what we are, in fact, trying to benchmark.

A further consideration is that looking at a single timed result, even though averaged, does not give us the full story of how our benchmark performed. Ideally, we want to capture the margin of error to understand the reliability of the collected value. If the error margin is high, it may point to an uncontrolled variable or, indeed, that the code we have written is not performant. Either way, without capturing the margin of error, there is no way to identify there is even an issue.

Benchmarking even a very simple sort can have pitfalls that mean the benchmark is wildly thrown out; however, as the complexity increases, things rapidly get much, much worse. Consider a benchmark that looks to assess multithreaded code. Multithreaded code is extremely difficult to benchmark, as it requires ensuring that all the threads are held until each has fully started up, from the beginning of the benchmark to making certain accurate results. If this is not the case, the margin of error will be high.

There are also hardware considerations when it comes to benchmarking concurrent code, and they go beyond simply the hardware configuration. Consider if power management were to kick in or there were other contentions on the machine.

Getting the benchmark code correct is complicated and involves considering a lot of factors. As developers, our primary concern is the code we are looking to profile rather than all the issues just highlighted. All the aforementioned concerns combine to create a situation in which, unless you are a JVM expert, it is extremely easy to miss something and get an erroneous benchmark result.

There are two ways to deal with this problem. The first is to only benchmark systems as a whole. In this case, the low-level numbers are simply ignored and not collected. The overall outcome of so many copies of separate effects is to average out and allow meaningful large-scale results to be obtained. This approach is the one needed in most situations and by most developers.

The second approach is to try to address many of the aforementioned concerns by using a common framework, to allow meaningful comparison of related low-level results. The ideal framework would take away some of the pressures just discussed.

Such a tool would have to follow the mainline development of OpenJDK to ensure that new optimizations and other external control variables were managed.

Fortunately, such a tool exists, and it is the subject of our next section.

Introduction to JMH

We open with an example (and a cautionary tale) of how and why microbenchmarking can easily go wrong if it is approached naively. From there, we introduce a set of heuristics that indicate whether your use case is one where microbenchmarking is appropriate. For the vast majority of applications, the outcome will be that the technique is not suitable.

Don't Microbenchmark If You Can Help It (A True Story)

After a very long day in the office, one of the authors was leaving the building when he passed a colleague still working at her desk, staring intensely at a single Java method. Thinking nothing of it, he left to catch a train home. However, two days later a very similar scenario played out—with a very similar method on the colleague's screen and a tired, annoyed look on her face. Clearly, some deeper investigation was required.

The application she was renovating had an easily observed performance problem. The new version was not performing as well as the version that the team was looking to replace, despite using newer versions of well-known libraries. She had been spending some of her time removing parts of the code and writing small benchmarks in an attempt to find where the problem was hiding.

The approach somehow felt wrong, like looking for a needle in a haystack. Instead, the pair worked together on another approach and quickly confirmed that the application was maxing out CPU utilization. As this is a known good use case for execution profilers (see Chapter 12 for the full details of when to use profilers), ten minutes profiling the application found the true cause. Sure enough, the problem wasn't in the application code at all, but in a new infrastructure library the team was using.

This story illustrates an approach to Java performance that is, unfortunately, all too common. Developers can become obsessed with the idea that their own code must be to blame, and thus miss the bigger picture.

Developers often want to start hunting for problems by looking closely at small-scale code constructs, but benchmarking at this level is extremely difficult and has some dangerous "bear traps."

Heuristics for When to Microbenchmark

As we discussed briefly in Chapter 3, the dynamic nature of the Java platform, and features like garbage collection and aggressive JIT optimization, lead to performance that is hard to reason about directly. Worse still, performance numbers frequently depend on the exact runtime circumstances in play when the application is being measured.

> It is almost always easier to analyze the true performance of an entire Java application than a small Java code fragment.

However, occasionally there are times when we need to directly analyze the performance of an individual method or even a single code fragment. This analysis should not be undertaken lightly, though. In general, there are three main use cases for low-level analysis or microbenchmarking:

- You're a developer on OpenJDK or another Java platform implementation.
- You're developing general-purpose library code with broad use cases.
- You're developing extremely latency-sensitive code.

The rationale for each of the three use cases is slightly different.

Platform developers are a key user community for microbenchmarks, and the JMH tool was created by the OpenJDK team primarily for its own use. However, the tool has proved to be useful to the wider community of performance experts.

General-purpose libraries (by definition) have limited knowledge about the contexts in which they will be used. Examples of these types of libraries include Google Guava or the Eclipse Collections. They need to provide acceptable or better performance across a very wide range of use cases—from datasets containing a few dozen elements up to hundreds of millions of elements.

Due to the broad nature of how they will be used, general-purpose libraries are sometimes forced to use microbenchmarking as a proxy for more conventional performance and capacity testing techniques.

Finally, some developers working at the cutting edge of Java performance may wish to use microbenchmarks to select algorithms and techniques that best suit their applications and extreme use cases. This would include low-latency financial trading but relatively few other cases.[1]

For the second two cases, it will normally make sense to include your JMH-based tests as part of your CI/CD pipeline and fail on a performance regression. This will detect not only changes in your own code but also in any library dependencies.

While it should be apparent if you are a developer working on OpenJDK or a general-purpose library, there may be developers who are confused about whether their performance requirements are such that they should consider microbenchmarks.

Generally, only the most extreme applications should use microbenchmarks. There are no definitive rules, but unless your application meets most or all of these criteria, you are unlikely to derive genuine benefit from microbenchmarking your application:

- Your total code path execution time should certainly be less than 1 ms, and probably less than 100 µs.
- You should have measured your memory (object) allocation rate (see "Allocation and Lifetime" on page 85 for details), and it should be <1 MB/s, and ideally, very close to zero.
- You should be using close to 100% of available CPU, and the system utilization rate should be consistently low (under 10%).
- You should have already used an execution profiler (see Chapter 12) to understand the distribution of methods that are consuming CPU. There should be at most two or three dominant methods in the distribution.

With all of this said, it is hopefully obvious that microbenchmarking is an advanced, though rarely used, technique. However, it is useful to understand some of the basic theory and complexity that it reflects, as it leads to a better understanding of the difficulties of performance work in less extreme applications on the Java platform.

The rest of this section explores microbenchmarking more thoroughly and introduces some of the tools and the considerations developers must take into account to produce results that are reliable and don't lead to incorrect conclusions. It should be useful background for all performance analysts, regardless of whether it is directly relevant to your current projects.

---

1 If you're developing a standard web service using something like Spring Boot or Quarkus, then you are almost certainly *not* going to benefit from using JMH.

The JMH Framework

JMH is designed to be the framework that resolves the issues we have just discussed.

> JMH is a Java harness for building, running, and analyzing nano/micro/milli/macro benchmarks written in Java and other languages targeting the JVM.
>
> —OpenJDK

There have been several attempts at simple benchmarking libraries in the past, with Google Caliper being one of the most well-regarded among developers. However, all of these frameworks have had their challenges, and often what seems like a rational way of setting up or measuring code performance can have some subtle bear traps to contend with. This is especially true with the continually evolving nature of the JVM as new optimizations are applied.

JMH is very different in that regard and has been worked on by the same engineers that build the JVM. Therefore, the JMH authors know how to avoid the gotchas and optimization bear traps that exist within each version of the JVM. JMH evolves as a benchmarking harness with each release of the JVM, allowing developers to simply focus on using the tool and on the benchmark code itself.

JMH takes into account some key benchmark harness design issues, in addition to some of the problems already highlighted. A benchmark framework has to be dynamic, as it does not know the contents of the benchmark at compile time.

One obvious choice to get around this would be to execute benchmarks the user has written using reflection. However, this involves another complex JVM subsystem in the benchmark execution path. Instead, JMH operates by generating additional Java source from the benchmark, via annotation processing.

> Many common annotation-based Java frameworks (e.g., JUnit) use reflection to achieve their goals, so the use of a processor that generates additional source may be somewhat unexpected to some Java developers.

One issue is that if the benchmark framework were to call the user's code for a large number of iterations, loop optimizations might be triggered. This means the actual process of running the benchmark can cause issues with reliable results.

To avoid hitting loop optimization constraints, JMH generates code for the benchmark, wrapping the benchmark code in a loop with the iteration count carefully set to a value that avoids optimization.

Executing Benchmarks

The complexities involved in JMH execution are mostly hidden from the user, and setting up a simple benchmark using Maven is straightforward. We can set up a new JMH project by executing the following command:

```
$ mvn archetype:generate \
        -DinteractiveMode=false \
        -DarchetypeGroupId=org.openjdk.jmh \
        -DarchetypeArtifactId=jmh-java-benchmark-archetype \
        -DgroupId=org.sample \
        -DartifactId=test \
        -Dversion=1.0
```

This downloads the required artifacts and creates a single benchmark stub to house the code.

The benchmark is annotated with @Benchmark, indicating that the harness will execute the method to benchmark it (after the framework has performed various setup tasks):

```
public class MyBenchmark {
    @Benchmark
    public void testMethod() {
        // Stub for code
    }
}
```

The author of the benchmark can configure parameters to set up the benchmark execution. The parameters can be set either on the command line or in the main() method of the benchmark as shown here:

```
public class MyBenchmark {

    public static void main(String[] args) throws RunnerException {
        Options opt = new OptionsBuilder()
                .include(SortBenchmark.class.getSimpleName())
                .warmupIterations(100)
                .measurementIterations(5).forks(1)
                .jvmArgs("-server", "-Xms2048m", "-Xmx2048m").build();

        new Runner(opt).run();
    }
}
```

The parameters on the command line override any parameters that have been set in the main() method.

Usually a benchmark requires some setup—for example, creating a dataset or setting up the conditions required for an orthogonal set of benchmarks to compare performance.

State, and controlling state, is another feature that is baked into the JMH framework. The @State annotation can be used to define that state, and it accepts the Scope enum to define where the state is visible: Benchmark, Group, or Thread. Objects that are annotated with @State are reachable for the lifetime of the benchmark; it may be necessary to perform some setup.

Multithreaded code also requires careful handling to ensure that benchmarks are not skewed by state that is not well managed.

In general, if the code executed in a method has no side effects and the result is not used, then the method is a candidate for removal by the JVM. JMH needs to prevent this from occurring, and, in fact, makes this extremely straightforward for the benchmark author. Single results can be returned from the benchmark method, and the framework ensures that the value is implicitly assigned to a blackhole, a mechanism developed by the framework authors to have negligible performance overhead.

If a benchmark performs multiple calculations, it may be costly to combine and return the results from the benchmark method. In that scenario, it may be necessary for the author to use an explicit blackhole by creating a benchmark that takes a blackhole as a parameter, which the benchmark will inject.

Blackholes provide four protections related to optimizations that could potentially impact the benchmark. Some protections are about preventing the benchmark from over-optimizing due to its limited scope, and the others are about avoiding predictable runtime patterns of data, which would not happen in a typical run of the system. The protections are:

- Remove the potential for dead code to be removed as an optimization at runtime.
- Prevent repeated calculations from being folded into constants.
- Prevent false sharing, where the reading or writing of a value can cause the current cache line to be impacted.
- Protect against "write walls."

The term *wall* in performance generally refers to a point at which your resources become saturated, and the impact to the application is effectively a bottleneck. Hitting the write wall can impact caches and pollute buffers that are being used for writing. If you do this within your benchmark, you are potentially impacting it in a big way.

As documented in the Blackhole JavaDoc (and as noted earlier), to provide these protections, you must have intimate knowledge of the JIT compiler so you can build a benchmark that avoids optimizations.

Let's take a quick look at the two `consume()` methods used by blackholes to give us insight into some of the tricks JMH uses (feel free to skip this bit if you're not interested in how JMH is implemented):

```java
public volatile int i1 = 1, i2 = 2;

/**
 * Consume object. This call provides a side effect preventing JIT to eliminate
 * dependent computations.
 *
 * @param i int to consume.
 */
public final void consume(int i) {
    if (i == i1 & i == i2) {
        // SHOULD NEVER HAPPEN
        nullBait.i1 = i; // implicit null pointer exception
    }
}
```

We repeat this code for consuming all primitives (changing `int` for the corresponding primitive type). The variables `i1` and `i2` are declared as `volatile`, which means the runtime must re-evaluate them. The `if` statement can never be `true`, but the compiler must allow the code to run. Also note the use of the bitwise AND operator (`&`) inside the `if` statement. This avoids additional branch logic being a problem and results in a more uniform performance.

Here is the second method:

```java
public int tlr = (int) System.nanoTime();

/**
 * Consume object. This call provides a side effect preventing JIT to eliminate
 * dependent computations.
 *
 * @param obj object to consume.
 */
public final void consume(Object obj) {
    int tlr = (this.tlr = (this.tlr * 1664525 + 1013904223));
    if ((tlr & tlrMask) == 0) {
        // SHOULD ALMOST NEVER HAPPEN IN MEASUREMENT
        this.obj1 = obj;
        this.tlrMask = (this.tlrMask << 1) + 1;
    }
}
```

When it comes to objects, it would seem at first the same logic could be applied, as nothing the user has could be equal to objects that the `Blackhole` holds. However, the compiler is also trying to be smart about this. If the compiler asserts that the object is never equal to something else due to escape analysis, it is possible that comparison itself could be optimized to return `false`.

Instead, objects are consumed under a condition that executes only in rare scenarios. The value for `tlr` is computed and bitwise compared to the `tlrMask` to reduce the chance of a `0` value, but not outright eliminate it. This ensures objects are consumed largely without the requirement to assign the objects. Benchmark framework code is extremely fun to review, as it is so different from real-world Java applications. In fact, if code like that were found anywhere in a production Java application, the developer responsible should probably be fired.

As well as writing an extremely accurate microbenchmarking tool, the authors have also managed to create impressive documentation on the classes. If you're interested in the magic going on behind the scenes, the comments explain it well.

It doesn't take much with the preceding information to get a simple benchmark up and running, but JMH also has some fairly advanced features. The official documentation (*https://oreil.ly/KsqHt*) has examples of each, all of which are worth reviewing.

Interesting features that demonstrate the power of JMH and its relative closeness to the JVM include:

- Being able to control the compiler
- Simulating CPU usage levels during a benchmark

Another cool feature is using blackholes to actually consume CPU cycles to allow you to simulate a benchmark under various CPU loads.

The `@CompilerControl` annotation can be used to ask the compiler not to inline, explicitly inline, or exclude the method from compilation. This is extremely useful if you come across a performance issue where you suspect that the JVM is causing specific problems due to inlining or compilation:

```
@State(Scope.Benchmark)
@BenchmarkMode(Mode.Throughput)
@Warmup(iterations = 5, time = 1, timeUnit = TimeUnit.SECONDS)
@Measurement(iterations = 5, time = 1, timeUnit = TimeUnit.SECONDS)
@OutputTimeUnit(TimeUnit.SECONDS)
@Fork(1)
public class SortBenchmark {

    private static final int N = 1_000;
    private static final List<Integer> testData = new ArrayList<>();

    @Setup
    public static final void setup() {
        Random randomGenerator = new Random();
        for (int i = 0; i < N; i++) {
            testData.add(randomGenerator.nextInt(Integer.MAX_VALUE));
        }
        System.out.println("Setup Complete");
```

```
        }

        @Benchmark
        public List<Integer> classicSort() {
            List<Integer> copy = new ArrayList<Integer>(testData);
            Collections.sort(copy);
            return copy;
        }

        @Benchmark
        public List<Integer> standardSort() {
            return testData.stream().sorted().collect(Collectors.toList());
        }

        @Benchmark
        public List<Integer> parallelSort() {
            return testData.parallelStream().sorted().collect(Collectors.toList());
        }

        public static void main(String[] args) throws RunnerException {
            Options opt = new OptionsBuilder()
                    .include(SortBenchmark.class.getSimpleName())
                    .warmupIterations(100)
                    .measurementIterations(5).forks(1)
                    .jvmArgs("-server", "-Xms2048m", "-Xmx2048m")
                    .addProfiler(GCProfiler.class)
                    .addProfiler(StackProfiler.class)
                    .build();

            new Runner(opt).run();
        }
    }
```

Running the benchmark produces the following output:

```
Benchmark                           Mode   Cnt      Score      Error  Units
optjava.SortBenchmark.classicSort   thrpt  200  14373.039 ±  111.586  ops/s
optjava.SortBenchmark.parallelSort  thrpt  200   7917.702 ±   87.757  ops/s
optjava.SortBenchmark.standardSort  thrpt  200  12656.107 ±   84.849  ops/s
```

Looking at this benchmark, you could easily jump to the quick conclusion that a classic method of sorting is more effective than using streams. Both code runs use one array copy and one sort, so it should be OK. Developers may look at the low error rate and high throughput and conclude that the benchmark must be correct.

But let's consider some reasons why our benchmark might not be giving an accurate picture of performance—basically trying to answer the question: "Is this a controlled test?" To begin with, let's look at the impact of garbage collection on the classicSort test:

```
Iteration   1:
[GC (Allocation Failure)  65496K->1480K(239104K), 0.0012473 secs]
[GC (Allocation Failure)  63944K->1496K(237056K), 0.0013170 secs]
10830.105 ops/s
Iteration   2:
[GC (Allocation Failure)  62936K->1680K(236032K), 0.0004776 secs]
10951.704 ops/s
```

In this snapshot, it is clear that there is one GC cycle running per iteration (approximately). Comparing this to parallel sort is interesting:

```
Iteration   1:
[GC (Allocation Failure)  52952K->1848K(225792K), 0.0005354 secs]
[GC (Allocation Failure)  52024K->1848K(226816K), 0.0005341 secs]
[GC (Allocation Failure)  51000K->1784K(223744K), 0.0005509 secs]
[GC (Allocation Failure)  49912K->1784K(225280K), 0.0003952 secs]
9526.212 ops/s
Iteration   2:
[GC (Allocation Failure)  49400K->1912K(222720K), 0.0005589 secs]
[GC (Allocation Failure)  49016K->1832K(223744K), 0.0004594 secs]
[GC (Allocation Failure)  48424K->1864K(221696K), 0.0005370 secs]
[GC (Allocation Failure)  47944K->1832K(222720K), 0.0004966 secs]
[GC (Allocation Failure)  47400K->1864K(220672K), 0.0005004 secs]
```

So, by adding in flags to see what is causing this unexpected disparity, we can see that something else in the benchmark is causing noise—in this case, garbage collection.

The takeaway is that it is easy to assume that the benchmark represents a controlled environment, but the truth can be far more slippery. Often the uncontrolled variables are hard to spot, so even with a harness like JMH, caution is still required. We also need to take care to correct for our confirmation biases and ensure we are measuring the observables that truly reflect the behavior of our system.

In Chapter 6, we met JITWatch, which gave us another view into what the JIT compiler is doing with bytecode. This can often lend insight into why bytecode generated for a particular method may be causing the benchmark to not perform as expected.

Microbenchmarking is the closest that Java performance comes to a dark art. While this characterization is evocative, it is not wholly deserved. It is still an engineering discipline undertaken by working developers. However, microbenchmarks should be used with caution:

- Do not microbenchmark unless you know you are a known use case for it.
- If you must microbenchmark, use JMH.
- Discuss your results as publicly as you can, and in the company of your peers.
- Be prepared to be wrong a lot and have your thinking challenged repeatedly.

One of the positive aspects of working with microbenchmarks is that it exposes the highly dynamic behavior and non-normal distributions produced by low-level subsystems. This, in turn, leads to a better understanding and mental models of the complexities of the JVM.

This, once again, raises the subject of statistics, as discussed in Chapter 2. The JVM routinely produces performance numbers that require careful handling—and the numbers produced by microbenchmarks are especially sensitive. It is incumbent upon the performance engineer to treat the observed results with a degree of statistical sophistication.

Performance Antipatterns Catalog

In this appendix, we will present a short catalog of performance antipatterns. The list is by no means exhaustive, and there are doubtless many more still to be discovered.

Distracted by Shiny

The newest or coolest tech is often the first tuning target, as it can be more exciting to explore how newer technology works than to dig around in legacy code. It may also be that the code accompanying the newer technology is better-written code that is easier to maintain. Both of these facts push developers toward looking at the newer components of the application.

Example Comments

"It's teething trouble—we need to get to the bottom of it."

"It is likely component X that I introduced and have been reading more about."

Reality

- This is often just a shot in the dark rather than an effort at targeted tuning or measuring the application.

- The developer may not fully understand the new technology yet and will tinker around rather than examine the documentation—often, in reality, causing other problems.

- In the case of new technologies, examples online are often for small or sample datasets and don't discuss good practice about scaling to an enterprise size.

Discussion

This antipattern is common in newly formed or less experienced teams. Eager to prove themselves, or to avoid becoming tied to what they see as *legacy* systems, they are often advocates for newer, "hotter" technologies—which may, coincidentally, be exactly the sort of technologies that would confer a salary uptick in any new role.

Therefore, the logical subconscious conclusion is that any performance issue should be approached by first taking a look at the new tech. After all, it's not properly understood, so a fresh pair of eyes would be helpful, right?

Resolutions

- Measure to determine the real location of the bottleneck.
- Ensure adequate logging around the new component.
- Look at best practices as well as simplified demos.
- Ensure the team understands the new technology, and establish a level of best practice across the team.

Distracted by Simple

The team targets the simplest parts of the system first, rather than profiling the application overall and objectively looking for pain points in it. There may be parts of the system deemed "specialist" that only the original wizard who wrote them can edit.

Example Comments

"Let's get into this by starting with the parts we understand."

"John wrote that part of the system, and he's on holiday. Let's wait until he's back to look at the performance."

Reality

- The original developer understands how to tune (only?) that part of the system.
- There has been no knowledge sharing or pair programming on the various system components, creating single experts.

Discussion

The *Distracted by Shiny* antipattern is often seen in a more established team, which may be more used to a maintenance or keep-the-lights-on role. If the application has recently been merged or paired with newer technology, the team may feel intimidated or not want to engage with the new systems.

Under these circumstances, developers may feel more comfortable profiling only those parts of the system that are familiar, hoping that they will be able to achieve the desired goals without going outside of their comfort zone.

Of particular note is that both of these first two antipatterns are driven by a reaction to the unknown. In *Distracted by Shiny*, this manifests as a desire by the developer (or team) to learn more and gain advantage—essentially an offensive play. By contrast, *Distracted by Simple* is a defensive reaction, playing to the familiar rather than engaging with a potentially threatening new technology.

Resolutions

- Measure to determine the real location of the bottleneck.
- Ask for help from domain experts if the problem is in an unfamiliar component.
- Ensure that developers understand all components of the system.

Performance Tuning Wizard

Management has bought into the Hollywood image of a "lone genius" hacker and hired someone who fits the stereotype to move around the company and fix all performance issues, using their perceived superior performance tuning skills.

There are genuine performance tuning experts and companies out there, but most would agree that you have to measure and investigate any problem. It's unlikely the same solution will apply to all uses of a particular technology in all situations.

Example Comment

"I'm sure I know just where the problem is…"

Reality

- Not many performance problems are precisely the same. A perceived wizard or superhero is unlikely to magically know how to address all issues at first glance.

Discussion

This antipattern can alienate developers in the team who perceive themselves to not be good enough to address performance issues. It's concerning, as in many cases, a small amount of profiler-guided optimization can lead to good performance increases (see Chapter 12).

This not to say there aren't specialists who can help with specific technologies, but the thought that there is a lone genius who will understand all performance issues from the beginning is absurd. Many technologists that are performance experts are specialists at measuring and problem-solving based on those measurements.

Superhero types in teams can be very counterproductive if they are not willing to share knowledge or the approaches they took to resolving a particular issue.

Resolutions

- Measure to determine the real location of the bottleneck.
- Ensure that any experts hired onto a team are willing to share and act as part of the team.

Tuning by Folklore

While desperate to try to find a solution to a performance problem in production, a team member finds a "magic" configuration parameter on a website. Without testing the parameter, the team applies it to production because it must improve things exactly as it did for the person on the internet…

Example Comment

> "I found these great tips on Stack Overflow. This changes *everything*."

Reality

- The developer does not understand the context or basis of the performance tip, and the true impact is unknown.
- It may have worked for that specific system, but that doesn't mean the change will even have a benefit in another. In reality, it could make things worse.

Discussion

A performance tip is a workaround for a known problem—essentially, a solution looking for a problem. Performance tips have a short shelf life and usually age badly; someone will come up with a solution that will render the tip useless (at best) in a later release of the software or platform.

One particularly bad source of performance advice is admin manuals. They contain general advice devoid of context. Lawyers often insist on this vague advice and "recommended configurations" as an additional line of defense if the vendor is sued.

Java performance happens in a specific context, with a large number of contributing factors. If we strip away this context, then what is left is almost impossible to reason about, due to the complexity of the execution environment.

> The Java platform is also constantly evolving, which means a parameter that provided a performance workaround in one version of Java may not work in another.

For example, the switches that control garbage collection algorithms frequently change between releases. What works in an older VM versions may not be applied in the current JVM versions. Even switches that are valid and useful in older versions are ignored or will prevent startup in newer versions of the JVM.

Configuration can be a one- or two-character change but have significant impact in a production environment if not carefully managed.

Resolutions

- Apply only well-tested and well-understood techniques that directly affect the most important aspects of the system.
- Look for and try out parameters in UAT, but as with any change, it is important to prove and profile the benefit.
- Review and discuss configuration with other developers and operations staff or DevOps.

The Blame Donkey

Certain components are always identified as the issue, even if they had nothing to do with the problem.

For example, one of the authors saw a massive outage in UAT the day before go-live. A certain path through the code caused a table lock on one of the central database tables. An error occurred in the code, and the lock was retained, rendering the rest of the application unusable until a full restart was performed. Hibernate was used as the data access layer and immediately blamed for the issue. However, in this case, the culprit wasn't Hibernate but an empty `catch` block for the timeout exception that did not clean up the database connection. It took a full day for developers to stop blaming Hibernate and actually look at their code to find the real bug.

Example Comment

"It's always JMS/Hibernate/A_N_OTHER_LIB."

Reality

- Insufficient analysis has been done to reach this conclusion.
- The usual suspect is the only suspect in the investigation.
- The team is unwilling to look wider to establish a true cause.

Discussion

This antipattern is often displayed by management or the business, as in many cases they do not have a full understanding of the technical stack and have acknowledged cognitive biases, so they are proceeding by pattern matching. However, technologists are far from immune to it.

Technologists often fall victim to this antipattern when they have little understanding about the code base or libraries outside of the ones usually blamed. It is often easier to name a part of the application that is commonly the problem, rather than perform a new investigation. It can be the sign of a tired team with many production issues at hand.

Hibernate is the perfect example of this; in many situations, Hibernate grows to the point where it is not set up or used correctly. The team then tends to bash the technology, as they have seen it fail or not perform in the past. However, the problem could just as easily be the underlying query, use of an inappropriate index, the physical connection to the database, the object mapping layer, or something else. Profiling to isolate the exact cause is essential.

Resolutions

- Resist the pressure to rush to conclusions.
- Perform analysis as normal.
- Communicate the results of the analysis to all stakeholders (to encourage a more accurate picture of the causes of problems).

Missing the Bigger Picture

The team becomes obsessed with trying out changes or profiling smaller parts of the application without fully appreciating the full impact of the changes. Engineers start tweaking JVM switches in an effort to gain better performance, perhaps based on an example or a different application in the same company.

The team may also look to profile smaller parts of the application using microbenchmarking (which is notoriously difficult to get right, as we explored in Appendix A).

Example Comments

> "If I just change these settings, we'll get better performance."

> "If we can just speed up method dispatch time…"

Reality

- The team does not fully understand the impact of changes.
- The team has not profiled the application fully under the new JVM settings.
- The overall system impact from a microbenchmark has not been determined.

Discussion

The JVM has literally hundreds of switches. This gives a very highly configurable runtime, but it also creates a great temptation to use all of this configurability. This is usually a mistake—the defaults and self-management capabilities are usually sufficient. Some of the switches also combine with one another in unexpected ways, which makes blind changes even more dangerous. Even in the same company, applications are likely to operate and profile in a completely different way, so it's important to spend time trying out settings that are recommended.

Performance tuning is a statistical activity, which relies on a highly specific context for execution. This implies that larger systems are usually easier to benchmark than smaller ones—because with larger systems, the law of large numbers works in the engineer's favor, helping to correct for effects in the platform that distort individual events.

By contrast, the more we try to focus on a single aspect of the system, the harder we have to work to unweave the separate subsystems (e.g., threading, GC, scheduling, JIT compilation) of the complex environment that makes up the platform (at least in the Java/C# case). This is extremely hard to do, and handling the statistics is sensitive and is often not a skillset that software engineers have acquired along the way. This makes it very easy to produce numbers that do not accurately represent the behavior of the system aspect that the engineer believed they were benchmarking.

This has an unfortunate tendency to combine with the human bias to see patterns even when none exist. Together, these effects lead us to the spectacle of a performance engineer who has been deeply seduced by bad statistics or a poor control—an engineer arguing passionately for a performance benchmark or effect that their peers are simply not able to replicate.

There are a few other points to be aware of here. First, it's difficult to evaluate the effectiveness of optimizations without a UAT environment that fully emulates production. Second, there's no point in having an optimization that helps your application only in high-stress situations and kills performance in the general case—but obtaining sets of data that are typical of general application usage but also provide a meaningful test under load can be difficult.

Resolutions

Before making any change to switches live:

1. Measure in production.
2. Change one switch at a time in UAT.
3. Ensure that your UAT environment has the same stress points as production.
4. Ensure that test data is available that represents normal load in the production system.
5. Test the change in UAT.
6. Retest in UAT.
7. Have someone recheck your reasoning.
8. Pair with them to discuss your conclusions.

Tuning by Folklore and *Missing the Bigger Picture* (abuse of microbenchmarks) are examples of antipatterns that are caused at least in part by a combination of the reductionism and confirmation biases. One particularly egregious example is a subtype of *Tuning by Folklore* known as *Fiddling with Switches*.

This antipattern arises because, although the VM attempts to choose settings appropriate for the detected hardware, there are some circumstances where the engineer will need to manually set flags to tune the performance of code. This is not harmful in itself, but there is a hidden cognitive trap here, in the extremely configurable nature of the JVM with command-line switches.

To see a list of the VM flags, use the following switch:

```
-XX:+PrintFlagsFinal
```

As of Java 8u131, this produces over 700 possible switches. Not only that, but there are also additional tuning options available only when the VM is running in diagnostic mode. To see these, add this switch:

```
-XX:+UnlockDiagnosticVMOptions
```

This unlocks around another 100 switches. There is no way that any human can correctly reason about the aggregate effect of applying the possible combinations of these switches. Moreover, in most cases, experimental observations will show that the effect of changing switch values is small—often much smaller than developers expect.

UAT Is My Desktop

UAT environments often differ significantly from production, although not always in a way that's expected or fully understood. Many developers will have worked in situations where a low-powered desktop is used to write code for high-powered production servers. However, it's also common that a developer's machine is massively more powerful than the small servers deployed in production. Low-powered micro-environments are usually not a problem, as they can often be virtualized for a developer to have one of each. This is not true of high-powered production machines, which will often have significantly more cores, RAM, and efficient I/O than a developer's machine.

Example Comment

"A full-size UAT environment would be too expensive."

Reality

- Outages caused by differences in environments are almost always more expensive than a few more boxes.

Discussion

The *UAT Is My Desktop* antipattern stems from a different kind of cognitive bias than we have previously seen. This bias insists that doing some sort of UAT must be better than doing none at all. Unfortunately, this hopefulness fundamentally misunderstands the complex nature of enterprise environments. For any kind of meaningful extrapolation to be possible, the UAT environment must be production-like.

In modern adaptive environments, the runtime subsystems will make best use of the available resources. If these differ radically from those in the target deployment, they will make different decisions under the differing circumstances—rendering our hopeful extrapolation useless at best.

In "Working with Remote Containers Using "Remocal" Development" on page 223, we introduced remocal development, which enables developers to directly connect their local environment to a production-like environment. With the introduction of CNCF platforms, *UAT Is My Desktop* has a lot more solutions than ever before. Container constraints do introduce a separate set of issues, which you can read more about in "Building Images" on page 203.

Resolutions

- Track the cost of outages and opportunity cost related to lost customers.
- Buy a UAT environment that is identical to production and look at technologies supporting remocal development.
- In most cases, the cost of a full UAT environment outweighs the cost of critical business impact, and sometimes the right case needs to be made to managers.

Production-Like Data Is Hard

Also known as the *DataLite* antipattern, this antipattern relates to a few common pitfalls that people encounter while trying to represent production-like data. Consider a trade processing plant at a large bank that processes futures and options trades that have been booked but need to be settled. Such a system would typically handle millions of messages a day. Now consider the following UAT strategies and their potential issues:

- To make things easy to test, the mechanism is to capture a small selection of these messages during the course of the day. The messages are then all run through the UAT system.

  This approach fails to capture burst-like behavior that the system could see. It may also not capture the warmup caused by more futures trading on a particular market before another market opens that trades options.

- To make the scenario easier to test, the trades and options are updated to use only simple values for assertion.

  This does not give us the "realness" of production data. Considering that we are using an external library or system for options pricing, it would be impossible for us to determine with our UAT dataset that this production dependency has not now caused a performance issue, as the range of calculations we are performing is a simplified subset of production data.

- To make things easier, all values are pushed through the system at once.

  This is often done in UAT, but misses key warmup and optimizations that may happen when the data is fed at a different rate.

Most of the time in UAT, the test dataset is simplified to make things easier. However, it rarely makes results *useful*.

Example Comments

"It's too hard to keep production and UAT in sync."

"It's too hard to manipulate data to match what the system expects."

"Production data is protected by security considerations. Developers should not have access to it."

Reality

- Data in UAT must be production-like for accurate results.
- If data is not available for security reasons, then it should be scrambled (aka masked or obfuscated) so it can still be used for a meaningful test. Another option is to partition UAT so developers still don't see the data, but can see the output of the performance tests to be able to identify problems.

Discussion

This antipattern also falls into the trap of "something must be better than nothing." The idea is that testing against even out-of-date and unrepresentative data is better than not testing.

As before, this is an extremely dangerous line of reasoning. While testing against *something* (even if it is nothing like production data) at scale can reveal flaws and omissions in the system testing, it provides a false sense of security.

When the system goes live, and the usage patterns fail to conform to the expected norms that have been anchored by UAT data, the development and ops teams may well find that they have become complacent due to the warm glow that UAT has provided and are unprepared for the sheer terror that can quickly follow an at-scale production release.

Resolutions

- Consult data domain experts and invest in a process to migrate production data back into UAT, scrambling or obfuscating data if necessary.
- Over-prepare for releases for which you expect high volumes of customers or transactions.

Index

A

AbstractQueuedSynchronizer, 357
abusing correlated logs antipattern, 253
access control, method handle, 350
access flags, 54
acknowledgment (ACK), 380
action bias, 46
actor-based task representation techniques, 367-368
AGCT (AsyncGetCallTrace), 319
agents, 63-64
  hprof heap profiling native agent, 333
  manual versus automatic instrumentation, 251
  OTel, 286, 296
  perf-map-agent, 317
  profiling, 306
aggregation
  avoiding percentile aggregation, 252, 277
  logs, 242
  metrics, 239, 250, 266
ahead-of-time (AOT) compilation
  code execution, 163-164
  for faster Java application launching, 221
  GraalVM, 71, 416
  versus JIT compilation, 59
  and zero-overhead principle, 57
alerting systems, purpose of, 306
allocation rates, 13
  cache hardware, 175-177
  garbage collection, 85, 101, 102
allocation, memory
  garbage collection, 97-102, 107
  mark and sweep algorithm, 77-79

  profiling, 329-332
  TLABs, 87-88, 93, 177, 331
Amazon Corretto, 71
Amazon EC2 virtual machines, 200
ambient context data, and scoped values, 411
Amdahl, Gene, 12
Amdahl's law, 12, 338-339
Andreessen, Marc, 170
Android project, 72
anewarray bytecode, 148
antipatterns, 249-254
  causes of performance, 26-28
  and cognitive biases, 44
AOT compilation (see ahead-of-time (AOT) compilation)
Apache Pekko framework, 368
AppendEntry, Raft, 387
Application class loader, 52
application performance monitoring (APM), 238, 288
application versus platform threads, 61
architecture robustness, 10
Argo CD, canary releases, 226-229
arithmetic bytecodes, 144
arraylets, Balanced collector, 130
arrayOops, 81, 83
arrays
  allocating large arrays in Balanced, 130-131
  anewarray bytecode, 148
  memory layout in Java, 421-422
  struct-like, 423
as-if-serial JMM guarantee, 345
Async Profiler, 319-320, 329
AsyncGetCallTrace (AGCT), 319

AsyncGetCallTrace() method, 319
asynchronous contagion, 373
asynchronous execution, 362-363
asynchronous messaging, distributed tracing for, 244
AtomicDouble class, 269
AtomicInteger class, 353-354
AtomicLong, 378
attach mechanism, in VisualVM, 67
attributes, role of, 54
automatic tracing, OTel, 296-297
automatic versus manual instrumentation, 250-252
average (simple mean), problems in latency testing, 19
Azul Systems (Zulu), 71

B

Bakker, Paul, 51
Balanced collector (Eclipse OpenJ9), 128-132
barriers and latches, concurrency, 360-361
@Benchmark annotation, 436
benchmarking (see microbenchmarking)
big-endian hardware architecture, 142
binary semaphore, 359
binding values to specific scope, 409
bindTo() method, 277
blackholes, in benchmarking code, 437-439
Blame Donkey antipattern, 44, 46, 448-449
blocking queues, 347
blocking threads
    avoiding, 355
    two-phase commit issue with, 380
    vthreads and I/O, 371
blue/green deployment technique, 224-225
Bootstrap class loader, 50-52
bootstrap method (BSM), 348
bootstrapping classes, initializing, 138
boredom, as cause of performance antipatterns, 27
branch prediction, 177
breaking point, latency and throughput, 19
Brooks pointers, 113, 124
BSM (bootstrap method), 348
buckets, in histograms, 35
"build and run" teams, 211
build cache, container image, 203
build phase, Quarkus, 165-166

Builder pattern, for vthreads in Thread class, 372
Burns, Brendan, 223
burst rate, bandwidth to memory, 174
bytecode
    Java agent's role in transformation, 63
    java.lang.instrument to modify, 63
    JVM execution, 52-56
bytecode interpretation, 137, 140-152
    families and categories, 142-149
    HotSpot specifics, 150-152
    simple interpreters, 149-150
bytecode weaving, 52, 251

C

C++11 model, 347
C1 and C2 JIT compilers in HotSpot, 156-157, 419
C or C++, 57, 59, 64
cache consistency protocols, 173
Cache interface, Infinispan, 391
cache lines, and mechanical sympathy, 190
call site, 146
call target, 348
Callable interface, 362
canary deployment technique, 226-229
CAP theorem, 383
capacity metric, 8
capacity planning test, 20
card tables
    HotSpot, 91
    Parallel collector, 120
cardinality, metric dimensions, 239
carrier threads, and vthreads, 180, 370, 372, 374
cascading failure, 259-260
Cassandra DB, 389-391
Cassandra Query Language (CQL), 389
causation versus correlation, 38-40
CDS (class-data sharing), Leyden, 418
centralized logging pattern, 242
cgroups, containers, 205, 233
Chaos Monkey, 21
Clark, Jason, 51
class files, bytecode, 52-56
class loading, 50-52, 138
Class object, 52, 81
class slot, as OpenJ9 object header, 129
class-data sharing (CDS), Leyden, 418
ClassLoader::getPlatformClassLoader, 51

J

M

magic numbers, 54

main branch, Fighting Animals, 207

main() method, 56

major generational collections, ZGC, 127

Majors, Charity, 236

Mak, Sander, 51

managed subsystems, Java's use of, 4

manual memory management, 85

manual tracing, OTel, 292-296

manual versus automatic instrumentation, 250-252

manual_tracing, Fighting Animals, 207

mark and sweep algorithm, GC, 75, 77-79

mark word, 81

Mastering API Architecture (Gough et al.), 217

maxage versus maxsize parameter, ring buffer in JFR, 326

measurement challenges with JVM applications, 5

mechanical sympathy, 179, 190

memory caches, 172-177

memory management, 4, 60
  (see also garbage collection)
  allocation rates, 13, 85, 101, 102, 175-177
  array layout, 421-422
  deployment of Java to cloud, 233-234
  hardware models, 178-179
  heap (see heap memory management)
  profiling, 329-333
  reading performance graphs, 13-14
  strong memory model, 343
  TLABs, 87-88, 93, 177, 331
  utilization metric, 8
  weak memory model, 343, 344

memory management unit (MMU), 179

memory performance, 171

memory pool, 91

MESI protocol, 173

Metaspace in HotSpot, 138

meter filters, 271-273

Meter interface, 267

MeterBinder, 277-278

MeterFilter interface, 272

meterFilter(), 273

MeterFilterReply enum, 272

MeterRegistry class, 270

meters and registries, Micrometer, 266-268

method call semantics (call-by-value), 80

method dispatch performance, 2

Method Handles API, 349-352

method handles, concurrency, 348-352, 353

method invocation (call) opcodes, 145

MethodHandle object, 349

methods, role of, 54

metric customers, Micrometer, 266

metrics, 238-241
  aggregation, 239, 250, 266
  architectural patterns for, 249-250
  capacity, 8
  counters, 239, 268, 339-342
  data volumes, 247
  gauges, 239, 269-271
  histograms, 35
  latency, 8, 18
  manual versus automatic instrumentation, 252
  Micrometer (see Micrometer)
  naming conventions, 249
  observable types, 7-11
  OTel, 298-300
  shoehorning data antipattern, 252-253
  SLO association, 255
  structure of, 247
  throughput (see throughput metric)
  utilization (see utilization metric)

microbenchmarking, 22, 59, 427-442
  case for avoiding, 432
  execution benchmarks (with JMH), 436
  heuristics for, 433-434
  versus integration tests, 307
  JMH framework, 435-442
  measuring low-level Java performance, 427-432

Micrometer, 266-278
  counters, 268
  distribution summaries, 274-277
  gauges, 269-271
  meter filters, 271-273
  meters and registries, 266-268
  and Prometheus, 280-285
  runtime metrics, 277-278
  timers, 273-274
  with OTel exporter, 299

Micrometer API, 267

micrometer_only, Fighting Animals, 207

micrometer_with_otel, Fighting Animals, 207

micrometer_with_prom, Fighting Animals, 207

About the Authors

Ben Evans, senior principal software engineer and observability lead at Red Hat Runtimes, is an architect, author, and educator. He's also a Java Champion who's written seven books on programming, including *Optimizing Java* and *Java in a Nutshell*. Previously, he was lead architect for instrumentation at New Relic, a cofounder of jClarity (acquired by Microsoft), and a member of the Java SE/EE Executive Committee.

James (Jim) Gough is a Distinguished Engineer at Morgan Stanley working on cloud native architecture and API programs. He's a Java Champion who has sat on the Java Community Process Executive Committee on behalf of the London Java Community and contributed to OpenJDK. James is also coauthor of *Mastering API Architecture* and enjoys speaking about architecture and low-level Java.

Colophon

The animal on the cover of *Optimizing Cloud Native Java* is a markhor goat (*Capra falconeri*). This species of wild goat is distinguished by its wizard-esque beard and twisting, towering horns. Found in the mountainous regions of western and central Asia, these goats inhabit high-altitude monsoon forests and can be found at 600–3,600 meters in elevation.

The markhor are herbivores that primarily graze on a variety of vegetation including grasses, leaves, herbs, fruits, and flowers. Like other wild goats, the markhor play a valuable role within their ecosystem as they munch the leaves from the low-lying trees and scrub, spreading the seeds in their dung.

The mating season takes place in winter, during which the males fight each other by lunging, locking horns, and attempting to push each other off balance. The subsequent births occur from late April to early June and result in one or two kids. Adult males are largely solitary and prefer the forest while the females and their young live in flocks on the rocky ridges high above.

Many of the animals on O'Reilly covers are endangered; all of them are important to the world.

The cover image is from *Riverside Natural History*. The series design is by Edie Freedman, Ellie Volckhausen, and Karen Montgomery. The cover fonts are Gilroy Semibold and Guardian Sans. The text font is Adobe Minion Pro; the heading font is Adobe Myriad Condensed; and the code font is Dalton Maag's Ubuntu Mono.

www.ingramcontent.com/pod-product-compliance
Lightning Source LLC
Chambersburg PA
CBHW080122220326
41598CB00032B/4929